M. Edward (Marshman Edward) Wadsworth

Lithological Studies

A Description and Classification of the Rocks of the Cordilleras

M. Edward (Marshman Edward) Wadsworth

Lithological Studies
A Description and Classification of the Rocks of the Cordilleras

ISBN/EAN: 9783337178147

Printed in Europe, USA, Canada, Australia, Japan

Cover: Foto ©ninafisch / pixelio.de

More available books at **www.hansebooks.com**

Memoirs of the Museum of Comparative Zoölogy
AT HARVARD COLLEGE.
Vol. XI. Part I.

LITHOLOGICAL STUDIES.

A DESCRIPTION AND CLASSIFICATION OF THE
ROCKS OF THE CORDILLERAS.

By M. E. WADSWORTH.

WITH EIGHT PLATES.

CAMBRIDGE:
Printed for the Museum.
October, 1884.

INTRODUCTORY NOTE.

UNDER the title of "Lithological Studies," a work is here presented to the public which is, in point of fact, a continuation of the publications of the Geological Survey of California, begun under my direction, in 1860. Had that Survey been completed, the investigation of the rocks of the State would naturally have been one of the matters to which our attention would, at the proper time, have been turned ; and, after the stoppage of the Survey, in planning for the elaboration of the materials in my hands, I, in 1877, determined that the lithological collections which I had accumulated, and which represented a wide area, should be described and classified. For this purpose Dr. Wadsworth was selected; and, a portion of his results being now ready, it is thought best that it should be published, without waiting for the completion of the entire work. It will undoubtedly seem to the reader that what is here furnished does not exactly correspond with or carry out the idea suggested on the title-page, namely, that this is a description and classification of the rocks of the Cordilleras. The reason is this : Dr. Wadsworth having been led by his investigations to place his work on a considerably different basis from that built upon by other lithologists, has found it desirable, and indeed necessary, to incorporate in it results obtained from the study of material not furnished by the Cordilleran collections. In the portion of the work herewith offered to the public, rocks more basic than the basalts are brought under consideration ; and in doing this, it has been found that it was not possible to arrive at the end sought to be gained without using the materials furnished by other regions and by other lithologists. Should this investigation be continued and completed — as it is hoped will be the case, a large amount of work having been already done with that end in view — the Cordilleran collections will yield the chief portion of the material drawn upon for the remaining portion of the volume, so that it will be found that the work is essentially based on the collections made on the western side of the North American continent, the study of which gave rise to the ideas presented in this first part.

J. D. WHITNEY.

CAMBRIDGE, MASS., October 18, 1884.

origin of rocks demanded by the results of petrographical study, 10. The associations of different rocks, and the difficulties in their separation, 10, 11. The microscopic and field evidence the only means of distinction, 10, 11. Eruptive and Sedimentary Rocks resemble each other through the alteration of both, 11. Sedimentary Rocks presenting peculiar and abnormal conditions not proper guides, 11, 12. Sedimentary Rocks found not to present the microscopic characters of Eruptive ones, 12. Requirements necessary to prove the passage of a Sedimentary into an Eruptive Rock, 12. Generally positive evidence that such passage does not exist can be obtained, 12, 13. The chemical resemblance of Sedimentary and Eruptive Rocks owing to the derivation of the former from the latter, 13. Minerals in Lavas of prior origin to the consolidation of the magma, 13; not derived from Sedimentary Rocks and characteristic of ancient and modern Eruptives, 13, 14. Field and microscopic evidence opposed to the theory of the derivation of Eruptive from Sedimentary Rocks, 14; the demands of that theory, 14. Volcanic or eruptive action began in the earliest ages of the Earth, 14; this action, although intermittent, is a dying one, 14, 15. The older Eruptives the same, originally, as the modern ones, 15; their present differences due to alteration, etc., 15. Under like conditions alteration is proportional to the age, 15. The presence of fragments of one rock in another is alone no proof of difference in geological age, 15. The alteration produced by internal molecular or chemical changes in the rock mass not to be confounded with superficial weathering, 15. Metamorphism not extended Pseudomorphism, 15. Pseudomorphism but an incidental phase in alteration, 15. The explanation of changes in rocks, 15, 16. Metamorphism inversely proportional to the contained silica in the original rock, when time and other conditions are the same, 16. Eruptive Action, including Thermal Waters, an efficient agent in Metamorphism, 16. Metamorphism dependent on the chemical composition of the rock and the metamorphic agents, hence lithological characters no criterion for determining geological age, 16. The constituents of rocks pass from an unstable towards a more stable condition, 16; this passage a factor in the dissipation of energy, 16. Rocks are produced, grow old, and decay, but are not raised again, 17. Crystalline Structure no proof of great age or of great depth, 17. Long time not always allowed for the formation of fine-grained and fossiliferous rocks, 17. Contraction tends to maintain a uniform temperature in the Earth's interior, 17, 18. Relative Progression in geological time from abundant Acidic to abundant Basic Eruptives, 18. All Eruptives derived from the Earth's interior material which had never solidified, or which has since been reliquefied, 18. Sonny's method of determining the origin of a rock misleading, 18. Association of Rocks is alone no proof of community of origin, 18, 19. Crystalline Schists naturally occur in a region of eruptive rocks, 19. Definition of Lamination, 19; this structure common in many eruptive rocks, 19. Joint Planes defined, 19; often mistaken in eruptive rocks for Bedding Planes, 19, 20. Cleavage defined, 20. Cleavage common both in Eruptive and Sedimentary Rocks, 20. Foliation defined, 20. Foliated Limestone mistaken for Mica Schist, 20. Foliation and Cleavage produced by the same cause at Squantum, Mass., 20, 21. Foliation common in altered eruptive rocks, 21; the planes being at right angles to the direction of pressure, 21. Schistose or Fissile Structure, 21. Fluidal Structure defined, 21. Schistose Structure often mistaken for Fluidal Structure, 21; the latter mistaken for Planes of Sedimentation, 21. Lines of chemical deposition taken for fluidal structure, 21. Arguments from analogy of doubtful value, 22; also from one region to another, 22. Evidence not sustaining the divisions of the Azoic System, 22, 23. Explanation of the structure of

CONTENTS. vii

districts of Crystalline Rocks, 22. Application of current views in American Geological Literature, 23. Association of Eruptive and Volcanic Rocks, 23. Origin of Crystalline Rocks, 23. Application of current views to Vesuvius in the time of STRABO, 24. Principles to be employed in studying regions of Crystalline Rocks, 24. Materials of the earliest formed Lands of eruptive origin, 24. Application of the term Eruptive or Volcanic in this work, 24. The younger Volcanic and the older Plutonic Rocks form a continuous series, 24.

SECTION III.

THE ORIGIN AND RELATIONS OF THE MINERAL CONSTITUENTS OF ROCKS . . . 25–30

The constituents of rocks fall into three classes, 25. Two divisions of the first class, 25; action of the Magma on Minerals of the first division, 25. Inclusions in eruptive rocks, 25, 26. Action of Lava on Inclusions, 26. Microscopic characters of Eruptive Rocks opposed to the theory of their derivation from Sediments, 26. Mineral products of the crystallization of a magma, 26. Mineral products of rock alteration, 26. The chemical constitution of altered rocks not essentially changed, 26. Cause of rock alteration, 27. Alteration a character of the rock mass as a whole, 27. Altered eruptive rocks tend to simulate the features of sedimentary forms, 27. The general tendency of rock alteration, 27, 28. The concentration of ores in rocks and veins attendant upon rock alteration, 28. Ores of mechanical and eruptive origin excepted, 28. Theory of ore deposits, 28. Mineralogy and Economic Geology chiefly sciences of abnormal minerals, 28. Unstable character of eruptive rocks, 28; their resemblance to chemical laboratories, 29; passage from unstable towards more stable chemical combinations, 29. Induration not always an indication of exposure to heat, 29. The glassy state of rocks is nearest their primitive condition, 29. Designations employed for the three classes of rock-forming minerals, 29. Distinction of cases of envelopment from alteration products, 29, 30. Application of the principles of Thermo-optics, 30. The pyrognostic characters of a mineral have little or nothing to do with its condition before its formation, 30. The conditions under which minerals crystallize from a cooling magma are different from those under which vein and alteration minerals are formed, 30.

SECTION IV.

CHEMICAL ANALYSIS OF ROCKS 31, 32

Chemical Analysis unable to determine the mineral constituents of rocks, 31, 32. While Chemical Composition remains nearly constant, great variation exists in the structure and mineral constituents, 31. What Chemical Analysis can do for the lithologist, 31. Relation of Chemical Analysis of normal rocks to rock species, 32. Analyses should be written in terms of the elements, instead of their compounds, 32.

SECTION V.

CLASSIFICATION BASED ON MINERAL COMPOSITION 33–45

Basis of the common classifications of rocks, 33; minerals used, and data required, 33. — THE FELDSPARS, 33-43. Their different modes of origin, 33. SCHEERER'S feldspar theory, 33, 34; DELESSE'S views, 34; HERMANN'S molecular

viii   CONTENTS.

theory, 34. WALTERSHAUSEN's theory, 34. Krablite a rock, and not a mineral, 34, 35. BUNSEN's view of Baulite, 35. HUNT's theory of the feldspars, 35. TSCHERMAK's theory, 35, 36; STRENG's views, 36; PETERSEN's objections to TSCHERMAK's theory, 37. DANA's method of accounting for variations in feldspars, 37. HUNT claims to have originated TSCHERMAK's theory, 37. HUNT's alteration of his direct quotation, 37. HUNT's theory not original with him, and not the same as TSCHERMAK's, 37. Writers who through misapprehension have acknowledged HUNT's claims, 37, 38; SILLIMAN charges TSCHERMAK with appropriation of HUNT's views, 38; LEEDS recognizes the difference between the views of HUNT and TSCHERMAK, 38. The charges of appropriation made against TSCHERMAK false, 38. DESCLOIZEAUX on the optical properties of the feldspars, 38; FRIEDEL's theory of their chemical constitution, 38; VOM RATH's views, 38, 39. DESCLOIZEAUX's discovery of microcline, 39. MALLARD and LÉVY teach that it is the same as orthoclase, 39. SCHUSTER's observations on the optical properties of the feldspars, 39. Feldspars not suitable to found specific distinctions upon, 39. No means of positively determining the feldspar species in rocks, 40. DESCLOIZEAUX's method of determining feldspars, 40; PUMPELLY's modification of, 40, 41; PUMPELLY anticipated by LÉVY, 41. The work of both independent, 41. HAWES on the distinction of feldspars, 41. BOŘICKÝ's micro-chemical method, 41, 42. SZABÓ's method, 42. GEO. H. EMERSON's invention of a method of distinguishing minerals by means of crystals formed in blowpipe beads, 42; amplified later by GUSTAV ROSE, W. A. ROSS, and H. C. SORBY, 42. The specific gravity method for determination of the feldspar species, 42. Objections to the above methods, 42, 43. The twinning not constant in feldspars, 43. The chief value in lithology of the determination of the feldspars, 43. — THE PYROXENE-AMPHIBOLE GROUPS, 44, 45. A variable series in them as in the feldspars, 44. Cleavage not a satisfactory basis for separating Diallage from Augite, 44. Augite found in Basic and Acid Rocks, and in the *older* and *younger*, 44. Alteration of Augite, 44. Secondary origin of some Pyroxenes, 44. Relation of Hornblende and Augite, 44. The same hand specimen both a Diorite and Diabase, 44. The Mica Series, 45. Secondary origin of Chlorite and Epidote, 45. — MINERALOGICAL NOMENCLATURE OF ROCKS. Rock Classification based on mineralogy alone, impracticable, 45. Rock Structure valueless for specific distinctions, 45.

SECTION VI.

NAMING ROCKS ACCORDING TO THE GEOLOGICAL AGE 45–47

Such nomenclature not natural, 45. No line can be drawn at the Tertiary Age, 46. Alteration under like conditions proportionate to age, 46. The petrographer's duty, 46. The presence of Fluid Cavities in rocks, 46. VOGELSANG and JULIEN on Fluid Cavities, 46. Fluid Cavities sometimes original and sometimes secondary in rocks, 46. Occurrence in Tertiary Rocks, 46. The cause of the Crystalline Structure in the older rocks, 46, 47. The Granitic Structure, 47.

SECTION VII.

METHODS OF CLASSIFICATION 47–51

Classification the framework of any descriptive science, 47. The mineralogical method of studying rocks, 47. The natural method, 47. The relation of minerals to rocks, 47, 48. Meaning of the Natural Classification, 48. Characterization of the Mineralogical Classifications of rocks, 48, 49. Compared with zoölogical methods, 49. Question of methods, 50. Earlier publication of these principles, 50. European classifications based largely on altered rocks, 50. To express perfectly the Natural Classification of rocks requires perfect knowledge of them, 50. The classification here introduced empirical, 50, 51. Elasticity of the classification, 51; its fundamental principles, 51.

SECTION VIII.

THE PRINCIPLES OF CLASSIFICATION 51, 52

SECTION IX.

GENERAL CONCLUSIONS IN REGARD TO SYSTEMS OF LITHOLOGICAL CLASSIFICATION 53–59

Universal law of degradation of energy, 53. Natural classification conforms to it, 53. The demands of Petrography, 53. Expansion of materials in passing from the liquid to the solid state, 53. Pressure tends to render the Earth's interior solid, 53. Sinking of the Earth's crust, 53. The structure of the Earth indicated by petrographical and geological facts, 54. Crystalline rocks, 54. Systems of classification, 54, 55. Chemical analyses of rocks, 56. Alteration of rocks, 56. Divisions of minerals and rock fragments in rocks, 56. The order of arrangement of rocks, 57. Determination of a rock by means of its unaltered groundmass, 57. Practical application of the principles of nomenclature and classification, 57. Specific and varietal names, 57. The use of the terms Melaphyr, Diabase, and Diorite, 57, 58. Sub-varietal names, 58. Trivial names, 58. Arrangement of the fragmental rocks, 58. Arrangement of rock names, 58, 59. Varietal and sub-varietal names not essential, 59. Use of a binomial and trinomial nomenclature, 59.

CHAPTER II.

THE SIDEROLITES AND PALLASITES.

SECTION I.

SIDEROLITE 60–68

Definition of SIDEROLITE, 60. Shingle Springs, Eldorado Co., California, 60. Stanton, Virginia, 60, 61. Coahuila, Mexico, 61. Gibbs meteorite, Texas, 61. Butler, Missouri, 61. Toluca, Mexico, 61. General structure of meteoric siderolites, 61; constituents of, 61. Widmannstättian figures developed in, 62; also in Greenland iron, 62. References to illustrations of Widmannstättian figures, 62. Further divisions of the Siderolites, 62; chemical analyses of, 62, 63; specific gravity of, 63; Iron in, 63; Nickel and Cobalt in, 63, 64; minor elements in, 64. Terrestrial Siderolites, 64, 65. Greenland iron, 65; its origin, 65. Doubtful meteoric origin of many Siderolites, 65. Chemical analysis made sole test of meteoric origin, 65, 66. Origin of masses of meteoric iron, 66; TSCHERMAK'S views, 66;

SORBY's conclusions, 66, 67; objections to their theories, 67. The organic origin of meteoric iron and graphite, 67. MASKELYNE's use of the term *Siderolite*, 68. The terms *Siderite* and *Holosiderite*, 68.

SECTION II.

PALLASITE 68–83

GUSTAV ROSE's use of the term, 68. Definition of Pallasite, 68; arrangement of, 68. — THE METEORIC PALLASITES, 69–75. Tucson, Arizona, 69. Hemalga, Peru, 69. Berdjansk, Russia, 69. Deesa, Chili, 70. Atacama, Bolivia, 70. Bitburg, Prussia, 70. Hommoney Creek, North Carolina, 71. Singhur, India, 71. Forsyth, Missouri, 71. Anderson, Ohio, 71. Krasnojarsk, Siberia, 71, 72. Potosi, Bolivia, 72. Rittersgrün, Saxony, 72. Breitenbach, Bohemia, 73. Steinbach, Saxony, 73. Atacama, Chili, 73. Sierra de Chaco, Chili, 73. Newton Co., Arkansas, 74. Moyollones, Bolivia, 74. Hainholz, Westphalia, 74. Lodran, India, 74, 75.

VARIETY. — **Cumberlandite**, 75–83.

Iron Mine Hill, Rhode Island, 75–79. State of the Iron of but little importance lithologically, 76. Microscopic veins, 76. Hercynite (?), 77. Tracing altered conditions of Cumberlandite, 77–79; specific gravity of, 79; diminishing specific gravity with alteration, 80. First published description of Cumberlandite, 80. Study of other iron-bearing rocks, 80, 81. Taberg, Sweden, 81. General description of Pallasite, 81; of Cumberlandite, 81, 82. Chemical analyses of Pallasite, 82, 83. Chemical analysis alone suggests, but does not prove, the specific relations, 83.

CHAPTER III.

THE PERIDOTITES.

SECTION I.

INTRODUCTORY 84, 85

ROSENBUSCH's use of the term *Peridotite*, 84. How employed in this work, 84. Order of arrangement in the Peridotites, 84. The needlessness of subdivisions of Peridotite, 84; yet subdivided here in conformity to general usage, 85. Definition of *Dunite*, 85. Proposal of the name *Saxonite*, 85. Definition of *Lherzolite*, 85. Proposal of the name *Buchnerite*, 85. Definition of the terms *Eulysite*, *Picrite, Serpentine, Porodite*, and *Tufa*, 85.

SECTION II.

THE METEORIC PERIDOTITES 86, 106

VARIETY. — **Dunite**, 86.

Chassigny, France, 86; glass in, 86, 105.

CONTENTS. xi

VARIETY.— **Saxonite**, 86-94.

Iowa Co., Iowa, 86-88. Origin of the chondritic structure, 86, 87. Occurrence of a lusse in meteorites, 87. Dhurmsala, India, 88. Kuyahinya, Hungary, 88-91; organic remains in, 89. The constitution of meteorites such that they could not have existed in conditions suitable for life, 91. Chondritic structure, 91. Gnadenfrei, Silesia, 91, 92. Gopalpur, India, 92; feldspar in it doubtful, 92. Butsura, India, 92, 93. Lancé, France, 93. Tourinnes-la-Grosse, Belgium, 93. Waconda, Kansas, 93, 94. Goalpara, India, 94.

VARIETY. — **Lherzolite**, 94-101.

Pultusk, Poland, 94, 95. New Concord, Ohio, 95, 96. Mocs, Transylvania, 96. Zsadány, Banat, 96, 97. Estherville, Iowa, 97-101. Iron globules in, 97, 98. Peckhamite, 99, 101. MEUNIER's theory of the origin of the Estherville meteorite, 99, 100; objections thereto, 100. Variations in structure of this meteorite, 100, 101.

VARIETY. — **Buchnerite**, 101, 102.

Tieschitz, Moravia, 101, 102. Peculiar character of its chondri, 101. Hungen, Germany, 102. Grosnaja, Caucasus, 102. Alfianello, Italy, 102.

MISCELLANEOUS, 103-105.

Bavarian Meteorites: Mauerkirchen, Eichstadt, Schönenberg, and Krähenberg, 103. Cabarras Co, North Carolina, 103, 104. Mezo-Madaras, Transylvania, 104. Alessandria, Piedmont, 104. Renazzo, Italy, 104; special study should be made of this form, 104. Linn Co., Iowa, 104. Ausson, France, 104. Nanjemoy, Maryland, 104. Drake Creek, Tennessee, 104. L'Aigle, France, 105. Weston, Connecticut, 105. Château Renard, France, 105. Hessle, Sweden, 105. Nobleboro', Maine, 105.

VARIETY. — **Tufa**, 105, 106.

Orvinio, Italy, 105, 106. Chantonnay, France, 106.

SECTION III.

THE METEORITES. — THEIR ORIGIN AND CHARACTER 106-118

MASKELYNE's teachings, 106, 107. SORBY's views, 107, 108. FORBES's microscopic observations, 108. MEUNIER's theory and FORNES's criticism of it, 108, 109. TSCHERMAK's idea of the tufaceous character of meteorites, and their eruptive origin, 109, 110. Objections to the preceding views, 110-112. The Chondritic Structure limited to a certain chemical and mineralogical type of meteorites, 110. Continuity of the Chondri and Matrix, 110, 111. Structure of meteorites rarely fragmental, 111, 112. Chondritic Structure produced by rapid crystallization, 111. Enclosures in meteorites, 111, 112. Meteorites derived from liquid, not solid material, 112, 113. The Sun, or some similar body, their most probable source, 112. Community of elements in the Sun and Meteorites, 112. Possibilities of Meteorites being thrown from the Sun, 113. Probable liquid condition of the Sun, 113. Meteoric constitution of some astronomical objects, 113. The theory that Meteorites are thrown from the Sun is old, 113, 114. Abundance of Metallic Meteorites in past times, 114. Meteorites not thrown from the Moon, 114; and not from the Earth in past times, 114. Need of further careful study of meteorites, 114, 115. Objections to Sorby's view that minerals of unlike specific gravity can intercrystallize, 115. Objections to Helmholtz's theory that the Earth is composed of meteoric fragments, 115, 116. Boulders in Northern Drift, fallen Meteorites, 116. Unscientific to suppose Meteorites have brought germs of life to the Earth, 116. Destruction of germs by the cold of space, 116. Meteorites not exposed to action of water and air, 116. Meteorites not vein formations, 117. Source of metals in veins, 117. Copper in Meteoric Rocks and Terrestrial Basic ones, 117. Metallic Iron in Terrestrial Basic Rocks, 117. Nickel, etc. in Meteoric and Terrestrial Masses, 118.

SECTION IV.

THE TERRESTRIAL PERIDOTITES 118–162

VARIETY. — **Dunite**, 118–125.

Franklin, North Carolina, 118; structure indicates eruptive origin, 118. Webster, North Carolina, and alterations in, 119, 120. Tafjord, Norway, 120. Dun Mountain, New Zealand, 121. Söndmöre, Norway, 121. Röbergvik, Norway, 121. Bonhomme, France, 121, 122. Karlstätten, Austria, 122. Tron, Norway, 122. Heiersdorf, Saxony, 122. Ronda Mountains, Spain, 122, 123. Serranía de Ronda, Spain, 123. St. Paul's Rocks, their origin and alterations, 123–125.

VARIETY. — **Saxonite**, 125–128.

Russdorf, Saxony, 125. Northern Norway, 125, 126. Thorsvig, Norway, 126. Birkedal, Norway, 126. Hovenden, Norway, 126. Rodfjeld, Norway, 126. Andestad See, Norway, 126, 127. Langenberg, Saxony, 127. Callenberg, Saxony, 127. The Ziegelei, Saxony, 127. Fatu Luka, Timor, 127. Rofna, Alps, 127, 128.

VARIETY. — **Lherzolite**, 128–147.

Lake Lherz, France, 128, 129. Serranía de Ronda, Spain, 129. Italy, 129. Ultenthal, Tyrol, 129. Colusa Co., California, 129–132; alteration structure in, taken for stratification, 130. Inyo Co., California, 132. Production of Magnetite during alteration, 132. Mohsdorf, Saxony, 132, 133. Rödhaug, Norway, 133. Baste, Harz, 133, 134. Christiania, Norway, 134. Gjorud, Norway, 135. Presque Isle, Michigan, 136–138. Formation of dolomitic rocks, 137, 138. Eruptive origin of this Peridotite, 138. Ishpeming, Michigan, 139. Dolomitic rocks, 139. Transylvania, Austria, 139, 140. Fichtelgebirge, Bavaria, 140. Jaina River, San Domingo, 140. Starkenbach, France, 140. Todtmoos, Baden, 141. Plumas Co., California, 142. Levanto, Italy, 142. Eubœa, 142. Philippine Islands, 143. Lizard District, Cornwall, 143. Troad, Asia Minor, 143–147. Dikes of Serpentine, 144. Diallage with Cleavage of Augite, 145. Schistose Rocks and their origin, 146, 147.

VARIETY. — **Eulysite**, 147–149.

Tunaberg, Norway, 147. Kettilsfjall, Sweden, 147, 148. Varallo, Sesia Valley, 148. Lepce, Austria, 148. Fontanapass, Greece, 148. Mohsdorf, Saxony, 148. Gillsberg, Saxony, 148, 149.

VARIETY. — **Picrite**, 149–152.

Austria, 149. Steierdorf, Banat, 149, 150. Inchcolm Island, Scotland, 150. Herborn, Nassau, 150. Ellgoth, Austria, 150, 151. Anglesey, 151. Dillgend, Nassau, 151, 152.

CONTENTS. xiii

VARIETY. — **Serpentine**, 152–161.

Fitztown, Pennsylvania, 152. Frankenstein, Silesia, 152. Lekö, Norway, 152. Waldheim, Saxony, 153. Thessaly, 153. Santiago, San Domingo, 153, 154. La Vega, San Domingo, 154. Brixlegg, Tyrol, 154. Il Pinno, Elba, 154, 155. Tasmania, 155. Windisch-Matrey, Tyrol, 155. St. Sabine, France, 155, 156. River Oisain, Timor, 156. Rivière des Plantes, Canada, 156. Melbourne, Canada, 156. Galicia, Spain, 156. High Bridge, New Jersey, 156, 157. Zöblitz, Saxony, 157, 158. Chip Flat, California, 158. Depot Hill, California, 158. Plumas Co., California, 158. Finland, 158. Klopfberg, Austria, 159. Nezeros, Thessaly, 159. Fatu Temann, Timor, 159. Westfield, Massachusetts, 159, 160. Formation of Talc, 159. Lynnfield, Massachusetts, 160. River Jon, San Domingo, 160. Newport, Vermont, 161. Colinae, Austria, 161. Texas, Pennsylvania, 161. Chester, Pennsylvania, 161.

VARIETY. — **Porodite**, 161, 162.

Fatu Luka, Timor, 161, 162. Strand, Timor, 162.

SECTION V.

PERIDOTITE. — ITS MACROSCOPIC CHARACTERS 162–165

Structure of the Meteoric Peridotites, 162. Structure of the Terrestrial Peridotites, 163–165; least altered forms, 163; alteration characters, 163. Appearance of the Olivine Groundmass, 163. Alteration of the Pyroxene Minerals, 163, 164. Segregations in Serpentine, 164. Translucency of Serpentine, 164. "Slickensides" in Serpentine, 164. Products of extended alteration in Peridotite, 164. Term *Serpentine* in Mineralogy, 164. Variability of Serpentine, 164; Schistose Structure in, 164. Production of Talc and Actinolite Schists, 164, 165; of Dolomitic Limestones, 165. Fragmental states of Peridotite, 165. Origin of Ophicalcites and brecciated Serpentines, 165. Introduction of the terms *Merolite* and *Merolitic* for pseudo-fragmental rocks, 165.

SECTION VI.

PERIDOTITE. — ITS MICROSCOPIC CHARACTERS 165–175

General Microscopic Structure of the Meteoric Peridotites, 165–167. The Base of, 166. The Chondri of, 166. The Olivine of, 166. The Enstatite of, 166. The Iron and Pyrrhotite of, 166, 167. The Chromite and Picotite of, 166. The Manbhoom Saxonite, 167. Union of Diallage and Augite Cleavage in Diallage, 167. Lherzolite, 167. Minor minerals in Meteoric Peridotites, 167. Fragmental Meteorites, 187. Microscopic characters of the Terrestrial Peridotites, 168–175; of Dunite, 168; alteration to Serpentine, 168. Transition in the varieties of Peridotite, 168. Characters of Enstatite, 168, 169; of Diallage, 169; of Augite, 169. Alteration of the Pyroxene Minerals, 169. Description of the alterations in the Peridotites as shown in the plates, 169–172. The *Eozoön* question, 172–174. Organic structure simulated in Felsites, 173. The supposed *Eozoön*, and other organisms, the more perfect, the more the rock is altered, 173. The inclination to unduly extend one's line of study, 173, 174. Crucial test in disputed problems, 174. The *Eozoön* in segregated or veinstone deposits, therefore not of organic origin, 174. Microscopic characters of Picrite, 174, 175.

xiv   CONTENTS.

Obliteration of original characters in the process of the alteration of Peridotites, 175. Production of Schistose Structure in, 175. The supposed conversions of Schists into Serpentine, 175. Absence of the Mesh Structure and Chromite or Picotite in Serpentine due to alteration, 175. Formation of Serpentine Veinstones, 175. Alteration minerals in Peridotite, 175. Ground covered by the text, 175.

SECTION VII.

CHROMITE AND PICOTITE. — THEIR RELATIONS 176–186

Fischer's observations, 176. Dathe's studies, 176. Thoulet's observations, 176. Translucency of Chromite first remarked in 1825, by C. H. Pfaff, 176. The writer's observations on some eighty specimens of Chromite, Picotite, and Ores of Iron, 177–180. Color and lustre of massive Chromite, 180. Hardness and streak of Chromite and Picotite, 180. Specific gravity of, 180. *Coffee-brown* color of, 180. Variability in color of, 180, 181. Observation of translucency, 181. Preparation of specimens, 181. Chemical relations of Chromite and Picotite, 181–183. Views of Genth and Rammelsberg on, 183. Microscopic relations of, 183, 184. Conclusions regarding mineral species and their variability, 184, 185. A natural system in mineralogy, 185. Strange history of a Chromite Analysis, 185, 186. Errors in published lists of Analyses, 186.

SECTION VIII.

PERIDOTITE. — ITS CHEMICAL CHARACTERS 186–189

Designation of the varieties of Peridotite, 186. Specific gravity of, 186, 187. The Carbonaceous Meteorites, 186. As specific gravity decreases, the Iron diminishes and Magnesia increases, 187. Microscopic characters of the Cold-Bokkeveld Meteorite, 186. Percentage of silica in Pallasite, 187; of silica in Peridotite, 187, 188. Special case of the Cabarras Meteorite, 187. Percentages of alumina, iron, lime, and magnesia in Peridotite, 188. The meteoric forms richest in Iron, 188. Alteration leads to decrease in the percentage of Iron, 188. Relation of Picrite to Basalt, 188. Minor elements in Peridotite, 188. Water proportioned to the amount of alteration, 188, 189. General chemical characters of Peridotite, 189.

SECTION IX.

PERIDOTITE. — ITS ORIGIN 189–192

Eruptive occurrence of Peridotite in the Cornwall, Troad, and Lake Superior districts, 189. Relations of Schistose Rocks and Peridotes, 189, 190. Association of Eruptive and Schistose Rocks, 189. The Schists produced by alteration of Peridotite, 189, 190. Detritus of Eruptive Rocks, 190. Peridotic Volcanoes, 190. Expected occurrence of Peridotites, 190; difficulty of the study of, 190. Production of Serpentine by alteration of Peridotite, 190. Migration of mineral matter, 190. Chemical precipitation of Serpentine from ocean waters, 190. Confusion between migrated serpentine material and that produced by alteration *in situ*, 190. Serpentine question allied to the phenomena of Eruptive Rocks and Veinstones, 190, 191. No proof that the Canadian Serpentines are stratified sedimentary deposits, 191. Believed inaccuracy of Dr. Hunt's writings, 191.

CONTENTS. xv

Production of Serpentine through alteration of other rocks than Peridotite, 191. Literature of the Serpentine question, 191. Talcose Rocks derived from Peridotites, 191, 192. Steatite Rocks alteration forms of Gabbro and Diabase (Diorite), 192. Actinolite and other schists derived from Peridotite, 192. Amphibole Schists, 192. Origin of Magnesian Limestones, 192. Explanation of the alterations, 192.

SECTION X.

PERIDOTITE. — ITS CLASSIFICATION 192–194

The use of Specific and Varietal Names, 192. Definition of Peridotite, 192. Basis of varietal distinctions, 193. Definition of the varieties, 193. Alteration varieties subordinate to the original mineralogical ones, 193. Probable varieties to be found by future study, 193. Most variety names not important, 193. *Limburgite* of ROSENBUSCH, 193. Terms applied to the fragmental forms of Peridotite, 193, 194. Tabular Classification of Siderolite, Pallasite, and Peridotite, 194. Essential terms in describing Peridotites, 194.

CHAPTER IV.

THE BASALTS.

SECTION I.

THE METEORIC BASALTS 195–206

VARIETY. — **Basalt**, 195, 196.

Stannern, Moravia, 195. Constantinople, Turkey, 195. Jonzac, France, 196. Petersburg, Tennessee, 196. Frankfort, Alabama, 196.

VARIETY. — **Gabbro**, 196–205.

Luotolaks, Finland, 196. Mässing, Bavaria, 197. Juvenas, France, 197. Shergotty, India, 197, 198. Maskelynite, 198. Páwlowka, Russia, 198. Le Teilleul, France, 198. Bishopville, South Carolina, 199–201. Chladnite, 199. Aqueo-igneous origin of Eruptives, 201. Manegaum, India, 201, 202. Busti, India, 202. Shalka, India, 202. Ibbenbühren, Westphalia, 202. Greenland, 202–205. Assuk, 203. Ovifak, 203, 204. Pfaff-Oberg, 204, 205. General Structure of the Meteoric Basalts, 205; not fragmental, 205. Nomenclature, 205. Future changes, 206.

SECTION II.

THE PSEUDO-METEORITES 206–208

Waterville, Maine, 206, 207. Richland, South Carolina, 207. Ignat, Russia, 207, 208. Waterloo, New York, 208. Concord, New Hampshire, 208. Andesite type, 208.

CONTENTS.

EXPLANATION OF THE TABLES 209

TABLES OF CHEMICAL ANALYSES . . . . ii–xxxiii
    TABLE I. Analyses of Chromite and Picotite . . . .   ii–v

TABLES II.–V. — *A Classified List of Complete (Bausch) Analyses of Meteoric and Terrestrial Rocks.*
    TABLE II. Siderolite . . . . vi–xv
    TABLE III. Pallasite . . . . xvi, xvii
    TABLE IV. Peridotite . . . . xviii–xxxi
    TABLE V. Basalt, Part I. The Meteoric Basalts . . . . xxxii, xxxiii

---

The black-faced figures in the text, e. g. **3001**, refer to the numbers of specimens in the Whitney Lithological Collection in the Museum of Comparative Zoölogy.

The letters A. E. prefixed, and G. and P. affixed, refer respectively to special collections, belonging to the Whitney Collection, made by Mr. Diller in the Assos Expedition, Professor W. M. Gabb in San Domingo, and Professor W. H. Pettee in California ; e. g. A. E. **324** ; **250** G. ; **46** P.

LITHOLOGICAL STUDIES.

CHAPTER I.

SECTION I. — *The Structure of the Earth.*

THE "natural system of rocks" ought to contain within itself a key to the history of the earth, and to be an exponent of that history. The entire physical universe seems to be under the government of a universal law, and our classification ought to accord with that law, so far as it has been expressed in the rocks themselves. This law has thus far been best formulated by Sir William Thomson as *the degradation and dissipation of energy*, — or, as it may be styled, the passage from the unstable towards a more stable condition, — the tendency towards harmony with the environment. This I regard as the law under which the universe has moved from its beginning, and under which it will continue its course uniformly towards the end, believing that no turning back can occur, and that no energy once lost can be restored except by the same Almighty Power which gave it birth.[*] It is in accordance with this law that I have tried to do my work, and to set forth the principles on which the rocks described are classified; in other words, this is an attempt to explain the present condition of the rocks by tracing out their past history.

The terms "lithology," "petrography," and "petrology" are so indefinitely employed that it seems necessary to give some fixed meaning to them here. For this purpose I define *Lithology* as that science which treats of the constitution and physical structure of rocks. It corresponds somewhat to the anatomy and histology of animals, including the study of morbid tissues.

[*] Science, 1883, i. 541.

Petrology treats of the origin, history, physical features, mode of occurrence, and relations of rock masses.

Lithology is essentially an in-door or cabinet and laboratory science; while *petrology* is exclusively a field study. The former needs for its pursuit hand specimens only; for the latter we must have the rocks *in situ*.

Petrography I define as that branch of science which embraces both *lithology and petrology*. It includes everything that pertains to the origin, formation, occurrence, alteration, history, relations, structure, and classification of rocks as such. It is the essential union of field and laboratory study.

So far as possible my work has been carried on according to petrographical rather than ordinary lithological methods, and with the belief that field evidence is stronger than any laboratory evidence can be in all matters relating to the origin of rocks.

The facts developed by petrographical study seem to me to demand for their explanation a former liquid condition of this globe, and the admission that all rocks, not of organic origin, now forming a portion of the earth's crust, are the results either of that molten condition, or of the action of atmospheric and hydrous agencies upon the formerly liquid material. The belief in the former fluid condition is in accord with the demands of geology and the results of physical and astronomical research; for it seems proper to hold, that, as is the present physical condition of the nebulæ, stars, sun, planets, and satellites, so was, or is, or will be, this earth. Indeed the various phenomena with which we are concerned seem to be but the concomitants and results of the passage of this earth from its active condition, as a hot fluid mass, towards a cold, inert, and passive state. Is it not our part to study matter in its present transitory stage, and from the facts thus gathered to reconstruct as far as possible its past history and infer its future course? To me the beginnings, the various transitory stages, and signs of what the end will be, are apparent in the rocks; and the effort of the classification here employed is to give voice to these changes, or to the unstableness of the rock constituents, while the classifications of others appear in general to be based upon the assumed stability of the rock constituents,—that is, they assume that as the rocks now are so they were, and always will be.

I am unable to explain the facts obtained in the petrographical study of the rocks except on the supposition that the eruptive rocks of all kinds came from the interior part of the earth, and from below the sedimentary deposits; moreover it would seem that they must come from a portion that has either never solidified, or which through some cause has been reliquefied. Here, then, it will be desirable that some examination should be made of the evidence derived from physical and mathematical laws on which is based the opinion held by many that the earth is solid.

This evidence may be considered under two divisions. 1°. That derived from the phenomena of precession and nutation, and of the tides. 2°. That derived from the action of matter under the combined influence of heat and pressure.

In the first case, the conclusions which have been reached have been obtained by assuming certain hypothetical globes with a certain definite structure, substituting for these the name earth, and then claiming that the conclusions applied to the *actual earth* instead of to the *hypothetical globes*, for which the name earth was used just as the algebraist uses x and y. Hopkins assumed for his globes: 1°, a homogeneous fluid mass enclosed in a homogeneous solid shell; 2°, a heterogeneous fluid mass enclosed in a heterogeneous solid shell. The transition between the entire solidity of the shell and the perfect fluidity of the interior mass was assumed by him as being an abrupt one. He further assumed that the circulation would go on in the mass until it lost its perfect fluidity in every part at nearly the same moment.*

Sir William Thomson, in the same way, drew his conclusions from globes assumed to have a thin shell, passing abruptly either into a homogeneous incompressible fluid, mobile like water; or into a heterogeneous viscid fluid interior.†

Likewise Professor George H. Darwin has taken as the basis for his discussions, if he is not misunderstood, homogeneous spheroids which are viscous and non-elastic, also those which are elastico-viscous, and those which are either elastic, plastic, or viscous.‡

The view that the phenomena of precession and nutation prove the earth to be solid was opposed by Hennessy,§ Delaunay,‖ Newcomb and

---

* Philos. Trans., 1839, pp. 381–423; 1840, pp. 193–208; 1842, pp. 43–55.
† Trans. Royal Soc. Edin., 1864, xxiii. 157–160; Phil. Mag., 1863 (4), xxv. 1–14, 149–151; Phil. Trans., 1863, pp. 573–582; Trans. Geol. Soc. Glas., 1878, vi. 38–40; Nat. Phil., 1867, I. 670–727; Nature, 1872, v. 223–224, 257–259.
‡ Phil. Trans., 1880, clxx. 1–35, 447–503; 1882, clxxii. 187–230.
§ Phil. Trans., 1851, pp. 495–547; Nature, 1871, iii. 420; 1872, v. 288, 289; Geol. Mag., 1871 (1), viii. 216–218.
‖ Geol. Mag., 1868 (1), v. 507–511.

others; and although strongly supported by Thomson for some fourteen years it was abandoned by him in 1876,* and is now generally given up.

The view that the phenomena of the tides prove the earth to be solid is still sustained by Thomson and Darwin, but their conclusions only apply to the *assumed globes* and not to the earth itself. Their conclusions are also opposed by Hennessy, Fisher, Airy, and many others.

The difficulty seems to be that it is beyond the power of any known transcendental mathematics to grasp the problem of the earth's structure, if its most probable condition be assumed. This condition may be described as being that of a globe having a density gradually increasing from the exterior inwards towards the centre, but with its materials heterogeneously arranged, and with the lighter crust gradually and irregularly passing into the heavier liquid beneath.

If our attention be now turned to a consideration of the evidence derived from the behavior of matter under the combined action of heat and pressure, which behavior is said to prove that the interior of the earth is solid, the important questions are: $1°$. What are the materials forming the earth's mass? $2°$. Do these expand or contract on passing from the liquid to the solid state?

In answer to the first question, it may be said that the results of petrographical study render it probable that the portion of the interior mass lying nearest the centre, and concerning which we have any data, is composed of iron,† either with or without nickel. As we recede from this portion we find pyrrhotite united with the nickel and iron. Then these minerals are further joined with olivine, or olivine and enstatite, in varying proportions, until a region is reached composed almost entirely of one or both of these silicates with or without diallage. From this we pass into the common basaltic rocks, then into the andesites, and so on outward into the trachytic, rhyolitic, and jaspilite forms. However true this order may have been for the liquid earth, it is certain that in the solid portions of the crust these materials are interlaced now with each other in every conceivable way, and that in the chemical and sedimentary deposits they have been intimately mingled. As to what may be the composition of the earth's mass nearer the centre, if there be anything there besides the iron and nickel, we have

---

* Report Brit. Assoc. 1876, xlvi. (sect.) 1-12.
† Whitney's Metallic Wealth of the United States, 1854, p. 434. Judd's Volcanoes, 1881, pp. 307-324.

no clew, unless it be that very possibly some of the rarer elements now found mixed with the iron may occur there.

It was claimed by Sir William Thomson* that the earth must have solidified from the centre outward in accordance with the "thermo-dynamic law" of his brother Professor James Thomson, which may be stated in these words: *All materials which contract on congelation have their melting point raised by pressure, while bodies which expand on freezing have their melting point lowered by pressure.* Thomson, in common with nearly all physicists, held that the expansion of water and that of bismuth on freezing, were exceptional cases; but that contraction was the rule, and that pressure would therefore overcome the increment of heat as the centre was approached. The mistake made here was, that the cold solid was compared with the hot liquid; the fact being overlooked that this law applies to the point of passage from the liquid to the solid, and not to the relative density of the two taken at temperatures differing hundreds and even thousands of degrees.

Experiments† by Mallet, Centner, Millar, Whitley, Hannay, Anderson, Nies, Winkelmann, and Wrightson show that in the case of steel, iron, tin, copper, zinc, bismuth, antimony, etc., compared, at a temperature just below the melting point, with the melted material at about its freezing point, the solid is the lighter; but that these metals contract so on cooling that when cold all, except bismuth, are then heavier. It would seem that if solids and liquids are compared together at about the temperature of their congelation the solid is the lighter; and that therefore the pressure at the earth's interior would cause these metals to remain liquid at a lower temperature than they would on the earth's surface.

The same law holds good for slag, and seems to do so for lava; in fact this is probably true of almost all rocks, although the evidence is far from being conclusive.

Experiments‡ made by Hopkins, Bunsen, Mousson and others indicate that to change the fusion point a few degrees an enormous pressure is required, and that the law of Thomson is really capricious and variable, if always true. Hence, so far as our knowledge extends in regard to the

---

* Trans. Geol. Soc. Glasgow, 1878, vi. 38–49.
† Proc. Roy. Soc., 1874, xxii. 366–368; 1875, xxiii. 209–234; Nature, 1874, x. 156, 157; 1877, xv. 529, 530; xvi. 23, 24; 1878, xviii. 397, 398, 464; Proc. Roy. Soc. Edin., 1879, x. 359–362; Sitz. Akad. München, 1881, pp. 63–112; Phil. Mag., 1881, (5), xi. 295–299.
‡ Report Brit. Assoc., 1854, xxiv. (sect.) 57, 58; Ann. Physik Chemie, 1850, lxxxi. 562–567; 1858, cv. 161–174; Everett's Deschanel's Nat. Phil., 1872, pp. 312, 313; 1883, pp. 331, 332.

action of matter under pressure and heat, there is far more reason for believing the earth to be liquid than for taking the opposite view.

From what has here been stated it would seem that there is no evidence drawn from mathematical and physical laws which obliges the petrographer and geologist to assume an interior structure for the earth different from that which the facts of geology and petrography would lead them to expect.*

Starting, then, with the accepted belief that this earth was once an intensely hot gaseous body, it follows that if the heavier gases tend to lie nearer the centre than the lighter ones, the dissipation of heat could only take place through the slow conductivity of gases. In like manner, when the earth cooled down to a liquid mass convection would soon cease, if it ever existed, on account of the different densities of the earth's materials; and here also the dissipation of heat would have to take place by the slow conduction of liquids. In the same way, in the solid portions of the earth the heat from the interior has to be conveyed outwards through broken, fissured, heterogeneous material. It would seem that all these conditions should be taken into account in all physical discussions of the age of the earth and sun; but thus far all calculations seem to have been based upon the laws of the relation of gases and liquids of about the same density. There should further be considered the heat disengaged by the chemical unions necessary to form the present mineral combinations now existent on the earth.

As the liquid earth cooled and its materials grew viscous, all interchange of materials would be retarded; and as the cooling continued, the lighter exterior liquid portion would form a hot crust, which would be lighter than the underlying liquid. On account of the viscous condition through which the earth's materials must pass before solidification, the crust would gradually shade into the underlying liquid, and both would be nearly in the same condition with each other as to temperature. It is not probable that the crust would break up and begin to sink, because, even if its surface grew cold, it would always have this hot solid base lighter than the underlying viscous liquid, which, owing to the increase of specific gravity as the interior is approached, would probably be more dense than any of the overlying cold crust. Even if the crust should become heavier, break up, and begin to sink, this sinking would be very slow, on account of the viscosity

* Whitney, Earthquakes, Volcanoes, and Mountain Building, 1871, p. 74; Dana, Man. Geol., 1880, p. 812.

of the liquid, and its constantly increasing density; while the heat imparted to the sinking material would tend to bring it to about the same specific gravity with the liquid portion as the sinking mass neared its melting point. But — what is of still greater importance — the sinking material would soon reach a liquid of different composition and greater density than the crust; and farther than this it could not sink. That sinking of the crust to the centre, which Sir William Thomson supposed would take place, could only do so in case the hot solid was heavier than the liquid interior, and that liquid homogeneous. But both these conditions appear opposed to what we know of the properties of matter and of the heterogeneous composition of the earth.

The structure of the earth that would naturally follow, from what has been above stated, would be a heterogeneous crust floating on a denser heterogeneous liquid, and one which the interior pressure tends to keep liquid at a lower temperature than on the surface, so far as it affects it at all.

In an earth like this, owing to the gradual passage of the crust into the viscous liquid interior, no shrinking of the nucleus from the exterior could take place, but the earth would contract as a whole. A linear shortening of the crust would occur that would crush it together, and cause its depression in some places and its elevation in others. The depression of any portion of the crust into the liquid interior would naturally cause an equivalent weight of the heavier liquid to rise, and perhaps overflow. This simple sinking of a portion of the crust on one side with its corresponding but less elevation on the other, with the attendant fissuring, would afford all the dynamic agencies needed to raise lavas to the tops of our highest mountains, and would account for the association of volcanoes with depressed basins, for fissure eruptions, etc.* The contraction could hardly be expected to be equal in every portion, while the depression of portions of the crust with the attendant outflows would cause an unequal thickness of the crust, with great irregularities in its base adjacent to the liquid interior. The outflows, themselves, would cause this crust to be tied through and through by the different eruptive materials.

This great irregularity in thickness, which the earth's crust is supposed to present, coupled with the viscosity of its interior portion next the crust, would apparently prevent any direct or special connection between different

---

* Whitney, Earthquakes, Volcanoes, and Mountain-Building, p. 90.

vents, even if they were near one another. The viscosity of the cooling liquid portion would, of itself, prevent any rapid flow of material from one point to another. But at the same time the liquidity of the interior mass would cause it to seek escape from pressure at any available opening, however far that vent might be from the point of pressure. Yet the more viscous the material, the less applicable would be the ordinary law of the transmission of pressures by liquids.

The part played by water in a volcanic eruption seems to consist mainly of its action on the lava during its passage upwards, instead of serving as the cause or *primum mobile* of the eruption. It is difficult to see how lava in ascending to the earth's surface could reach it without meeting water somewhere on its way. This water with its attendant phenomena seems to be the accident, rather than the cause of the eruption. As stated before, a different view of the present structure of the earth's interior can be taken, which may not be inconsistent with the facts of petrography. This is that the interior, or at least the portion from which our eruptive rocks come, is solid, but in such a state that it can be readily reliquefied. This reliquefaction may be brought about either from increase or diminution of pressure, according as future experiments may show the relative densities of hot solid and liquid matter to be. The supposition that eruptive rocks come from these re-fused portions of the earth's originally solidified primitive material, would perhaps explain the origin of the minerals of the first or foreign class, to be spoken of later, which occur in these rocks.

Section II. — *The Origin and Alteration of Rocks.*

The theory of the origin of rocks generally taught in America is the following, with some more or less important modifications: The sedimentary (chemical and mechanical) rocks derived from the ruins of the "primeval crust" form all that portion of the earth's crust which is now known. By ordinary denudation these rocks would be removed from one point and deposited in another locality, the result being that the underlying sediments would be still more deeply buried in one place, and exhumed in another. The portions thus more deeply buried would be invaded by the earth's central heat, this giving rise to a more or less intense chemical action in them. The seat of this action is known as the "zone of aqueo-igneous fusion" (solution), and all sediments, if sufficiently deeply buried, come within this hypothetical zone. The different portions of the sediments would be more or less affected and metamorphosed, according to their chemical constitution, and their proximity to the hypothetical zone. If they came within the zone, their fusion or solution would give rise to lavas and volcanic eruptions. Some authors hold that every form of eruptive rock comes from sedimentary materials which have been thus acted upon; while others maintain that, although the true lavas and intrusive rocks may have been derived from non-sedimentary material, yet the sedimentary rocks take upon themselves forms undistinguishable from those of the volcanic rocks. Other modifications of this theory are delegating the source of the eruptive rocks to re-fused portions of the original solidified crust of the earth, which has been fused again on account of relief from pressure by denudation. This last view has been founded, so far as present evidence shows, on a misconception of the apparent general action of matter in passing from a liquid to a solid (not cold) state; therefore this should be abandoned, and fusion by increase of pressure either through the earth's contraction or by the deposition of sediments substituted. Another theoretical view is simply a remodelling of the old Wernerian hypothesis, and its application to the crystalline rocks. According to this view we are taught that all these rocks were deposited in pre-Cambrian time, and that all eruptive rocks have been derived from these chemical ones by aqueo-igneous solution or fusion. These crystalline rocks and their derived eruptive forms are then divided according to their lithological characters into distinct geological ages, and their age is said to be recognizable whether the rocks themselves be seen in their original form or in that of dikes and lava-flows.

If the above views are correct, we should expect to find in some formations rocks which had suffered every degree of alteration, the same rock passing from an unmetamorphosed condition into a highly metamorphosed or even eruptive one, with every gradation between. At certain points, when denudation has succeeded a former epoch of accumulation, the more or less deeply buried sediments would again appear upon the surface, showing greater or less evidence of the conditions to which they had been subjected. By carefully selecting the localities to be studied, we naturally should expect to find every degree of change in the rocks, and various transitions by direct passage from rocks unmistakably sedimentary into those that are truly eruptive, in their present position, — from those rocks whose original fragmental structure is undoubted, to those that have been in a plastic, semi-fluidal, or fluidal state. All these changes should exist in the same continuous mass of rock, and we ought to be able to trace the gradations from one place to another. That such passages have been observed, has been repeatedly claimed, but when the localities where these facts could be observed were sought for, they could not be found.

The results of petrographical study seem to point to the following as the probable origin of rocks. If we start from a cooling liquid earth then all mechanically and chemically formed rocks have come from the liquid material originally. Furthermore, all the eruptive rocks appear to have come from below the sedimentary ones, and are only influenced by them in their composition, by the materials accidentally picked up during their passage through, or flow over the latter. In the case of volcanic rocks, we should expect to have associated with the lava, ashes, and in fact every kind of material projected from the crater, including débris and mud. All these would be naturally more or less intimately mixed together according as one was deposited on, or around the other, — or as one in its flow picked up, surrounded, or overlaid another. This would associate all loose materials and rocks of any kind that existed in the locality prior to the lava flow; while during that time and later the atmospheric agencies would tend to still more intimately mingle these diverse materials, and obliterate their differences. Wherever the lava was exposed to detrital action, there would be deposited about and around it detritus of the same material, mixed or not, as the case might be, with that from other rocks, — especially if the eruption took place on or near the shore line. In the case of massive or fissure eruptions and dikes, we should expect but few or none of the common accompaniments of an ordinary explosive volcanic eruption, but all eruptive material would be subject to degradation, and would under proper conditions become associated with its own detritus and that formed from other rocks. All the associated detritus, if of one kind, would suffer the same alterations which non-fragmental material of the same kind has to pass through. Under conditions otherwise identical, detrital material would doubtless be affected in a greater degree than the solid rock, owing to the former's greater perviousness to water. While in the unaltered condition we may be able to readily distinguish the fragmental from the non-fragmental forms by the unaided eye, this is no longer possible when both have been subject to alteration. They then closely simulate one another, and the microscope used in connection with the field evidence offers the only means of distinguishing the fragmental from the non-fragmental form. When rocks of more than one kind are mixed in the detritus, the alteration and appearance of the sedimentary rock formed from this undergoes a corresponding modification.

We should expect to find certain very intimate relations between all these various forms of associated rock, and it would be very difficult to distinguish, in the older and more altered forms, between the material picked up during the flow, the ashes or débris, and the solid non-fragmental rock. The greater the amount of secondary alteration which these different rocks have suffered, the greater the difficulty of distinguishing between them. In no case, however, would the fragmental pass into the non-fragmental form by insensible gradations or otherwise. It is true that they sometimes appear to do so, but that appearance is only superficial.

In order then to decide between the different theories proposed for the origin of eruptive rocks, it is necessary to make some examination of the evidence offered in their support by petrographical study. For this purpose the most important question is, do sedimentary rocks take upon themselves the characters of eruptive ones? In the writer's studies he has found a certain resemblance between both classes of rocks when they are of similar composition. This is, however, only in the case of rocks greatly altered, and arises from secondary changes in each; which result in the production of new mineral constituents, and in the obliteration of the original structure of both to a greater or less extent. Indeed, in some cases, this obliteration is total, the minerals and mineral characters — in fact all the characters — of the rocks thus changed being rendered unlike those which belonged to the original eruptive rock. These alterations are apparently more dependent upon the chemical composition of the rocks, and the conditions to which they have been subjected, than upon their having been in a fragmental or non-fragmental state. The result is, that the eruptive rock is degraded to the status of an altered sedimentary rock, not that the latter takes upon itself the characters of an eruptive one. Whether the two classes thus indicated can or cannot always be distinguished under the microscope in cases of extreme alteration, is a problem of the future, and perhaps the most difficult one with which the petrographer will be confronted.

Undoubtedly, a careful study of the field relations of rocks would, in the majority of cases, suffice to settle the question of their origin.

If sedimentary rocks should be found under peculiar and abnormal conditions, to present the characters regarded as typical of eruptive forms[*]

---

[*] Metamorphism produced by the burning of Lignite Beds in Dakota and Montana Territories. By J. A. Allen. Proc. Bost. Soc. Nat. Hist., 1874, xvi. 246-262.

this would not be a basis for assuming that normally sedimentary rocks take these characters; although this statement is one which is frequently made.

Examinations have been repeatedly made by the writer for the purpose of ascertaining whether any rocks whose sedimentary origin was undoubted had acquired the microscopical characters of eruptive forms, but nothing of the kind has yet been discovered by him.

In order to prove the passage of a sedimentary rock into an eruptive one, it is necessary to have on one side the undisputed fragmental form, and to trace it directly by continuous passage into the non-fragmental one. Not an inch of the parts lying between should be allowed to escape examination; and it must be positively known that no line of junction exists, but that the two rocks form a continuous whole. In no case on record, however, does it appear that passages of the kind indicated, and which have been claimed as existing, have ever been subjected to so close an examination as is here demanded. Eruptive and sedimentary rocks at their line of junction usually mutually influence one another, often appearing very much alike, especially when they have been subjected to later alterations by which both have been affected. It is, then, to be expected that the observer who is not practically familiar with these occurrences will pass directly over the lines of junction, especially if he has been taught that direct passages of one rock into another may occur. His evidence is of that negative kind which, for various reasons, can usually be obtained with ease. The evidence that the two rocks do not pass into one another is of the positive kind, for the line of junction when once seen can be examined and re-examined at any time; while hand specimens can frequently be procured which will show both kinds of rock and their junction in one fragment. We can then have positive field and laboratory (including microscopic) evidence that the two rocks are not the same but different ones. The writer has had frequent occasion to examine localities in which the direct passage of a fragmental rock into a non-fragmental one was said to occur, and in no case has he not been able to obtain positive evidence that such passage did not exist, when the conditions were such that a satisfactory examination could be made. When the evidence was lacking it was always owing to the junction being covered, or else shattered by jointing, frost, etc.

Practically, when the existence of these junctions had been shown, the observers who had previously denied their existence have always said: "That is not a typical locality; we were not quite sure about that place, but if you will go to such or such a locality, — indicating some new one, — you will find an undoubted passage of the sedimentary rock into eruptive forms." When this new locality is also examined and the statements are found to be erroneous, another one is mentioned, and so on; until one must demand hereafter of these observers that they shall select some locality on which they shall be willing to fully and finally stake their pet hypothesis, and abide by the evidence.

It has been claimed that the results of chemical analysis show that volcanic rocks are derived from sedimentary ones. While it is true that the former have a composition chemically like some of the latter, this resemblance is easily explained by the fact that a sedimentary rock ought to resemble chemically the massive rock from whose destruction it came. The chief difference between them would be that resulting from the change brought about by outside influences, the introduction of foreign material, etc. Hence the chemical resemblance between the two classes of rocks can naturally and readily be explained by the derivation of the sedimentary from the eruptive rocks; and there is no need to resort to the unnatural and hypothetical derivation of the volcanic from the sedimentary rocks. The former derivation is the one seen to take place every day, while the latter is unproved as yet, and those who hold it are apparently looking at the effect, and making it the cause. In other words, it seems to the writer that these observers have taken hold of the subject at the wrong end.

In examining the products of volcanoes, certain minerals appear to be characteristic of them, which are of prior origin to the consolidation of the lava. These minerals show evidence that a hot magma has directly acted upon them, and every gradation can frequently be seen between the almost untouched mineral, and the nearly destroyed one.

I regard these minerals, unless they were caught up by the lava during its passage from the earth's interior to its surface, as evidences that the material from which the lava was derived is no longer in its original condition, although this condition was not like that of any of our sedimentary rocks. Certain of these minerals are easily destroyed; two at least, suffering alteration readily on exposure, and it seems impossible that they could survive when the much less perishable materials of our sedimentary rocks have been entirely obliterated, if, as is supposed by many, they were ever there. These minerals are unlike, either in species, variety, or form, with possibly a few exceptions, any minerals occurring in sedimentary rocks as a metamorphic product, *i. e.*, not derived directly from the eruptive rocks. These minerals are characteristic not only of the modern lavas, but also of the most ancient eruptive rocks in which secondary alteration has not obliterated their characters; not only in the modern basalt, but also in the ancient melaphyr; not only in the modern rhyolite, but also in the ancient felsite. These characters are not confined to any single locality or age, but are, so far as known, world wide, and go back to the earliest times in which such rocks occur.*

We should then claim that the field evidence, as well as the microscopic, is opposed *in toto* to the prevailing theory that the eruptive rocks are derived from sedimentary ones. That theory demands immense duration of time, unstable continents, enormous forces, a solid earth that shall be more rigid than glass, and yet yield like a rubber ball to the slightest pressure of sediments, lava flows, or glaciers. The theory in question demands the removal of immense masses from one place, and their deposition in another, the elevation of billions of tons in order to avoid the necessity of admitting the elevation of hundreds, — for in order to have denudation that shall bring once deeply buried sediments to the surface, the entire mass must be lifted bodily above the surrounding region, or from the zone of aqueo-igneous fusion to the outer air. Which view requires the greatest force — to elevate and depress such enormous bulks in a solid earth, or to raise our lavas from a liquid interior — is plainly evident. This theory requires that volcanic action should be of modern birth — Tertiary — and that eruptive rocks of earlier date should have been produced by different forces — a view now known to be false. To the theory that the crystalline rocks are chemical precipitates arranged in regular succession, there arises the serious objection that the oldest form — the so-called Laurentian — is cut by dikes of rocks which, according to that theory, could not have existed below them; that is, they belong lithologically to the so-called Huronian and Norian systems.

In contradistinction to the views here indicated, the writer's petrographical studies lead him to hold, with some others, that all volcanic or eruptive action arises from the original igneous state of the earth — that it must have begun in the earliest ages of this globe. This action being a manifestation of a dying energy, must have been more active in the past than at present, although it may have been intermittent in character as all such forces seem to be. The products of this action have been the same from the earliest to

* See also David Forbes. Nature, 1870, ii. 283–286; 1873, vii. 259–261.

the latest geological periods; that is, a rhyolite, a trachyte, an andesite, or a basalt of the Azoic or Palæozoic times, was the same when erupted as is the rhyolite, trachyte, andesite or basalt of the present day, or of the Tertiary age. The difference at present existing between these ancient and modern forms — as the writer believes — is due to the greater alteration which the former have suffered; although possibly, a difference in the depth, or some peculiar condition prevailing at the time of the consolidation of the rock, may have had some influence in causing these differences.

Under uniformly like conditions, alteration is proportional to the age, in rocks of the same constitution and structure; but when rocks of like character are subjected to the same agencies, for the same length of time, like results would be produced, let the age be what it will. The original crust and the eruptive rocks must, then, have furnished the material for all the other rocks, directly or indirectly, except such as was derived from water and the atmosphere. To trace these changes, and to follow the rocks in all their variations is the work of the petrographer. As did Cuvier with fossil bones, so may the lithologist reconstruct the original rock from the fossil fragments of it found in other rocks. The presence of fragments of one rock in another, however, is not to be taken as proof of difference of geological age between them, unless it can be proved that the inclosed rock is of sedimentary origin. A lava flow on a sea-shore would have its fragments included in any rock then forming, and this would hold true of all volcanic ejectments. A dike, also, passing through a rock forming on the shore, would have all materials broken from it inclosed in the rock then forming, but both would be of the same age geologically, although differing in order of time.

In studying the alterations in rocks we ought not to confound the great molecular changes that go on through the rock mass as a whole, and those changes which are due to superficial weathering. The latter reproduce to some extent the characters of the former, but go to greater extremes, causing in the end destruction and disintegration of the rock mass itself. The internal changes are apparently chemical or molecular changes in the whole rock mass, instead of simple pseudomorphic changes of single minerals. In no sense is metamorphism to be looked upon as extended pseudomorphism; for pseudomorphic forms are but an accident in the process of alteration, and they may or may not occur, according to the amount of that alteration. All the changes in rocks are to be explained by taking into consideration the elements of the entire rock mass, and all elements brought into it by the percolating waters; the chemical reactions taking place between any or all of these elements according to the special conditions, and not being confined to simple interchanges between the constituents of two minerals, as pseudomorphs in mineral veins are usually explained. The failure to appreciate the above distinctions is believed to have led to the statement of much that is improbable in the works of many writers on pseudomorphic and metamorphic changes in rocks.

When we consider the petrographical structure of modern volcanic districts and the alterations their rocks have undergone, we ought not to be surprised at the magnitude of the changes which we find to have taken place in rocks which have been subjected to similar conditions during countless ages. But these changes are metamorphic, and the rocks thus altered are metamorphic rocks. Metamorphism, however, does not appear to be limited to rocks of one kind, but affects all classes. The amount of metamorphism any rock undergoes under the same conditions seems to be inversely proportional to the amount of contained silica; and this change apparently began as soon as any of the earth's solid material was exposed to the combined action of air and water, and has continued up to the present day. Volcanic or eruptive action, including a subsequent prolonged exposure to hot water, accompanying the dying eruptive force, appears to have been an efficient agent in metamorphism.

According to the above view, the metamorphic rocks produced would be dependent upon their chemical composition and the agency by which the changes were effected, but would not be at all dependent upon the geological age. Hence lithological characters would be valueless as a criterion for determining the age of such rocks.

The writer finds that the constituents of the eruptive rocks and their derivatives pass in their alteration from the unstable towards more stable compounds in the conditions to which they are subjected,—that is, they pass into forms that never can in the ordinary course of nature return to their original condition. In this there exists a potent factor for the dissipation of energy. The potential energy of the original chemical combination is in a greater or less degree lost, and cannot be restored except by some foreign power,— or, in other words, the original structure and composition cannot be normally regained. The advocates of the sedimentary origin of igneous rocks, however, require the restoration of that lost energy, and advocate a sort of perpetual motion. According to them these rocks are born, grow old, and die, and their remains are raised again and again, that the process may be repeated. The writer accepts the birth, old age, decay, and death; but he doubts the resurrection and believes that such views are opposed to physical laws.

A crystalline structure is indigenous in any eruptive rock, if it remains in a condition that allows it to slowly crystallize; and this structure is not therefore any proof of great age in a rock, or a sign that it was formed at great depth.*

From the above it would follow that such rocks as the felsites cannot be taken as characteristic of certain ages (Arvonian or Huronian); but if — as the writer, with others, holds — they are old rhyolites, they have been formed in all ages. Again, while they may have been deeply covered with detrital beds, there is no necessity for such a burial, or any proof that they were once thus covered, any more than there is that the modern rhyolites have been.

Also, the claim for long times for the formation of rocks which are fine-grained and fossiliferous cannot always be allowed; as for instance, the Florissant shales,† or a large deposit of fine, dust-like powder, observed in the vicinity of the Black Hills by my colleague, Mr. Samuel Garman. This powder is made up of minute fragments of volcanic glass, forming a bed several feet in thickness. If it had not been for the revelations of the microscope, would not some geologist be computing the number of thousands of years it would take to form these deposits "as Nile mud," when perhaps, a few weeks or even days were sufficient for this purpose. If the deposits in question had been subjected to sufficient alteration to obliterate the original texture, who would have been able to prove the falsity of the theory of a slow deposition of the material as an ordinary sediment?

Another illustration is afforded by the Lake Superior sandstone, which shows that extreme care is required to ascertain the conditions under which any deposit formed, before the length of time required for its formation shall be estimated.‡

To the objections offered to lavas being the same from all time, on account of the difficulty of believing that the same portions of the earth's

---

* Bull. Mus. Comp. Zool., 1880, vii. 111.
† Bull. U. S. Geol. Survey, 1881, vi. 286, 287.
‡ Bull. Mus. Comp. Zool., 1880, vii. 177, 118.

interior have been liquid since the Azoic time, it may be replied that if contraction suffices to keep up the heat of the sun to an approximate uniformity, so too the contraction of the earth would tend to maintain a uniform temperature in the earth's interior; a point that it is necessary to consider in all discussions relating to the earth's age. It may again be suggested that, while basic rocks of the same character as those seen to-day were erupted in the early ages of the earth, yet there has been on the whole a progression from the acidic to the basic, in relative abundance, from earlier to later times. Furthermore, owing to the irregularity in thickness with which the earth's crust has apparently solidified, great diversities would be expected to exist in that part immediately below the crust in different portions of the earth.*

Whether volcanic and all other eruptive rocks came from material that has never cooled to a solid state since the earth began to solidify, or whether they are derived from a portion that solidified, but has since been reliquefied, is a problem for the future, the solution of which hinges on the origin of the partially destroyed materials in the rocks themselves, — were they caught up on the passage of the lava to the earth's surface, or are they the remains of a prior crystallization?

If we turn to Sorby's method for determining the origin of rocks by the inclusions in the contained minerals, we find that it may possibly answer in recent, surface-formed rocks; but that in the old and altered forms it seems to carry us astray, and serves but to retard the advance of our knowledge of rock formation. This is especially the case if the secondary minerals, like quartz, have been formed later in the rock in question by the action of hot waters. Conclusions regarding the origin of a secondary or foreign mineral included in a rock ought not to be transferred to the rock itself, as those who use Sorby's method are in a habit of doing.

The somewhat common argument that a rock associated with crystalline schists must have the same origin as the schists, would make a dike in slate of the same origin as the slate. Association of rocks proves nothing, for in volcanic districts, in limited areas even, rocks of every character can be found together. Should we then hold that because some were sedimentary, all the others were so? Or, again, should we claim that because some were eruptive, all the rest were eruptive? No! we ought to prove the origin of each rock, and in every locality in which it occurs, so far as possible, and when evidence is wanting leave the question as undetermined.

* Whitney's Volcanoes, Earthquakes, and Mountain Building, pp. 69-107.

A region in which eruptive rocks abound is a region in which crystalline schists would naturally be expected to occur; for here the conditions of metamorphism are best developed, — conditions that affect and metamorphose all the associated rocks, both eruptive and sedimentary, according to their composition and physical structure. Eruptive rocks, whether in dikes or lava flows, ashes or detritus of any kind, frequently possess the characters of crystalline schists; must they therefore be regarded as being of sedimentary origin? The writer has seen dikes of crystalline schists cutting directly across schistose conglomerates and other sedimentary rocks. Was he to conclude that these dikes of schist were sedimentary, and had been intruded in the form of schists; or rather that they were of eruptive origin, — the original rock having been later metamorphosed into a schistose rock? He has also seen mica schists inclosed in distinctly eruptive granites. If the law of association is worth anything, then should it not be claimed that these schists were eruptive? Ought not the evidence and the facts of the origin, and not the association, to be taken as proof of what that origin was?

At this time, when the tendency is so strong to consider almost everything the result of stratification, it seems necessary here to call attention to some characters that for the most part are common to all rocks, whatever may be their origin. While these characters are taken as proof positive of sedimentation, in reality they have no bearing upon the question unless they are exclusively confined to one class.

Lamination in a rock is one of these characters; which may be defined as a structure, either original or superinduced in rocks of various kinds, causing them to *tend to split* into more or less parallel layers.

This structure is very common in many eruptive rocks, especially those of a fine-grained or glassy character, and which have become metamorphosed. In many rocks an appearance of lamination is brought about by the deposition of coloring matters in bands, and this pseudo-lamination even has been oftentimes taken for stratification.

Joint planes may be defined as fissures traversing rocks in a regular or irregular manner, independently of any other structural planes, induced during the time of the consolidation of the rock or later, and dividing it into masses of greater or less size.[*]

These planes are frequently mistaken for bedding planes, both in

---

[*] Faults and fissure veins are but modified joints.

sedimentary and eruptive masses, particularly in regions of crystalline rocks. Eruptive rocks subjected to pressure in dikes, or when they are metamorphosed, tend to take upon themselves a more or less parallel jointing, which superficially resembles stratification, and which to the writer's personal knowledge has been taken for bedding planes by some of the most prominent geologists in the United States.

Cleavage is another structure, which by many is supposed to be confined to sedimentary rocks; but this is evidently not the case. This may be defined as a tendency in rocks to split more or less indefinitely into thin plates, independently of any original structure in the rock masses. In the same series, the finer the grain the more perfect is the cleavage; therefore it is best developed in argillites, fine grained eruptive rocks, and volcanic ashes. The presence of cleavage characters in the last two series of rocks ought to make us careful in deciding upon the origin of any rocks from considerations connected with their cleavage alone: further evidence should be obtained, of a more decisive character.

Foliation is another rock structure belonging to rocks of diverse origin, and due either to the existence of bands or layers of different minerals, or to a more or less parallel arrangement of foliated minerals, like talc, mica, chlorite, etc. This structure may even be taken by rocks which are not composed of foliated minerals, as, for instance, limestone. Foliated specimens of limestone destitute of mica have been brought to the writer from Western Massachusetts, as being mica schist, and considered as supporting the view that in that region the limestone passes directly into mica schist.

It is very difficult to give any definition of foliation that will cover all cases of this structure, but it may in general be said to signify a structure induced (not congenital) in rock masses by the arrangement of certain crystallized minerals, or of a single mineral, in more or less parallel lines, along which the crystals lie, flatways or lengthways. It has been found that in sedimentary rocks the foliation may or may not correspond with the stratification planes, and until in each case it is proved to do so it cannot be taken as marking the original planes of deposition. The causes that produce cleavage in some rocks seem to induce foliation in others. An example of this is to be observed at the point of land south of Boston Harbor, known as Squantum. At this locality the stratification and cleavage of the argillite and sandstone are seen to differ considerably from one another, while the conglomerate lying between has its pebbles somewhat rearranged, giving rise to a schistose or semi-foliated structure. These foliation planes correspond with the cleavage planes, but not with the original bedding of the rock.

Foliation is of frequent occurrence in metamorphosed eruptive rocks, giving rise to schistose forms which are ordinarily taken for micaceous, chloritic, and other schists, which are usually regarded as sedimentary. All these are cases of similar structures and similar rocks, resulting from the alteration of rocks of diverse origin, but of similar chemical composition. Foliation usually corresponds to the lines of pressure, — either from the walls or from the surface downward, and is usually brought about by recrystallization of the rock constituents during the process of alteration. Since rocks of every kind are subject to metamorphism, and none more so than the basic eruptive ones, it is natural to suppose that highly altered eruptive as well as sedimentary rocks would display that character of structure which is designated by the term foliation.

Many rocks which can hardly be said to possess lamination or foliation, show nevertheless a schistose or fissile structure, which is a property of all more or less altered rocks, — a superinduced structure, and not a congenital one. Hence, this structure cannot be taken as being confined to a single class of rocks, and therefore a diagnostic for that class, as has been done by some geologists.

Fluidal structure is a character induced in eruptive rocks through their having moved or flowed when in a liquid or pasty condition. It is best seen in the glassy and acidic eruptive rocks and furnace slags. This structure belongs to, and is characteristic of eruptive rocks. It is by no means confined to lava flows, but is also to be seen in dikes. The difficulty in regard to employing it as a diagnostic character arises from the close resemblance of it to other structures in altered rocks, and its obliteration by secondary alteration in the rock mass. A schistose structure induced in rocks by alteration is the one structure that under the microscope is most often mistaken for fluidal structure. Fluidal structure has been taken for bands of sedimentation in a large number of instances, particularly in the older acidic rocks like felsite and granite.

The bands of chemical deposition, as in the case of silica from hot springs, have in some instances been confounded with the fluidal structure of eruptive rocks, although distinct from that both in character and cause.

In the employment of the fluidal characters in the older rocks, great care needs to be taken to prevent their being confounded with the superinduced structures in the same rocks, for such mistakes are of very frequent occurrence.

Arguments from analogy should only be permitted in deciding the question of the origin of any rock when no other evidence exists; and then such arguments should be admitted to be of a doubtful character, and not held to be proof positive. Another prominent fallacy in petrography is the argument that as the conditions are in one region, so must they be in another, — while no effort is made to find out what the real conditions are in the latter.

The origin of the older rocks, comprising the districts regarded as Azoic or Archæan, and the principles on which they have to be subdivided into groups, or ages, have an important bearing upon the classification of rocks. The prevalent views regarding the constitution of these older formations were looked upon, by the writer, as opposed to petrographical facts; hence it became necessary to make a careful examination of the published evidence in behalf of these views. This has been done and duly published,[*] with the result that no real evidence has been found sustaining the current views; and thus the petrographer is free to follow the data of his science.

The structure of the districts of crystalline rocks can in most cases be explained in the following way. Let the reader imagine a region covered by rock, either eruptive or sedimentary. Then suppose that here eruptive (volcanic) action begins, and ashes, mud, lava, and the other accompaniments of such action are mingled together. The earlier sedimentary rocks, and the volcanic material are later cut through and through by dikes — faulted and jointed, contorted, and if on a sea-shore, subjected to wave action before the latter are fairly cold.

We might thus have mingled in inextricable confusion lava flows, indurated and contorted sedimentary rocks, ashes, scoria, mud-flows, dikes, marine deposits, in short, every known form of rock which can be produced by the combined action of volcanic, pluvial, and marine agencies. After this, then imagine the decline of the eruptive power, with the accompanying gaseous and thermal water action. Imagine the changes in the rock structure that these agents would produce, as previously mentioned under rock alteration, including vein phenomena; and then consider what would be the effect upon such a district of the action of every conceivable geological agency during the countless years since the early geological ages. Then suppose that some

[*] Bull. Mus. Comp. Zoöl., 1880, vii. No. 1; 1884, No. 11.

geologist be placed upon this old volcanic ground worn down to its roots, its rocks altered or metamorphosed, its remnants of mingled lava flows, ejectamenta, and marine deposits, and let him be asked to give its history. If he were educated in the prevailing views current in American geological literature, it is probable that he would declare that this was an old chemical or sedimentary deposit, which had been buried thousands on thousands of feet deep under other sedimentary deposits, and in which, owing to the inclosed moisture and the rise of the internal heat, an aqueo-igneous solution had set in, rendering the formation plastic. He would also say, that owing to the generated gases and pressure, the lower portions of the deposit had been forced into the upper ones, and every gradation had been produced between the normal sedimentary rock and eruptive forms, which pass by insensible gradations into each other. How easy and simple would this explanation be!—nothing could be shown which the authors of such theories could not explain. But how false in our supposed case such an explanation would be. If we add to our supposed volcanoes massive eruptions, with or without fragmental ejections (explosive action), shall we not have the same petrographical features that now exist in regions of the older crystalline rocks?—and is the explanation generally adopted for them any more accurate?

The intermingling of eruptive and detrital deposits here supposed is described in almost every work on volcanic action, and it has been clearly shown, in many of these districts of older crystalline rocks, that the series of events here indicated has been very common.

That sedimentation has done its part the writer believes, and he has not the slightest wish to belittle its importance; but that it has done everything he does not believe. Whether any of the first-cooled masses may ever be found, is a problem for the future; but that we have to do with material that was fluid before sedimentation began, we consider is clearly established.

To volcanic phenomena, whether explosive or massive, and to the associated water action, appear to be due the phenomena of crystalline rocks, which occur in any and every age from the earliest times to the present.

Especial stress has here been placed upon the characters and phenomena of eruptive rocks, in hopes of bringing about a state of geology in which the opposing eruptive and sedimentary agencies shall both have their proper share,—which at present they do not have, on account of the extreme to which the advocates of sedimentation have now carried their views.

The views of sedimentation have been pushed so far that one wonders if Strabo, after he had described the volcanic characters of Vesuvius, was not told by his cotemporaries that it was all a mistake — that the peculiar character of the rocks was owing to chemical deposition or to mechanical sediments; that all showed the slow accumulations of millions of years on a slowly subsiding sea-floor; that the whole had been buried many miles under the accumulating sediments, rendered plastic, causing dikes to be formed; that all the different rocks passed by insensible gradations into one another, etc.; and that, finally, the whole mountain was carved out by the slow process of the removal of the sediments, and was undoubtedly, owing to the crystalline character of its rocks, one of the earliest formations of the globe.

In working in regions of crystalline rocks, the principles should be used that one would employ in studying districts in which modern volcanic action has existed, as about Naples, Mount Etna, Iceland, western North and South America, and Japan.

If this is done, and the older districts are examined by the aid of the light given by the modern eruptive formations, the writer believes that the present obscurity enveloping the former would be cleared away. The greatest difficulties in the study of such regions seem to have been in the theoretical views of the observers themselves. The question regarding such rocks should be, what are the facts, and not what are the theories.

It seems to the writer clear that the earlier formations of which we have any record in the earth's crust were not derived from the waste of earlier lands, but rather that they are for the most part eruptive, if not portions of the first formed crust; and that the fragmental portions were eruptive ashes, or were derived from the waste of eruptive material.*

The burden of proof rests upon the advocate of ancient destroyed continents, to show that the materials which he supposes came from such lands could not have been derived from the eruptive action of that early day.

The term eruptive, or volcanic, has been applied in this paper to all rocks coming from beneath the surface, showing signs that they have been in a fluid condition, — whether ancient or modern, — for nature has not, to my belief, drawn any line in her rocks between the younger volcanic and the older plutonic forms, but all form a continuous and harmonious whole.

* Geikie, Text Book of Geology, pp. 12, 13.

SECTION III. — *The Origin and Relations of the Mineral Constituents of Rocks.*

TAKING the consolidation of any rock as the initial point, particularly those of an eruptive nature, the constituents fall into one of three classes: I. Those of prior origin; II. Those formed at that time; III. Those of later origin.*

The minerals of the first class naturally fall into two divisions, in the eruptive rocks.

1. Those that are characteristic of the rock species.
2. Those that are accidental, being probably caught up in the passage upward or during the outflow. Similar divisions are found to a greater or less extent in the sedimentary rocks, according as they were derived from one or more rocks, and also according to the preponderance of different rock fragments and minerals in them.

The minerals, and fragments of minerals and rocks, occurring in rock masses that belong to the first-class, have an important bearing upon the questions of the origin and relations of rocks — so much so that more attention will be given to them in the future than has been the case in the past. These are in a great measure characteristic of the rock species, and should have a very great weight in the nomenclature of sedimentary rocks; for one of the most important questions regarding these is, what was the original material from which they were derived? In the volcanic rocks these minerals are distinguished generally by the effect that the magma has produced upon them — the blackening, breaking, tearing, and dissolving action which is so conspicuous in the case of olivine and hornblende; while in quartz it is shown in the fractures, the rounding of the grains, and the interpenetration of the magma. Frequently these foreign materials, especially quartz, have radiating rings of the groundmass surrounding them, these rings being largely composed of crystals standing perpendicular to the surface of the inclosed piece. In all rocks of an eruptive nature, the fragments are apparently either inclusions caught in the passage upward, or during the surface flow of the lava, or else derived from the remelting of the more crystalline portions of these or other rocks at the time of, or prior to the eruption; especially when the eruption

---

* A. Michel Lévy, Bull. Soc. Géol. France, 1874 (3), iii. 199-236; Ann. Mines, 1875 (7), viii. 341-346; Wadsworth, Bull. Mus. Comp. Zool., 1879, v. 277, 279.

took place in an old vent, from which the plug of lava and ashes must be removed before the outflow could occur.

The action of lavas upon these foreign inclusions seems to be that of a corrosive dissolving hot magma or solution, which penetrates and gnaws its way into the included fragments. Two classes of foreign materials seem to be characteristic of most of the eruptive rock species — simple minerals, and rock fragments. The latter are either the same as the inclosing rock or else they are the same as some rock known to have reached the earth's surface earlier in order of time. These mineral inclusions characterize the same rock type from the earliest times to the present, when- and where-ever they may occur. All this indicates some deep seated universal cause beyond the influence of sedimentary rocks.

These characteristic minerals, too, are not such as occur in sedimentary rocks; while no such admixture of material exists in the eruptive forms as would naturally be expected to occur if they were formed from sediments. Then too, the minerals and fragments of the more difficultly altered sedimentary rocks ought to have remained side by side with these easily alterable foreign minerals in eruptive rocks, if the latter rocks are the re-fused portions of the former. The microscopic characters of the eruptive rocks are to my mind utterly opposed to any theory that they come from sediments, or anything else than the original liquid material of the earth.

The second class of rock constituents naturally occupies the most prominent place in recent volcanic rocks, and a more subordinate one in the older eruptive and sedimentary ones. In eruptive rocks, the indigenous materials are the products of the magma when unacted upon by extraneous agencies. It is doubtful if any minerals come under this head — direct primary products of crystallization of the magma — except anhydrous silicates and oxides, a few phosphates, sulphides, and native elements, the other minerals in the rocks belonging to the other two classes.

The third class becomes very prominent in the older and altered rocks, and includes the hydrous and some anhydrous oxides and silicates, carbonates, and most sulphides.

These forms are the products both of alteration taking place in the rock mass and of material brought into the rock from extraneous sources. In one case the chemical constitution of the rock remains essentially unimpaired, while in the other that constitution is changed to a greater or less degree. The causes of these alterations in ancient and modern volcanic rocks is but imperfectly known, but the changes probably take place under the influence of percolating waters. That these changes are slow in many cases is rendered probable by the fact, that when rocks have been exposed to rapid alterations by hot and mineral waters, the result is a general destruction of the rock mass, a disintegration of it as a whole, and not such changes as are seen in rock masses in general. It is probable that both cold and thermal waters have contributed to the change, as the latter are abundant in volcanic regions at the present, and we have the right to infer that they were so in past time at the localities in which ancient igneous activity was manifested.

These alterations are considered to be molecular, or belonging to the rock mass as a whole, although some portions and some minerals are altered more rapidly than others. The general tendency of rock alteration seems to be the breaking up of the original constituents, and the formation of quartz and other minerals, that give to the rock characters closely simulating those of sedimentary rocks.

The sediments also undergo the same changes, and in extreme cases produce crystalline schists and gneisses. The changes in them are apparently brought about by the same agencies as the changes in eruptive rocks, and thermal waters may have been an important factor in producing crystalline structure in the former.

In the various alterations of the rocks of every kind the new mineral structures come apparently from the segregation of mineral matter, either from the rock or adjacent sources, in some place suitable for its deposition. The place may be some fissure or cavity, or it may be in the solid rock mass itself, by the removal of one or more chemical constituents from the immediate point of action, and the substitution of others. So far as the rock mass goes when no foreign material is carried into it, these changes may be defined as the migration or aggregation of the chemical elements, produced by their tendency to seek such unions as shall expose them under their present conditions to less disturbing elements than their former relations did — a tendency to pass from an unstable towards a more stable condition. The final result of these changes is, usually, to produce clays, ochres, quartz, and carbonates; the latter of which while not stable in position, are apt to be so in composition; *e. g.*, calcite, while readily soluble and removed, generally reappears as calcite — the position unstable, the union stable. The general principle of change is the same, whether the mineral matter be reprecipitated in the rock mass itself, or is carried out and deposited in any contiguous cavity or fissure, or borne away to be deposited from thermal or mineral springs, or from bog, river, lake, or ocean waters.

The efforts to explain the changes in rocks and in their mineral constituents by theories of pseudomorphism have generally failed, because the changes have been attributed to the single minerals, and not to the rock mass as a whole.

The concentration of ores in rocks, and the formation of mineral veins seem to be brought about by the same process as the more common alteration of the rock mass, or the storing up of the material in minute fissures in the rock.* The only difference is that the kind of material and its amount, owing to the size of the receptacle and the extent of the action, is such as to make it commercially valuable. In this statement there would be excepted all ores that can be proved, as some iron ores have been, to be of eruptive origin, as well as all mechanical deposits. In this connection it may be explicitly stated, the writer holds the view that the elements of most of the ores were disseminated through the original and eruptive rocks, and that when these rocks became exposed to the action of meteoric agencies, these scattered materials were collected and deposited in the veins and segregations in which they are now formed.† So far as now known, the only ore of eruptive origin, in masses sufficient for exploitation, is that of iron, which is so only in part of its occurrences. If this view is correct, it would follow that our veins and most of our ore deposits are superficial phenomena‡ of the earth, and that mineralogy and economic geology as ordinarily studied relate chiefly to the secondary products of mineral matter; or, they are the sciences of abnormal minerals.

The above described alterations in rocks and minerals, and the localization of mineral deposits, with the consequent essential original unity of ancient and modern rocks, naturally follow from the general law of the passage from the unstable towards a more stable condition. This results from the fact that the original materials of the earth, whether forming the original crust, or appearing on the surface as eruptive rocks, are in a higher state of energy than is adaptable to the surface conditions of this globe. They are unstable both in temperature and in the majority of chemical combinations formed on solidification, and heat is lost with a resulting

* Bull. Mus. Comp. Zool., 1880, vii. 123-130; Proc. Bost. Soc. Nat. Hist., 1880, xxi. 91-108.
† Eng. Min. Jour., New York, 1884, xxvii. 364, 365.
‡ Whitney, Aurif. Gravels, pp. 350-361.

dissipation of energy; while the chemical elements or the molecular combinations tend to seek new unions better adapted to the present circumstances of the rocks. These changes progress, going on from one form to another. It is not uncommon to find that as steps in the progress, the original minerals and glass are altered to other more or less well defined minerals, having sometimes perfect crystalline form; while these in their turn yield to the acting forces, and new mineral combinations are entered into, and so on downward in the course of the alteration. It may be said that an eruptive rock, when it has passed from the interior to the exterior of the earth, becomes a chemical laboratory, in which solutions, reactions, and precipitations are continually carried on — experiment after experiment, change after change, succeed one another, according to the materials, reagents, and conditions. But they always progress in one direction; the combination last formed is always more stable in the then conditions than the preceding combinations were; with any change of condition there would of course come change in relative stability.

The induration or hardening of rocks would thus oftentimes be no index of exposure to heat, for if the mineral formed or infiltrated into the rock mass is one which stands high on the scale of hardness, $e.\,g.$ quartz, then induration follows as a matter of course.

From the principle of passage or unstableness it follows that the glassy state is nearest the primitive condition, and is to be looked upon as the starting point of the indigenous and secondary minerals in rocks; hence it should come first in our study and be traced in its process of crystallization and alteration.

The three classes of products above discussed will be mentioned hereafter as products of the first, second, and third class, or as, 1st, foreign; 2d, indigenous; and 3d, alteration or secondary products.

The two first classes have been collectively and singly called by the writer *original* in contradistinction to the *secondary* products.

Cases of envelopment occur in minerals of the second class frequently, but they can be distinguished as easily under the microscope, in rocks not too far altered, from the foreign or secondary minerals, as a coarse conglomerate can be distinguished from a granite by the naked eye, or as a piece of wood joined to another by a mortise and tenon can be distinguished from the natural growth of a limb.

The various changes that rocks undergo in their alterations are determined under the microscope, the same as changes are determined in objects in botany, zoölogy, and astronomy. It is not necessary that one should see an acorn grow to an oak, an apple-seed grow to an apple-tree, a lamb to a sheep, a nebula to a star, before he can reason upon the growth of plants, animals, and stars.* It is sufficient to be able to study these in various stages of their growth, in order to make out their history — to examine numerous specimens that exhibit all the various phases of existence, to make out the general life history of the individual. So in lithology the history of the rocks and minerals can be made out as distinctly and certainly as the life history of the individuals in the other subjects before mentioned.

In applying the principles of thermo-optics to the mineral constituents of rocks, in order to determine at what temperature the rock was formed, it should be remembered that it is only the minerals of the first class to which they apply. These alone must have been subjected to the heat of the liquid magma and present permanent marks of that action. Of course, nothing can be asserted concerning the temperature to which a liquid has been exposed, from either the thermo-optical or pyrognostic characters of the resulting minerals arising from its cooling under various conditions;† in other words, the characters of a mineral after it is formed have little or nothing to do with what it was before it was formed, except so far as the relation may have been shown to exist, by experiment and by observation of the same conditions. Investigations upon the thermo-optical properties of minerals belonging to the first class would probably lead to interesting results, if care were taken to select such as are typical of the lava.

It should also be kept in mind that the conditions under which minerals are formed from the crystallization of a cooling magma are different from those under which minerals are formed in veins, fissures, and cavities, or by alteration of the rock mass; and that minerals truly of the second or indigenous class occupy a very subordinate position in our mineral cabinets.

* Peirce, Ideality in the Physical Sciences, 1881, p. 69.
† As well predicate what was the temperature of the water glass and hydrochloric acid, from the amount of heat it takes to fuse the chalcedonic silica which they form under suitable conditions, as to attempt to prove the heat of a liquid magma from the fusion point of some mineral crystallizing out of its cooling solution. The temperature at which a mineral fuses and the temperature at which it formed have no connection with one another, except in the case of crystallization from dry fusion ; if they do, how hot corals must be!

Section IV. — *Chemical Analysis of Rocks.*

At the present time the most that chemical analysis seems to be able to do for the lithologist is to give the composition of the rock as a whole. The many attempts that have been made to determine the mineralogical composition of rocks by unaided chemical analysis appear to have been in almost every case a failure. This is natural, for this method alone is unable to take into account the three different classes of minerals in rocks, and in its statements has to proceed as if all the minerals were the products of free crystallization in the rock. But while the chemical composition remains about the same, every gradation in structure and mineral composition is known to exist, — from a pure glass to mixed glass and crystals, to a purely crystalline rock, and to one in which all the mineral constituents are secondary or alteration products. Since the chemical composition of all these forms is essentially the same, the results of any calculation of the percentage and kind of minerals inclosed, would be nearly the same; but how different from the reality are the results of the calculation, except when the rock is composed of crystals of the second class alone. Even here the correctness of the result would be a matter of doubt.

Chemical analyses of rocks, showing their ultimate constitution, if made from specimens carefully selected and studied in the field, and further studied microscopically, would aid greatly in lithological research. Typical unaltered specimens are needed to establish rock species; and for such work the average specimens of collectors are too much affected by surface alteration, or weathering, to be used. But a large proportion of rock analyses appear to have been made from such unsuitable specimens, of whose structure, mineral composition, and field relations we know nothing, or next to nothing; this, too, when the chief value of such analyses is to enable us not only to institute comparisons between the chemical composition of the rock analyzed and that of other rocks, but also between that composition and its origin, structure, mineral composition, and physical relations.

Chemical analyses could be made of great service in lithology by taking a graded series of rocks, beginning with the unaltered form, and passing gradually into the extremely altered form, comparing step by step the chemical composition with the changes in structure and mineral composition.

CHEMICAL ANALYSIS OF ROCKS.

There is a vast amount of unconscious humbug in the constant attempts to use chemical analyses for a purpose foreign to their nature; that is, to determine, as before mentioned, the mineral composition by mathematical calculations founded on rock analyses. All these efforts appear to be based on an entire misconception of the nature of rocks. Nothing better illustrates the inutility of this method alone for the purpose of determining the mineral composition, than a comparison of the speculations of chemists regarding the minerals composing the stony meteorites and the actuality as obtained by microscopic examination.

The writer holds, as the result of his studies, that the chemical analysis of a normal rock corresponds with its species — that is, certain percentages of the more prominent elements can be laid down, beyond the extremes of which normal rocks belonging to that species will rarely if ever go, and within which normal rocks of other species will rarely if ever come. This, of course, applies especially to the eruptive rocks, for in the case of the sedimentary ones, every degree of composition is to be expected according to the sources from which the materials composing them were derived, and the amount of sorting, chemical replacement, etc., they have undergone.

The more highly altered or weathered eruptive rocks, especially if chemical constituents have been removed, and either replaced or not by others, would not be normal forms. If the analyses were written in the percentages of the elements, instead of their compounds, it is thought that the chemical relations between the different rock species and varieties would be more clearly apparent than at present, as Nordenskiöld has shown for the meteoric peridotites.[*]

From the manner in which many chemical analyses of rocks have been made (poor work, poor specimens, and no knowledge of the rock) the difficulties in the way of proving these relations are great; but the writer has prepared tables which show them in an approximate manner.

---

[*] Nature, 1878, xviii. 510, 511; Geol. Fören. Förhandl., 1878, iv. 45–61; Zeit. Deut. geol. Gesells., 1881, xxxiii. 14–30.

SECTION V. — *Classification based on Mineral Composition.*

IF the artificial schemes of lithological classification are examined, it will be found that they are generally based on the mineral composition, the geological age, and the structure of the rocks, some rocks even being defined by a statement of that which they are not, or that which they do not contain.

It does not accord with the limits of this paper to enter upon any thorough critical discussion of the application of such principles, but a certain examination of them may be made, so far as they bear on the method of classification it is proposed here to use. Amongst the minerals of which the chief use is made in classification there may be mentioned the feldspars, including leucite and nephelite, also olivine, quartz, the micas, pyroxenes, and the amphiboles; although any mineral is liable to assume in special cases sufficient importance in these artificial schemes to found specific distinctions upon.

Of these minerals the most important are the feldspars, and on their presence or absence, and on the species or type of feldspar present are founded some of the most important divisions of the rocks. In order to successfully use any mineral in classification it is necessary that it should be a determinate quantity — that is, it should always have in the rock one mode of formation only — that its specific limits shall be well marked, and that it shall be accurately determinable with fair facility.

The Feldspars.

That the feldspars originate in all three of the methods given previously for the origin of rock minerals — foreign, indigenous, and secondary — the writer thinks cannot be denied; although, for the most part, they appear to be indigenous. In classification of this kind, the most important question about the feldspars is, what are their divisions and the diagnostic characters of them. A sketch of the various prominent opinions regarding their constitution will best answer our question.

In 1846 Scheerer held that the feldspars were different grades of saturation, of a radical compounded of equal atoms of $\dot{R}$ and $\ddot{Al}$.[*] Later he remarked[†] that it was permitted to regard all known feldspars as chemical

---
[*] Ann. Physik Chemie, 1846, lxviii. 337; Am. Jour. Sci. 1849 (2), vi. 61.
[†] Ann. Physik Chemie, lxxxix. 19.

combinations of either (1) anorthite and labradorite, or (2) anorthite and albite (orthoclase), or (3) labradorite and albite (orthoclase).

In 1850 Delesse said: "I have already had occasion to remark that we have hitherto attached too much importance to the varieties of the feldspars of the sixth crystalline system, and that nature has not always been limited by the divisions established among them by chemists and geologists; the same rock sometimes containing several varieties of these feldspars."* In the last reference Delesse had also pointed out that the composition of the feldspar was not constant even in the same rock from the same locality.

In 1851 Hermann taught that in the feldspars were two molecules: one denoted by $\quad a = (\dot{R}\,\ddot{S}i_3 + \ddot{S}i_3)$,
and the other by $\quad b = (\dot{R}\,\ddot{S}i + \ddot{S}i)$.

Of these molecules the species were thus compounded (giving, however, from his list only those species of importance to-day):—

$$\begin{aligned}
\text{Orthoclase} &= a \\
\text{Albite} &= a' \\
\text{Anorthite} &= b \\
\text{Andesite} &= \tfrac{a+b}{2} \\
\text{Labradorite} &= \tfrac{a+3b}{4} \\
\text{Oligoclase} &= \tfrac{5a+3b}{4}
\end{aligned}$$

The union in this case was regarded as a molecular union, and not a chemical combination between the atoms.†

Sartorius von Waltershausen, in his work "Ueber die vulkanischen Gesteine in Sicilien und Island, und ihre submarine Umbildung," published in 1853, advanced the theory that there were three definite triclinic feldspars, *i. e.* anorthite, albite, and krablite, and that the other triclinic feldspars were formed by varying compounds of these. Krablite, or baulite,‡ was then supposed to be a definite silicate, with the atomic ratio 1 : 3 : 24, as determined by the researches of Forchhammer§ and Genth; ‖ but it has since been shown to be a mineral aggregate or rock, referred at first to the

---

* Bull. Soc. Géol. France, 1850 (2), vii. 526; see also Ann. Mines, 1847 (4), xli. 266, 267; 1849, xvi. 327, 328.
† Jour. Prakt. Chemie, 1851, lii. 256–258.
‡ Landgrebe, Mineralogie der Vulcane, 1870, pp. 60, 227.
§ Oversigt over det Kgl. danske Videnskabernes Selskabs Forhandlinger, etc., 1842, pp. 43–55; Jour. Prakt. Chemie, 1843, xxx. 394.
‖ Ann. Chemie Pharm., 1848, lxvi. 271.

quartz trachytes,* and later to the liparites or rhyolites,† which now include most of the quartz trachytes of the older authors. Bunsen, indeed, maintained both before and after 1853, that baulite was a mechanical mixture — a rock, and not a mineral. ‡

In 1854 Dr. T. Sterry Hunt stated that the triclinic feldspars constituted a genus, of which albite might be taken as one representative, and anorthite as the other. The intermediate feldspars might be distinct species, or they might be looked upon as variable mechanical mixtures of the two typical feldspars, albite and anorthite. A similar mixture of albite with a potash feldspar, and anorthite with a soda or magnesian one, as well as of orthoclase with a lime or potash feldspar, were regarded as probable. Hunt distinctly objects to any idea that these variable feldspars were formed by chemical unions between the different types, and makes it clear that he had in mind the process of envelopment and variable, mechanical, contemporaneous intercrystallization, on which he founded his doctrines of the origin of crystalline rocks, pseudomorphism, and metamorphism. In this he followed Scheerer's views regarding the relations of iolite and aspasiolite, and of olivine and serpentine. The proportions of these intermixtures of the feldspars were regarded by Hunt as entirely variable and indefinite, being "such mixtures of species as constantly take place in the crystallization of homœomorphous salts from mixed solutions," and he explained the process in every case in the same way as he did in the case of perthite. That this view of the mixture of the feldspars is the same as his explanation of pseudomorphism can be seen from his statement that the latter has resulted in many instances from the association and crystallizing together of homologous and isomorphous species. §

In 1864 Professor Gustav Tschermak advanced the theory that (excepting hyalophane and danburite) there were three distinct species of feldspar: Orthoclase, or potash feldspar; Albite, or soda feldspar; and Anorthite, or lime feldspar. He held that soda and potash were not isomorphous, and therefore all orthoclase crystals containing soda were mechanical mixtures

* Zirkel, Sitz. Wien. Akad., 1863, xlvii. (1) pp. 243, 244; Lehrbuch der Petrographie, 1866, i. 25; ii. 154–166.
† Zirkel Die mikroskopische Beschaffenheit der Mineralien und Gesteine, 1873, p. 341.
‡ Bunsen Ann. Physik Chemie, 1851, lxxxiii. 199, 201; Ann. Chemie Pharm. 1854, lxxxix, 98; Preyer und Zirkel, Reise nach Island im Sommer, 1860; pp. 317–324.
§ Proc. Am. Assoc. Adv. Sci., 1854, viii. 237–347; 1871, xx. 1-59; Am. Jour. Sci., 1853 (2), xvi. 218; 1854, xviii. 270, 271; Phil. Mag., 1855 (4), ix. 354–363; Geological Survey of Canada, Report of Progress, 1853–1856, pp. 373–383; 1858, p. 180; Canada in the London International Exhibition, 1862, p. 65; Geology of Canada, 1863, p. 480.

(interlaminations or intercrystallizations) of orthoclase and albite. Albite and anorthite were looked upon as two distinct species of triclinic feldspar, and it was held that labradorite, andesite, and oligoclase were formed from isomorphous mixtures of albite and anorthite, — that is, through the molecular union of albite and anorthite, in definite mathematical proportions. These mixtures Tschermak distinctly held were not mechanical, but molecular.

The finding of potash in the triclinic crystals formed from the molecular union of albite and anorthite was explained by Tschermak, by the supposition that some orthoclase was mechanically interlaminated. Oligoclase, labradorite, and andesite were united under the name of plagioclase. This term has, however, been employed since to include both albite and anorthite, and in this latter sense it is generally used.*

Tschermak, indeed, does not claim this theory to be entirely original with himself, for he remarks, "Dabei verschweige ich jedoch nicht, dass die Grundidee dieser Vereinfachung keineswegs neu sei und ich bemerke, dass durch die früheren Bemühungen der Forscher, welche eine solche Vereinfachung auf chemischer Basis anstrebten, also durch Sartorius von Waltershausen, Rammelsberg, Scheerer, der Gedanke endlich so weit entwickelt wurde, dass Andere wie Delesse, Hunt denselben als keines speciellen Beweises bedürftig hinstellten."

Tschermak's theory was variously opposed and advocated, and on one side or the other the most prominent chemical mineralogists arranged themselves. It has been especially discussed by Rammelsberg, Rath, Roth, Bunsen, Petersen, Streng, and others, with the result that it is the generally accepted view regarding the composition of the feldspars.

Tschermak's theory does not appear to be well understood in England or America, and although the present writer recognises his liability to also misinterpret it, he deems it right to point out some of those differences of opinion, believing that in the end it will lead to a more accurate conception of the theory than now seems to exist.

Streng later offered a theory for the feldspars, in which he held that they were silicates, in which the Ca partly replaces the Na_2, and R the Si_2; claiming that there were only two principal divisions; 1st, the potash feldspar, and 2d, the lime soda feldspar — the latter forming a number of varieties with variable composition.†

* Sitz. Wien.Akad., 1864, I. (2) pp. 566–613.
† Neues Jahr. Min., 1865, 411–434, 513–529; 1871, 598–618, 715–731.

Peterson objected to Tschermak's theory on the ground that orthoclase feldspars containing soda do not show any of the striations peculiar to triclinic feldspars, which, if the theory is correct, must be mechanically mixed with the soda-bearing orthoclase; also, that some potash-bearing plagioclases exhibit no trace of orthoclase.*

Professor J D. Dana, in 1867, also opposed Tschermak's theory, holding that the variations from the normal analyses were caused by, —

(*a*) Incorrect analyses.

(*b*) Impurities; and often, mixtures of different feldspars through intercrystallization.

(*c*) Alteration; caused either (1) by the infiltration of ordinary waters, carbonated or not — the rocks containing feldspars having been exposed to this action through long ages past — or (2) through the same process aided by mineral ingredients in the waters, resulting in the introduction of magnesia, oxide of iron, etc., and in other changes.†

In the meanwhile Tschermak's theory assumed great prominence, and in 1874, Dr. T. Sterry Hunt put forward the claim that he was the originator of it. In support of this assertion he quoted from a published abstract of his original paper (*ante*, p. 35), which had given his views in an indefinite manner, and in his direct quotation from this abstract a hypothetical statement was altered to a positive one. ‡

As pointed out in the preceding pages, Hunt's theory of the triclinic feldspars is nearly the same as Dana's (*b*) given above. Hunt held that they were indefinite, variable, mechanical aggregates, or intercrystallizations; while Tschermak held that they were formed by isomorphous molecular unions in definite proportions. Further, Hunt's theory does not seem to be at all original with him.

Yet a number of writers have acknowledged Hunt's claim, presumably because they have never read his original papers, or else have misunderstood Tschermak. The use of the term "mixture" with two distinct meanings — 1st, for mechanical aggregation (Hunt), 2d, for molecular combination (Tschermak) — has probably added to the confusion.

* Neues Jahr. Min., 1872, pp 576-586 ; Jour. Prakt. Chemie, 1873 (2), vi. 200-212.
† Amer. Jour. Sci., 1867 (2), xliv. 260, 399. See also System of Mineralogy, 5th ed., 1868, p. 336.
‡ Chem. Geol. Essays, pp. 438, 443-445.

Amongst those who have acknowledged Hunt's claim are both Danas,[*] Silliman,[†] Leeds,[‡] Rutley,[§] Hawes,[||] and Fouqué and Lévy.[¶]

Edward Dana says that the theory "was offered by Hunt, and has since been developed by Tschermak;" Rutley, that Hunt's conclusions are almost identical with those of Tschermak; again, James D. Dana, mistaking Hunt's views, stated of the latter, "In the view . . . with regard to the molecular relations of the feldspars, he appears to have anticipated Tschermak by ten years;" while Silliman goes so far as to say, "Here will be found developed his [Hunt's] views on the constitution of the feldspars, which were some years later adopted without acknowledgment by Tschermak." Leeds appears to have been the only one who recognized the essential difference between the indefinite mechanical-mixture view adopted by Hunt, and the definite molecular-union theory of Tschermak; but he failed to see the logical conclusion to be derived, — that Hunt[**] was in no sense the originator of Tschermak's theory, and that all the charges of appropriation made against the latter ought to be entirely withdrawn.

In 1875, Descloizeaux, from the optical properties of the plagioclastic feldspars, concluded that andesite was an altered oligoclase, but that labradorite and oligoclase are distinct species, and not isomorphous mixtures. He looked upon their optical properties as opposed to Tschermak's theory.[††] To explain the chemical composition, Descloizeaux calls attention to the theory of Friedel and others, that the several feldspars differ from one another only in their proportions of silica, forming a series whose common difference is SiO_2: e. g., anorthite $+ SiO_2 =$ labradorite; labradorite $+ SiO_2 =$ andesite; andesite $+ SiO_2 =$ oligoclase; and oligoclase $+ SiO_2 =$ albite.

While Descloizeaux admits that the composition of the feldspars may be explained as well by Tschermak's theory as by Friedel's, yet he holds that the latter accords better with the optical and crystallographic characters of the species.

Vom Rath, on the other hand, is of the opinion that the chemical constitution of the feldspars is most satisfactorily represented by Tschermak's theory, and holds that the formation of the intermediate triclinic feldspars

---

[*] Am. Jour. Sci., 1875 (3), ix. 102; Text Book of Mineralogy, 1877, p. 297.
[†] Amer. Chemist, 1874, v. 106.   [‡] Amer. Chemist, 1877, vii. 335.
[§] The Study of Rocks, 1879, p. 95.   [||] Geol. New Hampshire, 1878, iii. part 4, p. 89.
[¶] Miner. Microg., 1879, p. 206.
[**] Bull. Mus. Comp. Zool., 1884, vii. 370–374, 445–454, 458, 459.
[††] Ann. Chimie Physique, 1875 (5), iv. 429–444; Comptes Rendus, 1875, lxxx. 364–371; Neues Jahr. Min., 1875, pp. 279–284, 395–399.

by the molecular union of albite and anorthite is an established law, and not a mere hypothesis. He states that the supposition that the difference of composition in the plagioclastic feldspars is due to the successive addition of silica molecules, takes no account of the replacement of lime and soda, which is so intimately associated with the variation in the amount of silica. Andesite, he holds, is distinct from oligoclase.

In 1876,* Descloizeaux described a new potash feldspar (microcline) which is triclinic, although chemically the same as orthoclase. This discovery only added to the difficulties and confusion in the feldspar question. Mallard and Michel Lévy, however, taught later that orthoclase and microcline were the same, but that the cross-twinning had become so fine that it was no longer visible in polarized light, *i. e.*, the laminæ were excessively thin — so much so as to cause the feldspar to appear optically homogeneous.†

Extended observations were later made by Max Schuster on the optical characters of the feldspars. He claims that these characters show a gradual change or transition between anorthite and albite, *pari passu* with the variation in chemical composition; that is, each definite proportion in the mixture of anorthite and albite gives a variety whose optical properties approach one or the other of these feldspars, according to the predominance of either. From the optical characters of any feldspar crystal, there could be inferred its chemical composition, and the reverse. He claims that Tschermak's law is sustained by these observations, and such seems to be the prevalent opinion.‡ These observations of Schuster are in accordance with those of Sennamont on Rochelle salts.§ They not improperly may lead to very different views of mineral species from those commonly held.

From the above, it seems clear that the feldspars are either species with such indefinite boundaries that they (the feldspars) cannot be defined with any accuracy, or else they form a continuous series from anorthite to orthoclase. In either case it is improper to found definite groups and specific divisions of rocks on a variable and indefinite group of minerals, concerning whose nature the chemical mineralogists are not agreed.

---

* Comptes Rendus, 1876, lxxxii. 885–891; Ann. Chimie Physique, 1876 (5), ix. 433–499.
† Bull. Min. Soc. France, 1879, pp. 135–139; Neues Jahr. Min., 1880, i. pp. 174, 175; Zeit. Kryst., 1880, iv. 632, 633.
‡ Sitz. Wien. Akad., 1879, lxxx. (1), 192–200; Min. Mitth., 1880 (2), iii. 117–284.
§ Ann. Chimie Physique, 1851 (3), xxxiii. 420–437.

40 CLASSIFICATION BASED ON MINERAL COMPOSITION.

Even supposing the species were well established, have we any methods whereby these species or divisions can be positively discriminated?

In 1876, Descloizeaux gave a method, whereby he thought the different plagioclastic feldspars could be distinguished from one another. This method required a thin transparent section, either cleaved or ground parallel to the plane of easiest cleavage (O, OP, 001, p) — the triclinic feldspars being as a rule twinned, so as to show color bands parallel with the plane of the next easier (or less perfect) cleavage. The sections are placed on the stage of the polarizing microscope, with the color bands parallel to any diagonal of the crossed nicols (plane of vibration or plane of polarization); the section is then revolved until one set of color bands becomes dark, or the light is extinguished in them. The angle between this point and the former position of the section is taken. The section is then revolved in the opposite direction until extinction of light takes place in the alternate set of color bands. The angle between this point and the first or original position of the section is taken. If the section is properly cleaved, or ground, the two angles observed are equal. By experiment on feldspars of known composition, the angles between the nicol diagonal and the extinguished color bands, or the angle (double the others) between the two positions in which the alternate bands are rendered dark, have been determined; and it is assumed that all feldspars having the same angle of extinction as any one of these previously determined angles belongs to the same species of feldspar. Descloizeaux held that this supposed fixity of optical characters was opposed to Tschermak's theory.*

Prof. R. Pumpelly endeavored to make Descloizeaux's method practically applicable to thin sections of rocks, which he did in the following manner: If instead of cutting sections parallel to the principal cleavage they should be cut at any angle with that cleavage but in the zone $O : i\bar{\imath}$ (p: h'; 001: 100; O P: ∞ $\bar{P}$ ∞) we should have every variation of angle, from 0° up to the maximum for that feldspar. In a thick rock section in which the feldspars are cut at random, it is necessary first to ascertain whether any feldspar section has been cut in the zone $O: i\bar{\imath}$. This is done by ascertaining on trial if the extinction in the alternate color bands takes place at equal angles on opposite sides of the nicol diagonal. If it does, the section of feldspar was cut as required. A number of such sections

* Comptes Rendus, 1876, lxxxii. 885–891; Ann. Chimie Physique, 1876 (5), ix. 433–499.

are usually to be found in the slide, and their maximum angle is taken as the index of the feldspar. In actual practice, Professor Pumpelly took as oligoclase those feldspars of which several individuals in a rock section gave angles between 32° and 36°; as labradorite, those between 36° and 62°; and as anorthite those over 62°.

When more than one feldspar is present in the slide, only that one can be distinguished which has the highest angle; and this may be the minor or subordinate feldspar. It is even possible for a single crystal, only, of one feldspar, to change the conclusion as to the rest of the feldspars in the section. Then, again, the sections examined may be so cut as to give a lower angle than they should; therefore the observer concludes he has a different feldspar from the one actually present. It is scarcely possible by this method to distinguish between oligoclase and albite.*

Professor Pumpelly was, however, anticipated in order of time, in the publication of this method, by M. Michel Lévy, who discussed the subject mathematically, and applied the principles to many different minerals.†

That the work of both Lévy and Pumpelly was independent and original with both, can be inferred from the fact that the latter asked me early in the year 1876 to undertake a mathematical discussion of this subject, in order to aid his experimental work which he was then upon. The mathematical portion the present writer had then neither time nor inclination to perform, but the practical work of Professor Pumpelly resulted in that method of determination which has been given before. Schuster's results would, however, appear to render such determinations of but little value at present.

Dr. George W. Hawes in 1881, showed that the common method of distinguishing triclinic from monoclinic feldspars was unreliable in certain cases; for labradorite from St. Paul's Island and Canada, anorthite from New Hampshire, and oligoclase from Bodenmais, exhibited none of these supposed distinguishing features, i. e. striation in common and polarized light.‡

Amongst the methods used for the determination of the feldspars, as well as of other minerals, is the micro-chemical method of Dr. E. Bořický, which consists essentially in subjecting the specimen to the action of fluosilicic acid, hydrofluoric acid gas, chlorine gas, etc.; and microscopically

---
* Proc. Am. Acad. Sci., 1878, xiii. 253-309; Geol. Wisc., 1880, iii. 30.
† Ann. Mines, 1877 (7), xii. 392-169; Comptes Rendus, 1878, lxxxvi. 316-348.
‡ Proc. Nat. Mus., 1881, pp. 134-136.

examining the crystals produced, under proper conditions. This is simply a method of making qualitative tests upon material in bulk too small to be tested in the ordinary way.*

In 1876 Professor J. Szabó published† his method of determining feldspars by means of their fusion, reactions, and coloration produced in the Bunsen flame, which gave, according to him, a means for estimating the percentages of alkalies, etc., in the specimen examined.

Still a third method is from the crystals formed in blowpipe beads under proper conditions. This method was invented by Mr. George H. Emerson in 1863,‡ and later expanded by Gustav Rose,§ W. A. Ross,|| and H. C. Sorby.¶ The results are essentially similar to Bořický's method, qualitative, but can be used with small fragments.

The last and most important method is that of separating the feldspars by means of liquids of different specific gravities. In this way considerable material of a certain specific gravity can be obtained for chemical analysis, and its nature ascertained.** All these methods have their defects: as, for instance, the feldspars which give character to the rock are of more than one species, usually; they contain more or less glass and mineral impurities; and they are subject to alteration. These factors change their specific gravity and chemical relations, and make the determination of a few crystals of but limited value in fixing the condition and character of the remaining feldspars. Of all the methods the specific gravity one promises the most, but it is not believed at present to lead to any essentially valuable results in determining minerals like the feldspars, whose very species are so indeterminate. While the before-mentioned methods, and many others not mentioned, have added greatly to the knowledge of minerals, they seem to have blinded most observers to the general characters of the rocks they were studying.

In the coarsely crystalline rocks crystals of feldspar, of sufficient size for analysis, can often be obtained; but that analysis, to be of any value, must proceed on the supposition that the crystal is pure, unaltered, and

---

* Archiv der naturwissenschaftlichen Landesdurchforschung Böhmens, 1877, iii. 5th Abth., pp. 1–80.
† Ueber eine neue Methode die Feldspathe auch in Gesteinen zu bestimmen, Budapest, 1876.
‡ Amer. Jour. Sci., 1864 (2), xxxvii. 414, 415; Proc. Am. Acad., 1865, vi. 476–494.
§ Monatsb. Berlin Akad., 1867, pp. 129–147.
|| Chemical News, 1868 (Amer. Reprint), ii. 74–76, 147, 148, 157–160, 196; Pyrology or Fire Chemistry, London, 1875.
¶ Month. Micro. Jour., 1869, i. 349–352.
** Thoulet, Comptes Rendus, 1878, lxxxvi. 454–456; Bull. Min. Soc. France, 1879, p. 17; Church, Min. Mag., 1877, i. 237, 238; Goldschmidt, Neues Jahr. Min., 1881 (Beilage-Band), pp. 179–238.

typical of the predominating feldspar in the rock; microscopic analysis shows that the larger crystals in our rocks are generally abnormal, often foreign to their present surroundings, containing numerous inclusions, sometimes three fourths of the crystal being glass, microlites, etc. If a thin section is prepared before the chemical analysis is made, it only proves that the part examined is pure or impure, as the case may be, offering no proof regarding the rest, only a probability; further, the larger crystals are usually the subordinate ones, being unlike the generality in the mass of the rock. This method is, also, inapplicable in the cases where it is most needed; in the fine-grained and compact rocks, which contain few or no feldspars of sufficient size. The larger feldspars are most subject to alteration, passing from the basic towards the acidic,* some becoming greatly changed while the smaller crystals are untouched; yet the analyst names the rock from the altered, and not from the unaltered feldspar, — euphotide, for instance.†

The secondary formation of feldspars, like orthoclase in rocks, adds greatly to the difficulty of making the classification dependent upon the kind of feldspar present. In other cases the feldspathic material is seen to be largely replaced by quartz and other minerals — the presence of the first not being suspected until the crystal was examined under the microscope. The twinned character of the triclinic feldspars, seen both in common and polarized light, is not a constant character, as has been pointed out before. It has been customary to regard all unstriated feldspars in basic rocks as plagioclase, cut parallel to the brachypinicoid, but in the acidic rocks as orthoclase. Through the great alteration to which the feldspars have been subject in the older rocks, all signs of twinning have been frequently obliterated, thereby causing such crystals in granitoid rocks to be classed as orthoclase.‡ The chief value, therefore, of the optical method for distinguishing the feldspars is apparently to determine the predominance of plagioclase, or of orthoclase; while the chief use of the present micro-mineralogical study of the feldspars in lithology is the determination of the more or less acidic or basic composition of the rocks, according to the predominance of orthoclase or plagioclase in them. From the above it follows that a systematic classification cannot be properly based on any such variable, indeterminate materials.

* Geo. W. Hawes, Geology of New Hampshire, iii. part. iv. 90–92.
† T. Sterry Hunt, Am. Jour. Sci. (2), 1859, xxvii. 336–349; J. D. Dana, ibid. (3), 1878, xvi. 340.
‡ Bull. Mus. Comp. Zool., 1880, vii. 55, 56.

The Pyroxene-Amphibole Groups.

In the enstatite-hypersthene-pyroxene-amphibole group of minerals, a similar relation seems to exist as in the feldspars, and a like variability.

In these the distinctions are founded mainly on optical, crystallographic and cleavage characters. May there not be a similar relation between the orthorhombic and monoclinic pyroxenes as there is between the different feldspars? Specific distinctions between rocks have been based solely on a difference in cleavage in minerals otherwise identical. This is the case with augite and diallage, which thus become the means of separating diabase from gabbro. How valid this cleavage distinction is, may be learned from the fact, that the cleavages of augite and diallage are found sometimes united in a single crystal of pyroxene. While augite has been regarded as distinctive of the augite-andesites, basalts, and diabases, more recent observations show that it is not confined to any one species of rock, but exists in every species, from the pallasites to the rhyolites. So, too, it was regarded as entirely characteristic of modern or younger rocks, but this is found not to be true. This belief in the occurrence of augite in modern rocks has arisen mainly from its ready alteration to viridite, chlorite, hornblende, biotite, etc., which would thus cause it nearly or entirely to disappear in the older and more altered rocks. Again, the probability that pyroxene in some of its varietal forms, like sahlite, is of secondary origin, increases the difficulty of employing pyroxene as a species character.

In the case of hornblende but little distinction is made in nomenclature, whether the mineral is foreign, original, or secondary; but in all these modes of occurrence it is given equal value in classification. As a foreign product it occurs in the andesites, the augite apparently arising from the crystallization of the dissolved hornblende material, while in the older forms of the same andesites hornblende occurs as a secondary product, after both the foreign hornblende and original augite. But the same rock is given three different names, according to the predominance of augite, foreign hornblende, or secondary hornblende. This is done, however, unconsciously by lithologists, since they do not practically make these mineralogical distinctions. The writer has seen two sections taken from the same hand specimen; one of which pronounced the rock a diabase, the other a diorite.

Of other minerals, mica occurs in a series of species like the feldspars, and in rocks is found in all three forms — foreign, indigenous, and secondary; while chlorite and epidote are probably always secondary. From this it would appear that they are not suitable to designate species.

Mineralogical Nomenclature of Rocks.

As the result of my study, I have been obliged to regard classification based on mineralogy, unless it be for some varietal subdivisions, as impracticable, because it is not a natural but an artificial method; a system that requires constant change and readaptation; and further, one that is based too much upon theory, individual judgment, and weight of authority; a system that admits, even requires, the "dumping" of rocks into certain places without the slightest regard to their relations of any kind, except it be that they hold one or at most a few minerals in common. This relation is often vitiated by the observer's not taking into account whether these minerals are natural crystallizations in the rock, foreign, or secondary products.

When classification is based on structure it usually separates the rock into distinct species according as it is glassy, partly glassy, crystalline, or porphyritic. That these distinctions are valueless, the writer thinks, follows from the fact that the same rock mass may show all these cases; dikes often being glassy and non-porphyritic on the edges, and crystalline and porphyritic towards the middle. The granitic structure indicates probably a certain depth at the time of crystallization, but that this may practically be slight has been shown by the lava flows of Keweenaw Point, some of which are fine-grained on the surface, and coarsely crystalline (granitic or diabasic) towards the base.

SECTION VI. — *Naming Rocks according to the Geological Age.*

This question has been so well discussed by Allport,[*] Dana [†] and others, that but little needs be said upon the subject here. Chemical, microscopical, and geological evidence all point to the fact that this division is not a natural one; and so far as my work has gone, the original characters of the

---

[*] Geological Magazine, 1871 (1), viii. 249; 1875 (2), ii. 553; Quart. Jour. Geol. Soc., 1874, xxx. 529.
[†] Amer. Jour. Sci., 1878 (3), xvi. 336.

rocks are the same from the earliest times to the present. Other things being equal, the older rocks are more altered; but as other things are not equal, no abrupt line can be drawn at the tertiary age, as is now generally done; no characters exist whereby it can be done, and the line must remain an arbitrary one. Alteration produces characters in the rocks that can be used to indicate their greater age, or greater alteration — terms which are not synonymous, although usually taken to be. The subject can, perhaps, be best formulated as follows: all rocks upon the earth's surface undergo alteration, and when exposed to the same conditions this is proportionate to the age. It is the unquestioned duty of the petrographer to study these changes, and starting from the least altered rock trace the continuous series to the most altered one of that kind. Such a system of work has been attempted here, so far as time and means have permitted.

The presence or absence of fluidal cavities, which has been urged as a distinction between tertiary and pre-tertiary rocks, seems to be related more to depth, and the conditions to which the rocks have been exposed since consolidation, than to age. The modern volcanic rocks are but the froth of an eruption, compared with the massive eruptions that have taken place in past time. The specimens collected are generally of a surface nature, and would allow the very ready escape of the inclosed vapors; while at some depth the escape could not take place as readily. Our older rocks have in general suffered more denudation, and therefore are more likely to contain fluid inclusions. Should it be shown that these fluid cavities are in part, or entirely, of posterior formation to the rock, as has been urged by Vogelsang,* and shown by Julien to be so in one case,† it would require a new interpretation to be placed upon these and upon their occurrence. My work would indicate that while part of the fluidal cavities are original, some are posterior to the consolidation of the rock. A more fatal objection to their use in separating tertiary from pre-tertiary rocks is the finding of fluidal cavities in undoubted tertiary and post-tertiary rocks.‡ Why quartz should be the mineral chosen to found this distinction upon, and other minerals containing fluid inclusions in lavas should be ignored, is a difficult thing to understand.

The older rocks are, as a rule, entirely crystalline, a condition arising in

---

* Philosophie der Geologie, p. 155.

† Am. Quart. Microscopical Jour., 1879, i. 103–115.

‡ H. C. Sorby, Quart. Jour. Geol. Soc., 1858, xiv. 484; Franz Zirkel, Microscopical Petrography, vi. 142, 156, 157, 164, 166, 167, 170, 265; Zeit. Deut. geol. Gesell., 1869, xx. 117, 132.

part from the alteration of the non-crystalline materials, and in part from the fact of the more or less denudation which they have suffered. When buried enough to allow of a more or less slow solidification, the tendency is to form a completely crystalline structure, approaching more and more to the granitic. While the chief portion of the granitic structure, like that seen in gabbros, some diabases and diorites, true granites and syenites, is indigenous, all does not seem to be so, and great depth does not appear to be indispensable; the only requirement seems to be slow solidification.

Section VII. — *Methods of Classification.*

The framework of any descriptive or systematic science is its classification, and upon it depends much of the value and suggestiveness of the work. It hence becomes a most important and vital point that the classification used shall be as correct as possible. The common classifications of rocks are well known to be artificial, and the writer has found them unsatisfactory in his work. Instead, therefore, of endeavoring to invent a new one, he has striven to discover the laws and principles of the natural system, so far as the rocks studied might enable him to do so.

In studying rocks by any system, two methods are open to the observer. One is to simply describe the characters of the minerals in the rock, thus making the minerals the principal object, and the rock the subordinate one. In this case lithology becomes simply a mineralogical study, and the lithologist a mineralogist, who looks upon his rocks as small mineral cabinets, not realizing that the minerals are for the most part changing and changeable, and that the true method is to trace the history and variations of the rock as manifested in its mass and its constituents.

The other method is to study the rocks for the purpose of determining their natural relations, the various changes they have undergone, and the characters by which they may be known in all these various alterations. In this the rock is the unit, the paramount object, and the mineral the subordinate quantity. From this point of view the minerals in a rock answer to the teeth and bones in an animal — very important, but not superior in value to the animal as a whole. In a rock the mineral is the accident, it may or may not exist; and when the rock is entirely composed of crystallized minerals, they should be used as the teeth and bones are used in determination, when the zoölogist has them alone in his specimen — in subordination to his general knowledge of animal structure. The subordinate relation of the mineral to the rock is more obscure than the same relation of the bones to the animal as a whole, since it is true that the mineral makes up the whole of the majority of rocks. The subordination of the crystalline minerals to the rock unit has been above thus strongly insisted upon since the opposite view seems to be taken by many lithologists, who appear to study as microscopical mineralogists, instead of working as lithologists proper.

If it is possible to find the principles of the natural classification of rocks they ought to be applicable to any rock, whatever may be its age and condition. By the natural classification of rocks is meant that system which will place together those forms nearest allied in their general characters, composition, structure, and origin, when the rock as a whole is considered, and not certain of its characters only. The present artificial classifications of rocks pick out certain mineralogical characters, and render the rock characters subordinate to them. These classifications are, to a certain extent, natural, and afford a convenient method of arrangement, requiring on the part of the lithologist who follows them simply skill in the determination of minerals. The method works well in some places, in others it masses together a most heterogeneous collection of rocks in a single species — causing some rock names, like diorite for instance, to remind one of the old use of the term *schörl* in mineralogy. The employment of the minerals alone to determine the rock species is like Linnæus's use of the stamens and pistils in botanical classification — a convenient but artificial system. One in objecting to the sexual system in botany does not reject the use of the stamens and pistils in classification, but he does object to their over-riding all other characters. They are to have their just and proportionate weight, but no more. So, too, in lithology the minerals in rocks hold a similar relation to them that the sexual organs do in plants — they may comprise all or but little of the rock or plant. Minerals are entitled to their just and proportionate weight in rock classification but no more; they are not to be allowed, in my judgment, to become superior to the rock itself. No single character should be allowed to over-ride all the others, that is: the presence or absence of a single mineral ought not to remove a rock from the species to which all its other characters assign it. In the current classifications it frequently happens that the name given to the rock depends upon the particular portion of the hand-specimen from which the microscopic section was taken.

MODERN METHODS OF CLASSIFICATION CHARACTERIZED.

The present lithological methods of classification can best be characterized, in a homely way, by supposing that there were placed in the hands of a zoölogist a great number of specimens of one species of some carnivorous animal, in every condition, from a fresh state to that of an advanced stage of decomposition; also of those of the same species that had lived during distinct periods of time, as well as of those that had lived for different lengths of time. With these, too, let there be given to the zoölogist a number of packages of the bones of this animal, part of the bones having been worn and part unworn.

Now, imagine this zoölogist naming as new species every specimen more decomposed than a preceding one; as new species, those which showed different products of decomposition; as new species, those that gave any variation, through that decomposition, upon chemical analysis — as for instance, one and forty-seven one hundredths, or even nine-twentieths of one per cent. Continuing, let it be supposed that our zoölogist makes new species, or at least varieties, out of all specimens in which he finds any teeth or bones of other animals which have been swallowed; changing the species or variety as often as the inclosed fragments differ; creating new species out of all that have lived for different lengths of time; new species out of those whose bones are fractured crosswise, as distinct from those whose bones are broken lengthwise; new species out of the distinct packages of fragments; new species according as these fragments are worn or angular; also, above and beyond all, fixing an arbitrary date, and demanding that all the specimens of this animal that had existed prior to that time should be held as distinct species, and in general of different origin from those that were of a later period. Suppose, too, that in addition, our zoölogist should maintain that some, or all, of the animals submitted to him were made out of the remains of their defunct ancestors, by a species of fermentation; also, that this creative chemical action was brought about by the deposition of the more recent remains upon the older, and that then the older forms successively came from beneath and lay down on top, thus producing a perpetual cycle. Let the reader suppose all this and he will gain some idea of the principles and methods commonly employed in lithology, as well as, in a greater or less degree, in chemistry as applied to rocks.

This is no mere fancy sketch, but, so far as can be done by taking an illustration from a distinct science, shows some of the principles of lithology as taught *to-day*, and some of the methods upon which rocks, *even now*, are classified.

Of course, every degree of skill exists in the applications of any classification, and many men, even with erroneous principles, succeed better than others do who work with correct ones. In this, however, it is a question of methods and not of men; if it were the latter, then no discussion would be possible, since the older and more experienced would always, and justly, claim the right to have their views followed. Since it is a question of science and methods, it is often true that some young and fresh observer may, starting from the ground gained by others, push on a little way beyond them; this too, when he may not have a tithe of the ability of the others; and it is not to be taken as presumption, if he endeavors to hold and point out the ground he thinks he has gained.

The principles and methods employed herein were essentially enunciated by me in 1879,* the chief changes being the greater extension of the subject, owing to further investigations; and these principles have been used by myself and my students in papers published since. Owing to the condensed or abstract form of the first publication, it seems to have been but little understood by lithologists working in the mineralogical method of rock classification; but it is hoped that the publications made since then, including this, will make my meaning sufficiently clear. One thing is certain, that unless a lithologist has had an extensive range of study of both the unaltered and altered forms of rocks, and seen their relations in the field, such understanding will be difficult. Bearing upon this, it is to be pointed out that, outside of the rocks from a few volcanoes in Europe, every rock that I have seen from that country is altered, to a greater or less degree; but the European classifications are chiefly based on such altered rocks. Hence, a mineralogical classification would naturally be adopted there, and will be tenaciously held to. A lithologist who is dependent on the material that Europe alone can furnish him, has not the means at his command of judging accurately regarding the basis of much of my work, which has been founded upon much fresher and less altered specimens than his. The most that I can hope to do, however, is to call attention to, and point out, that which seems a better way than the one at present followed. To perfectly express the natural system of rocks requires a universal knowledge of them — a knowledge that it is not given to any man to possess.

No definite scheme of classification can be laid down in the beginning; it must result from the study of all available specimens, and be the best

* Bull. Mus. Comp. Zoöl., 1879, v. 275–287.

arrangement according to their natural affinities that can be ascertained by that study. Future studies, discoveries of new rocks, and other causes are liable, in this science as in botany and zoölogy, to change the particular arrangement; but the principles and methods, so far as they are natural, will remain the same.

The natural method is sufficiently elastic to allow of the incorporation of whatever new divisions future investigations may require; it can never expect to be fixed and rigid, until the sum of human knowledge shall be complete. These changes will result simply in removing the artificial portions which imperfect knowledge has incorporated with it, and bring the classification nearer and nearer to the perfect natural system. If none of the system here adopted is natural, then all will in time be removed.

The important principle that underlies the natural classification, as here advocated, is the belief that *the older rocks now classed as distinct species are rocks that once were identical with their younger prototypes — the present differences being due to alteration, and conditions of crystallization.*

Standing next to this, is the belief in *the changeableness of the mineral constitution of the rocks,* and the feeling that no classification should be placed entirely on so uncertain a foundation.

As a deduction from the preceding discussion, the following statements may be taken as guides in describing and classifying our rocks: —

Section VIII. — *The Principles of Classification.*

1. In the study of rocks, we should begin with the younger and glassy state, and follow the gradations step by step to the most crystalline one in the series — from the least altered to the most altered forms — tracing every change, and studying their history in their tufaceous, poroditic, metamorphic, or any other state in which they or their remains can exist.

2. Any rocks that can be followed in this way between certain limits, whatever may be the changes they have undergone, form a species. In every shape they should be retained under the specific name; the various modifications, when of sufficient importance, being regarded as varieties, and named as such.

3. All the petrological, lithological, and chemical characters should be used in determining rock species; that is, the rock as a whole and in all its relations should be considered.

4. The classification should be a natural one, therefore empirical, embodying all known characters of the rocks. A natural mineralogical classification of rocks is an impossibility, as it is based on part of the characters only — characters which are unstable. Minerals may serve for the establishment of varieties, but not of species.

5. Geological age has no value in the classification of rocks, and is not to be employed except incidentally in varietal forms.

6. The addition of new names in any science, unless they are absolutely necessary for its advancement, is a detriment: the needed names should be taken from those now in use, so far as possible, and they should be employed, as nearly as may be, in their most approved sense; when they belong to varieties they should be defined as such, and placed in their natural relations to the species of which they form a part.

7. In the classification of rocks, the original characters ought to hold priority over any of the secondary ones; and they should give name to the rock, and decide its relations, so long as they exist in a determinable state. If necessary, or convenient, variety names or adjective terms can be added, to mark the special peculiarities of secondary or other origin — but only in especially important cases.

8. If a rock is found to have the characteristics of any species as its prevailing characters, it should be referred to that species.

9. Chemical analysis alone, as a general rule, is insufficient to furnish data for naming a rock, since it is to be expected that rocks originating in different ways should have the same composition.

10. The relation of a rock to its associated rocks in the field is the principal criterion for determining its origin, especially in the altered rocks.

11. Association alone is an insufficient guide in determining the origin of a rock.

12. The origin of a rock should have an important bearing upon its classification.

13. The classification should be the exponent of some general law, which should embody all that is known at present of the rocks, and give promise for the future.

SECTION IX. — *General Conclusions in Regard to Systems of Lithological Classification.*

THE general results and bearing of the preceding can be briefly summarized as follows: —

As is claimed for the organic world, so there is for the inorganic universe a universal law of evolution or development expressed by the phrases: *degradation and dissipation of energy, the passage of the unstable towards the more stable condition,* — a law under which the universe has moved forward or "run down" from the beginning, and under which its course will continue uniformly to the end.

True and natural classification and work ought to give expression to that law and conform to it, and the classification and arrangement herein followed is an effort towards that end. In accordance with this, petrography seems to demand a former liquid globe and one whose interior portions are either now liquid, or in such a condition that they can readily become so. If the so-called physical and mathematical demonstrations of the earth's solidity be examined, it will be found that they have been based on certain hypothetical globes, of a constitution unlike that of the earth, and therefore not applicable to it, but to the hypothetical globes only. On examining the claim that the materials of which the earth's interior is supposed to be composed would tend to solidify under pressure, because they contract in passing from the liquid to the solid state, it is found that the best and more recent observations which compare the relation of the solid and liquid form — both taken at a temperature near the melting point — either prove or render it probable that iron and the various rock materials which are believed to compose the *infra*-sedimentary portion of the earth expand on passing from the liquid to the solid. Hence, according to Thomson's law, pressure would tend to render the earth's interior liquid instead of solid.

The alleged sinking of the earth's crust to the earth's centre could not, according to the above, take place; since the solid would be lighter than the liquid portion in contact with it. But if the crust were heavier it could not sink far, unless the earth was of homogeneous material; but since we know it to be heterogeneous — the materials varying also in specific gravity — the crust on sinking would soon meet with material of higher specific gravity, which would prevent any further subsidence. So, too, the heat imparted to the sinking crust would make it lighter, while the viscosity of the still liquid matter would retard the descent.

Since we may accept that which the facts of geology and petrography appear to indicate — an earth with a liquid interior — we may also hold, in accordance with observed petrographical facts, that all rocks originally came from the cooling molten material of the globe, and that the sedimentary and chemical rocks have resulted from the disintegration of that material, while all eruptive or volcanic (including plutonic) forms were derived from that material which either had never solidified or had been reliquefied; but they were not formed from either chemical or sedimentary deposits.

From this it would naturally follow that regions of crystalline rocks are, as a rule, regions in which eruptive, or mixed eruptive and sedimentary agencies have prevailed; and these rocks are of every geological age — meaning, by eruptive agencies, the original and secondary results of a cooling globe, including thermal waters. The original, including eruptive, rock materials appear to be the same for each species, no matter from what region they may have come. Hence the same principles should be employed in classifying them; and the classification, to be natural, ought to express their relationships.

This natural classification should be based on all the characters of the rocks, taken together. It must, of course, be an empirical one, as in zoölogy and botany, and ascertained by studying all known forms, considering all their relations, and arranging them according to their petrological, lithological, and chemical characters. With but one exception, all classifications in use at the present time are confessedly artificial; as can be readily seen by examining those proposed by Naumann, Blum, Von Cotta, Zirkel, Dana, Lang, Lasaulx, Rosenbusch, Roth, and many others. The exception is the classification of Richthofen, which however applies only to the modern volcanic rocks. This, although starting with many natural principles, has been rendered highly artificial in its practical applications. The classifications of rocks have usually been based on part of the characters only, to the exclusion of others; as, for instance, on age, structure, mineral composition, and upon almost every part of the rock separately, but not upon the rock as a unit. In the schemes based on the contained minerals, but little attention has been paid to the question whether the minerals were foreign, original, or secondary products in the rock. So long as the same minerals existed there, no matter how diverse their origin, all rocks containing them were called by the same name. Again, if the mineralogical classification is adopted it is found that the species of feldspar, which form the corner stone of that classification, and their relations, have not been definitely settled; and let the method of determination adopted be what it will, they cannot be accurately and surely distinguished from one another; therefore no system should be placed on such an uncertain foundation. Such classifications correspond to the Linnean artificial botanical classification, and hold about the same relations to the natural classification of rocks as that does to the natural classification of plants. The greater number of rocks separated by these classifications into distinct species seem to be mere varietal forms of certain natural species — the variation being due to alteration, or some change in condition. Distinction should be made between superficial weathering and the chemical and molecular changes that go on in all eruptive rocks, after consolidation and exposure to the action of infiltrating waters; that is, changes in the rock-mass as a whole — a change from an unstable to a more stable condition, a loss of energy. It is believed that to these changes is due in general the difference now observable between the ancient and modern eruptive rocks of the same types. In other words, to these changes is due nearly all, if not all, those distinctions which cause the eruptive rocks to be divided into older and younger, or into pre-Tertiary, and Tertiary and recent. It is, then, claimed that geological age has no bearing on classification beyond this: that the older rocks of the same type or species are, the greater is their alteration under like conditions; and that the greater number of the so-called rock-species of pre-Tertiary age are the altered forms of rocks which were once identical with Tertiary and modern rocks. The original or eruptive rocks of the universe appear to form a continuous series, from the most basic to the most acidic; but for convenience they are to be divided into definite species, types, or groups, which on the boundaries will naturally fade into one another. The preponderance of characters, and not the presence or absence of any one mineral ought to decide the place of any rock in the system, and the original characters ought to hold priority in classification over any that are of a secondary nature (alteration, etc.).

The natural classification, in its broader applications, can be employed in the field as well as in the laboratory; for, as a rule, all the characters of rocks are so related to one another that from one the others can be inferred with a fair degree of accuracy.

When complete (bausch) analyses are made of typical rocks, rock-species are believed to have in their broader features certain limits of chemical composition outside of which the normal forms rarely go, and inside of which the normal forms of other species rarely come; but the mineralogical composition is more or less unstable and variable, depending upon alteration and other conditions to which the rock has been subjected. It is thought that the chemical relation of rock species would be much better shown if the percentages were expressed in terms of the elements, instead of in their compounds — as Nordenskiöld has suggested for the meteorites.

All rocks, except meteoric and recent volcanic ones appear to be more or less altered; and it is evidently from these altered rocks that the classifications and principles of classification have been chiefly derived in Europe, on the supposition that as these rocks are now found to be, so they always were, and always will be.

Fragmental or derived rocks ought to be classed, so far as it is possible, under the rocks from which they were derived; the object of the classification both of these and the massive rocks being to show their relations and derivation so far as practicable.

The relation of one rock to its fellows in the field is the principal criterion for determining its origin — particularly in the case of altered rocks.

Taking the consolidation of any rock as the datum point, the minerals and rock fragments are found to be naturally divided into three distinct classes of different origin: —

1. Minerals and fragments of prior origin.
    (a) Those characteristic of the rock species.
    (b) Those that are accidental.
2. The products of the consolidation.
3. The products of alteration and infiltration.

All may exist together in a rock, or all except those of one class may be wanting; and far more depends, in lithology, on being able to determine the origin and relations of these different classes of minerals than on ability to name the mineral species correctly. Minerals of the third class are apparently formed through the agency of percolating waters, which may be hot or cold.

The alterations appear in general to take place slowly; while rapid alterations, such as would be produced by hot, intensely active waters, generally, if not always, seem to bear distinctive marks.

CLASSIFICATION IN LITHOLOGY. — GENERAL CONCLUSIONS.

In practically employing the principles given before, all kinds of rocks, whether from the earth or heavens, are naturally to be described and arranged, but only a limited portion of this work can be done here. In the execution of this the most basic rocks known will be taken, and the gradations between the different states traced as far as practicable.

The order will be to pass from the glassy to the most perfectly crystalline state; from the least altered towards the most altered; from the most basic towards the most acidic; from the non-fragmental to the fragmental or clastic. In the case of the fragmental rocks, it is intended to proceed from the least altered to the most altered; that is, from those little consolidated towards those most indurated; from the unaltered towards those most highly metamorphosed. In the wide range of rocks studied, it has been found as a rule that the macroscopic and microscopic characters could generally be inferred one from the other; and that, likewise, from these the chemical composition could be declared, within certain general limits. Indeed, by the method of classification pursued here, a bit of *unaltered* groundmass, not pure glass, sufficient to fill the field of a No. 7 or 9 Hartnack objective, is enough to enable one to tell the species to which the rock belongs, and to give some general idea of its composition, both chemically and mineralogically.

In applying the earlier given principles of nomenclature and classification, the following method has been practically adopted here: All the rocks, from one end of the series to the other, are divided into species or groups; and each of these species possesses the general characters that have usually found voice in the generally established nomenclature. Since the most typical forms are those of the modern eruptive rocks, their names, when practicable, have been selected, and in them the limits of the species is made as nearly as possible coincident with those made by the leading lithologists. Of course they are not absolutely identical, for natural boundaries do not correspond entirely with the artificial fences made by man. Under these specific or group names — such as basalt, andesite, trachyte, and rhyolite — are placed, as varieties, the altered, as well as older (pre-Tertiary) forms; which it is thought were once identical with the unaltered or modern forms. The variety names are also used as nearly as possible in their more general applications; but it is often found that the artificial boundaries of these varieties (regarded by other lithologists as distinct species) carry them into two or more of the species, as that term is used here; *e. g.*, melaphyr is, as a rule, a name given to the fine-grained older and altered rocks belonging to the species basalt, but in some cases the older forms of andesite have been described as melaphyrs. So, too, the term diabase includes under it, in the common artificial nomenclature, both old basaltic and andesitic rocks — a fact which has been imperfectly recognized in the division of the diabases into diabase and olivine-diabase. In this work the term melaphyr and diabase will be confined to the rocks belonging under basalt, which possess the general characters of the ordinary melaphyr and diabase type. In the case of some names — like diorite, which has been commonly used for a wide range of old and more highly altered rocks than those to which the names melaphyr and diabase have been usually given — a greater difficulty occurs in practical use. Such names are placed as sub-varietal names, after the names of the variety or species to which they belong, in order to indicate the line of derivation.

Many terms have been given in the past to rocks, indicating some special stage in their alteration, which are not of sufficient importance to be used as a variety or sub-variety form. These terms are sometimes inclosed in a parenthesis and placed after the specific or variety name. It is necessary to place those rocks, whose derivation is not clear, as nearly as possible in their apparently proper situation, leaving it to the future to correct and amend the classification.

The fragmental rocks are placed, so far as possible, under the rocks from which they are derived; but those whose derivation is unknown, it is intended to describe and classify according to the common method of nomenclature, as the best now practicable.

The recent or unaltered fragmental rocks will be placed as tufas under their proper species, while the older and altered forms will be classed as porodites,* under their respective species and varieties.

The object is to show the natural relations of the rocks so far as possible, and at the same time to interfere but little with the customary use of lithological names.

As illustrations of my meaning, the following examples may be given, the label of a melaphyr would be written as follows: Basalt, Melaphyr — the following term being always subordinate to the preceding one in this order: species, variety, sub-variety, etc., while any one of the names can be used in speaking of the rock.

If a rock to which the name diorite would be applied in ordinary nomen-

* Bull. Mus. Comp. Zoöl., 1870, v. 280.

clature is found, from its structure and composition, to come under either melaphyr or diabase, its label would be written as follows, according as it was one or the other:—

      Basalt, Melaphyr, Diorite.
      Basalt, Diabase, Diorite.

But if this diorite belonged apparently to the basaltic species, but could not be referred to either the melaphyr or diabase variety, its label would be thus: Basalt, Diorite.

When the names are trivial, or when they are not properly variety or sub-variety names of the species under which the specimen is placed, the label is written as follows: Basalt, Diabase (Calc-Diabase). For the fragmental forms it is written, Basalt, Tufa; or Basalt, Porodite; or Basalt, Diabase, Porodite — as the case may be.

The variety and sub-variety names are not here considered essential, but are employed out of deference to the common custom. However, in order to make the work symmetrical, such names, and even new ones, have been introduced, where it seemed necessary; but all can be dropped or continued, and expanded as the advance of the science may require.

The special nomenclature and its applications will be given in the descriptive portion of the work, with the account of the specimens, and to that the reader is referred. If, in course of time, a system of nomenclature like that employed in botany and zoölogy, should be desired, the system employed here would readily furnish it, by dropping the commas between the specific name and its variety and sub-variety, with the Latinization of these names. The names would then be in their proper order, and afford us both binomial and trinomial names, as the case might be.

CHAPTER II.

THE SIDEROLITES AND PALLASITES.

SECTION I. — *Siderolite.*

IN this, the first or most basic, species or group, the rock is composed chiefly of iron — either native or in its secondary states, as magnetite, hematite, menaccanite, etc. — and with or without nickel, schreibersite, pyrrhotite, graphite, etc.

It includes all those masses of iron and iron ore that have fallen as meteorites, or which formed an original, not secondary, portion of the earth, or are of eruptive origin, or directly derived, as fragmental deposits, from any of these. No veins or chemical deposits of iron ore are intended to be included in this species.

The characters of the supposed meteoric siderolites have been so fully described in numerous papers and treatises on the subject, that it is not necessary to describe them here in any detail. A few specimens only will be spoken of below, that the writer has seen, which will give a few of the characteristics.

In such meteoric siderolites as that from SHINGLE SPRINGS, ELDORADO Co., CALIFORNIA, the iron is in a nearly homogeneous mass, since only two small masses of pyrites have been reported to have been found in it. The etched surface of a specimen in Professor Whitney's collection shows an obscure granular structure, which under the lens is seen to be formed by some brilliant points, and small elongated ridges of like bright metallic lustre, rising above the dull gray surface left by the acid.

Professor B. Silliman states of a specimen in his possession that the etched surface showed under a lens "a reticulated structure with numerous brilliant points and v-shaped lines." *

The meteoric siderolite from STANTON, AUGUSTA Co., VIRGINIA, is a very

* Amer. Jour. Sci., 1873 (3), vi. 18-22.

compact mass of iron, showing only a few small nodules of pyrrhotite. A general description, with figures showing the structure of its etched surface, has been given by Professor J. W. Mallet.*

A specimen of the COAHUILA (MEXICO) siderolite in the Harvard College Mineral Cabinet shows a compact mass of iron, with irregularly distributed elongated cells filled with pyrrhotite. The chief portion of the iron seems to be free from these irregular masses of pyrrhotite, but some parts are quite filled with them.

The TEXAS (GIBBS) siderolite in the same collection shows a compact metallic mass, holding a few rounded and irregular cells containing pyrrhotite. This rock has been described by Professors Silliman and Hunt, who also give a plate representing the Widmannstättian figures.†

The specimen of the BUTLER (BATES COUNTY, MISSOURI) siderolite in the Harvard College Cabinet is very compact, but contains a few elliptical and irregular cells filled with pyrrhotite (troilite) surrounded by rings. These rings connect with the raised bands shown by etching. Some of the bands, indeed, appear as offshoots from the rings. In this specimen the etching has not brought out the Widmannstättian figures very clearly, yet the above relations can be distinguished. A brief description of this siderolite was given by Professor J. Lawrence Smith, with analysis of the iron alone. The nodules of troilite, according to him, were numerous, but free from any schreibersite. In his specimen the Widmannstättian figures were readily developed and found to be large and regular.‡

Some siderolites like that from TOLUCA, MEXICO, in the Harvard College Cabinet are composed of a very coarse sponge-like mass of iron, holding detached irregular masses of pyrrhotite, etc. In this the distance across the iron from one cell wall to another cell wall is greater than the diameter of the cells themselves.

The general structure of the meteoric form may then be said to be a mass of iron, or of iron inclosing more or less irregular and nodular masses of pyrrhotite, schreibersite, graphite, etc.

Associated with the meteoric iron, in intimate union with it or in combinations of their own, occur nickel, cobalt, magnesium, aluminum, calcium, silicon, chromium, phosphorus, copper, carbon, arsenic, sulphur, tin, manganese, potassium, sodium, chlorine, oxygen, beryllium, etc.

* Amer. Jour. Sci., 1871 (3), ii. 10-15, 1873; xv. 337, 338.
† Am. Jour. Sci., 1846 (2). ii. 370-376.
‡ Am. Jour. Sci., 1877 (3), xiii. 213.

In a large number of the siderolites, etching develops in the iron those structural planes, well known as the Widmannstättian figures, parallel to the planes of the isometric octahedron and cube. This structure is parallelized by the cleavage observed in magnetite, and by the observed structure produced in titaniferous iron during the process of its alteration to "leucoxene." Indeed, many of the altered titaniferous irons show a structure closely resembling some of the Widmannstättian figures. These latter figures can be taken no longer as proofs of the meteoric origin of any iron, since they have been developed in the terrestrial iron of the Greenland basalts. The Widmannstättian figures are so well known that it is unnecessary to reproduce them in the plates of this work, especially since good examples can be found in the following papers and works: —

Schreibers's Beiträge zur Geschichte und Kenntniss meteorischer Stein- und Metall-Massen, Wien, 1820; Clark on Metallic Meteorites, Göttingen, 1853; Büchner, Bericht Ober. Gesell. Giessen, 1869, xiii. 99–115; Haidinger, Sitz. Wien. Akad., 1855, xv. 354–360; 1862, xlv. (2), 65–74; xlvi. (2), 286–297; 1863, xlviii. (2), 301–308; Amer. Jour. Sci., 1846, (2), ii. 370–376, 1853, xv. 363; Brezina, Denks. Wien. Akad., 1881, xliii. 13–16; 1884, xliv. 121–158; Tschermak, Sitz. Wien. Akad., 1874, lxx. (1), 443–458; Denks. Wien. Akad., 1872, xxxi. 187–195; Gustav Rose, Abh. Berlin. Akad., 1863, pp. 23–161, etc.

It is possible that could chemical analyses be made that would yield the constitution of the siderolite masses as a whole, and thus enable their mineralogical and chemical constitution to be coördinated with their structure, that the species siderolite might be separated into several distinct, natural, and well marked species. The most probable divisions would be into those composed of metallic iron, and those formed from metallic iron and pyrrhotite. The first might possibly be separated into those bearing much nickel and those of nearly pure iron. Of course, no such subdivision of siderolite should be attempted unless the composition and structure both pointed towards the separation. This would require the study of a large number of siderolites, an opportunity for which the writer has not, even if satisfactory chemical analyses existed.

A list of chemical analyses has indeed been collected and will be appended; but it is far from being what could be desired, since it is the custom of chemists to select the purest portion of the iron for analysis. In fact but few analyses exist of siderolites that can be regarded as complete when the mass contains other minerals than the iron itself. Each separate mineral is analyzed, but the general average of the whole mass is unknown. Indeed, in many cases it may be difficult if not impossible, owing to its structure, to obtain the composition of the whole, except approximately.

Since the same mineral has nearly the same constitution, whatever may be its associations, the native iron would be expected to yield the same constituents whether in a large mass alone or in minute grains associated with other minerals. Consequently, the analyses of meteoric irons as now carried on afford but little clue to their structure, for a pallasite yields the same result as a siderolite, so far as the usual published analyses show.

The specific gravity of the siderolites varies considerably, but by far the greater portion lie between 7.50 and 7.90. The highest number is 8.31, and the lowest 5.75, but the average may be considered to be about 7.70. The analyses of the siderolites have been arranged according to their percentage of metallic iron, for in that way their relations could be best shown; but where there are several analyses of the same rock, all are placed together without regard to the percentage of the iron, except in the case of the first one in the given series. The predominating percentages lie between 87.00 and 97.00, the average being about 91.00. The highest percentage of iron is 99.81 and the lowest 37.00; but only seven analyses show a lower percentage than 80.00.

The percentage of nickel, as a rule, in the meteoric siderolites varies inversely with the iron; and if it is taken in connection with its associated cobalt and the iron — whether free, or united with sulphur or phosphorus — it is found that with but few exceptions the three elements make over 99 per cent of the mass. The nickel varies in amount from none, in seven analyses, and to .10 and .20 per cent, up to 12, 14, and 15 per cent. In three extreme cases it was found to be 24.708, 36.00, and 59.69 per cent. The percentage of nickel in the Greenland siderolites is low. One serious difficulty in estimating the relative proportions of the iron, nickel, and cobalt is the apparent unreliability of many of the analyses — a difference of about four per cent existing in the nickel as determined from the same siderolite; and in an extreme case one chemist obtained 14.70 per cent of nickel, and another none. As a rule, cobalt is in amount less than one per cent, but in a few cases reaches between two and three per cent, and in one instance is between three and four per cent. Probably it is always present with nickel, but is not found, owing to imperfect methods, which cause the cobalt to be wanting in a large number of analyses.

As a rule, the other elements found in siderolites are in very small amounts, if not entirely wanting; although in one case 15.859 per cent of sulphur was reported. The analyses indicate that phosphorus, sulphur, copper, and possibly carbon (graphite) are always present in the siderolites and can be found when searched for with sufficient care. The greater the skill, the greater the number of elements found, and both appear to be roughly and inversely proportionate to the amount of iron reported.

Of course it is to be remembered that these analyses were made from picked portions, and they do not give a fair average of the siderolite masses as a whole.

None of the analyses of the oxidized siderolites have been given in the tables; for while they are quite abundant, most of them are too imperfect to serve any useful purpose for comparison, since they have been made for commercial purposes only. In the case of these terrestrial siderolites, it is desirable to have them carefully selected, typical, and of known origin, and then most carefully tested for the rare elements.

It is to be presumed that the native iron, coming to the surface of the earth from below, would as a rule either be oxidized at that time or during its subsequent existence; hence in but few cases is it naturally to be expected that metallic iron would occur to any especial extent on that surface.

In its oxidized forms, and in association with a rock belonging at the other extreme of the lithological scale, siderolite occurs on the southern shore of Lake Superior.

Since the author has quite fully discussed the evidence that causes him to believe in the eruptive origin of most of the magnetite and hematite of the Marquette district of Lake Superior, it is unnecessary to discuss the subject farther here. The other chief works relating to these ores are the Geological Reports of Messrs. Foster and Whitney, and T. B. Brooks. A general discussion of the various theories and of the evidence, as well as a list of the works relating thereto, has been given by the writer in the papers referred to below.*

From the various accounts given of the occurrence of iron ores in this country and elsewhere, it is probable that many other eruptive iron ore

* Bull. Mus. Comp. Zoöl., 1880, vii. 1-157, 6 plates; Proc. Bost. Soc. Nat. His.,1880, xx. 470-479.

masses exist which properly should come under the species siderolite. However, it is an open question, and it will probably remain so until these deposits can be studied with the view of ascertaining the facts bearing upon their origin, unbiassed by any preconceived theories of that origin.

The native iron found in Greenland may properly be mentioned here, as it is possibly a portion of the earth's metallic core brought to the surface by the associated basalt. The iron is in large masses associated with basaltic rocks, as well as in fine grains intimately mixed with the basalt itself and taking the place of the ordinary iron ores that generally occur in that rock. It occurs with schreibersite, pyrrhotite (troilite) graphite, and magnetite, the same as native iron commonly does in meteorites. On etching, the Widmannstättian figures are produced, and thus this iron shows characters that have usually been regarded as exclusively belonging to meteoric irons. These figures are produced even on the little grains, six to seven millimeters in diameter, occurring in the basalt. Whether the Greenland iron came from the interior of the earth as metallic iron, as the writer thinks most probable, or was produced by the reducing agency of carbon on some ores of iron, as maintained by Steenstrup and Smith, there appears at present no doubt that it is of terrestrial origin.

Of the large number of metallic siderolites that have been described, but very few are known to be of meteoric origin, only some seven having been seen to fall; while the localities in which so many occur — in mountainous districts, and in regions in which eruptive action has been intense — are such that in regard to many, doubt must exist regarding their cosmic origin.* Indeed, if they are truly of meteoric origin, there is a most remarkable concurrence of localities in which telluric iron would naturally occur, if at all, and the places in which iron in relatively large amounts has fallen.

It would seem that chemical analysis should not be made the sole judge regarding the origin of these numerous supposed meteorites. It would appear to be necessary that a petrographical or geological study of the localities in which these bodies are found should be made; and they ought to be regarded as doubtful meteorites, unless the circumstances of their occurrence preclude their terrestrial origin. That no attempt has been made, as a rule, to ascertain the origin of these masses of iron, beyond chemical tests, will be seen from the following: —

* The conditions under which the Bahia siderolite was found renders it not improbable that this is of similar origin with the Ovifak iron. See A. F. Mornay, Phil. Trans., 1816, pp. 270-285.

"Chemistry has entirely dissipated all doubts in the matter, and now an examination in the laboratory of the chemist is entitled to more credit than evidence from any other source in pronouncing on the meteoric origin of a body. No question need be asked as to whether it was seen to fall, or whether this or that rock or mineral exists in the neighborhood where it may have been collected. The reagents of the chemist alone are unerring indications that suffice to set aside all cavilling in the matter." [*]

The above statement rests upon the assumption that no terrestrial material under any circumstances can possess the same chemical characters that meteorites do! This basis is the one upon which most investigations of supposed meteoric irons now proceed, and have proceeded for many years; [†] a basis that has never been carefully investigated, and which many would probably repudiate since the Ovifak discovery. Would it not be well if a more thorough study could be made of the conditions under which so many siderolites have been found in the southwestern portion of the United States, Mexico, and South America?

The origin of the meteoric masses of iron has been a question upon which speculation has been rife. It has been suggested that they and the other meteorites were formed in our own atmosphere; that they were thrown from terrestrial or lunar volcanoes; or thrown from the sun; the remains of a shattered planet; some of the spare material left over when the solar system was made, etc. It concerns this work principally to examine the views of those who have made microscopical studies of siderolites, and not to discuss the general theories of others; however, it will be necessary later to point out the probable origin of meteorites as deduced from their microscopic characters. One of the most prominent of the students of meteorites is Professor Gustav Tschermak, who stated in 1875 that

"the greater number of meteoric irons exhibit a structure which indicates that each has formed part of a large mass possessing similar crystalline characters. The formation of large masses so constituted presupposes, as Haidinger has pointed out, long intervals of time for tranquil crystallization at a uniform temperature, and these conditions could only prevail on one of the larger cosmical masses." [‡]

A microscopic examination of the figures observed upon the etched surface of meteoric and artificial irons, led Mr. Sorby to the following conclusions: —

"These facts clearly indicate that the Widmanstätt's figuring is the result of such a complete separation of the constituents, and perfect crystallization, as can occur only when

---

[*] J. Lawrence Smith's Mineralogy and Chemistry, Louisville, Ky., 1873, p. 290.
[†] Newcomb's Astronomy, 1st ed., 1878, p. 386; 4th ed. 1883, p. 397.
[‡] Phil. Mag., 1876 (5), i. 499; Sitz. Wien. Akad., 1875, lxxi. (2), 661–673. See also J. Lawrence Smith's Memoir on Meteorites, Ann. Rep. Smith. Inst., 1855, p. 158.

the process takes place slowly and gradually. They appear to me to show that meteoric iron was kept for a long time at a heat just below the point of fusion, and that we should be by no means justified in concluding that it was not previously melted. Similar principles are applicable in the case of the iron masses found in Disco; and it by no means follows that they are meteoric, because they show the Widmanstatt's figuring. Difference in the rate of cooling would serve very well to explain the difference in the structure of some meteoric iron [s], which do not differ in chemical composition; but as far as the general structure is concerned, I think that we are quite at liberty to conclude that all may have been melted, if this will better explain other phenomena." *

It would appear that these observers advocate the view that the siderolites must have been subjected to a long and slow cooling upon some body of sufficient size to yield the required conditions; but since the same structure can be developed in the iron of the stony meteorites, which show evidence of rapid cooling, the writer is compelled reluctantly to differ from these eminent observers, and to hold that while the Widmannstättian figures may have originated as they have claimed, they may occur as readily in a small mass, cooling at a comparatively rapid rate, and therefore their origin is to be explained in some other way. In other words, as yet, there is no evidence that Sorby's and Tschermak's views are correct.

It is probable that but few will claim that the siderolites of meteoric origin were formed by organic agencies. If they were not, it follows that the graphite contained in them could not have been so produced. This has a very direct and obvious bearing on the question whether the graphite in Azoic and other rocks *need* have been derived from animal or plant remains, and it negatives the supposition.†

To make graphite the evidence of life is the same kind of argument as it is to claim that no oxides of iron and no carbonate of lime could be formed without the intervention of life. One we knew to be oftentimes of volcanic origin, and the other to be frequently the product of the decomposition of rocks. It is too much to assume, because minerals are known to form in certain conditions, or can be formed in certain ways, that they must always be made in that way. None of the meteorites now known appear to indicate that they came from a region where life could exist as we know it; hence, it does not seem proper to claim that life must have intervened in their formation merely because a mineral is found in them that is ordinarily supposed to be of organic origin.

* Nature, 1877, xv. 498.
† J. Lawrence Smith, Mineralogy and Chemistry, 1873, pp. 284–310; Am. Jour. Sci., 1876 (3), xi. 388–395, 433–442; Walter Flight, Pop. Sci. Rev., 1877, xvi. 390–401.

The term siderolite, or rather aero-siderolite was proposed by Professor N. Story Maskelyne, for the meteorites to which Gustav Rose had previously given the name pallasite. Rose afterwards divided his pallasites, retaining the original term for all, except two specimens, which he classed as mesosiderites. These Maskelyne united again, but instead of using the term pallasite for all, proposed the name above given. The name pallasite belongs by prior right to these forms, while siderolite does not; therefore, I trust Prof. Maskelyne will permit the transference of his term siderolite, as his own, from the pallasites to the forms that I have herein classed under the former name. It is impracticable to use the term *siderite* — long ago proposed by Shepard — on account of the well known mineral of the same name. The term *holosiderite*, proposed by Daubrée, is too inaccurate, since the majority of the specimens are not wholly iron.

Siderolite ($\sigma\iota\delta\eta\rho\sigma$, $\lambda\iota\theta\sigma$) — a stone of iron, or an iron rock — seems to answer better than any other term for the specimens I have included under it here, and if the transference is permitted it will save the introduction of a new name.*

Section II. — *Pallasite.*

This name was first given by Gustav Rose to a class of meteorites, of which he made the olivine iron rock of Krasnojarsk, Siberia, described by Pallas in 1776, the type. Later, Rose separated this group into two divisions — pallasite and mesosiderite — the latter comprising two specimens only.†

The writer proposes to restore the term to its original use; and in addition, to place under it a few other meteorites and those terrestrial rocks that have a similar composition and structure. As in the case of siderolite, it is not intended to include any vein stones, but only original and eruptive rocks of this character and their derivatives.

Of this group or species there will be given, first, descriptions of those nearest the siderolites in structure and composition, passing then to those nearer and nearer allied to the succeeding species — peridotite.

---

* Maskelyne, Phil. Mag.,1863 (4), xxv. 49; Rose, Monatsber. Berlin Akad., 1862, pp. 551-558; 1863, pp. 30-34; Shepard, Amer. Jour. Sci., 1867 (2), xliii. 22-28.

† Monatsber. Berlin Akad.,1862, pp. 551-558; 1863, pp. 30-34; Abh. Berlin Akad., 1863, pp. 23-161.

The Meteoric Pallasites.

Tucson, Arizona.

This meteorite is represented by two forms, known respectively as the Carleton and the Ainsa meteorites.

The Carleton pallasite is composed of quite a compact sponge of iron, containing minute rounded grains of olivine (?) Some schreibersite in black angular grains also occurs.[*]

The Ainsa pallasite is composed of a compact metallic sponge, the minute cells of which are filled by a white siliceous mineral in rounded grains. These grains are arranged in rude lines, giving to the iron an appearance somewhat resembling that produced by fluidal structure. From the torn and broken surface of a specimen in Professor Whitney's collection a number of silicate grains were removed by a needle-point, imbedded in Canada balsam, covered and examined under the microscope. Most of the fragments present the optical characters of olivine, and some contain bubble-bearing stone cavities, arranged in irregular lines, the same as are the fluid cavities in quartz. A few of the broken grains presented the polarization characters of non-striated meteoric feldspar, but two fragments were seen which showed the polysynthetic twinning characteristic of plagioclase.

Both of the above pallasites, when sawn or polished, present a more or less compact appearance, like the common siderolites, and it is only where the Ainsa meteorite has been forcibly torn apart, after being partially sawn, that its true structure can be seen. Since the sawn and polished surfaces of the irons are such poor guides to their structure, it may be that some other irons now classed with the siderolites belong here.

While the silicates [†] of the Ainsa pallasites are nominally clear and transparent, a number of the fragments have been stained to a yellowish brown, owing to the oxidation of the iron.

Hemalga, Tarapaca, Peru.

This rock, as represented by a specimen deposited in the collections of the Boston Society of Natural History, is largely composed of iron, having irregular cavities filled with silicates, which are considerably decomposed in places.

Mr. R. P. Greg states of a specimen in his possession, that its cavities were found to contain pure lead, a very hard, grayish-black, semi-metallic mineral, and a yellowish-brown one of an earthy texture, and insoluble in acids. Sometimes the lead only partially filled the cavities, but at others it entirely filled them, some being large as a pea.[‡]

The specific gravity of this pallasite was found to be about 6.50.

Berdjansk, Russia.

According to Hiriakoff, this is composed of an iron sponge, with fine grains of olivine and troilite, and on etching shows Widmannstättian figures. Specific gravity, 6.63.[§]

---

[*] Whitney and Brush, Proc. Cal. Acad. Sci., 1863, iii. 30–55; Haidinger, Sitz. Wien. Akad., 1863, xlviii. (2), 301–308.
[†] Whitney, Proc. Cal. Acad. Sci., 1863, iii. 48–50.
[‡] Phil. Mag., 1855 (4), x. 12–14.
[§] Geol. Fören. Förhandl., 1878, iv. 72; Neues Jahr. Min., 1878, pp. 653, 654.

Deesa, Chili.

This is composed of a compact iron sponge, containing inclosed silicates. Dr. S. Meunier detected in it troilite, schreibersite, graphite, olivine, hypersthene, pyroxene, enstatite, chromite, etc. Specific gravity varies from 6.10 to 6.24, but no satisfactory analysis exists of it as a whole.*

Atacama, Bolivia.

The rock found in the Desert of Atacama, Bolivia, is described as a cellular or spongy, metallic mass; the cells filled with granular, greenish-white olivine. The cellular spaces instead of being rounded, as in the other rocks of this species, are stated to be angular. An analysis of this rock as a whole is much to be desired, although a rough approximation is given in the list of analyses. A correct chemical analysis would probably show this to be more basic than the Pallas rock of Siberia.†

A specimen in the Harvard College Mineralogical Cabinet is probably from the same pallasite. This shows a very coarse sponge of iron, holding angular and rounded grains of olivine. The olivine is yellowish-green in color — the yellowish tint owing in part to a ferruginous staining. The coarseness of the iron sponge allies this more nearly than any of the other pallasites seen, except that from Tarapaca, to the siderolites.

On one side it shows a surface closely resembling an ordinary slickenside, but on another side is to be seen the remains of a fused crust — the common mark of a meteorite. Some pyrrhotite was seen in this rock.

Figure 1, Plate I., is from a tracing made from the polished surface of this specimen. Owing to the dulness of the polished face — the polishing having been done many years ago — it was impracticable to get the outlines exact. The general structure is well shown for the spongy metallic iron, but the olivine grains are far more angular, as a rule, than the figure represents them to be.

Specimens of an Atacama meteoric iron in the Mineralogical Cabinet, received from Professor I. Domeyko, show that this formed a metallic sponge holding olivine. Only traces of the olivine are left, and beyond it nothing can be told regarding the silicates that might have been contained in this sponge. Some pyrrhotite was seen. This contains less iron probably than the Pallas iron.

Another specimen of Atacama iron in the same Cabinet, received from a Mr. Clay, of Philadelphia, is similar to that figured (Pl. I. fig. 1), but the sponge is not so coarse, and the olivine is more abundant. This mineral is considerably decomposed, and the iron much oxidized.

Bilburg, Prussia.

A coarse sponge of iron, containing in its cells light-greenish-brown olivine. The only specimen seen by the writer somewhat resembles the Atacama meteorite, but, perhaps, contains even more iron.

---

* Daubrée, Comptes Rendus, 1868, lxvi. 571, 572; Meunier, Cosmos, 1869 (3), v. 552–556, 570–586, 612–619.
† Trans. Roy. Soc. Edin. 1831, xi. 223–228; Clark, Metallic Meteorites, 1851, pp. 17–19.

Hommoney Creek, Buncombe Co., North Carolina.

A coarse cellular mass of nickeliferous iron, with most of the observed cells empty but a few containing dull, yellowish-gray olivine grains. The iron exhibits, on etching, Widmannstättian figures.*

Singhur, India.

The pallasite found at Singhur, Deccan, India, was from a basaltic hill. It is described as a vesicular mass of iron, with the cavities either empty or else containing "small, yellowish-white, earthy-looking bodies, about the size of peas" — olivine (?). No satisfactory analysis of this rock has been made.†

Its occurrence is similar to that of the iron from Disco, Greenland, and it may be of like terrestrial origin.

Forsyth, Taney Co., Missouri.

A white, sponge-like mass of nickeliferous iron containing greenish olivine, the latter being more abundant than the former.‡ Specific gravity, 4.46.

Anderson, Hamilton Co., Ohio.

This pallasite, which may properly be called the Little Miami meteorite, was found on an altar in one of the earthworks now being explored in Anderson Township, in the Little Miami Valley, Ohio. This was placed in the hands of Dr. L. P. Kinnicutt, for analysis, by Mr. F. W. Putnam, the curator of the Peabody Museum of Archæology, into whose possession it had come. The polished surface shows a coarse sponge of iron, holding, according to Dr. Kinnicutt, olivine, bronzite, and an unknown mineral. In the section figured in Dr. Kinnicutt's report, the iron appears to predominate over the silicates, but taking the mass as a whole the two form about equal bulk. In structure it closely resembles the Pallas iron, its olivine grains being as a rule rounded, and not so angular as the Atacama pallasite. The olivine forms the chief portion of the siliceous material. The specific gravity of the mass is 4.72. The etched surfaces show the Widmannstättian figures. Analyses of the iron and of the olivine were given by Dr. Kinnicutt, and from this a rough approximation is given of the composition of the mass as a whole, on the supposition that the iron and olivine form about equal portions of the mass. Since there was sufficient material it seems a pity that no complete analysis has been made.§

Krasnojarsk, Siberia.

The Pallas rock is formed by a coarse metallic sponge, whose more or less rounded cavities are filled with olivine. This sponge-like structure, or one approaching it, is characteristic of the pallasites, so far as known. No complete analysis of this rock has ever been published that the writer can find, except an old one of Laugier, ‖ in which the iron was estimated as an oxide.

* Shepard, Am. Jour. Sci., 1847 (2), iv. 70-82.
† Herbert Giraud, Edin. New Phil. Jour., 1849, xlvii. 56, 57.
‡ Shepard, Am. Jour. Sci., 1860, (2) xxx. 205, 206.
§ Ann. Rep. Peabody Mus. Am. Arch., 1884, iii. 381-384.
‖ Mém. Acad. St. Peters, 1870 (7) xv., No. 6, pp. 40, 4 plates. Clark, Metallic Meteorites, 1851, pp. 15-17.

A specimen in the Harvard Mineralogical Cabinet shows the same characters as those given in the various papers relating to this iron, including even the parallel minute tubes in the olivine; hence this specimen is doubtless authentic. A tracing of the polished surface of this specimen is given in figure 2, Plate I. Of course, from the method employed, the most that could be done was to show the relation of the iron to the olivine; for the pyrrhotite could not be separated from the metallic iron in making the tracing. This apparently has less iron than the Atacama pallasite.

A figure of a polished surface of the Pallas iron has been given by Dr. Carl V. Schreibers, which seems to be very good, except that the olivine has been too highly colored.*

Potosi, Bolivia.

Of a similar character is the Potosi rock, described in 1839 as a meteoric iron, "cavernous, filled with vacuities, most of which are irregular, but some have the form of a rhombic dodecahedron; some of them also are filled with a greenish vitreous substance, similar to the olivine of Pallas." †

Brahin, Russia.

This is said to contain somewhat less iron and more olivine than the Pallas rock, but otherwise to be of similar composition and structure.

Rittersgrün, Saxony.

The Rittersgrün pallasite was regarded by Weisbach as composed of 30 per cent of nickeliferous iron, and 70 per cent of an unmetallic brown mass. The latter was said by Winkler to be composed of bronzite (enstatite) pyrrhotite, schreibersite, with asmanite [tridymite].

Breithanpt had held that the silicate was olivine.‡

In Fouqué and Levy's Minéralogie Micrographique (Pl. LV. fig. 2) is given a microscopic section of the Rittersgrün rock which shows that it is composed of iron, diallage, olivine, and augite. The olivine contains octahedrons and grains of pleonaste. The structure is much like that of the pallasite from Cumberland, Rhode Island (Cumberlandite).

A specimen in the Harvard College Mineral Cabinet has been figured from the polished surfaces. In this, while the iron in places forms a coarse sponge, in other parts it is much less in amount and occurs in detached irregular grains. Considerable pyrrhotite is found in this, forming part of the sponge or in irregular grains, and in figuring (Pl. I. figs. 3, 4) has not been separated therefrom, since the design has been simply to show the general structure. The iron where etched shows the usual Widmannstättian figures. The silicates cannot, of course, be separated through the examination of a polished surface, except partially. However, this specimen appears to contain considerable well marked olivine.

* Stein-und Metall-Massen, 1820, Plate VIII. page 70.
† Phil. Mag., 1839 (3), xiv. 394; Chronique Scientifique, 1839, i. 31; Ann. Physik Chemie, xlvii. 470; Neues Jahr. Min., 1840, p. 229.
‡ Nova Acta Leop. Acad. Halle, 1878, xl. 333–382; Berg. Hütt. Zeit.,1862, pp. 321, 322.

Since this specimen was figured and the plate in the hands of the lithographer, A. Weisbach's account of it, with the accompanying beautiful plate, has been received.*
This plate, so far as the writer can judge, shows the structure exceedingly well, and, like the two figures drawn by him, indicates the two types of structure in this meteorite. In one it shows the sponge-like character of the iron, holding the silicates in detached grains and masses; in the other the iron appears to be in the detached grains lying in the mass of silicates. The sponge-like structure shows, however, in all the detached pieces of iron, but it is discontinuous.

A microscopic examination of this meteorite has been made by Tschermak, who states that the asmanite is tridymite, and that the meteorite is composed of meteoric iron, bronzite and tridymite.†

Breitenbach, Bohemia.

The pallasite from Breitenbach was described by Prof. N. S. Maskelyne in 1871. This was seen to be composed of a sponge-like mass of nickeliferous iron with some pyrrhotite, and inclosing in its cells bronzite (enstatite), asmanite (tridymite), and chromite. No complete analysis has been made.‡

If this is, as has been claimed, the same as the Rittersgrün pallasite, the microscopic section of that rock given by Fouqué and Lévy would indicate that its composition was considerably different from that given by Maskelyne.

Steinbach, Saxony.

The structure of this is the same as that from Rittersgrün, and these two with the Breitenbach pallasite are supposed to be portions of the same mass.

Atacama, Chili.

To the pallasites also belongs a meteorite found on a mountain pass, in the province of Atacama, Chili, which was described by Prof. Charles A. Joy. This rock seems to be composed of an irregular sponge-like mass of iron holding grains of olivine and enstatite or labradorite, most probably the former.§

The analysis given by Professor Joy is apparently the best and most complete yet made of any of the pallasites.

Sierra de Chaco, Atacama, Chili.

According to Tschermak, this is composed of an iron sponge, containing grains of iron and silicate. Plagioclase, with broad twin lamellæ, is quite abundant, and contains numerous inclusions, of bronzite, pale brownish glass, parallel layers of fine black needles, etc. Besides the plagioclase, there were seen greenish grains of bronzite, greenish-gray rounded grains of olivine, with dust-like inclusions, brownish augite grains, colorless particles of tridymite, some supposed cordierite, and a brownish glass. This is considered by Tschermak to be the same pallasite as that analyzed by Joy from Atacama.

* Der Eisenmeteorit von Rittersgrün im sächsischen Erzgebirge, Freiberg, 1876; 3 pp. and plate.
† Sitz. Wien. Akad., 1883, lxxxviii. (1), 348.
‡ Phil. Trans., 1871, pp. 359–365.
§ Am. Jour. Sci., 1864 (2), xxxvii. 243–249.

Newton Co., Arkansas.

A coarsely reticulated or sponge-like mass of iron, containing in its cells olivine and enstatite (?) Chromite and pyrrhotite also occur.

The enstatite is of a greenish-gray color, and more or less stained by the iron. The olivine is in part colorless and in part stained yellow by the iron oxide. The analysis does not afford data to give the composition of the rock as a whole.* The specimens seen indicate that it is closely allied to the peridotites, but probably belongs with the pallasites, with which it is here placed.

Meyellones, Atacama, Bolivia.

A specimen in the Harvard Mineralogical Cabinet from Meyellones, Atacama, Bolivia, shows the iron in irregular fine semi-sponge-like masses. Occasionally, it is aggregated into grains from one to three quarters of an inch in length, but in general the grains are minute. The iron everywhere is rough, pronged, and jagged. The silicates cannot be distinguished from one another, except in the case of a few rounded olivine grains. This, with the Hainholz pallasite, lies near the peridotites bearing iron, but does not seem sufficiently distinct to be placed in a different species from the pallasites.

Hainholz, Westphalia.

The Hainholz, Westphalia, pallasite, while much finer grained, possesses a structure similar to those portions of the Rittersgrün pallasite that contain the least iron, and this iron in detached masses. The former contains irregular grains and semi-spongiform masses of iron and pyrrhotite, while the silicates form irregular masses, partly included in the iron and partly surrounding it. The silicates apparently predominate, and show characters much like those of the Rittersgrün pallasite. So far as can be told from a macroscopic study of this specimen, it lies near the Rittersgrün meteorite, but forms a connecting link between it and the peridotic meteorites containing iron, like those from Mezo-Madras, Cabarras, Iowa Co., etc. The chemical analysis, if it is a fair index of the general composition of this meteorite, would carry it into the peridotites. This pallasite has been studied microscopically by Tschermak, who states that its included silicates are olivine and bronzite, with subordinate amounts plagioclase, augite, and a cordierite-like mineral. The olivine grains are from 30 to 40 cm. in length, and contain only few inclusions. The bronzite grains are smaller, and contain inclusions of brown glass and black grains. The plagioclase shows the usual twinned structure in polarized light, and contains grains of olivine and bronzite. A few grains of augite occur, having fine dust-like inclusions, as well as brown glass globules, and angular black grains. Only two grains of the supposed cordierite were seen. All the larger crystals lie in a groundmass, composed of the same minerals, with a little interstitial brown glass.†

Lodran, India.

The meteorite from Lodran, India, is described by Tschermak as a granular mixture of vitreous, bluish-gray, and yellowish-green grains, between which steel-gray and yel-

* J. Lawrence Smith, Mineralogy and Chemistry, Louisville, Ky., 1873, pp. 339–342.
† Sitz. Wien. Akad., 1883, lxxxviii. 310–351.

lowish metallic particles are to be seen. The microscopic and chemical examination showed that the rock was composed of nickeliferous iron, pyrrhotite, chromite, olivine, and bronzite. The nickeliferous iron forms the cementing mass, in a fine irregular network. In the finer meshes lie single crystals, and in coarser portions are inclosed aggregated grains and crystals of the above mentioned minerals. This iron is of a very light steel gray color, and, on etching its surface, shows under the microscope figures somewhat similar to those of the Senegal iron.

The olivine forms more or less perfect crystals, which occur both in the iron and as intergrowths with the bronzite. The olivine was determined by the crystallographic measurements of Professor Viktor von Lang to be of the same form as basaltic olivine. It is on the surface of a bluish-gray to a berlin-blue color, but in the thin section pale green.

Under the microscope no well marked cleavages were seen, but undulating fissures parallel to the basal pinacoid are common. Many of these cracks are bordered by a moss-like black mineral, which Tschermak regards as chromite, arising from a secondary alteration of the olivine. Judging from the figure given, the present writer would agree in this particular with Tschermak.

The bronzite occurs in grains and irregular crystals. From its crystallographic characters, as determined by Von Lang, it appears to be enstatite, the same as the bronzite in the Breitenbach meteorite. The enstatite has an asparagus-green to a yellowish-green color, and under the microscope is of a very pale green shade. It is traversed by the usual cleavage and fissure lines, and contains inclusions of three different kinds. The first is in the form of colorless rounded grains, which are regarded as feldspar. The next class of inclusions are minute, round, black particles, which are referred to chromite. The last class are fine hair-like bodies, like those commonly seen in terrestrial bronzite, but whose nature was not determined by Tschermak.

The pyrrhotite was seen united with the iron, and often between the silicates in yellow grains having a metallic lustre.

The chromite occurs in black crystals and grains, possessing a strong semi-metallic lustre. The planes of an octahedron, rhombic dodecahedron, and tetragonal trinkis octahedron were observed by Von Lang upon the chromite crystals. It was found in small amounts between the silicate, and also in the iron. For a fuller description and the figures, the reader is referred to the original paper with its accompanying plate.[*] It is doubtful whether this meteorite should be placed here, or classed with the peridotites.

Variety. — Cumberlandite.

Iron Mine Hill, Cumberland, Rhode Island.

No. 998. A dark resinous, almost black, crystalline groundmass, holding, porphyritically inclosed, long, striated, glassy, and milky plagioclase crystals. Powder strongly magnetic. This rock has been exposed on one side to weathering, and shows a dark brown mass holding grains of magnetite, and gives an earthy yellow streak. In some of the unaltered portions, the groundmass has the oil-green color of olivine. The fracture

---

[*] Sitz. Wien. Akad., 1870. lxi. (2), 465–475.

is rough, splintery, and conchoidal. The rock gelatinizes with hydrochloric acid, even in the cold, and gives a titanium reaction.

Section: A granular groundmass, composed of olivine and magnetite, holding porphyritically inclosed feldspar crystals. The magnetite forms more or less connected spongiform irregular masses. The olivine is in crystals and grains, united directly without any cement, and occupies the cells and interspaces between the magnetite masses. Grains of magnetite are of frequent occurrence in the olivine. The olivine is traversed by numerous fissures, and the majority of the grains show a well marked cleavage. The fissures usually have a ferruginous staining. Besides this, the olivine is comparatively clear and unaltered, exhibiting, however, in connection with the feldspar, a greenish alteration-product.

The plagioclase is in grains and irregular masses, which occasionally send tongues out into the olivine magnetite mass. It shows well marked cleavage planes, and is somewhat kaolinized along those lines, otherwise the feldspar is clear and glassy. In polarized light the larger feldspar masses were seen to be made up of several polysynthetic individuals. Some small microscopic grains of feldspar are scattered in the rock mass, but as a rule most of it is in large crystals, clearly seen macroscopically. A few reddish-brown biotite flakes were observed in the feldspar.

The sponge-like structure of the magnetite is the same as that of the iron in the supposed meteoric pallasites, and in a similar manner contains the inclosed olivine. As would be expected, as a rule, in any iron coming to the surface of the earth in a heated condition (eruptive), the iron in this rock has suffered the first stage of oxidation, and is a magnetite. The writer regards the state of the iron (its alteration) of but little consequence, so long as the structure and general chemical and mineralogical composition remain the same. This section is figured in Plate I. figure 5.

In this figure the black portions represent the magnetic iron, and the light yellow and whitish portions the fissured olivine.

No. **999** is, both in the hand specimen and section, similar to the preceding.

No. **1000.** This is weathered to a slight extent only, and shows the same characters as the unweathered portions of Nos. **998** and **999.** The sections show the same relation of the magnetite and olivine as in the preceding. The latter mineral contains many grains and crystals of magnetite, and is much fissured. These fissures are filled largely with magnetite granules and air cavities. It is stained yellowish and greenish in places, and was seen in some portions to have been changed into a greenish aggregately polarizing mass.

The feldspar is clear throughout the greater portion of the mass, but in parts is kaolinized, and contains fluid and air cavities. This mineral in one section is seen to be in small masses, as well as large, and holding such relations to the olivine and magnetite that it leaves no doubt that it is a later crystallization than either of the other minerals. A small fracture extends across a portion of the section, through the feldspar and olivine grains, forming a miniature vein. The materials deposited in this vein vary according to its position, whether in the feldspar or in the olivine, but, at the contact of the two minerals, contains ingredients derived from both. This might be taken on a miscroscopic scale to illustrate the variation of veins in passing from one rock to another. In the olivine the vein is filled with serpentinous material, but in the feldspar with silicious.

Biotite occurs as a secondary product in connection with the magnetite. It is seen forming a fringe about the latter, or joined on to some of its prongs, extending out into the olivine grains. The color is dark reddish brown, and the mineral shows strong dichroism and well marked cleavage.

In the magnetite filling some cavities and fissures, a dark green isotropic mineral, of irregular outline and unknown characters, was observed.* This is regarded by myself as a secondary mineral, formed like the biotite, in connection with the magnetite. In another section considerable earthy yellowish green and green aggregately polarizing alteration products were observed in connection with the feldspar and olivine.

In all of the preceding sections the olivine is the predominating mineral. The feldspar crystals are confined to one side of the hill composed of this rock, and they are therefore local, and not to be regarded as characteristic of the rock as a whole.

No. 1005, from the same locality as the preceding, but nearer the middle of the hill, shows a dark granular and crystalline groundmass in which, under a lens, can be seen olivine in yellowish green grains, magnetite, and clear greenish glassy actinolite with a well marked cleavage. Dark green serpentinous masses occur in the rock in irregular vein-like and nodular forms. The rock weathers to a dull brownish gray surface, while immediately beneath the surface crust the olivine is decomposed to a yellowish brown ferruginous earth.

Section: The general structure of the section is the same as that of No. 998, without the feldspar; that is, like the more compact portions of the section of that specimen. A certain amount of alteration, however, has taken place here. This specimen, like all except those in the immediate vicinity of No. 1000, is free from feldspar. The olivine grains are now separated in the majority of cases from the magnetite sponge by a narrow film of a pale greenish actinolitic alteration product, which also separates these grains from one another. The same product in places traverses fissures in the olivine, and replaces some of the smaller grains. The olivine further presents in part a cloudy, smoky appearance, arising from a dark-colored staining, extending in fine lines parallel to a crystallographic axis. This clouding extends sometimes over part only, and at other times over the entire crystal. A greenish yellow serpentine replaces the olivine to some extent, and extends in vein-like forms across part of the crystals. The actinolite in the section is in minute elongated, irregular crystals, usually forming an interlocked mass. The olivine contains fluid, glass, and gas inclusions, as well as detached secondary actinolite crystals.

No. 1002 is macroscopically almost identical with No. 1005; but microscopically, its olivine is less in amount, and the actinolite in better formed and larger crystals. In many portions of the section the latter mineral appears in long-bladed crystals with well marked longitudinal cleavage. In other cases when the crystals are cut across they show the characteristic amphibole cleavage rhombs. They are colorless, and exhibit very brilliant polarization colors. Some of the altered portions of the section are of a pale greenish hue, and formed of an interlaced mass of fibres and non-polarizing particles — the fibres being apparently actinolite. Other portions, more coarsely crystalline, show dichroism, varying from a pale green to a pale yellow.

* Dr. Geo. H. Williams thought that this might be hercynite, a mineral which he had been especially studying. Specimens of the rock were placed in his hands, but owing to the small amount of this mineral, together with its high specific gravity, he was unable to isolate it from the magnetite.

The magnetite has diminished in amount, and for the most part forms a discontinuous sponge. This discontinuity appears to have arisen from the solution of the magnetite along the borders of its fissures and edges, which solution in some places has removed nearly the whole of this mineral.

The removed portions are replaced by actinolitic material. The olivine is generally surrounded by a border of actinolitic material, whose general relation is shown in Plate II. figure 1, the black portion representing the magnetic sponge, the brownish parts the smoky, fissured olivine, and the gray and white portions the secondary actinolite.

In this the actinolite band is represented by the uncolored portion surrounding the olivine, and in its turn inclosed by the magnetite. Little granules remain in the actinolitic material, part of which are shown in the drawing. The olivine as before is "smoky," marking apparently the first stage in its alteration.

Nos. 1007 and 1008 are both in the section and hand specimen similar to the preceding number, only in some portions the alteration has not extended quite so far.

No. 1006 is somewhat more changed than No. 1002. The section is partially crossed by greenish actinolitic material, which replaces nearly all of the original matter. In other portions the original structure still remains, the olivine being partly replaced by actinolite, etc. The centres of the olivine are in part only dark smoky-brown, but in others are altered to a reddish-brown serpentinous like product.

The section is stained by a greenish, yellowish, and brownish product in many places. This section serves as the last link in the chain connecting the specimens which contain unaltered olivine with those in which the olivine is entirely changed.

No. 1001 is from the same locality as No. 1000, but nearer the centre of the hill. This is a dark greenish black rock, showing a greenish serpentinous groundmass sprinkled with titaniferous magnetite. Rounded and irregular patches of green serpentine, comparatively free from the magnetite, are irregularly distributed in the groundmass. In weathering, the magnetite is left projecting in a cellular sponge-like mass.

Section: This, like the preceding, is composed of an irregular sponge-like mass of magnetite, with the interspaces filled with pale greenish and grayish mineral matter. While the structure of the section is essentially the same as that of Nos. 998, 999, and 1000, the olivine is entirely replaced by serpentine. The forms of the olivine grains remain the same, and the fissures by which they were traversed are marked by magnetite grains arranged in lines extending through the serpentine. With a low power in common light the section is almost undistinguishable from one containing unchanged olivine. With a higher power, or in polarized light, the fibrous structure of the serpentine shows itself. The polarization colors are dull, and the platy fibrous masses show some resemblance to talc, as well as being obscured when the fibres are parallel to a diagonal of the crossed nicols. The original fissures of the olivine show well both in common and polarized light. Magnetite is included in the serpentine, not only in original grains, as seen in the olivine of No. 998, but also in scattered dust-like granules and irregular masses, or in lines along the fissures. The latter magnetite is apparently a secondary product formed during the conversion of the olivine to serpentine. The main magnetite sponge-like mass is not quite so closely united as in No. 998, neither does it occupy so great an extent of the section; i. e., the percentage of magnetite is somewhat smaller in this portion of the hill, and continues less in all parts of the hill not immediately adjacent to the porphyritic feldspar portion, so far as the writer has observed. The structure of this section is shown in Plate I. figure 6. In this the structure of the altered fissured olivine, closely resembling the olivine of figure 5, is clearly shown.

No. 1003 shows more serpentine characters than No. 1001, having less iron and more of the irregular serpentine masses. In the section the characters are essentially the same as those of No. 1001. Some talc in fine scales aggregated together was seen towards the interior of the larger serpentinized olivines, and in the macroscopically visible serpentine masses before mentioned. The serpentine in these masses is pale-green and isotropic. The serpentine replacing the olivine shows the same fibrous character as No. 1001, but the structure is better marked, and the fibrous plates polarized with brilliant colors. In portions of the section considerable actinolite was observed.

Nos. 1004, 1009, 1010, and 1011 are from the side of the hill opposite to No. 1000, and with the preceding specimens show the gradual change from one side, on which is to be found such material as No. 1000, to those masses which have suffered very great alteration. Part show ochery patches of ferruginous alteration. In general, the sponge-like structure of the magnetite still remains, and besides this the interspaces are variously filled with talc, serpentine, actinolite, etc. — the serpentinous material predominating over the others. Owing to the extreme alteration, some of these specimens have developed an imperfect fissile or laminated structure, which might be mistaken for bedding planes.

No. 1012. This was from an exposure near No. 1011, but separated from it by a rivulet, and its connection with the other described masses could not be shown in the field. This rock is much jointed, presenting an imperfect fissile structure, and is of a dark green color, with yellowish-brown ochery spots of decomposition. On the weathered surface, the magnetite shows the irregular sponge-like structure so characteristic of all these rocks. The character of the section is like that of those last described, but with the addition to its alteration-products of considerable dolomite. I have no hesitation in declaring my opinion, from the microscopic characters of this specimen, that this outcrop belongs to the same formation as the hill itself.

The specific gravity of the Cumberland pallasite varies according to the state of the rock — whether altered or unaltered. Dr. Charles T. Jackson states that it varies from 3.82 to 3.88. Mr. J. E. Wolff, Assistant in Geology in Harvard College, kindly made some determinations for me. The specific gravity of No. 998 was found to be 4.06 and 4.005. The former determination was made from a fragment containing almost no feldspar, while the latter was made from one containing considerable. Again, a specific gravity determination of No. 1001 gave as a result 3.56, and of No. 1003, 3.55.

The two latter determinations were made from the more highly altered portions of the rock.

Owing to the various alterations that this Cumberland rock shows, it would be very interesting if chemical analyses should be made of the different portions, in order to ascertain what changes in the ultimate chemical composition have taken place. They should be made from material microscopically examined, so that the specific gravity and chemical and mineralogical characters could be coördinated. The diminished specific gravity of the more highly altered portions of this rock, as above determined, would indicate that considerable changes had taken place in the chemical composition of the rock as a whole. Further, an examination should be made of the least altered portions of this and all similar rocks, for the purpose of ascertaining if they contain any of the elements so commonly found in meteoric pallasites and siderolites. It is not impossible that, on boring, in depth some of the iron might be found in the native state instead of being entirely oxidized.

This rock has been used as an iron ore, for an historical account of which the reader is referred to previous papers of the writer.*

The additions and changes made in these descriptions to those already published, have been caused by the preparation and examination of other sections, thus making the work more complete. At the time the former descriptions were written, the writer assigned this rock to the peridotites — the most basic olivine rock of terrestrial origin then known. Although its relation to the meteorites was recognized, yet, since the present study of the meteorites themselves was not undertaken until February, 1882, the writer may be pardoned for not earlier perceiving its distinctness from the peridotites, properly so called. It is now regarded as a pallasite in which the iron has been oxidized — probably at the time the rock was formed. The writer holds that the rock is eruptive, although no proof beyond its microscopic characters has been obtained; and if its relations to the country rock should be found to be non-eruptive ones, then this view would have to be abandoned.

If it is necessary to have a distinct name to indicate the pallasites above described, in which the iron is oxidized, the writer would propose that of *Cumberlandite*, from the locality in which it occurs in Rhode Island. He would have preferred that of *Tabergite*, from the earlier described rock from Taberg, Sweden, if that name had not already been in current use in mineralogy.

In this direction a vast field exists in the study of iron-bearing rocks

* Bull. Mus. Comp. Zoöl., 1881, vii. 183–187; Proc. Bost. Soc. Nat. Hist., 1881, xxi. 195–197.

containing actinolite, serpentine, etc.; and the question of the formation of certain schistose rocks by metamorphism of these terrestrial pallasites is an interesting one.

A similar structure to that of this Rhode Island pallasite has been reported in some New York and Canada iron-bearing rocks.

Taberg, Sweden.

Of a similar character to the Cumberland pallasite is the rock from Taberg, Sweden, so long known and so well described by Messrs. Sjören and Törnebohm.*

The section in the collection purchased from Richard Fuess of Berlin shows an imperfect sponge-like mass of magnetite, holding olivine and feldspar.

The olivine is much fissured and traversed along the fissures by serpentine and magnetite bands, while in places it is entirely replaced by the secondary serpentine.

The feldspar is in irregular, somewhat kaolinized masses, holding olivine and magnetite grains. The feldspar polarizes with a polysynthetic structure.

A reddish-brown secondary biotite is associated with the magnetite, but is more abundant than it is in the Cumberland rock.

For the full description of this rock the reader is referred to the original papers above mentioned. This rock is figured on Plate II. figures 2 and 3. Figure 2 shows the sponge-like magnetite with the inclosed olivine, while figure 3 shows a more highly altered portion of the same section in which the magnetite has partly disappeared and the silicates contain more ferruginous material. The reddish-brown portions are the secondary mica, usually associated with or replacing the magnetite.

The pallasites may then be described in general terms as composed of a ferruginous sponge-like or semi-sponge-like mass, holding olivine with or without feldspar, enstatite, diallage, augite, and chromite, or spinel minerals. The sponge is formed either by native iron with pyrrhotite, or by their secondary products, like magnetite.

The alteration of these original materials gives rise to serpentine, chromite (?), biotite, actinolite, etc.

The general structure of the Cumberlandite from Rhode Island may be summed up as follows: In the least altered condition it shows a dark resinous, crystalline, splintery and compact mass, holding porphyritically inclosed feldspars, which, although characteristic of one portion of the locality, are not essential. This rock passes into a form destitute of feldspar, but having the same groundmass, which contains patches of a dark-green, fine-grained alteration-product, which holds a similar relation to the groundmass as the feldspar in the preceding. In the succeeding forms the resinous groundmass

* Geol. Foren. Forhan., 1876, iii. 42–62; 1881, v. 610–619; 1882, vi. 264–267; Neues Jahr. Min., 1876, pp. 434, 435; 1882, ii. 66, 67.

becomes less, and the greenish serpentinous product more abundant, until they pass into a greenish-gray serpentinous rock spotted with secondary ferruginous products. In many of the intermediate forms, short, brilliant crystals of actinolite are to be seen, while the rock assumes a more or less perfect schistose structure.

In the microscopic sections the series passes from a more or less spongiform mass of magnetite, holding olivine and more or less feldspar, into forms that show in portions of the mass an alteration to a greenish serpentinous aggregate. It then passes into a form destitute of the feldspar, in which the partially altered smoky olivine grains are surrounded by a band of secondary actinolite, while the greenish serpentinous product increases in abundance. These changes go on with diminishing olivine and increasing actinolite and greenish serpentinous material, until they have entirely (especially the last) replaced the olivine. The structure remains the same, but the magnetite sponge is more discontinuous and in part dissolved, while talc appears. In others dolomite is seen.

In some sections the greenish secondary products, with little or no actinolite, replace the olivine. The figures 5, 6 (Plate I.), and 1, 2, and 3 (Plate II.), fairly represent the general structure of these rocks, and their resemblance to the meteoric pallasites.

No satisfactory analyses of the pallasites exist except that of Professor C. A. Joy of an Atacama meteorite, but the imperfect ones that have been found have been tabulated, so as to give a rough approximation to correctness. The specific gravity determinations are also not satisfactory as a whole, since they have not been made upon characteristic specimens, but upon selected ones. They run from a little above 7 to some below 4, but it is probable that the majority of typical pallasites lie between 4 and 6; although we must expect to find them graduating in specific gravity, as well as in other characters, into both the siderolites and peridotites. The silica ranges from 3 per cent up to 33 per cent, but the probable limits are between 5 and 30 per cent, averaging about 20 per cent. The magnesia ranges from 2 to over 30 per cent, but the average probably will be found, by correct analyses, to lie somewhere between 10 and 20 per cent. The iron in various conditions is a variable quantity, but averages about 60 per cent; while the nickel, with one exception, is less than 10 per cent. In the terrestrial forms (Cumberlandite) nickel is wanting, but from 6 to 15 per cent of titanic oxide occurs. Some tin, copper, zinc, cobalt, phosphorus, sulphur, chromium, manganese, lime, and aluminum have been found in part of the specimens analyzed. More and accurate analyses are needed before anything but general conjectural statements can be made. If the analyses of iron ores from regions of crystalline rocks be examined, like those given by Richard Åkerman in his work "On the State of the Iron Manufacture in Sweden," Stockholm, 1876, also from Canada and elsewhere, many can be found whose resemblance to those of Cumberlandite is so close as to warrant an examination of the structure and mode of occurrence of the ore analyzed. In these we should look for from 5 to 30 per cent of silica and magnesia, but not of necessity for any titanium. The mere analysis, without further evidence, does not prove the relationship — it merely suggests it.

CHAPTER III.

THE PERIDOTITES.

SECTION I. — *Introductory.*

THE term *peridotite* is employed by Professor Rosenbusch to designate the pre-Tertiary terrestrial rocks that are composed essentially of olivine, with or without enstatite, diallage, augite, magnetite, chromite, picotite, etc.* The writer would extend it so as to include all terrestrial and extra-terrestrial rocks of similar composition and structure, and all the derivatives of both. The state of the iron, as in the case of the preceding species, does not appear to him to be a sufficient reason for separating the rocks herein described into distinct species. The descriptions will be given of the meteoric peridotites first, and of the terrestrial ones later, as a matter of convenience only. The order pursued in the arrangement of the meteoric peridotites will be, so far as possible, the same as that followed with the terrestrial ones, — those composed of olivine first, or the dunite variety; then those containing olivine and enstatite (olivine-enstatite rocks); then those containing olivine, enstatite, and diallage, or the lherzolite variety; etc. In each case those approaching nearest to the glassy condition will be described first. Of necessity this scheme has many imperfections, owing to the limited number of specimens studied microscopically.

While the writer does not believe in the necessity or value of dividing the peridotite into either species or varieties — holding that they are all essentially of one type, whatever may be the especial mineral composition — he recognizes the fact that, excepting himself, lithologists, universally, do so divide these rocks. He then thinks it better to conform for the present to that method, so far as seems necessary and convenient to aid the science, and not to retard its progress. It seems necessary, then, in deference to the prevailing sentiment, that the olivine-enstatite-bearing rocks should be sepa-

* Mikros. Phys. ii. 524–545.

rated as a variety, the same as the olivine-enstatite-diallage ones have been erected into the variety lherzolite. Believing, as he does, that the same methods, rules, and principles should be employed in studying meteorites as those used for the terrestrial rocks, and that both classes are in reality the same, it follows that the same name should be used for both, and the differences expressed adjectively if necessary.

In accordance with this, the variety of peridotite distinguished by olivine should, both as meteorites and terrestrial rocks, be designated by the term already in common use for the latter — *dunite*. For that variety which contains olivine and enstatite, the German term *enstatit-olivinfels* employed by Dr. Dathe is too cumbersome for Anglo-Saxon use, or even for any general use. It is, then, proposed here to designate all these rocks by the term *saxonite*, from the country in which the terrestrial form was first so well described by Dathe.

The term *lherzolite* is here applied to those rocks characterized by enstatite, diallage, and olivine. The forms that are characterized by the presence of olivine, enstatite (bronzite), and augite, are designated by the term *buchnerite*, given in honor of Dr. Otto Buchner, to whose writings on meteorites we are so much indebted, and who gave the first description of a meteorite having this composition.

The term *eulysite* is employed for the olivine-diallage forms, and *picrite* for the olivine-augite variety. Of course, for all of the highly altered forms for which the term *serpentine* has been already used, that name is retained; but in many cases, when it is known from what special variety the serpentine has been produced by alteration, it has been described under that variety in order to show its relations. This has particularly been the case with forms coming from the same rock in a single locality, but showing different stages of alteration. The fragmental forms, of which only a few have been described, are classed under the term *porodite* * for the old and altered forms, and *tufa* for the unaltered. Thus far, in meteorites, the fragmental rocks are all tufas, and in the terrestrial peridotites, porodites.

* Bull. Mus. Comp. Zoöl., 1879, v. 280.

SECTION II. — *The Meteoric Peridotites.*

VARIETY. — **Dunite.**

Chassigny, France.

The meteorite of Chassigny * is, according to Damour, of a pale-yellow tint. Under a lens it is seen to be formed of a multitude of little rounded grains, with a vitreous lustre. In these grains occur some of a deep-black color. This description is identical with that which could be given of an unaltered dunite, like that from Franklin, N. C., for example.

According to Tschermak, microscopically, this meteorite is composed of a pale yellowish olivine, traversed by fissures, and containing brownish glass inclusions. Between the olivine grains there are to be seen here and there three-sided cavities, filled with colorless or brownish glass, from which often radiate the fissures traversing the olivines. In the glass can be seen with high powers colorless grains, needles, and brown crystals. Octahedrons of chromite occur irregularly scattered through the rock.†

VARIETY. — **Saxonite.**

Iowa County, Iowa.

The Iowa County, Iowa, meteorite in the Harvard College Cabinet presents a fine-grained groundmass, sprinkled with pyrrhotite and iron. On the polished surface it shows a well-marked chondritic structure.

This meteorite was described by Prof. C. W. Gümbel, in 1875, as composed of olivine, an augitic material, iron, troilite, chromite, reddish garnet-like inclusions, etc. He holds that the rock is entirely crystalline, but fragmental in character. The reader is referred to the original paper for Gümbel's figure and views.‡

Specimens of this meteorite were purchased for the Whitney Lithological Collection of the Museum of Comparative Zoölogy, from Ward and Howell, Rochester, N. Y., and sections made. The sections are colored gray, with patches of brownish-yellow staining from the iron. The gray groundmass contains irregular detached bits of metallic iron, about which the stain extends. The groundmass is composed of crystals and grains of olivine, enstatite, pyrrhotite, iron, and base. The section shows the usual chondritic structure, in which granules of olivine and enstatite are cemented by the base to form the chondri. I can find neither in this nor in any other meteorite that I have seen any evidence that they are *fragmental* in character, but rather evidence that the structure usually observed is the result of *rapid cooling* upon a *liquid magma* of this constitution. The crystalline structure of any mass depends upon the crystalline form its minerals tend to assume, under the conditions to which they were exposed during that crystallization. In the crystalline forms of olivine and enstatite, coupled with the rapid cooling,

* Comptes Rendus, 1862, lv. 591.
† Sitz. Wien. Akad., 1983, lxxxviii. (1), 361, 362.
‡ Sitz. Akad. München, 1875, v. 313-330.

the writer believes, resides the cause of the peculiar structure of the chondritic meteorites, while, if through any cause the mass cools more slowly, the result is to unite the detached grains into larger crystals, as in the Estherville meteorite and in the ordinary terrestrial peridotites. These structures, certainly, do not vary any more from one another than do the glassy, the glassy and globulitic, and the crystalline forms of basalt.

The base in this peridotite varies from a light to a dark ash-gray, and is fibrous-granular in its structure. The darker shades are generally associated with the olivine and the lighter with the enstatite. Various gradations are seen between that state of the base which does not affect polarized light, and that which shows feeble coloration — properly not a base. These gradations are owing to the differentiation in it of more or less granules of olivine or enstatite, causing the depolarization of the light. The feeble polarization appears to be owing to a differentiation of the base so as to leave but minute portions of it in the original state, although the difference between the two states is not noticeable in common light. The tendency of these granules is to unite into a homogeneous crystal, the base disappearing more and more, according to the conditions attending the solidification of the mass. Furthermore, as in other rocks, so in this, the base should be expected to be one of the first materials, after the iron, to suffer alteration. The writer supposes this base to be that which other writers have described as the matrix of fine dust, formed by the comminution of the meteoric material, — flocculent, opaque, white mineral;[*] also as felspathic material, etc.

A series of grains and crystals of olivine, arranged in spherical form and cemented by the *fibrous-granular* base, forms the olivine chondri. I do not regard these as rounded forms, owing their shape to mechanical action, for no abrupt line separates them from the surrounding material, as is the case when detached fragments are inclosed in a matrix. In the same way the granules themselves show that they are products of crystallization, and not broken fragments held in the matrix. As said before, I can see no structure, in this or in any of the other meteorites examined, supporting the mechanical theory of their origin; but everything observed, in my judgment, points to crystallization in a more or less rapidly cooling body. In some instances it is, indeed, true that an abrupt termination exists to some of the forms, but these appear to be fragments of base, sometimes partly differentiated, caught in the liquid mass, instead of mechanical forms torn from some previously existing rock.

This meteorite has also been described by Lasaulx, who states that it shows an evident brecciated structure, with olivine grains and rounded enstatite masses, in a fine-grained groundmass, containing grains and fragments of crystals, as well as iron and pyrrhotite. Plagioclase is said to be present, and the base is described as a gray, fine-grained, aggregate, cementing mass, resembling the granular microfelsitic groundmass of many porphyries.[†]

Figure 4, Plate II., shows well the finer-grained portions of this meteorite with the native iron. The portion to the left of the centre represents one of the chondri, composed of detached grains held in a dark base. The grains are found to be divided by polarized light into three sets, one of which occupies the lower portion and the other two the upper portion of the chondrus. The grains in each division act optically as a unit, and cause the chondrus to present the appearance of a crystal composed of three twinned portions; and it is here thought that had not the crystallization been arrested,

---

[*] Maskelyne, Phil. Mag., 1863 (4), xxvi. 138.
[†] Sitz. nieder. Gesells. Bonn, 1882, pp. 102–105.

the grains would have united from the crystallization of the base, and a three-twinned rounded crystal resulted. The remaining portion of the figure is composed of base, olivine, enstatite, chondri, iron, pyrrhotite, and, possibly, magnetite.

Figure 5, on the same plate, shows one of the large chondri composed of olivine and enstatite, which blends at the lower portion of the figure with the general groundmass, showing that they are only somewhat differently differentiated portions of the continuous mass. The grains are surrounded by a gray base, while the yellowish and reddish-brown tints represent the staining from the oxidation of the iron. In figure 4 the base is darker than represented, and in figure 5 lighter. The colors of the two should be exchanged.

Dhurmsala, Punjab, India.

This meteorite is described by Professor A. von Lasaulx as having a light-gray groundmass, sprinkled with yellowish rusty spots. Microscopically, it was seen to possess a chondritic structure, similar to the meteorite from Iowa County. The chondri are composed of olivine and enstatite, with the fibrous cementing material. Besides olivine and enstatite the rock contains iron and troilite, as well as chromite or magnetite.*

Knyahinya, Hungary.

The Knyahinya meteorite was examined microscopically by Professor Adolf Kenngott in 1869. His section was of a gray color spotted with yellow, semi-transparent, but containing opaque and dark-yellow spots. The whole appears finely grained to the unaided vision, but spheroidally grained under a low magnifying power. The granules are gray, and some of them more or less angular. Besides the metallic and opaque particles two crystalline minerals were seen. One is colorless and transparent, the other gray and translucent. Some of the spherules consist essentially of one or the other of these minerals. The opaque substances are subordinate, and are interposed between the rounded or angular granules. Kenngott regards this spherulitic structure as the result of a process of crystallization within the substance of the meteorite, and not from an aggregation of separately formed bodies.

The opaque substances are light-gray metallic iron, grayish-yellow pyrrhotite, and a black material. In reflected light the iron appears dark-gray and translucent, the pyrrhotite blackish-yellow and faintly diaphanous, and the black substance opaque. The silicates are regarded as enstatite and olivine.

Descriptions of the granules (chondri) were given by Professor Kenngott. One is said to possess a striped appearance, owing to alternations of a delicate transparent substance with a gray one. The bands are partly parallel and partly divergent. When the power is 900 the structure is resolved into a more aggregation of gray and hyaline particles. The gray mineral (enstatite) constitutes essentially many of the round or rounded granules, while other granules are formed from a union of the olivine and enstatite. The two silicates crystallized simultaneously, one or the other of them, according to circumstances, having accumulated around certain centres in a spherical form, thus imparting to the meteorite as a whole a somewhat oölitic aspect. The original paper is illustrated by drawings of the granules.†

* Sitz. nieder. Gesells. Bonn, 1882, pp. 105–107.
† Sitz. Wien. Akad., 1869, lix. (2), 873–880 ; Phil. Mag., 1869 (4), xxxviii. 424–428.

Later, Dr. Otto Hahn thought he had discovered in this meteorite a plant form composed of olivine. This plant he named *Urania Guilielmi*. It was regarded as lying between algæ and ferns.* Since Hahn found his plants in granite, gneiss, serpentine, basalt, and meteorites, even in the metallic nickel-iron from Toluca, and in that of the Pallas meteorite, the conclusion would follow that he would be able to find them almost anywhere. His language is such that it is difficult to believe that his paper is a sober production, and not a parody on the Eozoön literature, especially since he claims to have found Eozoön structure in the Pallas meteorite. Perhaps this is not so remarkable, since Carpenter found the same in graphic granite. †

Whatever may have been Hahn's design in the publication of "Die Urzelle," he was evidently in earnest in his "Die Meteorite (Chondrite) und ihre Organismen," Tübingen, 1880.

This work is devoted chiefly to the structure of the chondri observed in the Knyahinya meteorite, and it gives very fair photographs of these. Hahn believed the chondri were sponges, corals, crinoids, etc., while *Urania* was in this book placed under the sponges.

There are some things which pass discussion, and Hahn's works belong to that class; for the kingdom to which such forms belong must be largely a question of belief rather than of decisive evidence. The artificial formation by Meunier, of Hahn's sponges, corals, and crinoids in a red-hot porcelain tube is perhaps the most decisive fact against their organic origin. ‡

The writer believes that this is one of the very common cases in which mineral forms have been taken to be organic ones, especially by those who were familiar with the latter and not with the former,—cases to some of which attention has been called in the "Azoic System." §

Later, Dr. D. F. Weinland continued the discovery of organic forms, principally in the Knyahinya meteorite. He gives but two figures; that of *Pectiscus Zittelii* is apparently an eustatite crystal, and that of "*Hahnia meteoritica*, a coral !" is evidently a series of olivine grains.‖

These and other such forms can be found in all chondritic meteorites, while almost every rock, especially if altered, will afford structures that can be tortured into organic forms, if the imagination or desire be strong enough. After this has been done, who shall say that the authors were not correct? Is not the case similar to that of the *Eozoön Canadense*—dependent solely on *weight of authority*? Yet the Eozoön occurs in rocks proved to be veinstones !

The specimen of the Knyahinya meteorite in the Whitney Collection shows on the fracture a gray color and a chondritic structure.

Section : The sections show a gray chondritic mass, marked in places by a yellowish-brown ferruginous staining; and they are seen under the microscope to be composed of a crystalline granular and chondritic mass, the parts often held by the dark-gray and light-gray fibrous base and semi-base. The chondri in these sections are seen to be composed

* See Die Urzelle, Tübingen, 1879, pp. 54–56, and Plate XVII.
† Nature, 1876, xiv. 8, 9, 68.
‡ Comptes Rendus, 1881, xciii. 737–739 ; Am. Jour. Sci., 1882 (3), xxiii. 155, 156.
§ Bull. Mus. Comp. Zoöl., 1884, vii. No. 11.
‖ Ueber die in Meteoriten entdeckten Thierreste. Esslingen, 1882. See also Die hypothetischen Organismen-Reste in Meteoriten, von Dr. F. Rolle, Wiesbaden, 1884 ; and Les Prétendus Organismes des Météorites, par Carl Vogt, Genève, 1882.

of enstatite, olivine, enstatite and base, olivine and base, enstatite and olivine, and of base and minute granules of either olivine and enstatite.

One of the chondri is seen to possess an approximately square centre of enstatite with some projecting points. Surrounding this, and also partially held in it, is the gray base and semi-base, showing over much of its surface a feeble polarization, which extinguishes at the same time with the enstatite. The latter shows traces of zone building, and lying parallel to the sides are other small masses of enstatite, which appear to form constituent portions of the enstatite crystal. In polarized light, the entire chondrus appears as a homogeneous enstatite, except that certain portions show more feeble coloration. The structure seems to me to be that of a mineral crystallizing out of a magma, the processes being arrested before it was complete. Another chondrus shows a bouquet-like mass of the fibrous gray matter in the centre, surrounded in part by long masses of enstatite, which hold included between and in them portions of the base. This is figured in Plate II. figure 6, at the centre and on right of the central portion of the figure. The lighter bars surrounding and cutting the yellowish-gray fibrous portion are enstatite, which polarize conjointly as a single crystal. They contain portions of the base forming the grayish parts. The central fan-shaped portion is composed of base mixed with enstatite fibres and iron grains, and stained by oxide of iron. At the bottom of the figure is another chondrus composed of mixed enstatite fibres and base, while towards the left and bottom of the figure is a fissured enstatite. The rest of the figure is composed of enstatite, olivine, and base, showing in places imperfect chondritic structure.

In another, the fan-like radiation of the base with the enstatite granules begins at opposite ends of the chondri, meeting and interlocking towards the middle, but leaving a non-differentiated oblong nebulous mass in the centre between them. The two portions interlock in such a manner that they evidently form the same crystal mass — the rudiments of a twinned crystal.

Some chondri are composed of a rude network of base — the meshes being filled with olivine grains. This is shown in Kenngott's figure 8. One chondrus is composed of an enstatite crystal surrounded by a narrow border of gray matter, apparently crowded out by the crystallization of the enstatite, as is often the case in the crystallization of the feldspars in modern lavas.

Chondri are seen composed entirely of olivine grains, the lines bounding the grains answering to the network of base before mentioned. One formed by an enstatite mass with black ferruginous grains (magnetite) is found to continue across its apparent boundary into the adjoining enstatite, the cleavage fractures and fissures extending from one to the other, both forming in common and polarized light a continuous enstatite crystal.

Another chondrus is composed of a sea-fan-like interior made up of base and fine granules of olivine (?) surrounded by a coarser granular mass destitute of base, the entire chondrus showing in common and polarized light that it was a homogeneous mass, out of which the granules have crystallized.

In others, the base is irregularly scattered through the crystals, and held as the base is in minerals in recent lavas. The base in this meteorite is often completely dark during the entire revolution of the stage, and every gradation exists between this state and that in which it affects the polarized light considerably — nearly crystallized into the enstatite and olivine forms. While the color of the base is usually a gray, in some cases it is of a brown to a black color in transmitted light. The descriptions of the chondri might be greatly extended, but it would seem that enough has been given to show that the olivine and enstatite crystallize out of the base, and that in the state of incipient crystallization these minerals, coupled with the base, assume the forms that have been taken for organic ones. The irregular distribution and relations of the base to the crystal grains show that even apparent organic forms are wanting except in selected cases. The mineral constitution of the meteorite is such that it could not have been exposed to air and water without alteration of the minerals, but must have been formed under such conditions that those agencies could not have produced their customary effects, i.e., under the action of heat. Action that was sufficient to crystallize enstatite and olivine out of a fossiliferous deposit, surely would have been sufficient to obliterate every trace of such delicate microscopic organisms as these supposed corals and crinoids. If these forms were organic, then, as Professor J. Lawrence Smith has justly observed, carbonate of lime ought to be found in them, which is not the case. The entire mass of the meteorite is made up of enstatite, olivine, iron, base, pyrrhotite, and apparently a magnetite.

Its chondri appear, with possibly a few exceptions, to be secretions in the mass formed by the tendency to crystallization, as was pointed out in the case of the preceding meteorite, since they pass as a continuous mass into the surrounding material, and have not the well-defined boundaries of a foreign or included mass. The possible exceptions are of a few forms that appear as if, while in a liquid or plastic state, they might have been inclosed in a liquid or plastic mass, and partly united with it. The supposed fragmental portions, or the grains, appear to me to be formed by crystallization, the same as the grains are formed in common peridotic rocks, and not by attrition. Some of the chondri are deformed by others, as would be natural in such a crystallizing mass.

Gnadenfrei, Silesia.

This meteorite has been described by Professors J. G. Galle and A. von Lasaulx as having a chondritic structure. The groundmass is colored light-gray, and contains numerous spherules, colored white, gray, or dark-gray. Particles of iron of varying size occur, while under the lens there are clearly seen little granular particles of bronze-colored pyrrhotite and brass-yellow spangles of troilite. Rusty-brown spots occur, arising from the rapid oxidation of the iron.

Under the microscope, the thin sections were found to contain nickeliferous iron, pyrrhotite, troilite, chromite, enstatite, and olivine. The iron is in irregular pronged masses.

Our authors separate the troilite from pyrrhotite, the former being rare in little yellowish grains, and the latter more abundant, in small granular aggregates having a bronze color, also in little grains in the silicates and in the iron. The chromite is in small octahedrons in the olivine. The enstatite appears both in the groundmass and in the spherules. It contains inclusions of brown and colorless glass with fixed bubbles, and black metallic particles; also a black dust-like substance. All the inclusions are more or less elongated in the direction of the cleavage lines.

The olivine occurs both in the groundmass and in the spherules. It is in rounded grains or crystal fragments of irregular contour. The grains are colorless except when discolored by the oxidation of the metallic iron. The olivine contains brown glass inclusions with one or two bubbles, also a black dust-like substance, the same as that inclosed in the enstatite.

The chondri are composed principally of olivine and enstatite, and show the usual variations; but for the descriptions the reader is referred to the original paper.*

Gopalpur, India.

The Gopalpur meteorite was microscopically studied by Tschermak. Its color is grayish-brown, but in the interior whitish-gray. The groundmass is filled with numerous little spherules, which are of a brownish-gray or a clear gray color. Throughout, the groundmass glitters with yellowish points of pyrrhotite. Cellular, pronged grains of iron could be seen in the section.

This meteorite belongs to the chondrites of Rose. The whitish groundmass is earthy, tufaceous, containing angular fragments of anisotropic minerals of various sizes. The larger fragments show a fibrous or stalk-like structure with an evident cleavage parallel to their longer direction; or they are traversed only by irregular fissures. The groundmass contains particles of pyrrhotite and iron of various sizes. Immediately about the iron is to be seen a small amount of a dust-like, untransparent, dark-brown material which Tschermak regards as chromite.

The larger spherules are composed principally of a radiating fibrous mineral, which is taken to be bronzite (enstatite). Sometimes a granular mineral was observed in them. Other spherules are made up of irregular fissured grains which are referred to olivine; and still others are thought to be composed of feldspar. From the figures and descriptions given, the present writer thinks that the presence of feldspar is doubtful, although Tschermak is one of the best authorities on that point. The author hopes that a careful re-examination of the sections will be made.

The large, dark, opaque particles in the spherules and groundmass are iron and pyrrhotite.

The spherules are said not to be different in composition from the groundmass. In both can be recognized, as the essential constituents, bronzite (enstatite), olivine, iron, and pyrrhotite. The only difference is that in the spherules the crystal grains are smaller.

Tschermak holds that the chondritic structure displayed in this meteorite was the result of a mutual attrition of the different particles, the whole afterwards being cemented together. He regards the whole structure as different from any terrestrial structure yet observed.†

Butsura, India.

The Butsura meteorite was described by Professor N. S. Maskelyne in 1863, as having a yellowish-brown groundmass containing numerous points of metallic iron. Irregular dark stains were observed surrounding the iron. The iron is very evenly distributed in small, isolated, irregularly formed and sometimes crystalline looking particles. Under the microscope the chief mass of the meteorite was regarded as olivine, associated with a gray and an opaque white mineral. The gray mineral constitutes entire nodules in the meteorite, and sometimes seems mingled in the apparently brecciated mass, containing olivine crystals that form other nodules in it. It presents the appearance in the former case either of a dark mottled surface spangled with dark points, or of a mineral presenting very regular and minute parallel cleavage-planes, with dark-gray bars running

* Mon. Berlin Akad., 1879, pp. 750-771.
† Sitz. Wien. Akad., 1872, lxv. (1), 135-146; Min. Mitth., 1872, pp. 95-100.

along them, often in divergent rays. Another mineral was observed which was transparent and presented cleavages nearly perpendicular to each other. The specific gravity of this meteorite is 3.60.*

From the above description it is inferred that this peridotite is composed principally of olivine and enstatite.

Lancé, Loir-et-Cher, France.

The Lancé meteorite was examined microscopically by Dr. Richard v. Drasche. It belongs to the chondritic type of Rose, and in the thin section showed a confused groundmass holding a great number of rounded forms of varying structure, together with isolated crystal fragments. The spherules were found to be composed either of olivine or of bronzite (enstatite). Iron and pyrrhotite also were seen.

Drasche sums up the structure of the rock as follows: The meteorite is formed by many isolated olivine crystals, and here and there a bronzite, together with a large number of spherules of two different kinds, lying in a tufaceous powder. The spherules are either regularly or irregularly arranged aggregates of olivine, or they are formed of bronzite needles radiating eccentrically. Plates with a full description of the meteorite were given by Drasche.†

Tourinnes-la-Grosse, Belgium.

The Tourinnes meteorite was studied microscopically by the Rev. A. Renard, S. J.

He found that upon the fractured surface the rock was of a grayish-white color, finegranular in structure, and with but little coherence.

Under a lens small spherules of a grayish-brown or a pale-gray color were seen, also yellowish points of pyrrhotite. This meteorite belongs to the chondritic type of Rose.

Under the microscope the groundmass is found to have but little coherence, and to be formed by an agglomeration of particles, the chief of these being non-cemented grains of olivine of irregular contour. Porphyritically inclosed in this granular groundmass were observed iron, pyrrhotite (troilite), enstatite, and olivine.

The nickeliferous iron is in the form of indented, cellular grains. The enstatite is gray or colorless, and possesses a fibrous structure.

The olivine shows the same characters as it does in the terrestrial peridotic rocks. It does not appear that the irregularity of the grains was necessarily due to mechanical action, since the same structure is to be seen in the terrestrial peridotic rocks, as for instance that from the St. Paul's Rocks.

The chondri were separated into two groups: those formed from prisms and fibres of enstatite, and those formed from an agglomeration of olivine granules.

Renard held that the chondritic structure was different from any terrestrial form, and that it was produced through the projection of incoherent volcanic matter, which through its agglomeration formed the tufaceous-like meteorites.‡

Waconda, Mitchel Co., Kansas.

Some description of this meteorite has been given by C. U. Shepard and J. L. Smith.§ According to the latter it is composed of iron, pyrrhotite (troilite), olivine, and

* Phil. Mag., 1863 (4), xxv. 50-58. † Min. Mitth., 1875, pp. 1-8.
‡ Mem. Soc. Belge Micros., 1879, v. 43-50.
§ Am. Jour. Sci., 1876 (3), xi. 473, 474; 1877, xiii. 211-213.

pyroxene minerals. The specimens purchased for the Whitney Collection from Ward and Howell show an ash-gray groundmass, stained with brownish spots of rust, and containing grains of grayish-brown olivine.

Section: a yellowish-brown and grayish groundmass containing iron. On one side a black band forming the exterior (rind) of the meteorite is preserved. The groundmass is composed of olivine grains with some enstatite. The yellowish-brown color is owing to a ferruginous staining of the silicates, while the rind is composed of the same minerals as the interior, but owing to the heat to which it has been exposed it has been burned black. Clear grains of untouched silicates (olivine and enstatite) are to be seen both in the interior and in the crust.

In one corner of the section a small amount of a fine ash-gray semi-base was observed cementing olivine grains.

The mixed enstatite and augite with iron, and a ferruginous stained groundmass are shown in figure 4, Plate III.

Goalpara, India.

The Goalpara meteorite, according to Tschermak, is a dark-gray granular rock, having a porphyritic structure. In the deep-gray groundmass are inclosed clear colorless and yellowish grains.

On microscopic examination the meteorite was found to be composed of enstatite, olivine, iron, and pyrrhotite.

The enstatite shows well-marked cleavage-planes running in two directions, forming an angle of 92° with each other. The olivine has no cleavage, and does not occur in distinct crystals, but in minute grains united together. The groundmass in which the olivine and enstatite are inclosed is very fine-grained. Microscopically it is seen to be composed of minute transparent grains, apparently olivine, and untransparent forms. These last are of three different kinds: iron, pyrrhotite, and coal-like bodies. The iron forms a sponge-like mass, with extremely thin cell-walls composed of cubic crystals. The coal-like bodies are described as being in all their properties similar to soot (graphite?). The groundmass is said to appear in branching, leaf-like, thread-like, and dot-like forms, winding between and around the grains forming the olivine clusters.

The student is referred to Tschermak's paper for the complete description and figures illustrating the microscopic structure.*

VARIETY. — **Lherzolite.**

Pultusk, Poland.

The Pultusk meteorite on the fresh fracture shows, according to Werther, as a light-gray rock, part very fine-grained, and part of a somewhat coarser texture. This is interspersed with numerous white and yellowish points, showing metallic lustre, also brownish-yellow spots in the groundmass. He regards the rock as composed of nickel-iron, olivine, enstatite(?), and chromite.†

This meteorite was further described by Dr. G. vom Rath as composed of a fine

---

* Sitz. Wien. Akad., 1870, lxii. (2), 855–865.
† Schriften, Köngsberg Gesell., 1868, ix. 35–40.

granular to compact groundmass, containing nickel-iron, pyrrhotite, spherules, olivine, white crystal grains, and chromite. He states that the nickel-iron occurs in three different forms: in large grains, in laminæ, and in ramifying, pronged grains sprinkled through the groundmass. The surrounding groundmass is sometimes stained, through the alteration of the iron, to a brown color.

The pyrrhotite occurs in small irregular grains and granules of a tombac-brown color, which, through a slight alteration, change to a dark steel-gray.

The chromite is in very small black non-magnetic grains, and only in minute amounts.*

The specimen purchased from Ward and Howell for the Whitney Collection has an ash-gray color and shows a chondritic structure. It contains pyrrhotite and iron.

Section: composed of a light-gray chondritic mass, containing grains of iron and pyrrhotite. The groundmass is composed of olivine, enstatite, and some diallage. The chondri are formed, in part, of grains and crystals of olivine and of enstatite, cemented by a gray, fibrous base. Like those examined by the writer in other meteorites he regards these as the product of an arrested crystallization in a rapidly cooling mass — the solidification taking place before crystallization was complete. Part of the enstatite chondri do not show the usual eccentric structure, but a parallel, or sometimes a very irregular one.

The arrangement of the pyrrhotite and iron about some of the chondri reminds one of the similar arrangement of the rejected or "pushed out" material about the feldspars in some andesites.

The iron is in part outside of, and in part entirely surrounded by, the pyrrhotite.

Figure 1, Plate III., shows a large chondrus at the base of the figure, composed of enstatitic, aggregately polarizing, fibrous material. The form shows the rounded indentations seen by Tschermak in the Tieschitz meteorite, and at its upper portion blends with the groundmass, although distinct from it elsewhere. Under the microscope its boundaries appear to be those of a crystallizing mass and not those of a foreign inclusion in the groundmass. At the left of this chondrus is another radiating fibrous one, composed of enstatite ribs cemented by connective tissue of gray base, holding metallic iron grains. The remaining portions of the figure are composed of mixed chondri and the constituents of the rock.

Figure 2, Plate III., shows the structure of a chondrus composed of olivine, enstatite, iron, base, etc., with its blending at the bottom of the figure into the groundmass.

Figure 3, Plate III., shows the relations of a mass of pyrrhotite (troilite) to an inclosed mass of metallic iron, and the whole surrounded by the chondritic groundmass.

New Concord, Guernsey Co., Ohio.

A crystalline granular rock containing pyrrhotite and iron, and showing yellowish-brown spots of staining around the latter.

Section: a light-gray crystalline mass of olivine, pyroxene and enstatite, and containing iron and pyrrhotite. The groundmass is stained a yellowish-brown in many places.

* See further the original paper of vom Rath. Abhandlungen aus dem Gebiete der Naturwissenschaften, Mathematik, und Medicin als Gratulationsschrift der niederrheinischen Gesellschaft für Natur-und Heilkunde zur feier des fünfzigjährigen Jubiläums der königlich rheinischen Friedrich-Wilhelms-Universität. Bonn. Am 3 August, 1868, pp. 135-161, with plate.

The enstatite, pyroxene, and olivine are in clear grains when unstained, and are much fissured and broken.

Some of the enstatite shows the same structure as the chondri of other meteorites except that it wants the cementing base. That is, these grains are formed from minute grains arranged in rod-like forms, and lying side by side. The iron and pyrrhotite is in irregular masses and granules. Some colorless irregular patches were observed, giving a pale color in polarized light and resembling nephelite.

Figure 1, Plate IV., shows the general structure of the groundmass, with its inclusions of iron, pyrrhotite, etc., and its ferruginous staining. This groundmass is fine-granular, with some traces of chondritic structure.

Mocs, Transylvania.

This meteorite has been described by Koch, Tschermak, and Brezina, and the following is condensed from Tschermak's description. On the fresh fracture the rock appears as a gray and white, rough, friable mass, flecked with little brown and yellow spots, and traversed by fine black veins. The grayish-white groundmass contains small spherules of varying size, small grains of iron and pyrrhotite, and occasionally larger grains of iron. Those chondri which are granular and vary from a white to a yellowish color are composed of olivine, but those of a white color and of a fine rod-like or fibrous texture are composed of enstatite. Under the microscope the stone was found to contain olivine, enstatite, diallage, plagioclase, iron, pyrrhotite, rarely chromite, and a black undetermined mineral. The olivine is pale-yellowish green, and contains irregular inclusions of a fine black dust, angular black grains, and glass. The enstatite has a pale-greenish color, and contains brownish, rounded glass inclusions, spherical and lens-shaped vapor cavities, and small black spheres. The diallage contains inclusions of abundant black dust and grains, and glass, with some microlites. Part of the diallage presents the characters of diopside. The plagioclase appears in colorless rounded grains, containing many irregular, brownish, glass inclusions. In polarized light many of the feldspars show well-marked characteristic twinning. The iron is in small spheres in the groundmass and in the chondri, as well as in rounded and elongated rough grains, sometimes showing a cubic cleavage. The pyrrhotite occurs in minute grains.*

Zsadány, Temesvar Comitat, Banat.

Dr. E. Cohen made a microscopic study of the Zsadány meteorite in 1878. Macroscopically, the following constituents were observed:—

1. A fine-crystalline, light-gray groundmass, in which appeared scattered grains with a conchoidal fracture and a vitreous lustre. These were mostly water-clear or else of a pale honey-yellow color.

2. Grains of the color of pyrrhotite, and grains or leaves of nickeliferous iron.

3. Numerous dark gray crystalline spherules, with a rough surface, and a faint resinous lustre on the surface of fracture. On the polished surface they show an elliptical form.

In the thin section two classes of these spherules were seen. One is composed of small columns of an enstatite-like mineral. This contains a few small pores, and

* Koch, Min. Mitth., 1883, v. 234–244; Sitz. Wien. Akad., 1882, lxxxv. 1, pp. 116–132; Tschermak, ibid., pp. 195–200; Brezina, ibid., pp. 335–343.

between the columns a cloudy substance was observed. Cohen is in doubt whether this substance is an alteration-product or has intruded.

The second is formed from aggregations of round or angular olivine grains and a cloudy substance. The olivine and enstatite also occur in the groundmass. The enstatite incloses some opaque grains and colorless microlites. The olivine contains some pores which are for the most part empty, but some of them appear to hold a little fluid.

Cohen thought that an accessory mineral observed was hypersthene. Pyrrhotite and nickeliferous iron were also seen. Between all these constituents lies a cloudy, very rarely feebly transparent substance which appears to be identical with that observed in the spherules.

Cohen seems to adopt the mechanical theory for the origin of chondritic structure, but, following Gümbel, holds that the eccentric radiated structure of many of the spherules is owing to a secondary formation.*

Cohen's cloudy substance is doubtless the gray, fibrous, base and semi-base observed by the present writer in other meteorites — like the Iowa one, for instance.

Estherville, Emmet Co., Iowa.

The Estherville meteorite has a grayish granular groundmass, holding irregular grains of olivine and diallage. The olivine grains are of various sizes, from minute ones to those two inches in diameter. Scattered through the mass, in irregular nodular jagged forms, occurs the iron. Some bluish-gray fragments were seen inclosed, but of an unknown nature, although they may be olivine. The groundmass is identical in appearance with that of the finer-grained peridotites, and, excepting the iron, the rock is strikingly similar to some from North Carolina.

Two or three patches composed of yellowish-green olivine, and a glassy white mineral were seen. The latter resembles feldspar or quartz, but it would probably not be found in the section, or by chemical analysis, unless especial portions were taken for examination. The iron shows imperfect dodecahedral forms with striated faces. One imperfect form resembled a cube face modified by two pentagonal dodecahedral planes. A few small black grains were seen resembling picotite or chromite. The crust in some places shows that it was derived from the fused olivine; hence if the fusion point of this olivine could be ascertained, it would give the minimum temperature of the surface during its passage through the air. The specimen above described, in the Harvard College Cabinet, is said to weigh twenty-eight pounds, and it affords, on account of the large extent of its fractured surface, a good opportunity to study the macroscopic characters of this peridotite. This specimen, in some places, shows the remains of an internal cavernous structure, its cell-walls being lined with minute crystals.

Section : a grayish groundmass, holding grains of enstatite, olivine, and diallage, with iron and pyrrhotite. The groundmass is composed of a crystalline, granular aggregate of these minerals.

The olivine is in clear, rounded grains, of irregular outline. Lying in the olivine are numerous grains and irregular masses of iron, which are usually confined to certain portions of the mineral, and are wanting in some crystals. Besides the larger, easily recognizable, irregular, semi-sponge-like masses of iron surrounding, projecting into, or included in the olivine, drop-like forms are seen extending in irregular lines from

* Verh. Natur. Med. Verein, Heidelberg, 1878, ii. (3), 154-163.

points on the larger iron masses through the silicate. These globules are of every size, from those whose metallic lustre and character can be readily recognized with low powers to those that remain a fine dust when magnified one-thousand times. It cannot be said that the finer dust-like portions, resembling the globules in the basaltic base, are the same as the larger globules of iron; but the gradual transition in size between the grains of different sizes, and, with the increase in power, the increase in number of globules that can be recognized as metallic iron leads one to suspect that all these granules, whatever may be their size, are of the same origin and material — iron. These forms, in the minute state, are similar to some of the inclusions in the olivine of the Cumberland pallasite, but in the latter case the iron, if occurring, would be oxidized. Some of the olivine grains show a fine cleavage adjacent to the cross fissures.

The enstatite is in irregular and oval masses, with a perfect longitudinal cleavage and a cross fracture. The extinction takes place in polarized light parallel to the cleavage. The enstatite contains inclusions of olivine and of iron, the same as previously described in the olivine.

The diallage has an irregular longitudinal cleavage, its forms being the same as those of the enstatite. The cleavage lines of the diallage are either cut by irregular cross-fractures, or connect by oblique fissures, so as to give an irregular network over the face, rendering it more obscure and cloudy. The extinction is oblique to the principal cleavage planes. It contains the same inclusions as the enstatite. While the olivine, enstatite, and diallage are all clear, transparent, and colorless in the thin section, yet their cleavage characters are so distinct that in general they can readily be distinguished from one another without the use of polarized light.

The iron and pyrrhotite are in detached granules, droplets, irregular jagged masses, and in imperfect sponge-like forms. In some cases they form an irregular net-work in the groundmass, and in an imperfect ring surround the larger grains of olivine, enstatite, and diallage. The material for the above described sections was purchased from W. J. Knowlton of Boston.

Figure 5, Plate III., represents a central crystal of diallage with the surrounding groundmass of olivine, enstatite, diallage, iron, pyrrhotite, and the ferruginous staining.

Figure 6, Plate III., shows the semi-sponge-like mass of iron and pyrrhotite with their inclosed silicates, forming a groundmass holding two porphyritic crystals of diallage and enstatite, showing their characteristic cleavages and inclusions, although the latter are imperfectly represented.

Attention was originally called to this very interesting meteorite by Prof. S. F. Peckham, who stated that a preliminary examination showed that the metallic portion was an alloy of iron, nickel, and tin. "Full half the mass consists of stony matter which appears in dark-green crystalline masses embedded in a light-gray matrix. . . . Some of the crystalline masses are two inches in thickness, and exhibit distinct monoclinic cleavage. Under the microscope, in thin sections, olivine, and a triclinic feldspar appear to be imbedded in a matrix of pyroxene. . . . A small piece of the metal polished and etched exhibited the Widmanstättian figures very finely."[*] Prof. C. U. Shepard, in the same volume (pp. 186–188), gives a further description of this meteorite. He writes: "It is marked by the unusual prevalence of chrysolite and meteoric iron, the former probably constituting two-thirds its bulk; also by the size and distinctness of the chrysolitic individuals, together with their pretty uniform, yellowish-gray or greenish-

[*] Am. Jour. Sci., 1879 (3), xviii. 77, 79.

black color; and by the ramose or branching structure of the meteoric iron. Nearly one-half of the chrysolite, however, is more massive, approaching fine-granular, or compact. Yet in this condition it is still highly crystalline, and difficultly frangible. This portion is of an ash-gray, flecked with specks of a dull greenish-yellow color. The lustre is feebly shining. . . . Especially is it observable that the stony portions nowhere present traces of the oolitic, or semi-porphyritic structure, so common in meteoric stones. . . .

"The meteoric iron, besides being in ramose branches, is also in enveloping coatings around the chrysolite, somewhat as in the Pallas and Atacama irons. . . . The presence of schreibersite in the metal is apparent to the naked eye." The minerals that Shepard supposed that he found were chrysolite, schreibersite, chromite, troilite, a "feldspathic mineral, presumably anorthite," and an "opal-like mineral of a yellowish-brown color, which I take to be chassignite."

Later, J. Lawrence Smith made a further examination of the Estherville meteorite.* He found olivine, bronzite, nickeliferous iron, troilite, chromite, and an opalescent silicate. The last has a light, greenish-yellow color, and cleaves readily. It was regarded as formed from one atom of bronzite plus one atom of olivine. Smith further says: " I examined carefully for feldspar and schreibersite, but the absence of both lime and alumina (except as a trace) clearly proved the absence of anorthite; and the small particles of the mineral that might have been taken for schreibersite, were found on examination in all instances to be troilite."

Dr. Smith's chemical analysis was made in such a manner that it is impossible from it to draw any conclusions as to the relative proportion of the elements in the mass as a whole.

Later,† Smith named the "opalescent silicate" *peckhamite*, and thought from his farther analyses that it was probably composed of two atoms of bronzite to one of olivine

In 1882 Dr. Stanislas Meunier described the microscopic characters of the Estherville peridotite, which he referred to the *logronite* type of meteorites — one of the 43 types proposed by him in 1870. ‡ He found the following minerals: olivine, bronzite, *peckhamite ?* pyrrhotite, schreibersite, magnetite, and nickeliferous iron.

The olivine is in very large crystalline fragments, yielding in polarized light a most brilliant colored mosaic. In common light they are colorless, often cleaved and filled with crystalline inclusions. Liquid bubbles in spheroidal cavities, remarkable for their large size, were seen. In converging light the crystals show two systems of brilliant rings, whose axes show strong dispersion.

The bronzite is in poorly formed crystals, clearly dichroic, and showing a well-marked parallel rectilinear cleavage.

The *peckhamite* is in large, feebly colored crystals, composed of alternations of laminæ, inversely affecting polarized light. The action of acids upon them causes one to regard this mineral as composed of extremely thin interlaminated layers of bronzite and olivine.

The magnetite is in perfect octahedrons.

M. Meunier concludes as follows: " In presence of these different characters of composition and structure, it is seen that the identity is complete with the logronite already

---

* Am. Jour. Sci., 1880 (3), xix. 459–463, 495, 496.
† Am. Jour. Sci., 1880 (3), xx. 136, 137.
‡ Cosmos, 1870 (3), vi. 70–73, 95–98, 152–155, 186–188, 210–215.

described. We must believe with respect to the Estherville form, that the primitive mass in the condition of debris, in part stony, in part metallic, accumulated in some crevice, has been subjected to metalliferous emanations, of which the product, under the form of a fine network, has soldered together the components previously disconnected. The spaces — so remarkable — existing sometimes between the modules of iron and their rocky matrix, are artificially reproduced in the process of metallic cementation of the dust of peridot, by a method which I have already described." *

The present writer finds himself obliged to dissent from M. Meunier's views regarding the origin of this meteorite, for the following reasons: He (the writer) can nowhere in the sections find any evidence that its materials ever held any different relation than the present, and no sign of a former fragmental state is observable to him; but he does see evidence that is convincing to him that the entire mass has been formed by cotemporaneous crystallization, i. e., it has the same structure that a terrestrial lava of the same composition, cooling under conditions that would allow the entire mass to crystallize, would have. The inclusion of the iron in the silicates, indicating their later solidification, would show that the iron was not a posterior emanation. Such a formation as M. Meunier supposes could not take place without leaving a record behind of its action.

It has been hoped that a complete microscopic description would have been published by Professor C. W. Hall, of the University of Minnesota (see Professor Peckham's paper before referred to, page 98); but thus far he has been unable to get time for the work. Professor Hall has very kindly sent me some of his sections for examination, and the additional information obtained from them is given below.

The sections sent by Professor Hall are, in their general and mineralogical characters, so unlike those already described, that were it not for the source from which they were obtained, it would be very difficult to believe that they came from the same meteorite.

They have a confused light-greenish-yellow groundmass, holding irregular masses of olivine, enstatite, and feldspar. The groundmass appears to be composed of olivine, enstatite, feldspar, pyrrhotite, and magnetite. But little native iron is to be found in the sections. The groundmass is stained a ferruginous yellow in many places, and the commencement of a serpentinous alteration was seen in some of the olivines.

The feldspar is in irregular glassy masses, and in imperfect crystals, showing striation and extinction oblique to the nicol diagonal. They contain inclusions apparently of olivine, enstatite, magnetite, bubble-bearing glass cavities, etc.

The olivine and enstatite contain also glass inclusions, magnetite, etc. The enstatite in some places is dichroic along its cleavage planes, owing to its slight greenish alteration.

These sections, having been prepared by a student, are of such thickness, and ground with so uneven a surface, that the study of them is very difficult. A few grains resemble quartz, but they are probably unstriated glassy feldspars. My thanks are due Professor Hall, and I regret that I cannot profit more by his kindness. These sections are so much unlike those previously described, that I trust he will have further and thinner sections made, and publish a complete description of them himself. †

From the various descriptions given it is to be concluded that the Estherville peridotite varies considerably in its mass, in different portions — from those parts entirely iron,

* Comptes Rendus, 1882, xciv. 1659-1661.

† It is probable from their alteration that the material from which these sections were made had been exposed to atmospheric agencies for some time.

those of a sponge-like iron mass holding silicates, those of but little iron with the silicates, and those that are pure or nearly pure silicates. If detached portions should be taken and analyzed chemically and microscopically, it could be claimed that this meteorite is a siderolite — a pallasite — a peridotite, and all be equally correct so far as the portion examined would show; but studying this meteorite as a whole, its proper place both chemically and microscopically appears to be with the peridotites. The variations in the descriptions given by the different observers who have examined this meteorite, are doubtless owing, in many cases, to the actual variation in the rock itself. It offers a striking illustration of the need of some more general method than a purely mineralogical one in naming rocks.

Since the preceding was written, specimens of this meteorite, containing peckhamite, have been received from Professor Peckham. The sections present for the mass of the meteorite the same composition and structure as those obtained from Professor Hall. The peckhamite presents the optical characters and cleavage of enstatite, but is filled entirely full of vapor cavities, iron, glass, brown grains, etc. To these inclusions is apparently owing the coloid appearance of peckhamite, and the variation in its analysis; while Meunier probably mistook plagioclase for this mineral.

VARIETY. — **Buchnerite.**

Tieschitz, Moravia.

A microscopic study of the Tieschitz meteorite has been made by A. Makowsky and G. Tschermak. The color of the meteorite on its inner surface is ash-gray, and it has a chondritic structure. It shows many minute deep-gray, or dark-colored globules and splinters, and occasionally larger spherules of the same color ; also, little white globules and fragments, which are subordinate in amount to the former. Lying between them were seen an ash-gray earthy groundmass, and a very few yellowish particles showing metallic lustre. Certain characters of some of these spherules had never been described previously in any other meteorite. Some show a concave impression upon them, indicating plasticity during their formation. Some of these latter spherules also show outside of these concavities an excrescence having a round or pointed termination. These characters not harmonizing well with Tschermak's friction theory of the formation of the globules, which will be later given in this work, (pp. 109, 110), he adopted a new theory, that while these grains are the result of volcanic eruption and explosion, their form could be derived from their plastic condition, instead of from the friction of solid particles as he had held before.

The general characters of the meteorite were much the same as those of the preceding. Olivine, bronzite, enstatite, augite, pyrrhotite, and nickeliferous iron were the mineral constituents observed.

The olivine was found in the groundmass, and in some of the spherules. Inclusions of black angular grains, and of brownish glass with fixed bubbles, were seen.

The bronzite is principally in stalk-like and fibrous forms. It contains also inclusions of brown glass, with immovable bubbles.

The enstatite has about the same form as the bronzite, contains the same inclusions, and is white or of a pale color. It occurs in chondri and fragments. Augite was found in small amounts in globules, having the same inclusions as the olivines.

The pyrrhotite occurred in small grains, not only in inclusions in the globules and fragments, but also in the groundmass.

The iron is mostly in irregular pronged particles in the groundmass. *

Hungen, Germany.

The Hungen meteorite has been described both by Buchner and Tschermak. Tschermak stated that the section showed quite large particles of iron, a few small grains of magnetite, with fragments of minerals and spherules in the groundmass. Some small untransparent grains without metallic lustre were thought to be chromite or picotite.

The other minerals were olivine and bronzite, besides brown angular grains that were supposed to be augite. This, like nearly all the meteoric peridotites, is chondritic. Needles and grains of a water-clear mineral, and fine grains of chromite were seen in the olivine. The enstatite contained brown needles and grains, as well as the chromic iron dust.†

Grosnaja, Caucasus.

The color of the interior of the Grosnaja meteorite, according to Tschermak, is a blackish-gray, sprinkled with clear to whitish-colored points. In the section the groundmass is black and opaque, while many of the inclusions were either opaque or transparent only in spots. Other inclusions were transparent, and showed mostly a spheroidal structure, although a few pieces were angular.

Tschermak distinguished five different minerals: a clear-green olivine, bronzite, augite, pyrrhotite, and a carbonaceous mineral. Iron in very small amounts was also found.

This meteorite showed chondritic structure, as seems to be usual with the olivine-enstatite ones.‡

Alfianello, Brescia, Italy.

This meteorite has been microscopically studied by Baron von Foullon. It has a chondritic structure and is composed of nickeliferous iron, olivine, bronzite, an augitic mineral, pyrrhotite, and maskelynite. The fresh fracture shows a pale-grayish white finely crystalline surface sprinkled with pyrrhotite. The olivine is of a light color and generally in grains. The bronzite is somewhat of a light-yellowish to brownish-yellow color, and shows cleavage lines. The maskelynite was found as an intergrowth with the bronzite, occurring as a colorless, water-clear substance.

The chondri are irregular and show about the usual structural varieties. §

---

* Denks. Wien. Akad., 1879, xxxix. (2), 187–202, 5 plates; Sitz. Wien. Akad., 1878, lxxviii. (1), 440–443, 580–582; Verh. Nat. Verein, Brünn, 1879, xviii. 40, 41.
† Min. Mitth., 1877, pp. 313–316.
‡ Min. Mitth., 1878 (2), i. 153–164.
§ Sitz. Wien. Akad., 1883, lxxxviii. (1), 433–443.

MISCELLANEOUS.

Bavarian Meteorites.

In 1878 Prof. C. W. Gümbel gave an account of his microscopic examination of five meteorites that had fallen in Bavaria at different dates during the 18th and 19th centuries. Four of these are described below, and one later under *The Basalts*.

1. *The Mauerkirchen Meteorite.*

This rock is of a light-gray color, with black spots of metallic iron, which in places show oxidation. It has a very fine-grained groundmass, which incloses blackish and yellowish grains. The stone shows the chondritic structure, and has the usual characters. The groundmass contains fragments and grains of the various minerals.

Gümbel holds that this meteorite contains olivine, a feldspathic and an augitic mineral, pyrrhotite, chromite, and iron.

2. *The Eichstadt Meteorite.*

This rock also belongs to the chondritic meteorites, and was thought by Gümbel to contain an augitic and two feldspathic minerals, as well as olivine, iron, pyrrhotite, and chromite.

3. *The Schönenberg Meteorite.*

This, like the preceding, belongs to the chondritic type, and was thought by Gümbel to contain the following minerals: olivine, iron, pyrrhotite, chromite, schreibersite, a feldspathic, a scapolitic, and an augitic mineral.

4. *The Krähenberg Meteorite.*

According to Gümbel this chondritic rock contained olivine, pyrrhotite, iron, chromite, an augitic mineral (bronzite?) and a feldspathic mineral (labrador?).[*]

It is not probable that the meteorites above described by Gümbel in reality differ much in mineralogical characters from the common forms, the determinations being here thought to be imperfect. It is therefore to be hoped that in the light of the advances made in the knowledge of the microscopic characters of minerals, a reëxamination will be made to these meteorites.

Charlottetown, Cabarras Co., North Carolina.

This stone is described as having, on the fresh fracture, a dark, bluish-gray groundmass, holding porphyritically inclosed crystals and grains of a grayish-white mineral, with a tinge of lavender-blue.[†]

The specimen in the Harvard College Cabinet shows the usual chondritic structure, and contains considerable iron. The grayish-white minerals, with a tinge of lavender-blue, are the chondri, which are well marked in this meteorite. It possesses a striking

---

[*] Sitz. München Akad., 1878, viii. 14–72.
[†] C. U. Shepard, Proc. Am. Assoc. Adv. Sci., 1850, iii. 149–152.

similarity to the Iowa Co. meteorite, although the chondri are somewhat smaller. Judging from the general characters of the Cabarras meteorite, it is probable that Shepard's analysis is incorrect, and it is hoped a new one will be made.

Other specimens of meteoric peridotites in the Harvard College Mineral Cabinet, macroscopically examined by the writer, are: —

Mezo-Madaras, Transylvania.

This shows a somewhat coarse chondritic structure, and contains grains of iron and pyrrhotite.

Alessandria, Piedmont.

This has a grayish groundmass showing an imperfect chondritic structure, and contains considerable iron in grains and in films running through it.

Renazzo, Ferrara, Italy.

This has a dark surface or groundmass, holding grayish-white rounded grains or chondri. Since this specimen shows no fresh fracture, but little can be said about its characters. It resembles closely, in external appearance, some of the Cordilleran andesites, possessing a dark, glassy groundmass holding rounded, glassy feldspars.

This meteorite has been described before as similar to an obsidian-porphyry and possessing a compact, black, enamel-like groundmass, holding numerous light-gray spherules.*

This meteorite ought to be studied microscopically, for it promises to be one of the most interesting specimens examined by that method, and will probably throw much light upon the origin of meteorites, especially if it should prove to be, as it appears, less devitrified than other meteorites microscopically examined.

Hartford, Linn Co., Iowa.

This has a light-gray granular groundmass showing chondritic structure, and is sprinkled with metallic particles.

Ausson, Haute Garonne, France.

The specimen shows a gray groundmass, and possesses a well-marked chondritic structure.

Nanjemoy, Maryland.

This is the same as the Ausson rock, except that its structure is of a finer character.

Drake Creek, Sumner Co., Tennessee.

This has a light-gray, fine-granular groundmass, sprinkled with iron in various forms. This stone closely resembles that from Hartford, Linn Co., Iowa.

* Buchner, Meteoriten in Sammlungen, 1863, pp. 46, 47.

L'Aigle, Orne, France.

This possesses a gray groundmass, holding chondri. One of the chondri shows a concave depression, the same as those described by Tschermak as occurring in the Tieschitz meteorite. (See ante, page 101.)

Weston, Connecticut.

This shows the same gray groundmass as the preceding, and an excellently developed chondritic structure.

Château Renard, France.

This has a light-gray groundmass, sprinkled with metallic points.

Hessle, Sweden.

This has a grayish chondritic groundmass.

Nobleboro', Maine.

This specimen is apparently fragmental in character, and closely resembles a trachytic or rhyolitic ash. The specific gravity, according to Webster, is 2.08, but, according to Rumler, 3.092. It is probable that Webster's chemical analysis is not correct, the specimen, if authentic, not bearing out any such analysis as that published by him.*

This meteorite ought to be reëxamined chemically, and studied microscopically.

Variety. — Tufa.

Orvinio, Italy.

The structure of the Orvinio meteorite is described by Tschermak as uncommon and remarkable. The rock is composed of clear-colored fragments, surrounded by a compact, dark, cementing mass.

The fragments are yellowish-gray, and contain spherules and particles of iron and pyrrhotite. The cementing material is blackish, compact, and splintry, holding nearly uniformly-distributed particles; and near its contact with the fragments shows an evident fluidal structure. This makes it in the highest degree probable that the cementing material was once in a plastic condition and in motion. The fragments are darker, harder, and more brittle at the junction with the inclosing mass than they are in the middle. From this it would seem that the matrix had been at a very high temperature when plastic.

The fragments and matrix both have almost the same composition, density, and mineral characters.

This meteorite resembles a volcanic rock in which a fine matrix holds fragments of rock of the same character. The structure is the same as it is when a younger compact lava breaks through an older and more crystalline one.

The fragments have the usual chondritic structure. They contain, besides iron and pyrrhotite, olivine, bronzite (enstatite), and possibly some feldspar. For the further

* Bost. Jour. Phil., 1824, i. 356–389; Buchner, Meteoriten in Sammlungen, 1863, p. 46.

description and figures the reader is referred to the original paper.* If Tschermak is correct this meteorite must have come from a body either partly solid and partly liquid, or one in which cooler fragments fell into the liquid mass.

Chantonnay, Vendée, France.

This is described by Tschermak as composed of olivine, bronzite, a finely-fibrous translucent mineral, nickeliferous iron, and pyrrhotite. Its structure is similar to the Orvinio meteorite; that is, is composed of chondritic fragments cemented together by a black, glassy and semi-glassy material. †

SECTION III. — *The Meteorites. — Their Origin and Character.*

It is thought most convenient to enter upon these questions here in connection with the largest class of authenticated meteorites. And in doing this the views of those persons who have studied them microscopically will be especially referred to.

Professor N. S. Maskelyne taught, in 1863, regarding the chondritic meteorites: —

"that there have been stages in the progress of the slag-like mass from the first origin of the spherule — in perhaps a seething lake of mixed and molten metals on which a rare oxygenous atmosphere was acting and fermenting out as it were the more oxidizable elements — to the final state of compact continuity in which the spherules are found agglutinated together or imbedded in a magma of mineral." ‡

The previous year he had said : —

"The spherules which characterize this structure are often composed of a single crystalline and homogeneous mineral, with a radiating structure; often they are breccias made up of several crystals of the same or of different minerals united by a granular network of mineral. These spherules are often surrounded by a shell of meteoric pyrites or iron, and are set in a mixed mass, often highly porphyritic, composed of similar ingredients with the spherules. The solidification of this ground-mass marks, probably, a second stage in the history, the former indicating the very gradual separation by cooling of some of the ingredients of the aërolite, and the latter the result of the further gradual cooling of the residuary mass. There is no glass or uncrystallized matter apparent in any aërolite yet examined." §

Professor Maskelyne's views were set forth again in 1875, but with great caution and indefiniteness. The following extract gives the chief additional point bearing on the chondritic structure : —

"We may, perhaps, go so far as to suppose that if groups of the individual particular units of a meteor cloud once should approach each other to a distance small enough to

---

* Sitz. Wien. Akad., 1874, lxx. (1), 459–465.   † Sitz. Wien. Akad., 1874, lxx. (1), 465–472.
‡ Phil. Mag., 1863 (4), xxv. 440.   § Proc. Brit. Assoc., 1862, xxxii. (sect.) 188–191.

give their mutual gravitation a sensible influence, they might gradually collect into masses, and acquire a cohesion more or less compact according to the conditions imposed on such masses during their subsequent history. . . . We may, indeed, assert that the meteorites we know have, probably all of them, been originally formed under conditions from which the presence of water, or of free oxygen, to the amount requisite to oxidize entirely the elements present were excluded; for this is proved by the nature of the minerals constituting the meteorites, and by the way in which the metallic iron is distributed through them." *

In 1864, Mr. H. C. Sorby announced the presence of glass and gas cavities in the olivine of meteorites. He stated that

"the vitreous substance found in the cavities is also met with outside and amongst the crystals, in such a manner as to show that it is the uncrystalline residue of the material in which they were formed. . . . It is of a claret or brownish color, and possesses the characteristic structure and optical properties of artificial glasses."

Of the chondritic structure Mr. Sorby says, it appears that

"after the material of the meteorites was melted, a considerable portion was broken up into small fragments, subsequently collected together, and more or less consolidated by mechanical and chemical actions. . . . Apparently this breaking up occurred in some cases when the melted matter had become crystalline, but in others the forms of the particles lead me to conclude that it was broken up into detached globules whilst still melted." †

The same year Mr. Sorby remarked that the earliest condition of meteorites was that of igneous fusion, but he thought that the Pallas iron afforded

"physical evidence of having been formed where the force of gravitation was much smaller than on our globe, either near the surface of a very small planetary body, or towards the centre of a larger, which has since been broken into fragments." ‡

In 1865, Mr. Sorby developed his views still further, stating: —

" The character of the constituent particles of meteorites and their general microscopical structure differ so much from what is seen in terrestrial volcanic rocks, that it appears to me extremely improbable that they were ever portions of the moon, or of a planet, which differed from a large meteorite in having been the seat of a more or less modified volcanic action. A most careful study of their microscopical structure leads me to conclude that their constituents were originally at such a high temperature that they were in a state of vapour, like that in which many now occur in the atmosphere of the sun. . . . On cooling, this vapour condensed into a sort of cometary cloud, formed of small crystals and minute drops of melted stony matter, which afterwards became more or less devitrified and crystalline. This cloud was in a state of great commotion, and the particles moving with great velocity were often broken by collision. After collecting together to form larger masses, heat, generated by mutual impact, or that existing in other parts

---

* Nature, 1875, xii. 485-487, 504-507, 520-523.
† Proc. Roy. Soc., 1863-64, xiii. 333, 334 ; Phil. Mag., 1864 (4), xxviii. 157-159 ; Report Brit. Assoc., 1865, xxxv. 139, 140.
‡ Geol. Mag., 1864 (1), i. 240, 241 ; Report Brit. Assoc., 1864, xxxiv. (sect.) 70.

of space through which they moved, gave rise to a variable amount of metamorphism. In some few cases, when the whole mass was fused, all evidence of a previous history has been obliterated; and on solidification a structure has been produced quite similar to that of terrestrial volcanic rocks. Such metamorphosed or fused masses were sometimes more or less completely broken up by violent collision, and the fragments again collected together and solidified. Whilst these changes were taking place, various metallic compounds of iron were so introduced as to indicate that they still existed in free space in the shape of vapour, and condensed amongst the previously formed particles of the meteorites. At all events, the relative amount of the metallic constituents appears to have increased with the lapse of time, and they often crystallized under conditions differing entirely from those which occurred when mixed metallic and stony materials were metamorphosed, or solidified from a state of igneous fusion in such small masses that the force of gravitation was too weak to separate the constituents, although they differ so much in specific gravity. . . . I therefore conclude provisionally that meteorites are records of the existence in planetary space of physical conditions more or less similar to those now confined to the immediate neighborhood of the sun, at a period indefinitely more remote than that of the occurrence of any of the facts revealed to us by the study of Geology — at a period which might, in fact, be called *pre-terrestrial.*"*

These views of Mr. Sorby were again given to the public, with additional matter, in 1877. He then stated that

".it is very probable, if not absolutely certain, that the crystalline minerals were chiefly formed by an igneous process, like those in lava, and analogous volcanic rocks. . . . Some [of the spherules] are almost spherical drops of *true glass* in the midst of which crystals have been formed, sometimes scattered promiscuously, and sometimes deposited on the external surface, radiating inwardly; they are, in fact, partially devitrified globules of glass, exactly similar to some artificial blow-pipe beads. . . . I . . . argue that some at least of the constituent particles of meteorites were originally detached glassy globules, like drops of fiery rain. . . . We cannot help wondering whether, after all, meteorites may not be portions of the sun recently detached from it by the violent disturbances which do most certainly now occur, or were carried off from it at some earlier period, when these disturbances were more intense." †

David Forbes stated that meteoritic stones are seen under the microscope

"to be an aggregation of fragmentary matter resembling a volcanic ash or breccia, in which, whilst some of the particles have been in a molten state (the presence of both glass and air cavities in them indicating that they were in the molten state when gases or vapours were being given off), others show no signs of fusion; so that the structure of meteorites confirms the views that they have been formed out of the débris of some previously existing larger mass, or even out of the ruins of some planetary body."‡

Dr. Stanislas Meunier has done much work in the study of meteorites, published a large number of papers, and holds some decidedly original views regarding their origin. He maintains that all have a common origin, and

* Geol. Mag., 1865 (1) ii. 447, 448. † Nature, 1876-77, xv. 495-498.
‡ Geol. Mag., 1872 (1), ix. 232-235.

possess types corresponding to rocks and structures of terrestrial origin, i. e. to lavas, dunite, lherzolite, serpentine, breccias, pumice, metallic veins, metamorphic rocks, etc. David Forbes thus concisely gives the views of the former:—

"Meunier, who has of late written more copiously than concisely on the subject of meteorites, whilst believing them to be fragments of broken-up planets, regards these bodies as but the last stage in the evolution of planetary bodies, and suggests that the moon is rapidly coming to this stage from the irregularities and incipient fissures visible on its surface, its dissolution not having taken place before, owing to its greater magnitude; arguing still further, that once broken up into fragments, these would arrange themselves concentrically according to their densities, those which before formed the central part of the planet, which he regards as most heavy and metallic, on the outside; and the others, according to their weight, in the interior. This arrangement he considers accounts for siderites or meteoric irons having first fallen in the earliest ages of the world, then the siderolites [pallasites], and afterwards the stone or aërolites proper; and owing to the meteorites of some recent falls, particularly that of Hessle in Sweden, having contained considerable carbon, he predicts the fall of a totally different class of meteorites in future. These hypotheses seem, however, to be but mere assumptions incapable of proof, for although only some very few instances of siderites [siderolites] having fallen in historic times are recorded, as compared to the much larger number of aërolites; still there is no proof that the proportion was different in prehistoric times, especially as it is well known that the latter would be infinitely more likely to escape observation than the former." *

Prof. Gustav Tschermak, in 1875, taught that meteorites were the result of the disruption of cosmical bodies by explosive agencies. He stated that

"the constitution of many of the meteorites shows that they are the result of a gradual tranquil crystallization; while others, on the contrary, are composed of fragments, and are the product of disintegrating forces. The majority are made up of minute flakes and splinters and of rounded granules."

Following Haidinger, he regarded the chondritic meteorites as tufas, and states that the spherules have the following characters:—

"1. They are imbedded in a matrix consisting of fine or coarse splinter-like particles.

"2. They are invariably larger than these particles.

"3. They are always distinct individuals, never merging into each other or joined together.

"4. They are quite spherular when composed of a tough mineral, and in other cases merely rounded in form.

"5. They consist sometimes of one mineral, sometimes of several minerals, but always of the same material as the matrix.

"6. The structure of the interior of a spherule is in no way related to its external form. They are either fragments of a crystal, or have fibrous structure (the fibres

* Geol. Mag., 1872 (1), ix. 234.

taking an oblique direction towards the surface), or have irregularly barred structure, or are granular.

"These chondra bear no indications of having obtained their spherular form by crystallization. . . . They resemble rather the spherules which are frequently met with in our volcanic tuffs. . . . As regards the last mentioned chondra, we know them to be the result of volcanic trituration, and to owe their form to a prolonged explosive activity in a volcanic 'throat,' where the older rocks have been broken up, and the tougher particles have been rounded by continued attrition. The characters of the meteoric chondra indicate throughout a similar mode of formation. . . . It is certain, in short, that the spherules are the result of trituration.

"The [meteoric tuffs] are peculiarly characterized as containing no trace of a slag-like or vitreous rock, nor enclosing distinct crystals in the matrix; in short they exhibit nothing which their formation from lava would lead us to look for. All that is to be seen in them is the triturated product of a crystalline rock. Some of the tufaceous meteorites bear evidence of a later modification wrought by heat. . . . Others, again, exhibit phenomena which can only be explained on the theory of their having undergone a chemical change subsequent to their formation. . . . Still, with the many proofs which we possess of the action of heat, we have not yet met with a meteorite which resembles a volcanic slag or a lava. Although the meteorites are comparable to volcanic tuffs and breccias, this comparison cannot be extended beyond a certain point. The volcanic activity, of which the meteorites furnish evidence, consisted in the disintegration of solid rock, in the modification, by heat and otherwise, of already solidified masses. . . . It is, then, by explosive activity, and that alone, that the breccias and tuffs which we find in meteorites have been formed. . . . The volcanic activity of which those mysterious masses of stone and metal are evidence, may be compared to the violent movements on the solar surface, the more feeble action of our terrestrial volcanoes, or the stupendous eruptive phenomena of which the lunar craters tell the history. . . . Volcanic activity is a cosmical phenomenon in the sense that all star-masses at a stage of their development exhibit a phase of volcanic activity." *

The objections to the theoretical views of Tschermak, Sorby, Forbes, and Maskelyne, can be briefly stated as follows:—

The chondritic structure appears to be limited to meteorites of a peculiar chemical and mineralogical character, while all, even of this special kind, do not possess such structure. Hence, if it was purely mechanical, one can hardly see how this structure could be so localized, not even being universal for this special class. Again, if the spherules are the broken-up, and rounded fragments of prior existing rock, they should have the composition of that rock as a whole, instead of generally being composed either of olivine and base, or of enstatite and base. Also, they ought to show in their interior the structure of the rock from which they were derived; while distinct lines of demarkation, and a want of continuity, ought to exist between

* Phil. Mag., 1876 (5), i. 497–507; Sitz. Wien. Akad., 1875, lxxi. 661–673.

each spherule and the adjacent matrix, as is the case with terrestrial rocks so organized. Such a relation does not appear to exist, except rarely in meteorites, but the chondri usually pass into the adjacent matrix the same as the secretions formed by a cooled lava do into the surrounding magma. So, too, we find different materials mixed in terrestrial tufas; and since different kinds of rock fall in meteorites, these supposed meteoric tufas, if of mechanical origin, ought to contain all these different forms, instead of only the same material as the groundmass.

As stated previously, it seems to me, from microscopic study of these structures, that they do not show any evidence of fragmental origin, but they show rather that they have been produced by rapid and arrested crystallization in a molten mass; the result being in part due to the forms which the olivine and enstatite tend to assume on crystallization. If time enough had been given, an entire crystallization of the material would have taken place, as in the Estherville peridotite, and in the common terrestrial peridotites. Of the latter, the crystallization is either complete, or else the original structure has been obliterated by alteration. If we could find rapidly cooled, unaltered terrestrial peridotic rocks, I should expect to find in them the chondritic structure, the same as the Estherville meteorite possesses the structure of an unaltered terrestrial peridotite, and the meteoric pallasites possess that of the terrestrial ones.

A similar method of crystallization, with the production of a similar structure, has been observed by me in the crystallization of watery vapor on the windows of horse-cars during extremely cold weather. When the window is untouched the crystallization is after the usual manner, familiar to all as occurring in our houses; but when the car-window has had this first deposit removed, as is frequently done by passengers, for the purpose of looking out, the abundant vapor of the crowded car is rapidly deposited on this cold surface, and in such abundance as to give rise to similar elliptical and spherulitic figures, which in form and appearance resemble the chondritic forms the more closely the more they interfere with the development of one another. They also possess the eccentric-fan and ribbed structure so commonly seen in the enstatite chondri — the radiation starting from one side. Again, on interfering with one another, they tend to take a rounded, instead of an angular or irregular form.

That rounded, drop-like masses should be inclosed in meteorites is naturally to be expected, in case they came from the sun or any similar body, for material is continually being thrown up from their surfaces and falling back again; and it is to be expected that some of these drops would be inclosed and thrown up in other masses before they had been entirely liquefied, although they were probably viscous.

So far as meteorites have been examined by me, they do not appear to be fragmental in the sense of consolidated cold masses joined together. It is possible that they may be composed in part at least, of molten globules — originally united in a pasty condition; but the uniformity of composition of each spherule is a remarkable circumstance, if they are formed from drops. One would suppose that each chondrus would possess all the elements of the meteorite as a whole.

So far as can be learned from the structure of most meteorites, it appears to the writer that they must have come from a liquid mass, and that in the majority of cases the length of time in which they passed from the liquid to the solid condition was not great. The silicates held in the interstices of metallic masses, like the pallasites, would have time to crystallize through the effect of the heat of the surrounding iron, and the chondritic structure would not be developed in this class as a rule, if at all; while Professor Ball's[*] claim that meteorites must have been torn from a solid rock does not seem to be borne out by the structure of the meteorites themselves. Starting with the hypothesis that all cosmical matter was originally in a gaseous state, and that this gas, through condensation or otherwise, was intensely hot, the writer believes that the meteoric material, reaching the earth, was thrown from some one or more of these condensing bodies, formed from this cosmical matter during its liquid or partially solid state. He holds that of these bodies, the most probable one serving as the source of meteorites is the sun, as suggested by Sorby — they either being thrown from it now, or in past time, through eruptive agencies, whose action can now be seen upon its surface. It is of course possible that any of the celestial bodies, when in the incandescent condition, while eruptive forces were sufficiently active, might be the originator of meteorites; but before any meteorites are attributed to them, it is necessary that it should be shown that their probable constitution corresponds to that of the meteorites in question.

The number of elements common both to the sun and meteorites lends some support to their relation as advocated here. These elements are iron, titanium, calcium, manganese, nickel, cobalt, chromium, sodium, magnesium,

[*] Science for All, iv. 31.

THE ERUPTIVE ENERGY OF THE SUN. 113

copper, hydrogen, vanadium, strontium, aluminum, sulphur (?), oxygen, lithium, tin, and carbon.

The question whether it would be possible for meteorites to be derived from the sun by their being thrown off from it by eruptive agencies, is a problem for physicists; if it can be shown that the sun's constitution is such as to render it not improbable that meteorites could have this origin. The immense velocities of the eruptive prominences — from 100 to 200 miles per second, or, according to Proctor, 500 miles — indicates, with their great height of sometimes from 150,000 to 350,000 miles, a violence of eruption tending to hurl solid materials far away from the sun into space. The elements seen in the spectrum of these prominences, iron, sodium, magnesium, titanium, calcium, chromium, manganese, and probably sulphur, are with one exception, common ingredients in meteorites.*

If the above-mentioned velocity may, on investigation, be deemed sufficient to project matter into space, the prevailing view of astronomers that the sun as a whole is gaseous, and neither liquid nor solid, would certainly be opposed to the solar origin of meteorites. As before stated, their constitution would, so far as we are acquainted with the action of gaseous substances, demand that the meteorites should be derived from a hot liquid. The body from which they came might be for the most part solid, or gaseous, or both, but that the portion from which they came should be liquid seems a necessity. The liquid condition of the sun is also the best explanation of the eruptive phenomena now observed upon it.†

Should it be shown that meteorites might come from the sun, its eruptive energy being sufficient, it would be rendered probable then that meteorites might have been thrown from the sun when larger, as well as from the planets and their satellites during their condensation — if the nebular hypothesis is accepted. It would certainly seem that the present view of the partial or entire meteoric constitution of the corona, the zodiacal light, the *Gegenschein*, of Saturn's rings, and of comets, bears directly on this question. If our sun may do this, is it not consistent to suppose that other suns may do the same, and thus account for the comets, their varied orbits, as well as for the supposed diverse constitution of the August and November meteors.

The theory that meteorites come from the sun is by no means a new one,

---

* Young, The Sun, 1881, pp. 202, 207–212.
† Young, *l. c.*, p. 211.

being as old as the days of Diogenes Laertius, and in recent times has been advocated by Hackley,* Wilcocks,† Williams,‡ Sorby, and others.

If, in the process of condensation of the sun from a gaseous to a liquid state, the metallic portion liquefied before the silicates, would it not in some measure account for the metallic meteorites being so common in the past and rare at the present time, and for the periodic ones being the common type now? On account of their specific gravity, meteorites, as a rule, could not be derived from the moon; unless it should be held that its interior is now much hotter than the earth's interior, and its density made less through that means. This is an improbable supposition on account of its small size, compared with that of the earth, which would lead to its more rapid cooling. Since the specific gravity of the moon, as a whole, is about that of the more common meteorites, and if the law of the increase of density from the surface to the centre is the same as that observed upon the earth, it follows that the moon's surface formations must have far less density as a whole than those belonging to the earth. The law of eruption as observed upon the earth is, that the lighter eruptive material as a whole is most abundant, while the rocks approaching the mean density of the earth are comparatively rare, so much so that their presence is generally denied. This law ought also to hold good on the moon, and eruptive material from it, forming meteorites, ought to have less specific gravity as a whole than our granites. The astronomical reasons have usually been regarded as sufficient to show that meteorites could not come from the moon, and that theory is not now especially urged by any one.

Such a view as advocated by Messrs. Ball and Rodwell,§ that meteorites were thrown from the earth in past times, is negatived by their general composition, which, as a rule, is different from the exterior portions of the earth. If they were originally terrestrial, these meteorites ought to more commonly possess the characters of basalts, andesites, trachytes, etc.

Whether the view that meteorites came from the sun demands too great a loss to his mass, since accurate records have been kept, is a problem for the physical astronomer.

Since it is possible that careful examinations of meteorites by chemical and spectral methods will throw light on the constitution of the celestial

* Proc. Am. Assoc. Adv. Sci., 1860, xiv. 4–6.
† Proc. Am. Phil. Soc., 1864, ix. 384–387.
‡ The Fuel of the Sun, London, 1870, pp. 131–142.
§ Science for All, iv. 32; Nature, 1879, xix. 493–495.

bodies — especially concerning the strange lines in the sun's spectrum — it would appear that meteorites ought to be studied more critically than ever for the rarer elements, as well as for some at present unknown.

Careful examinations ought also to be made on microscopic sections of recently fallen meteorites, in order to ascertain if any changes have taken place in the rock since it was first formed, but before it reached this earth, since all changes now seen in them are referred to the action of our atmosphere after the fall of the meteorite. It is not to be expected that in any way can any clue be obtained as to how recently or how long ago the meteorite left its parent mass, since no alteration in its substance can be expected to have taken place in inter-solar space.

Mr. H. C. Sorby's view* that it is impossible for minerals of so diverse specific gravity as iron and olivine to crystallize together in the pallasites and other metallic meteorites on the surface of the earth or any large body, but that they came from the metallic centre of small bodies, or else formed small planets by themselves, does not seem to be well founded. The same method of reasoning would prove that magnetite could not be formed with leucite, or feldspar, or augite in any lava-flow on the earth's surface; yet they are minerals of common occurrence together in lavas. Hence it is claimed here that the crystallization of silicates with metallic iron might, so far as gravity is concerned, take place on the surface of the earth as it has been proved to have done in Greenland. So too, if such a structure and arrangement of iron and olivine could not take place on the surface of a body like the earth, then the rocks of Cumberland, Rhode Island, and of Taberg, Sweden, ought not to exist since they have this structure and are at the surface of the earth. The difference between the magnetite and olivine is not so great as that between the native iron and olivine, but yet it is sufficient to cause a separation, if Sorby's view is correct.

Helmholtz's theory that the earth is built out of meteorites is negatived by the following facts: the geological formations in and of themselves are not composed of detached fragments like meteorites; meteorites, so far as known, are not found in the geological formations; and the chemical composition of the latter is different from that of the meteorites. His view seems to be a pure theory without any regard being paid to the actual known structure and composition of the earth and meteorites. As well

* Quart. Jour. Sci., 1864, i. 747.

might the physicist explain the dispersion of boulders in the northern drift,* or the origin of the large nuggets in the gold placers by supposing that they were meteorites, as to explain the earth's structure by the meteoric theory.

The further supposition that the earth has been formed from meteoric matter that became entirely fused from the impact of the falling masses is one that makes an assumption and then deprives us of every means of disproving or proving it.

Everything relating to the state of the earth prior to its fluid condition is of course a matter of conjecture, and theories relating to it are beyond scientific discussion, as belonging to the unknown and unknowable.

The origin of meteorites, as shown by their structure, yields but little assistance to the theory of the introduction of life upon this planet through their agency; since the conditions under which they were formed, and those, so far as can be ascertained, to which they have been since subjected are not compatible with life as understood upon this globe.†

In other words it may be said that meteorites show in their structure that they have been formed from molten liquid material, while their chemical composition is such as to show that they could not have been exposed to air and water upon any globe in conditions compatible with life as we understand it. If their structure points to an igneous origin, and their composition shows that they could not have been exposed to conditions such as earth-life demands, then Sir William Thomson was not right in claiming that it was scientific to suppose that life was brought to this earth by meteorites. It certainly only pushes the question of life a little farther off; it begs the question but does not solve it, even could it have been shown that life might have been thus brought here. Zöllner was indeed right in opposing this theory and regarding it as unscientific. Assuredly, the germs inclosed in crevices would be destroyed by the cold of space, as much as the exterior ones would be by the heat generated by the passage of the meteorite through the air. It is not intended to state that water or air could not be present on the body from which meteorites come, but that the meteorites could not have been exposed any length of time to such agencies, or their constitution would have been changed.

* Since the above was written such an explanation has been published, entitled: "Ragnarok — the Age of Fire and Gravel," — by Ignatius Donnelly.
† W. Thomson, Proc. British Assoc., 1871, pp. civ., cv. ; 1877 (Sect.), p. 43 ; A. Thomson, ibid., 1877, p. 75 ; Helmholtz, Popular Scientific Lectures (Sec. Ser.), 1881, pp. 193, 196, 197 ; Nature, 1875, xi. 212 ; J. C. F. Zöllner, "Ueber die Natur der Cometen, Leipzig," 1872, p. 24 ; Walter Flight, Pop. Sci. Rev., 1877, xvi. 390–401 ; David Forbes, Geol. Mag., 1872 (1), ix. 234, 235.

Again since mineral veins appear to have been formed on the earth by the action of percolating waters, none of the meteorites can be of such vein formation, as has been claimed by M. Meunier, since they show by their composition that they have not been exposed to or formed in the presence of water; and so far as the present writer is concerned, he sees nothing in their structure supporting such a theory, even if, as Meunier seems to think, these veins were formed by sublimation.

The finding of many of the metals, in larger or smaller amounts, in meteorites points to a relation between them and terrestrial eruptive rocks. The association of metallic veins with eruptive or metamorphosed rocks, coupled with other characters, indicates that our metals, as concentrated in veins, have generally been derived by aqueous and chemical agencies from eruptive rocks and their débris. This deposition may be direct or indirect, but primarily the starting point is believed to have been the original molten material of the earth.*

The more common association of metalliferous veins with basic rather than acidic rocks points towards the deeper-seated origin of the former, as has been claimed by many.†

The occurrence of copper in so many of the meteoric forms has, it seems to the writer, an important bearing on the question of the origin of the native copper of Lake Superior. He holds that it was derived from the associated basaltic rocks as he has set forth in another paper.‡

If copper is an almost constant associate of meteorites, ought it not to naturally be associated with eruptive rocks which are held to be part of the original materials of which the solar system is composed? The basic rocks are naturally, then, the ones with which the copper should be associated, and it is with basaltic rocks — diabases and melaphyrs — that it is commonly found, as, for instance, on Lake Superior, Bay of Fundy, and in Newfoundland.

The metallic iron in the basalt of Greenland, the native iron found in basalts by Dr. Andrews, that found in gabbros from New Hampshire, by Dr. George W. Hawes, and in gabbros from the west of Scotland, by Mr. J. Y. Buchanan, all serve to connect the meteorites with the terrestrial rocks.§

* Whitney, Aurif. Gravels, pp. 310, 311.
† Whitney, Earthquakes, Volcanoes and Mountain Building, p. 85.
‡ Bull. Mus. Comp. Zoöl., 1880, vii. 130.
§ Report Brit. Assoc., 1852, xxii. (Sect.) 34, 35; Geikie's Text Book of Geology, 1882, p. 64; Geol. New Hampshire, 1879, iii. part 4, p. 24.

118   PERIDOTITE.

In the same way the presence of nickel, chromium, tin, copper, and cobalt in the group of terrestrial olivine minerals, serves to connect the earth and meteoric bodies; as also does the presence of nickel in the terrestrial pyrrhotite and magnetite.

SECTION IV. — *The Terrestrial Peridotites.*

VARIETY. — **Dunite.**

Franklin, North Carolina.

5134. An oil-green, crystalline-granular rock, weathering from a yellowish-green to a reddish-brown. Composed of a granular mass of olivine, holding irregular grains and crystals of chromite and long needles of tremolite. It contains some talc and dark-green chlorite.

Section: a clear, pale-yellowish, fissured mass, composed of olivine, with some talc, chromite, and tremolite. The olivine is in clear transparent grains, tinged slightly yellow along the fissures. It contains some chromite and glass inclusions, — the two often being associated. The talc is in clear irregular plates, showing a longitudinal cleavage. The polarization is generally simple, but sometimes aggregate. An earthy, white substance was observed in some cases lying between the laminæ.

The chromite is generally in octahedral crystals, although a few minute grains of irregular form were seen. The chromite was opaque in every instance. A few minute rounded grains were observed, that may possibly be picotite.

The section, to my mind, presents the characters of a granular rock, resulting from a cooling igneous magma — an eruptive rock. The olivine is in grains which are separated only by fine cracks, every irregularity in one being matched by corresponding irregularities in its neighbors. If these grains were olivine sands aggregated by wind or water, such uniformity would not exist. The grains would be irregularly massed together, with interstitial portions filled with binding material. The cracks which separate the different individual grains are the same as those which separate different portions of the same grain. The absence of any signs of wearing to the grains, and their matching one another as they would in this substance when completely crystallized, point towards an eruptive origin for the rock. In addition, long, lenticular, much broken grains are seen, whose parts show in polarized light that they belong to the same individual. They are arranged at every angle with one another; but if these grains had been deposited as a shore sand, it is difficult to see how they could have retained their sharp thin cutting edges. Again, these grains and the general structure of the rock are like those observed in the Estherville meteorite, which I think no one would be inclined to regard as a beach deposit. The granular structure appears to me to be due to the crystallization of a mineral inclined to take such a rounded form as olivine usually has. The same structure and arrangement of the grains from a cooling eruptive rock had been previously seen by the writer in quartz in some granitoid rocks from Lake Superior, part of which are known to be in dikes, while the others are probably also eruptive.*

Many of the larger olivine grains show a faint banded polarization, the bands being nearly parallel with a crystallographic axis. The structure of this section is shown in Plate IV. figure 2; the darker bands indicating the fissures in the grains.

* Bull. Mus. Comp. Zoöl., 1850, vii. 53-55.

Webster, North Carolina.

5135. A crystalline-granular rock, of a yellowish-brown color on the fresh fracture. Lustre resinous and greasy, fracture uneven-conchoidal. Weathered to a granular pale-yellow mass, on the exterior portions. Contains grains and crystals of picotite.

Section: of a pale-yellow color; composed of olivine, enstatite, diallage, picotite, and serpentine. The olivine forms the chief portion of the rock, and is in irregular fissured grains. It is clear-transparent, and holds grains of picotite, some of which are in minute lenticular forms. The picotite is very abundant, but mostly in minute microscopic grains of a coffee-brown color. The macroscopic picotites are opaque, except in the thinnest portions.

The enstatite and diallage are in small, transparent, irregular masses, lying between the olivine grains. Both are traversed by longitudinal fissures, but in general the enstatite cleavage is better marked and more finely fibrous than that of the diallage. The latter mineral was observed sometimes to have the irregular, approximately right-angled cleavage of augite. Although the enstatite could sometimes be separated from the diallage by its cleavage, in general the distinction was made solely by optical methods.

The serpentine is mainly of a pale-yellowish color, although in some places a darker or brownish color was observed. It follows the fissures, making a network, enveloping the fragments of olivine, enstatite, and diallage. Many of the olivine grains now separated by serpentine are seen by their optical characters to be parts of the same original crystallographic mass. The serpentine is plainly a secondary product, formed from the alteration of part of the original minerals, comprising this peridotite. In some parts of the section in which the mineral fragments were small, the minerals have been changed entirely to serpentine, forming ganglion-like masses in this plexus of serpentine. The serpentine shows the common fibrous polarization, the fibres standing perpendicular to the walls of the channel.

Plate IV., figure 3, shows well the yellowish and greenish serpentine alteration along the fissures, and surrounding the clear olivine grains. The brown spots are picotite grains.

Dr. F. A. Genth, in 1862, made an examination of some Webster (Jackson Co., N. C.) peridotite, and stated that they gave "evidence that chrysolite is probably the mineral from which talc slate and many of the serpentines have been formed." *

Dr. Alexis A. Julien regards the North Carolina peridotite as formed by consolidated olivine sand — a detrital deposit derived from the wearing down of older eruptive rocks. He describes the rock as occurring in long lenticular masses, that show a laminated structure; giving his reasons why he regards this lamination as due to the sorting of sediments deposited in water. His reasons for holding that the dunite is a sedimentary rock are good so far as they go, but they do not appear to be conclusive; since the same condition of things could readily exist in an eruptive rock. The rock, when altered near the surface of disintegration, is, according to Julien, bound together by a network of quartz or actinolite fibres.

The alterations in the rock-mass, as traced out by Dr. Julien, are very interesting. Briefly, they are as follows: 1. Chalcedonic; 2. Hornblendic; 3. Talcose; 4. Ophiolitic; 5. Dioritic.

In the first, the silicates are decomposed, the silica forming chalcedony or chert, while the bases remain as soft ochreous grains, or are entirely removed.

* Am. Jour. Sci., 1862 (2), xxxiii. 199–203.

In the second case, the alteration consists in the formation of a few crystals, and in every gradation from that to a state in which the dunite has been transformed into a more or less schistose rock, largely composed of hornblende, and actinolite or tremolite. A few grains of olivine usually remain unchanged even in these extreme alterations.

The third change is brought about either by the direct alteration of the olivine, or by the conversion of the secondary actinolite itself into talc. Through this alteration talcose rocks are formed, like talc-schists; as well as amphibolitic or olivine ones bearing talc.

The fourth alteration has been described by me in the preceding account of the Webster peridotite, and hence I will not here quote from Dr. Julien, farther than to say that according to him talc is frequently associated with the serpentine, thus forming a talcose serpentine.

The fifth and last alteration is "confined to a single locality, and consists of an internal conversion of the olivine into amphibole — a bright grass-green variety which Dr. Genth has identified as smaragdite or koksclaroffite — and albite, sometimes with abundantly disseminated particles of ruby red corundum, producing a peculiar variety of diorite or gabbro. Again, this very rock has been subsequently attacked by a secondary process of alteration, the albite grains being enveloped by an alteration-crust of margarite, and the condition of hornblende modified. The result of this action is a coarse margaritic gabbro."

Dr. Julien believes that many of the amphibole and talc-bearing schists and serpentines along the Appalachian belt are the equivalents of the North Carolina dunite.

The North Carolina peridotites have been described in previous papers by Genth, Jenks, Kerr, C. D. Smith, Shepard, J. L. Smith, Raymond, and others.*

In most of the above papers, corundum is especially treated of, since it has been largely found associated with the peridotites of the Southern States. This mineral Genth regards as original, but Julien as a secondary product of alteration. Various opinions have been advanced concerning the North Carolina peridotite — that it is of chemical, sedimentary, and eruptive origin. Messrs. Kerr and C. D. Smith who have, except Julien, studied the rock most in the field, regard it as eruptive, but the published evidence given by them is, like Julien's, not conclusive. The reasons that the present writer has for believing this rock to be of eruptive origin have already been given. It hardly seems possible that the olivine could have been deposited as a loose sand, exposed to water and air, consolidated, and remained until the present time unchanged.†

Tafjord, Norway.

The rock from Tafjord, Norway, as seen in a section purchased from Richard Fuess, Berlin, is composed principally of rounded grains of olivine, with some enstatite, coffee-brown picotite or chromite, and a little magnetite. The structure is essentially the same as that of the peridotite from Franklin, North Carolina. The form and arrangement of the enstatite are very similar to those of the talc in No. **5134.**

Möhl describes this rock as being similar to the one from Rödfjeld, but with less enstatite, and some magnetite. ‡

---

* Am. Phil. Soc. Proc., 1873, xiii. 361–406; 1874, xiv.; 1982, 216–218, 381–404; Quart. Jour. Geol. Soc., 1874, xxx. 303–306; Geol. of North Carolina, 1875, vol. i. 129–130; Appendix D, pp. 91–97, 102–107; 1881, vol. ii. 42, 43; Am. Jour. Sci., 1872 (3), iii. 301, 302; iv. 109–115, 175–180; 1873. vi. 180–186; Pop. Sci. Monthly, 1874, iv. 452–456; Trans. Am. Inst. Min. Eng., 1878, vii. 83–90.

† Proc. Bost. Soc. Nat. Hist., 1889, xxii. 141–149. See also Science, 1884, iii. 486, 487.

‡ Nyt Mag., 1877, xxiii. 115, 116.

Dun Mountain, New Zealand.

The peridotite (dunite) of New Zealand is described by Hochstetter as a Mesozoic eruptive mass, associated with serpentine and hyperite, also of eruptive origin. This dunite is a crystalline-granular rock, of light yellowish-green to a grayish-green color on the fresh fracture, and weathering to a dirty, rusty, sometimes yellowish, sometimes reddish-brown color. Fracture uneven, granular, angular, and coarse-splintery. It was found to be composed of granular olivine, holding octahedrons of chromite, with rounded edges. The serpentine was formed by the alteration of the peridotite *in situ*.*

M. Renard has given a brief description of the microscopic characters of this rock. The section is composed of irregular grains of olivine, but of larger size than those in the St. Paul's peridotite, to be described later. "With this exception, the other microscopical characters are the same in both rocks: the fissures, more or less regular, marked by black lines, intense chromatic polarization of the olivine, roughness of the surface, etc., etc. The sections of chromic iron in dunite are larger than those in the specimens from St. Paul, but in other respects they present the same features." †

Söndmöre, Norway.

The thin sections of this rock, according to Brögger, contain predominating olivine, with (very sparingly) beautiful green smaragdite, here and there a grain of brownish-yellow enstatite, and chromite in little grains. The olivine is fresh, clear-green, and in the section colorless, and fine-granular. Some grains show one cleavage parallel to the longer direction of the crystals, and another perpendicular to the same. Only a trace of alteration to serpentine was observed. The smaragdite is of a green color, fresh, and shows pleochroism. The only two grains in the section were elongated in the direction of the vertical axis, and show cleavage lines running in the same direction. The enstatite occurs in a few scattered grains. They are fresh, brownish-yellow, finely striated, and crossed by cleavage-planes. The chromite appears in little, irregular, rounded grains.

This peridotite is associated with and lying in schists, and is called by Brögger an olivine-schist. ‡

Röbergvik, Skrenakken, Norway.

This rock was described by H. von Möhl as composed principally of olivine grains, containing octahedrons of picotite and deep hair-brown, transparent, chromite crystals. Magnetite was present, and some of the olivine grains showed a change to fibrous chrysotile. Lamellæ of fibrous enstatite were seen. §

Bonhomme, Bluttenberg, Vosges, France.

A blackish-green rock, with a rough, splintery fracture, showing a brilliant shimmer from numberless minute points, and traversed in part by many blackish veins. In thin splinters it is clear-green and translucent. In the section the olivine grains are seen to

---
* Zeit. Deut. geol. Gesell., 1864, xvi. 341-344; Reise der Novara, Geologie von Neu-Seeland, pp. 217-230.
† Report Challenger Expedition, Narrative ii. Appendix B. pp. 22, 23.
‡ Neues Jahr. Min., 1880, ii. 187-192.
§ Nyt Mag., 1877, xxiii. 114.

be clear and fresh, but in some points a change to serpentine has taken place. Picotite and a reddish garnet (?) were observed.
The other accessories were a few plates of amphibole minerals and iron ores.*

Karlstätten, Austria.

Tschermak describes a grayish-green, fine-grained rock from this locality, as composed of olivine, united with serpentine, grass-green smaragdite, and little, black, pitch-like, or semimetallic grains of picotite.†

Tron, Oesterthal, Norway.

This is similar to the serpentine from the Andestad See to be later described. The olivine grains are changed, along their boundaries and fissures, into a chrysotile. This is in part of a platy-granular structure, and part composed of parallel fibres. In some portions grains of olivine with unaltered centres are to be seen. Considerable magnetite was observed.

Enstatite is comparatively rare, and when present contains some picotite grains and crystals, a few of which were seen in the olivine.‡

A section of this rock obtained from R. Fuess is entirely altered to serpentine. The gray, serpentine groundmass is traversed by bands of ferruginous and gray material, resembling closely those represented in figures 1, 2, and 4 of Plate V. Dark-brown, translucent picotites were observed scattered through the serpentine, their borders jagged and opaque, probably as a result of alteration. The serpentine is filled with minute black grains of some iron ore.

Heiersdorf, Saxony.

According to Dathe, the Heiersdorf rock is medium grained, containing pale-red garnets, and showing under a lens quartz and feldspar, with light-greenish and brownish olivine, as well as black, lustrous crystals. The principal portion of the section is olivine. This is seldom fresh, but generally cloudy or altered to serpentine, forming the usual network, and containing some dust-like ore. The olivine contains some picotite or chromite grains.

Plates of magnesian mica occur in the neighborhood of the garnet and ore particles. The garnets are of the size of a pin's head, and are somewhat altered. The majority are entirely changed from the singly-refracting garnet substance to a doubly-refracting, radiately-fibrous material. This has a pale-blue aggregate polarization color, but in common light is greenish and feebly dichroic. The minority of the garnets have a small alteration zone surrounding them, of colorless fibres, probably asbestus, arranged perpendicular to the garnet boundary. Light-brownish zircon grains also occur. §

Ronda Mountains, Spain.

The serpentine of the Ronda Mountains, covering an area of nearly 600 square miles has been described as eruptive by Joseph Macpherson.‖ With the serpentine were

* Bruno Weigand. Min. Mitth., 1875, pp. 180–192.
† Sitz. Wien. Akad., 1867, lvi. 275–279.
‡ Nyt Mag., 1877, xxiii. 120, 121.
§ Neues Jahr. Min., 1876, pp. 227–229.
‖ On the Origin of the serpentine of the Ronda Mountains, J. Macpherson, Madrid, 1876, 20 pp. 2 plates.

found imbedded large masses of peridotite. The peridotite is irregularly disseminated through the serpentine, showing an intimate connection of the two. The peridotite is found to be composed of olivine grains, traversed by numerous fissures, and containing irregular fragments and octahedrons of picotite. The rock itself usually varied from a greenish-gray to various shades of green.

The serpentine is generally of a dark-green color, traversed frequently by veins of chrysotile, and not uncommonly charged with crystals of diallage. It is said that in some places the serpentine "is traversed by great parallel planes of fracture, which at first sight might be mistaken for stratification."

The alteration of the olivine takes place along the fissures, the iron separating in the serpentine as magnetite and chromite. This serpentinization gradually extends until only small grains of olivine are left, and then on until the entire rock is altered to serpentine. A perfect and gradual transition was traced from the beginning of the process to the complete transformation. The alterations are shown very well in the figures accompanying Macpherson's paper.

Serranía de Ronda, Spain.

This rock, according to Macpherson, is of a clear, greenish-gray color, with a lustre between a greasy and vitreous. The section is composed of a crystalline-granular aggregate of olivine fragments, containing numerous picotite grains. The olivine shows brilliant polarization colors, and sometimes a striation parallel to the plane of extinction, while it is traversed by irregular fissures.*

St. Paul's Rocks.

These rocks were described by Darwin as unlike any rock he had met. He states: "The simplest, and one of the most abundant kinds, is a very compact, heavy, greenish-black rock, having an angular, irregular fracture. . . . This variety passes into others of paler-green tints, less hard, but with a more crystalline fracture. . . . Several other varieties are chiefly characterized by containing innumerable threads of dark-green serpentine, and by having calcareous matter in their interstices. These rocks have an obscure, concretionary structure, and are full of variously colored angular pseudo-fragments. . . . There are other vesicular, calcareo-ferruginous, soft stones. There is no distinct stratification, but parts are imperfectly laminated, and the whole abounds with innumerable veins, and vein-like masses, both small and large." Darwin states that the rock is not of volcanic origin — not necessarily meaning by this anything more than that it was not a modern eruptive formation like that of the other islands visited.†

These rocks being the haunts of birds, a phospatic incrustation had been formed on part of the surface, and Professor Wyville Thomson states "that they look more like the serpeutinous rocks of Cornwall or Ayrshire, but from these even they differ greatly in character. . . . Mr. Buchanan is inclined to regard all the rocks as referable to the serpentine group. So peculiar, however, is the appearance which it presents, and so completely and uniformly does the phosphatic crust pass into the substance of the stone that I felt it difficult to dismiss the idea that the whole of the crust of rock now above water might be nothing more than the result of the accumulation, through untold ages, of the

* Anal. Soc. Esp., Hist Nat., 1879, viii. 251, 252.
† Volcanic Islands, 1851, pp. 31–33, 125.

insoluble matter of the ejecta of sea-fowl, altered by exposure to the air and sun, and to the action of salt and fresh water." *

According to Rev. A. Renard, the rock is composed essentially of very small olivine grains similar to those of the New Zealand dunite. Fluid cavities were also observed. Chromite (picotite) is abundant in irregular, generally lenticular grains, of a brownish-yellow color. Renard further described a pale green mineral of irregular outline, and a cleavage forming an angle of 124°, which he assigned to an amphibole mineral. Enstatite in colorless or clear greenish-yellow sections was observed, possessing an evident lamellar structure. A structure seen in the sections by Renard was regarded by him as a fluidal structure.†

In a later publication, M. Renard seems to have abandoned his idea of the eruptive origin of these rocks, and inclines to the view that they are formed from crystalline schists, the supposed fluidal structure being really schistose structure instead. He regards this peridotite as remarkably fresh and unaltered. Color, "blackish-gray, bordering green, which when deep looks perfectly black." Its component minerals, as determined by M. Renard, are olivine, chromite, actinolite, enstatite, and a pyroxenic mineral. For a fuller description the reader is referred to the original papers. ‡

M. Renard thinks that the association of olivine rocks with schists proves their similar origin, and therefore much peridotite is sedimentary; overlooking the fact that a region of eruptive rocks is one in which the sedimentary rocks are most likely to become schistose. Furthermore, many eruptive rocks are schistose, through secondary changes in them after eruption. Again, many eruptive rocks have associated with them ashes and other fragmental material of eruptive character, as well as sedimentary deposits, all of which brings into intimate relations metamorphosed eruptive rocks and schists. This is a case to which the principles earlier given in this volume apply. It is especially difficult to see how denudation could take place to the great depth in the ocean required when, as M. Renard admits, there is no evidence of depression.

Two specimens of this rock were kindly sent me by Mr. John Murray, of the Challenger Expedition. One shows on the fracture a dark grayish-green color, and as M. Renard remarks, closely resembles a quartzite. Weathers to a yellowish and brownish-gray. The section is seen to be composed of olivine, enstatite, diallage, picotite, chromite or magnetite, pyrite, actinolite, and serpentine.

M. Renard remarks that the minerals have their longer axes placed parallel with the supposed schistose or fluidal structure. In this section the larger grains stand in every direction, some of the olivine grains having their longer axes exactly at right angles to one another. No structure has been observed by me that I should regard as schistose. A slight schistose appearance has been produced in my judgment by the secondary alteration of the rock. Fortunately, one of the specimens sent me is of the rock said by M. Renard to be entirely fresh and unaltered. He also states that the structure of this rock is peculiar, and unlike that of other olivine rocks. In one section a portion of the rock is only slightly altered, and this portion shows the common structure of peridotites. The main mass of the rock, described by M. Renard as the groundmass, is in my opinion greatly altered, and contains only the remnants of the original minerals, surrounded by their alteration products. M. Renard regards this groundmass as composed entirely of

* Voyage of the Challenger, ii. 100-108.   † Neues Jahr. Min., 1879, pp. 389-394.
‡ Report of the Scientific Results of the exploring Voyage of H. M. S. Challenger, 1873-76. Narrative, vol. ii. Appendix B., 29 pp., 1 plate; Description Lithologique des Récifs des St. Paul. extrait des Annales de la Société belge Microscopic, 1882, 53 pp.

olivine grains, but of this I have grave doubts. The characters as seen microscopically do not appear to me to be those of ordinary olivine, but rather those of one or more minerals of secondary origin. That this groundmass is of secondary origin, for the most part, is shown by its occurrence along the fissures in the unaltered olivines, by its relations to the minerals which it surrounds, which are the same as those existing in other rocks between the original minerals and their secondary products, and by the secondary schistose structure. In such cases as these much depends upon the experience and especial kind of work that the observer has done, and unfortunately such evidence cannot be placed in words so as to enable others to judge of its correctness.

It is contrary to the laws of physics and chemistry that a mineral in altering should produce itself again — there is rather a passage from an unstable compound in the conditions in which it then is, to one more stable in the same conditions. If I am right regarding this alteration of the olivine the resulting mineral or minerals must belong either to another variety of olivine or to a distinct species.

The actinolite, chromite, picotite, magnetite, pyrite, and serpentine, I regard in this case as secondary products in the rock, and not original ones.

As said before, in places the section shows the olivine unaltered, and having the same relation between the grains that exists in other rocks when the granular structure is due to crystallization from an igneous magma, and not from detrital action. M. Renard has pointed out that the actinolite is more abundant in the fine groundmass than elsewhere in the sections, which is in accord with my view of their origin. One section shows at one end that it is composed chiefly of a confused mass of pale-greenish monoclinic crystals, showing cross fracture, and which are here referred to actinolite.

An examination of sections from the more highly altered rock shows that on further alteration the fine groundmass becomes changed from a clear to a dirty-yellowish one, but slightly polarizing. The hand specimens sent me bear evidence that they are surface and weathered specimens — to which probably much of the difficulty in their study is due; for, judging from M. Renard's descriptions, he had similar specimens to mine. In this I would by no means judge of what M. Renard saw, but only of the sections that I have myself studied.

It is to be hoped that should these rocks ever be visited again great pains would be taken to procure specimens as deep in the solid rock as it is possible to obtain them.*

VARIETY. — **Saxonite.**

Russdorf, Saxony.

Dathe described a peridotite from Russdorf, Saxony, as fine-grained, and of a light-green color. Olivine formed the essential portion of the rock-mass. This mineral was slightly altered on its edges to a granular substance of a light-yellowish to brownish color; also, along the fissures the olivine grains are changed to a light-yellowish, almost homogeneous mass. Inclosed in the olivine are black octahedral crystals of picotite or chromite. The enstatite shows in colorless, finely-striated sections. Olivine in small grains and small black needles was observed inclosed in the enstatite.†

Northern Norway.

Holland describes some of the peridotites from Northern Norway as composed of fresh olivine, containing picotite, together with enstatite and grains of iron ore. Serpentine

* Science, 1883, i. 590-592.   † Neues Jahr. Min., 1876, pp. 233-235.

from this region was found composed of serpentine, with olivine fragments, and magnetite. Another serpentine rock contained only serpentine, diallage, and magnetite.*

Thorsvig, Norway.

This rock is stated by Möhl to contain 60 per cent of olivine, 30 per cent of enstatite, and 10 per cent of anorthite and magnetite. The olivine and anorthite were in grains, and the enstatite in table-like forms, without crystalline contour.†

Birkedal, Norway.

From Birkedal, Norway, according to Möhl, was obtained a peridotite composed of olivine and enstatite, with some magnetite, chromite, mica, and anorthite — the latter mineral composing about 10 per cent of the rock-mass.‡

Hovden, Horningdal, Norway.

This peridotite, according to Möhl, is composed of olivine grains and enstatite plates, with magnetite and brown mica. The enstatite is in part of a light yellowish-gray, and in part a very strong nacarat color. It is cut through by parallel fissures, is fibrous, and contains many loose aggregates of brown needles and laminæ.§

Rodfjeld, Norway.

Dr. H. von Möhl described a rock from Rodfjeld, Muruajö, Norway, as made up of olivine grains, enstatite, and a little ledge-formed feldspar. The olivine in places is described as suffering a total change to chrysotile. ||

Andestad See, Aure, Norway.

This stone, according to Möhl, is composed of 75 per cent of olivine in angular grains, 20 per cent of enstatite and tabular-formed aggregates, and 5 per cent of chromite in granular aggregations.

Only a small portion of the olivine remains clear and fresh. Around the contour of the freshest grains wind strings of a dirty greenish-yellow chrysotile. The grains themselves are sometimes of a dirty grayish-yellow color or cloudy, and show aggregate polarization. Here and there a grain is entirely changed to a nearly opaque liver-brown serpentine.

The enstatite is nearly colorless, beautifully cleaved, and here and there is finely fibrous — the fibres being parallel. ¶

In part, this rock is so far changed to serpentine, that only here and there do the olivine grains show any clear central portions remaining. The enstatite remains in part as fresh as in the preceding, except in its cross fractures, which are filled with chrysotile. In part, the enstatite is completely serpentinized, but recognizable on account of its platy pores and its parallel fibrous structure. The chromite remains unchanged.**

A section of the Andestad-See peridotite, purchased from Richard Fuess, of Berlin,

* Neues Jahr. Min., 1879, p. 422. † Nyt Mag., 1877, xxiii. 115.
‡ Nyt Mag., 1877, xxiii. 116. § Nyt Mag., 1877, xxiii. 116.
|| Nyt Mag., 1877, xxiii. 113, 114. ¶ Nyt Mag., 1877, xxiii. 118, 119.
** Nyt Mag., 1877, xxiii. 119, 120.

has the following characters: A yellowish-green groundmass, holding several crystals of enstatite. Under the microscope the section is seen to be formed by a serpentine plexus holding olivine, enstatite, and chromite. The olivine remains only in small grains, surrounded by the serpentine, to which the remainder of the olivine mass has been changed. The olivine is generally very pure and clear, but its fissures are traversed by the serpentine; grains, even some little distance apart, showing in polarized light that they are portions of the same crystal.

Figure 4, Plate IV., shows the structure of this section. The greenish portion represents the serpentine, the grayish-white portion at the upper part of the section is the partly altered enstatite, the white grains inclosed in the greenish serpentine mass are olivine, and the dark grains are chromite.

Langenberg, Saxony.

A dull, black, serpentine mass, holding numerous brownish-black bronzite (enstatite) crystals. In the thin section the bronzite crystals show an extraordinarily fine, wavy, fibrous structure, parallel with the extinction plane. It contains arranged along the planes of the fibres little opaque needles, and pellicles of hydrous oxide of iron, and is partially altered to a feebly doubly-refracting substance — serpentine. Sometimes the crystals are cloudy and altered — bastite. The olivine has been altered to serpentine, having the usual *maschen* texture. Magnetite (?), and little crystals of chromite (?) were also observed.*

Callenberg, Saxony.

This rock has a blackish-green to brown color, and contains little bronzite crystals. In the section the olivine is seen to have been replaced by serpentine, with the usual network structure. The bronzite is also more or less altered, and chromite, hematite, and other iron ores were observed.†

The Ziegelei, between Russdorf and Meusdorf, Saxony.

A leek-green serpentine, containing bastite (enstatite) crystals. The section shows the mesh structure of serpentine divided from olivine, and fibrous-bastite (enstatite) with chromite and other iron ores. ‡

Fatu Luka and Fatu Termanu, Timor.

This rock, according to Wichmann, is of an oil-green to blackish-green color, and holds bronzite and chromite. Under the microscope the serpentine shows the mesh structure, indicating its alteration from olivine. The meshes are light-green to colorless, and the interstitial spaces of a brownish-green color. The bronzite (enstatite) in the section is colorless, and free from all inclusions, except secondary products. §

Rofna, Alps.

A compact, dark, purplish-green rock, containing folia of enstatite, having a jointed, crushed structure, with the sides coated with greenish serpentine, and presenting a schis-

* Dathe, Neues Jahr. Min., 1876, pp. 338, 339.   † Dathe, Neues Jahr. Min., 1876, pp. 339–341.
‡ Dathe, Neues Jahr. Min., 1876, p. 339.
§ Jaarboek van het Mijnwezen in Nederlandsch Oost-Indië, 1882, pp. 211–213.

tose aspect. The section shows a reticulated network of opacite, with interspaces having a fibrous border and a granular centre of serpentine. The section further contains some enstatite altered to serpentine, magnetite, and a little picotite, or chromite, and hematite. This is regarded as an altered olivine-enstatite rock. Further examination of these Alpine serpentines showed that they were either derived from rocks of this character, or else from olivine-augite-enstatite rocks.*

VARIETY. — **Lherzolite.**

Lake Lherz, France.

The famous lherzolite occurring about Lake Lherz, and at various localities between that lake and Vicdessos and Sem, in the department of Ariége, in the Pyrenecan region of Southern France, has been described by Professor T. G. Bonney as a crystalline aggregate of olivine, enstatite, and diallage (diopside), with some picotite; the texture varying from a finely to a coarsely granular. Color on the fresh fracture, a dark greenish-gray or olive-green. The rock on close inspection shows specks of emerald-green diallage, waxy looking, dull-green serpentine, resinous, pale-brown enstatite, and minute grains of picotite, inclosed in the predominant dull-colored, or glassy, olivine mass.

The sections are grayish to water-clear aggregates of olivine, enstatite, and diallage, holding picotite. The section is traversed by a network of fissures, and is thus coarse or fine-granular in different portions. The olivine is in rounded, water-clear, more or less irregular grains, and is the predominant mineral, forming, according to Zirkel and Bonney two-thirds of the whole mass of the rock. The enstatite is clear, colorless, and sometimes shows a slight, silky texture. The diallage, like the enstatite, is in irregular fragments, sometimes clear and transparent, and at others shows a faint tinge of green. Both it and the enstatite are often feebly dichroic, varying from colorless to various pale shades of green. Sometimes the diallage varies simply in the depth of the green tint. These minerals are not to be certainly distinguished one from the other, except by their optical characters.

The picotite occurs in coffee-brown, irregular masses and grains, the latter often grouped together in little masses, scattered along from the ends of some larger mass. The color is sometimes a yellowish-green, and Professor Bonney describes some as being of a deep olive-green. I should regard the picotite as being the first formed mineral, instead of the last, as he regards it. In some portions of the sections serpentine has been formed along the fissures, showing fibrous polarization, the fibres sometimes lying parallel, sometimes perpendicular to the walls. Near these serpentine veins the olivine is darkened along its fissures, apparently from the separation of magnetite or chromite in a fine powder. In some cases these black grains are united into irregular, branching, spiney masses. Masses of these black aggregations are seen arranged in the centre of the veinlets of the serpentine, like islets in a stream. Professor Bonney, in his sections, was able to trace the alteration of the olivine to serpentine, one of his sections showing a network of serpentine veins surrounding and penetrating the other minerals. In the sections before me, the olivine is in some cases changed to a pale-greenish serpentine, holding minute aggregations of the ferruginous grains. These serpentine masses are generally isotropic, although showing in a few points the fibrous aggregate polarization of serpentine.

* Bonney, Geol. Mag., 1880 (2), vii. 539-512.

This isotropic character of the early stages of the alteration-products of minerals, has been frequently observed by the present writer in the case of many other minerals.

The sections herein described are of two slides, from Voigt and Hochgesang, purporting to come from Viedessos (European Collection, Nos. 71 and 165). Some additions have also been made from the excellent description of Professor Bonney, to which the student is referred.*

This lherzolite was regarded by Bonney as undoubtedly eruptive, on account of its observed relations to the adjacent rock.†

Serranía de Ronda, Spain.

This rock, according to Macpherson, has a greenish groundmass of olivine, holding emerald-green diopside. Under the microscope it is seen to be composed of olivine, enstatite, and diallage (diopside).

The diallage is of a clear green color, dichroic, and has a fibrous structure. The olivine is clear and fissured, but shows in places a partial change to serpentine. The enstatite resembles the diallage in its general characters, but has a yellowish color. Picotite is common.‡

Italy.

Numerous peridotites — lherzolites and serpentines — have been described from Italy by the Italian lithologists, particularly by Professors Alfonso Cossa and Torquato Tarmelli. These appear to be composed principally of olivine, enstatite, diallage, and picotite, and their secondary products. Most of the serpentines seemed to have been formed by the alteration of the lherzolite variety of peridotite. Cossa's work contains many valuable chemical analyses of the olivine rocks which have been tabulated, and for the general descriptions and plates the student is referred to Cossa's Ricerche Chimiche e Microscopiche su Roccie e Minerali d' Italia, Turin, 1881; and to the publications of the "Accademia dei Lincei" of Rome.

Ultenthal, Tyrol.

A coarse, granular, greenish-white rock, according to Sandberger, holding bronzite, chromdiopside, and picotite, in grains and rounded octahedrons. A fine-grained variety shows a schistose structure, and holds rose-red and deep blood-red pyrope. This rock is altered in part to serpentine.§

Ridge between Indian and Bear Valleys, Colusa Co., Cal.

3001. A yellowish and grayish-brown groundmass, containing porphyritically enclosed somewhat bronze-like crystals of enstatite and diallage. Under the lens the groundmass shows a greenish network, holding a yellowish or gray substance between the meshes. Section: a greenish-white crystalline mixture of olivine, enstatite, and diallage.

---

* Geol. Mag., 1877 (2), iv.-59-64.
† See also Charpentier, Journal des Mines, 1812, xxxii. 321-340; Essai sur la Constitution Géognostique des Pyrénées, 1823, pp. 245-264. Ann. Physik, 1814, lvii. 201-208; Delamétherie, Théorie de la Terre, 1797 (2d ed.), ii. 281, 282; Leçons de Minéralogie, 1812, ii. 206, 207; Picot de Lapeyrouse, Mém. Acad. Toulouse, iii. 410; Lelievre, Journal de Physique, 1787, xxx. 397, 398; Vogel, Journal des Mines, 1813, xxxiv. 71-74; Zirkel, Zeit. Deut. geol. Gesell., 1867, xix. 138-148; Damour, Bull. Soc. Géol. France, 1862 (2), xix. 413-416; J. Kühn, Zeit. Deut. geol. Gesell., 1881, xxxiii. 398.
‡ Anal. Soc. Esp. Hist. Nat., 1879, viii. 253-258.
§ Neues Jahr. Min., 1865, pp. 449, 450.

The whole is traversed by a reticulated series of fissures, which in each mineral partakes of its usual mode of fracturing.

The olivine is the predominating mineral. It forms rounded irregular grains traversed by numerous fissures. Larger fissures surround the main olivine masses, these veins being marked by a yellowish-brown central line of earthy ferruginous and serpentinous material, on each side of which extend borders of pale-green serpentine. The borders are of various widths, and usually ramify in little veinlets of serpentine through the fissures intersecting the olivine individual. In places, the entire olivine is altered to serpentine. The serpentine in polarized light usually shows fibrous polarization, the fibres being arranged perpendicular to the sides of the fissures. The yellowish-brown earthy material that marks the medial line of the main veins has entirely replaced the olivine in some portions of the section, giving rise to brownish patches. The serpentine is filled, along various planes and especially along the central line of the veins, with innumerable minute fluid cavities, so minute that even magnified over nine hundred diameters they remain as fine black globulitic specks, totally reflecting the transmitted light. Occasionally one larger than the rest shows the narrow outline of the common full fluid cavity.

The enstatite is in elongated crystals and irregular grains, traversed by the usual fine, fibrous cleavage. The surface of the crystals is somewhat smooth and silky, and the principal cleavage is broken occasionally by fractures running obliquely across the crystals. The larger enstatites frequently show a greenish fibrous alteration extending along the fissures and sometimes reaching the main body of the crystal.

The diallage is, like the enstatite in most of the sections, clear and colorless. It can generally be distinguished from the latter mineral by the roughness and irregularity of its cleavage, owing to the acute angle at which two of the cleavages meet in most of the grains. Like the smaller enstatites, the diallage is in irregular grains and masses, and both occasionally contain rounded grains of olivine, and crystals and grains of picotite. In one or two cases grains were observed showing the cleavage of augite. Some of the diallage plates have an earthy-white or cloudy appearance, marking a certain amount of alteration. Sometimes both the enstatite and diallage are traversed by serpentine veins, and the smaller grains surrounded by that mineral.

Picotite occurs in yellowish-brown octahedrons, as well as in irregular masses, opaque for the most part, but translucent and of a yellowish-brown color in places. How much of this might properly come under the head of chromite can not be told. In the yellowish-brown serpentine veins are arranged grains showing the lustre of magnetite, which mineral is also seen in some portions of the before-mentioned opaque irregular masses of picotite (?).

The microscopic structure of the rock is shown in figure 1, Plate V., which indicates the grayish, fissured, partly altered olivine and enstatite grains, the dark picotite grains, and the brownish veins traversing the rock-mass.

This rock was described by the collector, Mr. W. A. Goodyear, as metamorphic, but with the stratification generally almost obliterated. Mr. Goodyear probably took a somewhat banded arrangement of the minerals, as observed in No. **3002**, and a tendency to split into platy masses, for stratification. Since both of these are common in eruptive rocks, the latter showing especially on alteration and weathering, further evidence is required upon the subject. Microscopically and lithologically they belong to rocks which the best evidence pronounces to be eruptive. It is to be hoped that future geologists, in visiting the locality, will endeavor to settle the question of the origin of these most interesting rocks by an examination of their relations to the associated rocks. Of the occurrence Mr. Goodyear states: "The great mass of the rock throughout the whole ridge consists of, apparently, a serpentinoid matrix, filled with foliated crystals of a hard, green mineral, which I suspect to be pyroxene, forming a rock similar to that of which large quantities occur near Guenoc and Coyote Valley. But there are also immense quantities of serpentine without these crystals."*

The associated rocks, according to Mr. Goodyear, were some hard metamorphic sandstones, and a few shales.

No. 3002 is from the same locality.

This has a reddish-brown groundmass, holding crystals of enstatite and diallage. The same reticulated network is observed in the groundmass as in the preceding, but the inclosed portions are of a yellowish- or reddish-brown color. A roughly banded appearance is produced by a somewhat linear arrangement of the enclosed crystals. Both this and the preceding are surface specimens. Some of the crystals in No. 3002 show the well-marked characters of bronzite. Section: this is composed of a reticulated network of serpentine veins, holding rounded and irregular grains of olivine, enstatite, and diallage; while larger enstatite crystals are porphyritically enclosed. This rock was evidently once a crystalline-granular mass of olivine, enstatite, and diallage, but now it exhibits a stage of alteration somewhat in advance of that shown in No. 3001. The same reticulated network of serpentine, with the same reddish-brown medial line, is to be observed as in the preceding; in fact, the structure of the two rocks is identical. The serpentine extends from the medial line of the veins inward along the fissures, until only portions of the original minerals are left surrounded by it. In many cases the serpentine has replaced the entire mass of the rock, but still retains the marks of the fissures along which the alteration took place. The serpentine extending out from the reddish-brown portion of the veins is of a pale greenish-yellow color, and shows fibrous and aggregate polarization — the fibres, as usual, being perpendicular to the sides of the vein. While part of the olivine lying inclosed in this network is unchanged, much of it has been altered to a reddish-brown serpentinous mass like that forming the centre of the veins. In many cases this last extends only partly through the olivine grain leaving a central portion of unchanged olivine, but in others the alteration is complete. This reddish-brown alteration shows a tendency to extend in fibres parallel to the crystallographic axis, or along the latent cleavage planes. The general characters given in describing the minerals in No. 3001 hold good here. The enstatite is more highly altered to the greenish fibrous product, while it is frequently crossed by fissures at right angles to the principal cleavage. The serpentine veins in this and in the diallage are more abundant and pronounced than in No. 3001; but these minerals evidently are more slowly altered than the olivine. Of the enstatite and diallage, the former is the more readily changed. Picotite or chromite occur as before, but in somewhat larger masses.

Figure 2, Plate V., shows the general microscopic structure of this rock, the dark to black portions representing the iron-ore grains; the white portions are the unchanged olivine, the orange-brown and yellow colors mark the differently altered portions of the olivine (serpentine), while the dark-brown bands are serpentine veins like those which are shown to some extent in figure 1 of this plate.

Figure 3, Plate V., is from the same rock, and shows the structure of the partly altered enstatite. The main portion of the figure is that mineral with its cleavage lines

* Unpublished Report made to Professor J. D. Whitney.

and alteration-products represented by the gray and brown lines running from top to bottom. The enstatite crystal is crossed from right to left by a yellowish serpentine vein connecting two portions of the altered olivine mass represented by the mixed brown, yellow, and white. The dark grains are the iron ores, or picotite.

Figure 1, Plate VII., represents an enstatite crystal from the same rock, in a more highly altered condition. The primary cleavage runs from right to left, and the secondary from top to bottom. The greenish color shows the earlier stages of the alteration, and the yellow color the following or serpentine stage, although part of the serpentine material may have been brought in from the surrounding olivine mass not shown in the figure.

Foot of divide between Round Valley and Bullfrog Creek, Inyo Co., Cal.

3003. A compact oil-green groundmass, holding bluish-black and bronze-like crystals of enstatite. The rock is traversed by a few veins of pale-green serpentine, while a chrysotile vein occurs at one end.

Section: a yellowish-green groundmass, holding porphyritically enclosed some dark enstatite plates. The groundmass shows under the microscope the same reticulated network of veins as that seen in **3001** and **3002**, the veins being readily distinguishable both in common and polarized light. While the structure remains in general the same as in **3001** and **3002** the entire groundmass is changed to serpentine: that is, it is a distinct pseudomorphous replacement by serpentine of all the essential structural characteristics of the preceding rocks. Even black opaque masses are seen having all the structural features of the picotite of Nos. **3001** and **3002**.

Much magnetite or chromite is seen scattered throughout the groundmass, or collected into open aggregations. The enstatite in some cases retains its usual polarization characters, with the well-marked cleavage. In others it has been so highly altered that only traces of the cleavage and the orthorhombic extinction in polarized light remain of its usual diagnostic features. All the enstatites are filled with grains of magnetite, which in some crystals are arranged along the cleavage lines. The powder of the enstatite crystals is magnetic, and it is to the magnetite that their bluish-black color is due. The magnetite is regarded as a product formed during the conversion of the rock into serpentine. The evidence afforded by the microscopic structure of this rock, it seems to me, is proof positive that this serpentine was formed from the metamorphism of a peridotite, the beginning of which change is to be seen in No. **3001**, and still further advanced in No. **3002**.

The general structure of this section is shown in figure 4, Plate VI., which displays an altered enstatite crystal with its secondary magnetite, surrounded by the serpentine replacing the olivine.

Mohsdorf, Saxony.

This rock, according to Dr. E. Dathe, is compact, blackish-green, and contains crystals of diallage and enstatite, which show a mother-of-pearl to silky lustre, and a light-yellowish color, while they are finely striated. The principal material of the section is olivine, part of which is in large rounded grains with few fissures, and part in smaller grains, traversed by cracks, and more or less altered to a greenish-fibrous serpentine. The olivine contains little octahedral crystals of chromite or picotite, with rounded angles. The enstatite is in light-greenish, elongated sections, sometimes holding olivine grains, and traversed by cleavage lines parallel to 010. Diallage also occurs, recognized by its optical relations and cleavage. Greenish, crumpled chloritic plates and fibres, forming rosette-like aggregates, are associated with the garnet as an alteration-product. Also, brownish plates, with the strong dichroism of biotite, were seen. Besides the secondary chlorite and biotite, magnetite and hydrous oxide of iron have been produced by the alteration of the garnet. The latter mineral is next in abundance to the olivine, and in its fresh state is traversed by fissures.*

Rödhaug, Gusdals See, Norway.

This peridotite is stated by Mühl to be formed of a regular mixture of olivine grains, enstatite plates with some grass-green diopside, and chromite grains and octahedrons. The olivine is in part changed to serpentine, but in general it is water-clear and free from pores and inclusions. The grains often show a grayish-yellow ferruginous tint, and the serpentinized portions are composed of short fibres, causing the fissures to appear broader, impellucid, and of a grayish-yellow color.

The enstatite is in single scales, which are numerous and of a nacarat color.

The very pellucid, leek-green chromdiopside is in feebly dichroic, ledge-formed pieces, filled with round and pipe-formed glass pores.

The chromite forms rounded grains or octahedrons with rounded edges. Portions of these grains are of a dark hair-brown color when viewed by transmitted light.†

Baste, Harz.

5062. A grayish-black rock, with grayish-white spots. It shows the characteristic *schiller* of the enstatite (bastite), with its enclosed olivine grains. Considerable brown biotite can also be seen.

Section: dark greenish-gray, and composed of an irregular sponge-like mass of enstatite, diallage, and feldspar, with their alteration-products, holding rounded, partially altered olivines. The least altered olivines are traversed by numerous fissures, most of which extend through the adjoining pyroxene. These serve as channels for the percolating waters, and more or less black ferruginous material exists in them. In those olivines that are further changed the ferruginous bands increase, and a greenish serpentine is observed bordering the sides of the fissures, while the amount of clear, unaltered olivine between the meshes made by the fissures grows less. Every gradation of alteration can be observed in this section, from that above mentioned to those olivines in which an entire alteration has taken place, a serpentine mass remaining, which shows by its structure and ferruginous bands the former fissure lines of the olivine. In some highly altered portions a few grains of olivine can be found, a mere remnant of the larger grain once there. The enstatite and diallage are traversed by numerous cleavage lines and fracture planes, which are bordered by a greenish serpentine. The pyroxene minerals are of a pale-yellowish tinge, slightly dichroic, and in places much altered to the serpentine. The feldspar in part retains the characteristic polysynthetic twinning of plagioclase, which here has the same broad banding as that commonly observed in the feldspar of gabbros. For the most part it is altered to a clear or gray fibrous mass, with brilliant aggregate polarization similar to that of liebenerite. In some places it has been changed to a dirty-green viriditic mass.

Picotite and iron ores occur in the mass of the rock, the former mineral being found

* Neues Jahr. Min., 1876, pp. 230-232. † Nyt Mag., 1877, xxiii. 117, 118.

even in the feldspar. A little brownish-biotite was observed as a secondary product. The structure of a portion of this section is shown in figure 2, Plate VIII.

Another section, purchased from Voigt and Hochgesang, shows similar characters, but part of the olivine and enstatite is not so much altered as in the preceding. While in the former the diallage largely predominated, in this only enstatite was observed.

A section of so-called serpentinfels of Baste, purchased from R. Fuess of Berlin, shows a gray and greenish-brown sponge-like mass holding serpentinized olivines. The general structure is like the preceding ones described from Baste, as well as those to be later given from Christiania and Gjørud, Norway, but the alteration has progressed considerably further. Talc and amphibole occur as secondary products, as does a pale bluish-green mineral associated with a mineral of pale pinkish or grayish color. From their association and relations the bluish-green form seems to be a better developed state of the gray mineral. Since both are isotropic, and have the usual structure and relations observed belonging to garnet, I am inclined to refer them to that mineral. Associated with these are coffee-brown picotite or chromite grains, which also appear to be of secondary origin, and closely resemble those found in the St. Paul's peridotite.

No. **5041** is another specimen of the so-called schillerfels from Baste, Harz, obtained from Voigt and Hochgesang. This is a greenish-black rock, showing the schiller of the altered pyroxenes, and holding rounded grains of serpentinized olivine. Weathered on one side to a rusty-brown. The section of this is very similar to the one last described, but contains more picotite, and none of the pale bluish-green mineral has been so far observed.

Streng states that the schillerfels of the Harz is a mixture of anorthite, protobastite, diaclasite, compact schillerstein, schillerspath, serpentine, and chrome-bearing magnetite.[*]

Figure 1, Plate VIII., shows a portion of the structure of an enstatite mass with its enclosed olivines — the characteristic fissuring of both minerals being shown. The dark grains in the olivine are picotite and the greenish portion indicates the beginning of change in the enstatite.

Figure 2 of the same plate indicates a change in the rock still further advanced, and shows the olivine discolored by secondary iron ores bordering the fissures, and more or less changed to serpentine, while the enstatite is considerably altered. Figure 5 on the same plate exhibits a phase of extreme alteration, the rock, while retaining its structure, having its olivine entirely, and its enstatite and diallage nearly, if not entirely, replaced by serpentine and various secondary products.

Christiania, Norway.

5063. A dark, nearly black rock, showing in places the *schiller* of the pyroxene minerals, and occasionally exhibiting grayish-white spots. At one end it presents an appearance similar to that of the forellenstein of Volpersdorf. One side is coated with serpentine and dolomite.

Section: a grayish-white spongiform mass, enclosing greenish, serpentinized olivines. The olivine is much altered, showing the usual reticulated network of magnetite with the later greenish and yellowish serpentine. Part of the olivine enclosed between the meshes remains intact, or only slightly smoky. In some of these elongated tubes of minute size

---

[*] Neues Jahr. Min., 1862, p. 521.

occur similar to those observed in the olivine of the Siberian pallasite (*ante*, p. 72). These tubes lie parallel to the plane of extinction in the olivine.

The grayish-white groundmass is composed of enstatite, a little diallage, and various secondary products. The enstatite varies from a clear transparent mineral to a pale-brown and a reddish-brown. The last is so associated with the first as to indicate that it is a partially altered state of the first. This reddish-brown portion owes its color to the same included plates as those commonly seen in bronzite and hypersthene; and it could be well called the former, or, because the mineral is feebly dichroic, the latter. Whether the altered portions of the groundmass are derived in part from the alteration of feldspar or entirely from the pyroxene minerals, is not known. No distinguishable feldspar was seen. The pyroxene minerals are in part changed to serpentine, and in part to an indefinite aggregately polarizing mass, usually surrounded by one or two bands of secondary minerals standing perpendicular to the bounding surface. The outer band possesses a polarization similar to that of enstatite, while the inner resembles an amphibole mineral. In some cases on the olivine side, another band composed of serpentine was observed. A similar structure frequently exists in altered gabbros, but in this case the products are not sufficiently well defined to be determined. Considerable dolomite was seen in the more highly altered portions of the rock. Altered picotite or chromite (slightly translucent and reddish-brown in spots), as well as iron ore produced during the conversion of the olivine into serpentine, was found. Only a small portion of this ore remains in the parts where the conversion of the entire olivine mass is most complete.

Figure 3, Plate VIII., shows the general structure of this rock. The white portions have the granules still unchanged in the greenish secondary serpentine material, which in part replaces the original olivine. The brownish portions forming a matrix for the altered olivine are the enstatite and diallage, which for the most part are changed. The bluish band on the right is one of the alteration-borders between the olivine and enstatite.

Gjørud, Norway.

This, according to Möhl, is principally composed of rounded and obtuse-angled olivine grains, which form from sixty per cent to seventy per cent of the mass.

Along the contours and fissures the olivine is changed to a bright leek-green, gray-green, and grass-green chrysotile, whose fine fibres are arranged partly across, and partly parallel to, the direction of the veins. The centre of these chrysotile veins is generally filled with a fine black line of magnetite or by aggregations of magnetite grains.

Some hypersthene or an augitic mineral occurs in the section. This is dichroic, of a chocolate-brown color, but altered in part to a cloudy-grayish and yellowish-white substance, supposed to be a magnesium carbonate.*

In a section of Gjørud serpentine purchased from R. Fuess, a gray, sponge-like mass is seen holding the greenish, serpentinized olivine. Excepting that the alteration has progressed some further, the description of the Christiania peridotite would apply to this section. If the dichroism of the rhombic pyroxene arises from alteration, as I suspect it does, there seems to be no reason for calling it hypersthene, instead of enstatite.

Its structure and alteration are shown in figure 4, Plate VIII.

* Nyt Mag., 1877, xxiii. 122, 123.

Presque Isle, Michigan.

65. A dark grayish-black to black rock, showing in places the irregular shimmer of enstatite holding olivine.

Section: grayish-green, and composed of an irregular mass of enstatite, olivine, diallage, magnetite, and various secondary products like feldspar, viridite, dolomite, serpentine, etc. The olivine with its secondary products forms in places the principal portion of the section; in other parts the enstatite and diallage are the chief minerals; while the olivine and magnetite are held in grains in the interior. The olivine crystals are comparatively large, but much fissured and altered along the fissures and exterior. The interior portions are clear or smoky, except where the olivine material has been completely changed. The alteration shows in the form of cloudy bands of magnetite traversing the crystal along the fissure lines, while a further change is shown by the formation of greenish and yellowish serpentine along the same lines. The change continues until the olivine is entirely altered. The magnetite usually assumes an irregular grating form or network extending through the serpentine, as well as being arranged in lines which show the former position of the olivine fissures.

The enstatite and diallage have a slight tinge of green, and are slightly pleochroic. They are traversed by longitudinal, transverse, and irregular fissures, the latter being more abundant in part of the diallage. They form together an irregular sponge-like mass holding olivine, and thus present a structure not unlike that of the Atacama and Siberian pallasites, in which they play the *rôle* of the iron. They seem to form the same identical continuous mass, but with a high power the line of union can be faintly seen. It probably would have never been discovered if polarized light had not directed attention to it.

The enstatite polarizes with a pale greenish tint differing but little from the natural color, while the diallage shows brilliant hues of mixed yellow, red, and violet. Both are more or less altered along the fissures to a greenish or a yellowish-green serpentinous product, which is dichroic, varying from a green to a yellowish-brown shade. Similar dichroism, but less marked, was observed in the secondary portion of the olivine. In the highly altered portions of the section are lath-shaped crystals, branching from a centre in a fan-shaped mass. These appear to be feldspars, some of which possess plagioclastic characters. Associated with these occur brown biotite, a little apatite, and some augitic material. The structure of these patches closely resembles that of some diabases. The entire section is traversed in places by a pale greenish serpentine in veins holding dolomite, the latter mineral occurring elsewhere in the section. Some actinolite was observed. The magnetite is in octahedrons and irregular grains, as well as in the secondary forms before mentioned. The cloudiness of the olivine seems to be due to magnetite granules.

Besides the serpentine, a bluish-green fibrous viriditic product occurs, associated with brown biotite plates in such a manner as to lead to the belief that this product is an earlier stage in the formation of biotite, which is evidently an alteration product here. The structure of the enstatite portion is shown in figure 3, Plate VII.

73, from the same locality, is a dark grayish-black to black rock, mottled with minute specks of grayish-white, as well as with pyrite. Weathers to a rusty brown. Section: of a dirty green color, and composed principally of olivine grains and crystals, with magnetite held by a light green mass of enstatite, diallage, and various secondary products. The alteration of the olivine is greater here, as a rule, than in No. **65**. The magnetite bands along the fissures are wider, and fewer portions are left showing the olivine polarization. The secondary products are as in the preceding, but more abundant and well marked. Much less enstatite and diallage exist here than in No. **65**, and they are more highly altered. The interspaces between the olivines more commonly contain pale greenish serpentine, bluish-green and yellowish biotite (?) material, dolomite, magnetite, etc. Much of the serpentine shows the coarse fibrous laminæ so commonly observed in the serpentines described in this volume. In portions of this section and in another slide from the same hand specimen the change of the rock mass to serpentine is nearly, and sometimes quite complete, the forms of the olivines being distinguishable through the arrangement of the magnetite and the serpentine.

The general structure of section is shown in figure 4, Plate VII.

67, from the same locality, is composed of the same dark grayish-black rock, which here presents a brecciated appearance on account of its being traversed by rambling veins of light-yellowish serpentine. In the section the rock appears as a dirty greenish mass traversed by greenish-white veins. It is composed of serpentine pseudomorphs of olivine, filled with beautiful dendritic growths of magnetite, as well as with irregular masses of the same mineral. The interspaces contain the various secondary products before described : micaceous (viriditic) material, serpentine, magnetite, feldspar, dolomite, etc. The veins are composed principally of dolomite grains and serpentine, the former predominating.

74, from the same locality, is much like No. **65,** but the grayish spots are more abundant. Under the microscope it is seen to be composed of a coarsely fibrous lamellar serpentine traversed by the irregular network of magnetite so common in the serpentinized peridotites. It contains a little dolomite and one plate of a micaceous mineral was observed. This was feebly dichroic, greenish and yellowish, extinguished parallel to the nicol diagonal, and polarized with a beautiful purplish-blue tint. It presents a fine micaceous cleavage parallel to the line of extinction, and it is probably partially formed biotite.

71, from the same locality, is a grayish-green rock traversed by grayish-white veins of dolomite, which give to it a rude appearance of foliation. The rock contains a number of reddish-brown patches formed from a breccia of the decomposed rock held by minute reticulated veins of dolomite. The section is composed of yellowish and bluish green, and reddish-brown pseudomorphs of olivine held in a granular mass of dolomite. Crystals and grains of magnetite are scattered throughout the rock. The olivine in the greenish pseudomorphs has been entirely replaced by serpentinous and ferruginous material with dolomite, the first predominating. The reddish-brown pseudomorphs have the ferruginous material the most prominent, and it is these pseudomorphs which form the reddish-brown patches before referred to. The fissures of the olivine are represented by ferruginous and sometimes by dolomitic bands, and these bands can sometimes be seen in the dolomite, showing the form of the pseudomorph when the latter has been almost entirely replaced by dolomite. A portion of the structure of the section is shown in figure 5, Plate VII., the gray groundmass being dolomite and the greenish patches the pseudomorphs after olivine.

69, from the same locality, is a pale oil-green serpentine, banded and spotted with dark and light brown. The section is composed of a granular and fibrous mass of serpentine and dolomite, with ferruginous and earthy material, all holding brownish-yellow earthy pseudomorphs after olivine, which are traversed by the ferruginous bands representing the olivine fissures. These pseudomorphs are wanting in portions of the section. Much of the serpentine shows the fine fibrous polarization of chrysotile.

66, from the same locality, is a dark greenish-brown rock traversed by a network of oil-green serpentine veins, giving it a roughly foliated appearance. The section is very similar in character to that of the preceding.

70 is a dirty green rock coming from the upper portion of the mass at Presque Isle. Section grayish, and composed principally of a granular mixture of dolomite and serpentine with some ferruginous and micaceous materials, etc.

72 is from a portion of the Presque Isle peridotite which has been so filled by dolomitic material as to form a vein. The rock is brownish-gray with a slight pinkish tinge, and composed of granular dolomite holding masses and grains of the decomposed peridotite. It presents the usual structure observable in veins formed by the decomposition and the partial removal of the original rock, and its replacement by vein material. This more properly comes later, in the portion of this work in which the vein-stones are described; but on account of its connection with the previously described peridotite it is given here. The sections are composed of a dirty gray granular dolomite, holding patches of ferruginous material, both dark and light yellowish-brown. In places the darker portions show the cherry-red color of hematite, and appear in part at least to replace olivine.

The Presque Isle peridotite was microscopically studied by Dr. A. Wichmann, who gave a short description of it under the name serpentine, stating that it consisted only of olivine, serpentine, and magnetite.[*] No chromite was found, on making proper tests, in the Presque Isle rock, either by Professor Whitney [†] or myself;[‡] but Dr. Rominger states[§] that it contains two per cent of chromic iron in small octahedrons readily attracted by the magnet, although he does not remark whether this iron was tested to prove the presence of chromium or not.

This peridotite is confidently believed to be eruptive from the following observed evidence. On the southeastern side the overlying Potsdam sandstone dips quite irregularly from twenty to thirty degrees southerly. Its strata follow continuously the curve of the underlying peridotite, and even in places form anticlinals. The surface of the peridotite is an irregular knobby one, while it forms as a whole an immense knob. To this knobby structure the layers of the sandstone conform continuously, as layers of blankets would, and they show no signs of deposition against or around the knobs, but rather a structure as if the sandstone layers had themselves been indented and bent by the peridotite itself. The sandstone with its conglomeritic portion for some two or three feet above the peridotite has been greatly indurated and changed, showing heat action, particularly that of thermal waters. It is filled with vein and chalcedonic quartz; and indurated and reddened as such rocks are known to be when in contact with eruptives of later date than themselves. These indurated portions show, on examination under the microscope, that much of the quartz is a secondary water deposit formed since the deposition of the fragments composing the rock. Above this indurated portion comes the ordinary unaltered sandstone. No fragments of the peridotite could be found macroscopically in the field or microscopically in the laboratory in the sandstone. Now the sandstone does not hold such relations to the Azoic rocks of the district when in contact with them, and it seems right to maintain that this peridotite is younger and an eruptive rock, intruded in the form of a laccolite since the Potsdam sandstone was laid down.[||]

[*] Geol. Wisc., 1880, iii. 618. [†] Am. Jour. Sci., 1859, xxviii. 18.
[‡] Bull. Mus. Comp. Zoöl., 1880, vii. 61. [§] Geol. Mich., 1881, iv. 136.
[||] See Foster and Whitney, Geology of Lake Superior, 1851, ii. 17, 18, 92, 121, 122; Bull. Mus. Comp. Zoöl., 1880, vii. 2, 3, 6, 9, 10, 23, 60–65.

Sec. 29, *T.* 48, *R.* 27. *Three and one-half miles northwest of Ishpeming, Michigan.*

242. A gray, somewhat fibrous rock. Section: a gray mass traversed by a network of magnetite. It is composed of a light gray and colorless transparent mass of serpentine with some dolomite, and has the usual reticulated arrangement of the magnetite so characteristic of the serpentines produced from the alteration of olivine rocks.

244, from the same locality, is a greenish- and reddish-brown rock traversed by greenish-gray serpentine veins. Weathers light yellowish-green. The reddish-brown color is owing apparently to a ferruginous staining of the serpentine foliæ. Section is brownish-gray and composed of a pale greenish-yellow serpentine traversed by irregular reticulated magnetite bands, and spotted by irregular ferruginous stains of reddish- and brownish-yellow. While in the hand specimen these stains present the appearance of distinct micaceous foliæ, I am unable by the microscope, either in common or polarized light, to find any structure peculiar to them and distinct from the serpentine, beyond that belonging to ordinary ferruginous stains. The serpentine shows an irregular fibrous and lamellar structure in polarized and common light.

245, from the same locality, is similar to the preceding. Its staining is deeper, and the rock is coated on one side with a chrysotile and dolomite vein. In the section the fibrous structure, the magnetite network, and the ferruginous staining are all more strongly marked than in the preceding.

243, from the same locality, is a greenish-gray rock with the ferruginous staining showing in a few spots only, — principally along fissures. The section is gray, and under the microscope is seen to be composed of pale greenish-yellow serpentine with cloudy spots. These appear to be occasioned by a fine magnetite dust, which is generally associated with an approach to crystallization on the part of the surrounding material, which somewhat affects polarized light. Numerous pale greenish scales occur in abundance in the serpentine, and have the polarization characters of talc. Crystals and grains of magnetite are scattered throughout the section.

235, from the same locality, is a clear translucent green serpentine containing magnetite grains. It weathers light-colored, even to a chalky-white. The section forms a clear almost colorless mass spotted with crystals and grains of magnetite. The same mineral also traverses the section in the form of a vein. In common light the clear serpentine mass shows fibrous structure, which is beautifully brought out in polarized light. The magnetite appears as a secondary product.

Associated with these are other specimens of greenish- and reddish-brown serpentine often traversed by dolomite veins. In large masses this dolomitic material with talc seems to have replaced nearly all of the serpentine, giving rise to a rock called locally limestone. Much chrysotile also occurs.[*]

Transylvania, Austria.

Tschermak describes a schillerfels [†] from this region as a dark-green rock with white spots composed of olivine, bronzite, diallage, magnetite or chromite, and a little anorthite.

---

[*] See further, Bull. Mus. Comp. Zoöl., 1880, vii. 65, 66; Wright, Mineral Statistics of Michigan, 1879, pp. 201-206; Rominger, Geol. Michigan, 1881, iv. 137-143.

[†] Herbich appears to class this with eruptive rocks. Verh. Mitth. Natur, Hermannstadt, 1865, xvi. 172-183.

The olivine is traversed by a network of dark-green serpentine fibres, and the diallage and bronzite are both somewhat altered. Associated is a compact dark-green serpentine holding some chysolite and chromite. Another rock from the same district is of a dark olive-green color, flecked with white spots; and contains a platy greenish-brown shining diallage, a deep green finely granular mass of olivine, and small white grains of anorthite. The olivine is here traversed by a network of dark-green serpentine.*

Fichtelgebirge, Bavaria.

These rocks are composed principally of olivine with enstatite, chromdiopside, augite, and magnetite. The olivine is more or less altered into a serpentine, showing the usual network structure. The enstatite is in elongated, fibrous, brilliant clear wine-green needles, and the chromdiopside in roundish, compact, somewhat fissured particles. The groundmass consists of a mixture of chlorite, serpentine, etc.†

A Pebble from the Jaina River, ten to twelve miles N. W. of Mt. Mariana, Chico, Prov. San Domingo, San Domingo.

252 G. A compact dark-green groundmass holding crystals of brownish pyroxene and traversed by veins of chromite.

Section: a gray groundmass holding iron ore and crystals of enstatite and diallage. The groundmass is composed almost entirely of clear beautifully polarizing serpentine, which shows in its structure traces of the bounding planes of the minerals from whose alteration it was derived. A little white plagioclase, traversed by cleavage planes, was observed, portions of which had been rendered gray and nearly opaque by kaolinization. Only a few small fissured olivine grains were observed. The enstatite and diallage can here as a rule be distinguished by their cleavage, the latter being much less regular than the former, and closely like that of augite. Both are in irregular grains, more or less altered to a greenish- and yellowish-brown product. Where the change has progressed far, the ordinary serpentine of the groundmass is the result. Sometimes the serpentine resulting is filled with minute black globules, or with minute microlitic forms, arranged in lines forming definite angles with one another. The iron ore is in part in crystals and part in irregular grains and masses. The structure is shown in figure 6, Plate IV.

This rock was collected by Professor W. M. Gabb.

Starkenbach, Bluttenberg, Vosges, France.

According to Weigand this is soft black rock containing brownish-yellow and brass-yellow crystals. In the thin section the rock is seen to be composed of bronzite (enstatite), diallage, olivine, magnetite, hornblende (smaragdite?), and picotite, with more or less serpentine. The enstatite and olivine are more or less traversed by fissures filled with serpentine. The hornblende is in minute plates, while the bronzite is the predominating mineral.‡

* Sitz. Wien. Akad., 1867, lvi. 261-274.
† C. W. Gümbel, Die paläolithischen Eruptivgesteine des Fichtelgebirges, 1874, pp. 38–41.
‡ Min. Mitth., 1875, pp. 192–196.

Todtmoos, Baden.

5000. The specimen from this locality in the collection is a blackish-green compact one, containing a few enstatite and diallage crystals. It weathers to an earthy rusty-brown, showing the network method of decomposition frequently observed in the peridotites. This with the sections was purchased from Voigt and Hochgesang, Göttingen.

One section has a greenish groundmass holding crystals and grains of enstatite, diallage, olivine, and picotite. The enstatite is in part clear and unaltered, holding picotite grains, and in part it has suffered a greenish and yellowish serpentinous alteration. The same can be stated of the diallage. Both are in rounded crystals and irregular masses, and show the usual cleavage lines.

The olivine when unchanged is in clear grains, the remnants of the original larger crystals and grains. That a series of these grains now separated by the serpentine bands once formed the same crystalline mass, is shown conclusively by their possessing the same optical orientation. The major portion of the original olivine has been changed to serpentine, the structure showing the successive stages of alteration. The serpentine formed first along the fissures has a dividing line indicating the fissure, and on both sides the serpentine fibres stand at right angles to that line. The color of this serpentine is generally a light yellowish-green. The interior portion occupying the interspaces left between the network lines above described, is occupied by serpentine of a different shade of green, sometimes lighter, sometimes darker. This serpentine, which replaces the olivine grains before described, shows not only by its color, but also by its structure, both in common and in polarized light, that it possesses a distinct organization from that of the network, and is distinctively a later product. The serpentine forms the chief portion of the groundmass and is feebly dichroic. While it is usually of some shade of yellowish-green to pale-green, in some cases, especially about the ferruginous products, it is of a bluish-green color, doubtless owing to the ferrous oxide. Some secondary actinolite and talc exist associated with the pyroxene minerals. The picotite is in coffee-brown and pale-greenish irregular grains scattered throughout the section in the different minerals. The larger grains along their fissures and edges are altered to a black ferruginous product, probably chromite. This alteration sometimes extends nearly, and sometimes quite, through the entire picotite grain. Considerable secondary iron ore exists, which is either chromite or magnetite.

Another section has a yellowish-green groundmass containing grains of enstatite, diallage, and picotite, and traversed by veins of talc. The groundmass is a network of serpentine of a pale yellowish-green color, surrounding portions of a deeper green representing the unfissured parts of the olivine, while the meshes follow the fissures. The enstatite and diallage are in places only slightly altered; but for the most part they are traversed by threads of the serpentine web, and possess a fibrous alternation-structure showing a more or less aggregate polarization; yet in the majority of cases they retain their relative extinction. This serpentine is very beautiful in polarized light. The picotite is in irregular fissured grains, sometimes opaque, but more commonly with dark brown to black edges, and with a light brown to dark reddish-brown interior. Much ferruginous material in grains and irregular patches is distributed through the section.

This serpentine has been referred by Rosenbusch to the lherzolites.

From *Spur between Deadwood and Poker Flat, Cal.*

111 P. A dark-yellowish and brownish-green rock containing enstatite grains and talc scales; and traversed by light-greenish serpentine veins. Section: a greenish-gray mass flecked with magnetite grains and traversed by a grayish-yellow serpentine vein. The chief portion of the section is serpentinous material, in which besides the magnetite are scattered the remains of enstatite crystals and a few grains of olivine and diallage. The serpentine varies in color from white to yellowish and green. In places clear white leaves of talc associated with magnetite occur; while some hematite is to be seen. Along the sides of the serpentine vein before mentioned the section is black with the rejected magnetite. Much of the enstatite contains the same inclusions that the bronzite variety is accustomed to hold.

The structure is shown in figures 3 and 6, Plate VI.

Levanto, Italy.

One specimen described by Prof. T. G. Bonney from this locality is a purplish- or brownish-black rock veined occasionally with dull green, and flecked with crystalline folia of glittering bronzite, while another specimen is of a more granular texture, greener color, and rougher fracture than the preceding, but otherwise similar. The second rock, in the thin section, is seen to consist chiefly of olivine grains separated by threads of serpentine. It contains opacite, enstatite, augite, and perhaps a little diallage. Opacite [magnetite] occurs in the enstatite and a little picotite was observed.

The first specimen was seen under the microscope to have been completely altered, no olivine remaining intact. Much opacite was found, which often forms continuous strings, and is present to a greater or less extent in the grains that were formerly olivine. It forms bands towards the exterior of the grains, or is disseminated throughout them. Diallage and enstatite are both present, the latter being surrounded by a border of a serpentinous mineral, into which are continued the principal cleavage planes, often marked by opacite lines. Thin bands of serpentine indicate the prismatic cleavage.*

Near Limni, Eubœa.

A black splintery rock, which, as described by Becke, contains lustrous bronze-colored grains of enstatite. Under the microscope it shows the evident *maschenstruktur* of the serpentine which holds lens-formed masses of fresh olivine. This groundmass porphyritically contains fresh enstatite of a pale brownish color and a marked fibrous texture. This mineral is sometimes altered to a feeble bluish polarizing product. This alteration extends from the exterior along the fissures towards the interior. Diallage, reddish-brown octahedrons of picotite, and secondary magnetite also occur.

Similar to this is a rock from Mantoudi, in the northern portion of Eubœa. This is brownish, and contains numerous plates of enstatite in a fine-grained groundmass. No diallage was observed, but the brownish color of the rock is due to brown hydrated oxide of iron.

Similar to this is a rock from the district of middle Eubœa, between Chalcis and Gides, which has a reddish-brown groundmass holding tombac-brown enstatite (bastite). No olivine remains unaltered to serpentine.

---

* Geol. Mag., 1879 (2), vi. 362–371.

A rock of similar character was obtained between Kumi and Kastrovolo, in middle Eubœa, possessing diallage instead of enstatite. The diallage is partly altered into a greenish substance and partly into talc plates.

A serpentine from Kumi was found to contain much chromite, magnetite, and some green ouvarovite.*

Oberlauf, Luzon, Philippine Islands.

A dark blackish-green serpentine-like compact rock, with crystals of clear green diallage and brownish enstatite. The principal cleavage planes show a mother-of-pearl lustre. Microscopically the rock possessed the usual mesh structure, and contained magnetite and picotite.†

Lizard District, Cornwall.

The serpentines of this district were found to present intrusive relations to the adjoining rocks by Prof. T. G. Bonney. They send tongues and dikes into the latter and hold included fragments of them, while the adjacent rocks at their junction with the serpentine were often altered and contorted. The microscopic examination indicated that the serpentine resulted from the alteration of lherzolite. The following is condensed from Professor Bonney's description of the rocks and sections. The rock from Coverack Cove is a dull mottled, red and green rock with flakes of a silky bronzitic mineral in the green portion. Under the microscope the serpentine forms golden-colored and reddish- and greenish-brown reticulated veins, which enclose colorless olivine, as well as augite, enstatite, and diallage. Original and secondary iron ores occur. A rock from Mullion Cove has a similar composition and structure, but the alteration of the olivine has progressed further, with a differentiation of the common black ferruginous dust. A few small grains resemble picotite.

At Guc Graze a similar but more decomposed rock was obtained, which appeared to contain a pseudomorphic product after feldspar. From the Lower Pradanach and the Rill quarries similar rocks to that from Mullion Cove were obtained, but in one from Helston Road a little hornblende was observed.

The rock from Goomhilly Downs is a banded dull-colored light-greenish serpentine, containing in the section, besides the serpentine, olivine, hornblende, magnetite, and some picotite. A number of other sections were examined, but they are mainly similar to the above, or else have been more highly altered, so that the olivine was entirely changed; but the reader is referred to the original paper for the particulars.‡

Two other areas of serpentine were later examined in the Lizard district, one of which shows excellent junctions and is clearly intrusive in the associated schist. Bonney also re-examined the other portions of the district previously studied by him, and found the strongest evidence of the intrusion of the serpentine into the associated sedimentary rock.§

From the Troad, Asia Minor.

Owing to certain arrangements, and for a consideration, the lithological collection of the Assos expedition has become the property of Professor Whitney, and passed over to

---

* Min. Mitth., 1878 (1), i. 477–485.
† Konrad Oebbeke, Neues Jahr. Min., Beilage Band, 1882, i. 499.
‡ Quart. Jour. Geol. Soc., 1877, xxxiii. 884–928; 1883, xxxix. 21–23.
§ Phil. Mag., 1882 (5), xiv. 478; Quart. Jour. Geol. Soc., 1883, xxxix. 21–23.

my charge. Mr. Diller (who collected the specimens) has kindly consented that I should use his written description of the Assos serpentine rocks, not yet published except in abstract,* and it is given below, with a few verbal changes to adapt it to the present work.

"Serpentine occurs in the Troad at Qarà-dagh . . . derived from the alteration of eruptive rocks; also about the summit of Mt. Ida in small lenticular masses in talcose schist, and belongs to the stratified rocks; also . . . forming low rounded conical hills near the base of Qarà-dagh. The rock is usually of a deep green color, but varies, becoming bluish or reddish, often presenting smooth fibrous surfaces like slickensides, and occasionally an imperfect columnar structure. Although locally uniform, it is generally made porphyritic by a fibrous or lamellar mineral, whose cleavage plates between crossed nicols show an acute bisectrix with the plane of the optic axes at right angles to the fibrous structure. The mineral is bastite, and in all probability has been produced by the alteration of enstatite.

"Under the microscope the composition of the rock is seen to vary greatly. Sometimes it is composed almost wholly of a network of serpentine containing a few grains of unaltered olivine, bastite, and much iron ore. In other cases the serpentine is a subordinate constituent, and olivine forms the chief mass, in which are imbedded enstatite, for the most part changed to bastite, and also very rarely a colorless mineral, with prismatic and pinacoidal cleavage. It appears to belong to the pyroxene group, but with the few sections present its optical relations could not be determined. It is evident that the serpentine of Qarà-dagh is derived from an *olivine enstatite* rock.

"In the Kemar Valley, a short distance east of where it opens into the Trojan Plain, loose blocks of serpentine containing numerous very bright silvery crystals of bastite have been observed. In the thin section, besides serpentine, olivine, enstatite, bastite, and irregular dark grains, there occur numerous small black crystals whose square rhombic and hexagonal sections indicate that they may belong either to spinel or magnetite; but as they are not translucent, they are most likely magnetite.

"Further up the valley the serpentine is indistinctly porphyritic, and occurs intimately associated with schists and crystalline limestone, through which it appears to penetrate in the form of irregular dikes. Its specific gravity is 2.593. The microscopical structure of these rocks is strongly contrasted with that of the serpentine from Qarà-dagh. Between crossed nicols they appear rather coarsely microcrystalline, and throughout the greater portion of the section are not only uniform, but show no trace of the characteristic reticulated structure of serpentine derived from the alteration of olivine.† However, here and there a few meshes of the old net are still preserved, and there appears to be a passage from this portion into the other, in which the same structure cannot be traced. The porphyritic crystals, as in the other cases, are bastite, with considerable quantities of carbonates. According to Mr. Frank Calvert the serpentines in the vicinity of the Kemar Valley occur as distinct dikes cutting the crystalline limestones, so there can be no doubt concerning their eruptive nature, and they are in all probability derived from olivine enstatite rocks.

"Near the centre of Mt. Ida the oldest rocks crop out, and among them are talcose schists, which by the addition of olivine pass into small lens-shaped masses composed

---

* Papers of the Archæological Institute of America, Classical Series, i. 201, 203; Science, 1883, ii. 255–258.

† Hussak, after studying microscopically a number of Alpine serpentines, concluded that in the serpentines derived from schistose rocks the characteristic reticulated structure, chromite, and picotite are wanting.

almost exclusively of the latter mineral. According to the nomenclature of Brögger, the rock of these patches should be called olivine schist. By alteration it gives rise to serpentine with the characteristic reticulated structure which ever marks the serpentine derived from olivine.* Occasionally the fibrous serpentine forms veins of considerable size in the adjacent rocks. The olivine schist when purest has no schistose structure. The passage from pure talc schist in which no olivine occurs to that composed almost completely of olivine, takes place sometimes within a short distance. The chief mass of the rock, however, is a middle stage between the two extremes, having a distinct schistose structure and composed for the most part of olivine and talc, besides considerable quantities of pyroxene as well as other minerals not yet determined."

Differing in some points from Mr. Diller, although agreeing with him in the main, it has seemed best to add more special descriptions of the individual rocks and sections in question. It is further necessary to do this in order to point to the gradations and alterations which are conspicuous in them. Part appear to belong to the lherzolite variety, while others are so far altered that it cannot be predicated what was their original composition as a whole.

A. E. 324, from Mitylene, is a greenish-black compact rock containing lighter green crystals of enstatite. The section shows a grayish-brown groundmass, holding crystals of enstatite and diallage. This groundmass is formed by a network of grayish-brown serpentine, holding olivine, enstatite, diallage, and iron ore. Much of the enstatite is altered to a grayish-brown fibrous serpentine, but some portions remain intact in part of the crystals, while other crystals are entirely unaffected. The diallage is abundant, but in small irregular grains and imperfect crystals. Part of this appears to be an augite-diallage, for it has well developed both the prismatic cleavage of augite and the orthopinacoidal cleavage of diallage, as well as traces of a clinopinacoidal cleavage. Elongated dashes of iron ore are occasionally arranged parallel to 010, forming with the well-developed cleavage parallel to 100 a rectangular grating. Part of the iron ore is secondary, occurring in grains arranged in the centre of the serpentine veins, but part appears to be the product of alteration of picotite, since the interior portion still is of a translucent reddish-brown color. From its general characters the ore is probably chromite with some magnetite.

A. E. 208, from Qara-dagh, is of a similar character, but has less enstatite and diallage, and more olivine. In some places the olivine has suffered almost no alteration, while in others the change is complete. The rock is compact, greenish-black, containing light-greenish enstatite crystals, and coated with a greenish "slickenside" of serpentine.

A. E. 209, from near Mt. Daydah by the Plain of Troy, is a grayish-green rock holding enstatite crystals altered into a talcose-like material (bastite) and presenting a greenish to silvery-white appearance. The section is similar to the preceding, but more highly altered, the serpentine predominating. The diallage is abundant, and in its structure closely resembles that of the meteorites, being composed of a series of granules aggregated together into larger masses, and separated by little patches of different material.

A. E. 481, from the southeast part of the Chiplak, Mt. Ida, is a dark-green rock weathering brown and containing talc scales and grains, and bands of chromite. The section is grayish, and presents a schistose appearance, owing to the arrangement of its iron ore, etc. It is composed principally of a serpentine network enclosing olivine. A little enstatite and diallage were observed, also iron ore and secondary talc.

* With this statement of Mr. Diller the present writer is unable to agree.

A. E. **207,** four miles northwest of Eanedeh, is a compact greenish-brown rock, weathering rusty-brown, and contains enstatite crystals. Section: greenish-gray and composed principally of secondary serpentine, with its network structure holding later altered olivine grains, and altered enstatite crystals containing much iron ore, and traversed and stained by ferruginous material. Many of the olivine grains between the meshes appear in common light as unchanged olivine, but in polarized light the change to serpentine is seen to be complete. Some dolomite occurs, while portions of the section present a similar structure to that given in figure 4, Plate VI.

A. E. **482,** from the central part of the Chiplak, Mt. Ida, is a greenish-gray schistose rock closely resembling some mica schists owing to its contained talc scales. It holds actinolite and yellowish-brown altered olivine. Section · greenish-gray and composed of olivine, iron ore, secondary serpentine, talc, and actinolite. I am inclined to regard this rock as an altered massive rock, instead of a metamorphosed sedimentary one.

A. E. **265,** from the summit of Mt. Ida, is a similar schistose rock, composed of olivine and actinolite, with talc scales lying between the lamination planes. The section is composed partially of olivine, which is somewhat altered to a dirty-green serpentine, and partially of actinolite crystals. Iron ore and talc also occur. Mr. Diller has called this a talc schist; but I am unable to agree with him, for it appears to me to be a metamorphosed peridotite, in which the actinolite and talc are alteration-products. The foliation appears to me to have been produced during the metamorphosis, and not to be congenital.

A. E. **485,** from the northwest summit of Mt. Ida, is a schistose rock of a grayish-green color. The schistose structure appears to be due to alternation and to the production of talc scales. Section: composed of a network of greenish serpentine containing olivine and secondary actinolite and talc. The form of the olivine grains, and their relation to one another and to the other minerals, are such that I am unable to look upon them as either of mechanical or of metamorphic origin. The actinolite is clearly an alteration-product, and frequently separates portions of the same olivine individual.

There are two rocks numbered A. E. **483.** One, coming from the central part of the Chiplak, Mt. Ida, is a compact greenish-black rock containing talc scales and weathered brown. The section is composed of serpentine, olivine, actinolite, talc, and iron ore. The alteration of the olivine has been quite extended in this. The second A. E. **483** is from the northwest summit of Mt. Ida, and is a dark compact rock with little trace of a schistose structure. The section is composed chiefly of serpentine, talc, iron ore, actinolite, and a little olivine.

A. E. **473,** from the summit of a ridge east of Mt. Ida, is a dark greenish and grayish rock weathering brown. It is a surface specimen. Section composed of a network of greenish serpentine holding olivine grains, and associated with actinolite, talc, iron ore, etc.

A. E. **217,** from the Kemar Valley, is a compact dark grayish-green rock with greenish and grayish porphyritically enclosed enstatite crystals. The section is composed principally of a clear pale greenish and yellowish serpentine, holding diallage, enstatite, some talc, and iron ore. The serpentine shows traces of the structure of the minerals from which it was formed.

A. E. **216,** from the same valley, is a similar rock, and in the hand specimen presents considerable resemblance to that described from High Bridge, N. J. The section is much like that of A. E. 217. The altered enstatite and diallage have ferruginous material so arranged in their fissures as to give them a close resemblance to bronzite and hypersthene.

A. E. **214**, from the same locality, is a similar, but more highly altered rock, which contains talcose material.

The greenish talcose schists from Mt. Ida are stated by Mr. Diller to be associated with and to pass into the olivine-bearing rocks above described from that locality. Accepting the accuracy of his statement, it is proper to touch upon their microscopic characters so far as they bear upon this relation.

A. E. **484** is a greenish talcose schist containing grains and crystals of magnetite. Stained slightly with yellowish-brown ferruginous material from the decomposition of the magnetite. The section is composed principally of talc holding magnetite and patches of partly altered olivine and enstatite, traversed by a peculiar eozoön-like network of iron ore, with the longest and best marked portions approximately parallel with an optic axis.

A. E. **274** is a coarser greenish-gray talc schist, composed of talc and actinolite (Diller's pyroxene) with iron ore and the remains of partially altered olivine.

A. E. **270** is a beautiful green talc schist, containing crystals of actinolite and grains and crystals of iron ore. Only a few olivine grains were seen.

It seems to me from the study of these rocks, coupled with similar evidence obtained from the examination of other rocks, like cumberlandite, that these schists and schistose forms are the results of the alteration of peridotites: that is, the schists are derived from the olivine rock, and not that from the schists. This view is, of course, opposed to that of Mr. Diller and the majority of lithologists and geologists.

VARIETY. — **Eulysite.**

Tunaberg, Norway.

The rock from which this variety is named was first so called and described by Axel Erdmann, in 1849, as a granular mixture of diallage, garnet, and altered olivine.*

According to the later studies of H. von Möhl, it contains fresh clear angular grains of olivine cut by numerous fissures and holding much magnetite in powdery grains, while the olivine is here and there altered into serpentine. A pale sea-green diallage occurs, forming large grains in the rock. This diallage shows a fine fibrous parallel structure (cleavage), which is often crumpled. This mineral often contains layers of very minute laminæ, which make with the cleavage planes angles varying from 20° to as much as 60° or 70°. They are arranged in parallel lines. Pale almandine-red garnet in drop-like rounded grains, and magnetite also, form constituents of the rock. Möhl estimates the percentages of the minerals as olivine (fayalite) 60 per cent, diallage 35 per cent, magnetite 3 per cent, and garnet 2 per cent.†

The above description by Möhl answers very well for the section in this collection purchased from Richard Fuess. The general structure and relations of the crystals indicate that the diallage and garnet, if not all of the minerals, are the results of a recrystallization of the rock materials; i. e. it appears to be a rock whose structure has been produced by alteration and secondary crystallization, with but little if any of the original structure and minerals remaining.

Kellilsfjäll, Sweden.

According to Törnebohm, this rock is a fine granular one, greenish on the fresh fracture, and weathering yellowish. Microscopically it is composed of irregular olivine

* Neues Jahr. Min., 1849, pp. 937, 938.   † Nyt Mag., 1877, xxiii. 119.

grains, colorless pyroxene (diopside), colorless mica, and chromite. The olivine is fresh, and with the pyroxene is almost free from inclusions. The chromite is brownish on the edges, and is often surrounded or accompanied by the mica.*

This rock is said to be associated with schists, and to be a concordant part of them.

Varallo, Sesia Valley.

Prof. A. Stelzner described a fine-grained greenish-black rock from Varallo, in Sesia Valley, as composed of olivine, hornblende, and bronzite in nearly equal amounts. Green grains were observed which were isotropic and regarded as probably chlorospinel. †

Lepce, Austria.

A blackish fine-grained olivine mass with light greenish-gray foliated diallage having a metallic lustre.

The section is composed of predominating somewhat serpentinized olivine, whose fissures are filled with a black powder; as well as a light reddish-colored diallage, which is fibrous and shows a feeble dichroism between light red and light green.‡

Fontanapass, Locris, Greece.

According to Becke the rock from this locality is a light-colored fresh *olivinfels*, holding porphyritic crystals of diallage.

In the thin section it is seen to contain the following minerals: olivine in irregular colorless fresh grains, traversed by numerous irregular fissures; serpentine in thin plates along these fissures; diallage, very fresh, and traversed by cleavage planes, but sometimes this mineral is changed to a rhombic fibrous alteration-product; and picotite, in little reddish-brown, translucent quadratic or hexagonal sections.

A somewhat similar rock comes from Pyrgos, at the foot of Hymettus, in Attica. This has a black and green spotted groundmass holding large crystals of enstatite which are much altered (bastite).

In the section the rock shows the ordinary network of serpentine, to which the olivine has been entirely changed. Picotite and magnetite occur.§

Mohsdorf, Saxony.

This rock, Dathe states, contains as its most prominent mineral diallage. Sometimes along the fissures are alteration-products of calcic carbonate and iron. The olivine which is held by the diallage is generally altered to serpentine, which is filled with a powder of iron ore. Some garnet occurs.‖

Gillsberg, Saxony.

According to Dathe, this is a dark green rock composed of dark brown to black elongated crystals, which in the thin section are dichroic from light brown to dark brown,

---

* Geol. Fören. Förh., 1877, iii. 250; Neues Jahr. Min., 1880, ii. 107.
† Zeit. Deut. geol. Gesell., 1876, xxviii. 623–625.
‡ C. v. John, Jahr. Geol. Reichs., 1880, xxx. 447.
§ Min. Mitth., 1878 (1), i. 475–477.
‖ Neues Jahr. Min., 1876, pp. 233.

and have the cleavage of hornblende, garnet, olivine altered to serpentine in part, biotite strongly dichroic and containing little opaque needles, diallage, and iron ore.*

A similar serpentine was described by Dathe from Crossen, near Mittweida, in Saxony; but it appears to be a somewhat more altered rock (*l. c.*, p. 245).

VARIETY. — **Picrite.**

Austria.

Picrite, according to Tschermak, when in a fresh or little changed state, has a dark green color, and varies from a finely crystalline to a plainly crystalline character.

That from *Söhle* has a blackish groundmass containing a large number of olivine crystals. Microscopically the groundmass holds granular feldspar, grains of magnetite, scales of black mica, and little hornblende crystals.

The *Freiberg* and *Gümbelberg* picrite shows a dark groundmass holding olivine crystals traversed by numerous fissures filled by a serpentinous mineral; also blackish-green grains of diallage. The groundmass is similar to that of the Söhle picrite: granular feldspar, biotite scales, magnetite grains, and a few hornblende crystals, with here and there thin strings of serpentine.

The picrite from *Schönau* has a blackish-green groundmass holding olivine and dark-green mica. The mica forms aggregations of scales. Much serpentine also occurs in the rock. The groundmass consists of a granular feldspathic mass, grains and octahedrons of magnetite, blackish-green augite crystals, rarely some needles of apatite, also calcite grains, and some serpentine.

An altered picrite from *Söhle* is a dark greenish-gray rock flecked with pistacite green spots. It contains altered diallage and olivine crystals, hornblende prisms, dark-green mica plates, magnetite grains, and silicates like gymnite and palagonite.

Another altered picrite from *Bystryc*, has a clear gray very fine-grained groundmass, holding inclusions of bluish-gray to apple-green and blackish-green colors. Pseudomorphs after diallage and olivine occur, while the rock further contains magnetite and fine fissures filled with calcite.

The above picrites are stated to be eruptive in the Cretaceous.

Steierdorf, Banat.

A blackish rock resembling basalt, and containing porphyritically enclosed olivine and quartz. It is somewhat porous, and holds calcite amygdules. The section shows that the principal minerals are olivine, augite, and hornblende. Calcite occurs as an alteration-product, and quartz as an inclusion, while an isotropic base was seen. The olivine is in large, well-defined crystals, and in smaller rounded forms. It is for the most part fresh, but it shows here and there along its edges and the borders of its fissures an alteration to a dark brown radiated fibrous aggregate. The olivine contains inclusions of glass, augite, hornblende, and picotite. The latter is in large brown isotropic sharply defined octahedrons. The augite is of a light-reddish color, and the crystals are fresh with a feeble pleochroism. It contains inclusions of glass and picotite. The hornblende is of a dark brown color, with strong pleochroism, and contains glass particles. The hornblende is

* Neues Jahr. Min., 1876, pp. 244, 245.

often associated with the augite. The quartz is in water-clear, beautifully polarizing fissured grains containing fluid and glass inclusions, as well as apatite needles.*

Inchcolm Island, Scotland.

An apparent intrusive mass is described by Dr. A. Geikie as composed of a serpentinous base holding honey-yellow grains of olivine, dark lustrous augites, and a few plates of brown biotite. In the section the olivine is in a great measure undecomposed, though presenting the usual exterior band and transverse threads of serpentine. The augite is of a pale yellow color, and in large and well-defined prisms, often enclosing olivine. A little milky plagioclase full of fissures and decomposition products was observed. Long scales of rich brown biotite occur here and there; also a few plates and grains of probable titaniferous iron. One of the most conspicuous constituents is a rich emerald-green to grass-green decomposition product, filling up the interstices and running in veins and irregular streaks or tufts through the rock. Other pale or colorless aggregates, which are sometimes distinctly fibrous, also occur. These various decomposition products sometimes show the polarization of serpentine, and sometimes that of chlorite. Some zeolitic fibrous tufts were seen.†

Herborn, Nassau.

The section purchased from Richard Fuess is composed of pale brownish-yellow augite and clear fissured olivine surrounded and held by the secondary serpentinous products. The augite in places is changed to a pleochroic green fibrous mineral, whose extinction, being parallel to the nicol diagonal, presents a strong contrast in polarized light to the monoclinic augite. The augite holds numerous rounded grains of olivine, the same as enstatite commonly does in other rocks. The olivine is in rounded fissured forms, surrounded and traversed by the plexus of alteration material. Part of the latter is dichroic, varying from a green to brownish-yellow, and from its relations to the secondary brownish-yellow biotite it is regarded as a transition stage in the formation of the biotite. It is in irregular fibrous forms, the fibres being crumpled and aggregated together. In other portions some whitish fibrous material occurs, which affects polarized light in the same manner as part of the actinolite does in the *cumberlandite*. However, the chief portion of the alteration material is serpentine. The olivine is in part very clear, and in part changed to a pale-yellowish serpentine filled with globulites and margarites of iron ore. They are seen in the serpentine veins ramifying through the olivine, and projecting like pseudopodia from the surrounding material into the partially or entirely altered olivine. The ore also forms black grains and crystals (some of which are octahedrons) in the olivine, and in the network of alteration material. It frequently forms black bands, rows of grains, or fine powder, along the fissures or centres and sides of the serpentine veins. The biotite is in irregular yellowish-brown scales and grains, some of which are surrounded by the black ore grains. It is strongly dichroic, and shows oftentimes a wavy, fibrous polarization. (Plate VIII. figure 6.)

Ellgoth, Austria.

This rock is described by Dr. H. v. Möhl as having a black to blackish-green serpentinous groundmass holding many mica and hornblende particles.

The section is in part a very fine tufted serpentine, and in part a scaly fibrous one, of

* E. Hussak, Verhandl. Geol. Reichs., 1881, pp. 258–262.
† Trans. Roy. Soc. Edin., 1879, xxix. 506–509.

all possible colors from a pale apple-green to a brilliant grass-green, bright ochre-yellow, siskin-green, and reddish-brown, one color running into the others. Further, there occur remnants of the olivine grains having a light or ochre-yellow tinge, and also magnetite and göthite. The olivine remnants when untouched by alteration are colorless, very pellucid, beautifully polarizing, but extraordinarily rich in fissures, whose edges are cloudy with minute magnetite grains. Some show a light blue color, owing to exceedingly minute powder-like grains. Vapor, glass, and fluid cavities, as well as spinel inclusions, occur sparingly.

The serpentine mass includes fiery reddish-brown mica; very light grayish-brown, finely fibrous, or step-like, rough, feebly dichroic enstatite; a little clear light-brown, feebly dichroic augite, traversed by irregular fissures; and strongly dichroic fissured hornblende, varying from clear ochre-yellow to a deep blackish-brown. A little apatite and plagioclase were also observed. This is a cretaceous or tertiary eruptive rock.*

Pen-y-carnisiog, Anglesey.

According to Bonney this rock in the section is seen to be composed of augite, hornblende, actinolite, magnetite, opacite, serpentinous material, etc.

Augite occurs in colorless grains and crystals, some of which show a characteristic cleavage. The hornblende, including actinolite, is in (1st) innumerable small acicular or blade-like crystals, in irregular tufted groups, which are pale greenish or colorless, and feebly, if at all, dichroic; (2d) small crystals often exhibiting characteristic cleavages and even crystallographic planes, green-colored and strongly dichroic; and large brown crystals, supposed to be pseudomorphs after augite. These minerals occur in a serpentinous or chloritic groundmass containing no unchanged olivines, but pseudomorphs after that mineral were thought to be observed. Some talc (?) was seen, as well as other micaceous secondary products.†

Later Professor Bonney found a number of boulders of this rock on the western coast of Anglesey. In general these were similar to the one just described, although in one some decomposed feldspar and some diallage were observed. A little apatite, mica, etc. were seen in some of the sections.‡

Near the River Dill ("Dillgegend"), Nassau.

This rock in the fresh condition has a blackish-green color, and contains copper-colored mica, green chromdiopside, hypersthene, picotite, and magnetite.

The olivine is in water-clear to pale yellowish-green grains, traversed by fissures along which occurs a fibrous greenish or yellowish-green serpentine containing magnetite grains, etc. The chromdiopside appears as a rule in irregular leek-green grains showing cleavage, and is sometimes altered to a leek or smaragdite-green serpentinous aggregate.

The hypersthene is pale-brownish, and shows an evident brachypinicoidal cleavage. It contains the usual violet-brown laminæ, and olivine grains.

The mica shows a reddish-brown color darker than the hypersthene, is dichroic, and associated with the magnetite. The picotite is in deep black octahedral crystals, which are dark brown, and feebly translucent on the thin edges.

* Neues Jahr. Min., 1875, pp. 700-703. † Quart. Jour. Geol. Soc., 1881, xxxvii. 137-140.
‡ Quart. Jour. Geol. Soc., 1883, xxxix. 254-260.

152   PERIDOTITE.

Beside the magnetite, there occurs a whitish opaque mineral substance, which is considered to be magnesite.

A similar rock, which comes from the nickel mine *Hülfe Gottes* in the Weyherhecke, Nassau, is described as a granular to compact serpentine of a dark-green color. In the dark groundmass lie many minerals; as, for instance, calcite, magnesite, chrysotile, schillerspar, pyrite, chalcopyrite, and millerite. The olivine is much changed to serpentine, as also is the hypersthene. The chief difference between this and the preceding appears to be mainly in the greater amount of alteration.*

VARIETY. — **Serpentine.**

Fitztown, Berks Co., Pennsylvania.

1562. Section: a greenish-yellow serpentine holding crystals of grayish-white dolomite. Under the microscope in part of the section the serpentine is seen to form a network following the fissures in the clear, unaltered olivine, and enclosing grains of it, the fibres being generally parallel to the direction of the serpentine veins. In other portions only traces of the olivine remain, while in still others only the structure of the serpentine shows its origin. The direct conversion of olivine into serpentine is well illustrated in this section. The dolomite is in rhombohedrons, and irregular, sometimes geniculated grains. The larger forms mostly contain an irregular central portion of a clear, fissured mineral, closely resembling olivine in its clearness; but it is isotropic, and belongs to spinel. One grain, however, showed a pale grayish color in polarized light. The dolomite is surrounded by a white border of aggregately polarizing fibrous serpentine, which in places occupies considerable of the section. The serpentine about the olivine is in the middle of the fissures of a clear greenish-yellow color, but next the olivine frequently passes into a clear nearly white serpentine. (Plate VII. figure 6.)

The rock is composed of a mixture of greenish and yellowish serpentine and grayish-white dolomite. Many colorless and pale bluish octahedrons of spinel were observed in the dolomite. Three of the sides of the specimen show a "slickensided" surface coated with serpentine, dolomite, and white mica (phlogopite?). This rock is an "ophicalcite."

Frankenstein, Silesia.

Prof. T. Liebisch describes this rock as a siskin-green to oil-green serpentine mass holding chromite. In the section it shows the usual network of serpentine enclosing colorless olivine grains, minute crystals of actinolite, and whitish talc-like plates.†

Lekö, Norway.

The section shows portions in which the olivine is still unaltered, but it is rendered cloudy by a magnetite dust scattered through it.

In other portions the magnetite is very abundant, and in polarized light the rock is seen to contain numerous plates and fibres, having a similarity to sericite, or to talc and chlorite. It contains grains of a magnesium carbonate.‡

* Konrad Oebbeke, Inaug. Diss., Wurzburg, 1877, 38 pp.
† Zeit. Deut. geol. Gesell., 1877, xxix. 732.   ‡ Möhl, Nyt Mag., 1877, xxiii. 121.

Waldheim, Saxony.

5002. A dark grayish-green rock, purchased from Voigt and Hochgesang, mottled with spots of lighter grayish-green, and containing chromite.

Section: greenish-gray with a reticulated network of iron ore. Chiefly composed of clear colorless or pale yellow and pale green serpentine. This retains in part the structure of the fissured olivine, and in part that of the enstatite crystals which it has replaced. In the latter, the plane of extinction is the same as that of the enstatite, while in the serpentine replacing the olivine we have the reticulated network following the fissures, with the polarization of the serpentine first formed along the fissures differing from that later replacing the central portions of the grains. This difference is to some extent observable in common light, so that one is able to trace out the forms of the original enstatites, and then those of the olivine grains which were enclosed in them. The structure of the rock thus revealed shows that it was originally composed principally of olivine with comparatively small amounts of enstatite.

The Waldheim serpentines have been studied by Dathe, who describes that from the *Tunnel* as a blackish-green stone holding small garnets and many clear vitreous points. The section is composed of well-marked olivine grains, with the secondary serpentine, magnetite, garnet, picotite or chromite, and diallage. That from the *Quarry* on the Gebersbach is a dark-green serpentine showing olivine grains. In the section the olivine shows various degrees of alteration to an ore-bearing serpentine, forming the usual reticulated network. It also contains diallage and garnet, the latter of which is sometimes altered into chlorite. The serpentine from the *Breitenberg* is of two kinds: one a dark green serpentine, hard and brittle, and carrying garnet, and the other softer, tougher, and wanting garnets. The former answers in character to the Tunnel and Quarry serpentines, while the latter shows the network structure of serpentine, and holds iron ore and enstatite (bastite).*

Kokkino-Nero, Thessaly.

Dark, nearly black compact rock, traversed by strings of yellowish-green fibrous serpentine. In the section it shows the usual network of serpentine associated with altered diallage or enstatite crystals.

Similar to this is a rock from *Polydendri* which contains both altered diallage and enstatite, as well as garnet and picotite grains.

A similar rock from *Neokhori* shows comparatively fresh diallage traversed by fine parallel fissures along which are arranged small needles and plates.†

Between the Rivers Dajao and Cenobi, Province of Santiago, San Domingo.

120 G. A dark-brown rock flecked with greenish spots. Contains a little talc, and is traversed by serpentine veins having greenish borders and a dark central line owing to the iron ore in it. (W. M. Gabb, Collector.)

Section: banded greenish-yellow and black. The greenish-yellow portions are seen to be composed of yellowish pseudomorphs of serpentine after olivine, traversed by fissures and surrounded by a network of whitish fibrous serpentine with the fibres arranged perpendicular to the course of the veinlets. In other portions the remains of some apparent pyroxenic mineral occurs, while elsewhere the serpentinous material is quite compact, but

---

* Neues Jahr. Min., 1876, pp. 239–243.   † Becke, Min. Mitth., 1878 (1), i. 472, 473.

shows to some extent the characters of serpentine replacing olivine. The dark band is formed of irregular masses and grains of iron ore, arranged in the serpentine in a vein-like form. Some of the serpentinous material is isotropic. The structure of a portion of the section is shown in figure 1, Plate VI.

At the foot of the first rise on the ridge, edge of the river on the road from La Vega to Jurabacoa, Province of La Vega, San Domingo.

142 G. A dark reddish-brown compact rock, breaking with a conchoidal fracture. Traversed by some veins of a greenish-white serpentine. Contains many bronze-like crystals of altered enstatite (?). (W. M. Gabb, Collector.)

Section: a brownish and greenish mass composed of serpentine, dolomite, picotite or chromite, and ferrite products. The usual arrangement of the serpentine, in a network following the outlines and fissures of the original olivine grains, is seen; this is marked by veins formed by brown and black dust and grains of ferruginous material mixed with serpentines, having a similar arrangement to that observed in the California peridotites. Bordering these veins is a band of whitish serpentine, which sometimes occupies the entire interspace. In the majority of cases the portions between the veinlets are composed of a greenish-yellow serpentine having the form and outline of the fractured olivine grains.

Lying in the sections are a number of white, greenish, and grayish patches, of the same outline as the pyroxene minerals usually occurring in the peridotites. They enclose rounded portions of the serpentinized olivine; and in part have the fibrous cleavage of enstatite, while in part their structure is irregular. They show aggregate and fibrous polarization as a rule, but occasionally the optical characters of altered enstatite. Picotite or chromite occurs in irregular masses of a black and translucent deep coffee-brown color. Its grains are traversed by fissures and black bands, part of which, in reflected light, show metallic lustre with numerous crystalline facets.

Some dolomite with well-marked cleavage occupies a portion of one section, in the form of irregular somewhat rounded patches. A few veins traverse the mass, having been formed after the main serpentinous alteration of the rock. The whole section is sprinkled with black-brown and yellowish-brown grains, dust, and aggregations of ferruginous material. The structure of this rock is shown in Plate V. figure 4.

Brixlegg, Tyrol.

According to Von Drasche this shows a compact network of magnetic iron grains, with a fibrous serpentine mass, which encloses some remaining grains of olivine and diallage. The serpentine is said beyond question to have resulted from the alteration of olivine and diallage.*

Il Piano, Elba.

A greenish-brown mass traversed by talcose (?) veins, and containing altered enstatite crystals.

Under the microscope it is seen to be composed of brownish, greenish, and yellowish serpentine largely filled with black dust-like granules, having a network structure and

* Min. Mitth., 1871, i. 2. See also E. Hussak, Ibid., 1882 (2), v. 76, 77, who found augite in this rock, and throws some doubt on the correctness of Drasche's work.

cut by talcose (?) veins which are crossed by later chrysotile ones. The enstatite is in part altered to the talc-like material, and in part to serpentine. It is probable that olivine predominated over the enstatite when the rock was unaltered. This was purchased from Voigt and Hochgesang.

Launceston, Tasmania.

5170. A dark green rock, purchased of Ward and Howell, sprinkled with chromite and talc scales. Weathers greenish-white.

Section: greenish-gray with cloudy blotches. Composed of a pale yellowish fibrous serpentine showing brilliant polarization, and altered enstatite crystals, talc scales, and chromite. The talc is grayish-white, of feeble polarization, and usually associated with the iron ore. In some cases it is dichroic, varying from a gray or yellowish-gray to a pale bluish tint. The enstatite in some cases retains its original plane of extinction, although altered to a pale yellowish serpentine mass. The cloudy spots are caused by innumerable grains of iron ore locally concentrated.

Windisch-Matrey, Tyrol.

According to Von Drasche this serpentine is interbedded in a calcareous mica schist. The color varies from a light green to a deep green or brown, and the rock is sprinkled with calcite, asbestos, and chrysotile grains and fibres. Drasche placed the specimens in two divisions.

1. This is an olive-green rock flecked with yellowish-brown spots, and contains diallage, ankerite, and a white scaly mineral with irregular outlines. The section under the microscope shows a groundmass formed from a compact network of a rhombic mineral, which occupies the principal portion of the section. In addition grains of magnetite and diallage were seen. Some talc was also observed.

2. The other variety is a dark-green very fine-grained rock sprinkled with light-green diallage crystals and white talc plates. The section under the microscope is seen to contain the network formed by the rhombic mineral, magnetite arranged in bands, diallage, etc.*

The section in the Whitney collection from Voigt and Hochgesang, from this locality, has the following characters. Color pale green, but broken by veins and spots of black iron ore. In polarized light the section shows the usual structure of a serpentinous rock produced by the alteration of a peridotic one. It contains scales of talc and granular masses of pyrite. Some of the iron ore is in forms resembling the picotite grains in the Lake Lherz rock. These forms are traversed by fissures, and in reflected light it is seen that the ore bordering them is crystalline showing metallic lustre, while the remaining portions do not present these characters. The talc is so arranged that it appears to have arisen from the conversion of enstatite material. The rock apparently contained originally olivine, enstatite, and picotite at least. The section is traversed by veins of serpentine and talcose material.

St. Sabine, Vosges, France.

5169. A greenish-black compact rock, weathering grayish-brown.

Section: pale green, and composed of serpentine in which a few altered enstatite grains were observed. A few nodules occur which are formed in the interior of grayish

---

* Min. Mitth., 1871, i. 3–8. See also E. Hussak, Ibid., 1882 (2), v. 78–80.

fibrous material having a feeble polarization and containing irregular brownish-yellow spots, which affect polarized light more than the enclosing material does. The exterior portion of these nodules is formed of pyroxene granules (diallage) somewhat serpentinized with irregular grains of a deep-green color and isotropic, — picotaste.

River Oisain, Timor.

Dr. A. Wichmann describes from the River Oisain a serpentine of a dark bluish-gray color, porphyritically holding bronzite crystals and small grains of calcite.

Microscopically the serpentine has the usual mesh structure, and contains within its interstices colorless patches showing aggregate polarization. Opaque grains of iron ore are common. The bronzite is altered, and contains along the cleavage lines a blackish-brown aggregate of minute plates as well as black needles. Chromite in brown translucent grains, and calcite also, were seen.*

Range 11, Rivière des Plantes, Canada.

According to Mr. Frank D. Adams, this serpentine contains a few remains of a rhombic pyroxene (enstatite), which are slightly pleochroic and have numerous black needles arranged parallel to the cleavage and rhombic axis.†

Melbourne, Canada.

According to the preceding observer, this rock is of a dark-green color, and composed of a serpentine mass containing some irregular fragments of a rhombic pyroxene (enstatite). These show pleochroism varying from green to a reddish color, and have a well-marked cleavage or fibrous structure.†

Galicia, Spain.

The serpentines of this country are composed, according to Macpherson, principally of serpentine produced from the alteration of olivine, and holding the remains of enstatite or diallage crystals, etc.‡

High Bridge, Hunterdon Co., New Jersey.

1403. A mottled rock of black and oil-green, having a reticulated and somewhat banded structure. The powder of the rock is attracted by the magnet, and tests show the presence of chromium.

Section: greenish-white with black and dirty-brown spots. The least altered portions are the dark spots, with their included crystal forms. The spots show the structure in common and polarized light of serpentinized olivine, while the crystal forms present a cleavage similar to that of some enstatite, but more like that of diallage. Both spots and crystals are now completely changed to serpentinous material. The main mass of the section is white, slightly tinged in places with a pale yellowish-green color. It is traversed by fissures, and contains much disseminated iron ore in dust, grains, and irregular aggregations. In common light this groundmass shows but little evidence of its origin, but in polarized light there is distinctly revealed the usual network of serpentine fibres when formed from the alteration of an olivine rock. The story of the change can

---

* Samml. Geol. Mus. Leiden, 1884, ii. 105–110.   ‡ Anal. Soc. Esp. Hist. Nat., 1881, x. 50–53.
† Report of Progress; Geol. Survey of Canada, 1880, -81, -82, p. 19 A.

be read as clearly as in those rocks which are only partially altered. The picture was there; the polarized light served as the developer only. Figures 5 and 6, Plate V., show the structure of this rock.

1404, from the same locality as the preceding, is a greenish- and brownish-black rock, with lighter greenish spots, and coated with light greenish serpentine on "slickenside" surfaces.

Section: a yellowish and gray mass sprinkled with black spots of iron ore and in places traversed by a reticulated network of the same. It is composed principally of serpentine containing crystals and granules of iron ore, besides being traversed in much of its mass by the network of the same. It is also stained brownish-yellow by oxide of iron. In portions of the section are grayish spots, which sometimes show in their interior greenish grains. These interior grains are remnants of the original olivine, while the gray portions are formed of the serpentinized olivine traversed by numerous fissures filled with innumerable dust-like granules. The iron ore in a few points is feebly translucent, and in part shows no metallic reflection, but it is traversed by bands that do show the metallic lustre. Therefore it is probably a mixture of chromite and magnetite, which appear to be commonly associated in the majority of serpentines. The general structure is represented in figure 5, Plate IV.

1567 is a rock that in the hand specimens appears to be the same as No. **1404,** but no sections of it have been prepared.

1563, from the same locality,* is very similar to No. **1403,** but is more altered and weathered. It contains chromite and talc. It has a yellowish-green groundmass of serpentine traversed by innumerable reticulated veinlets of a dark green to black serpentine. These veinlets give a structure to the rock that might be taken by some for stratification.

Section: a grayish-green mass formed of translucent, feebly polarizing, grayish, finely granular serpentinous material, traversed by a network of innumerable veins of clear, more or less brilliantly polarizing serpentine. Much chromite occurs in irregular pronged masses, grains, and heaps of grains, principally arranged along the serpentine veins. While some may be original or else picotite altered *in situ*, the chief portion appears to be of secondary origin in the serpentine.

1564, from the same locality, is a dark-greenish rock filled with talc scales and weathering to a yellowish rust-like product, with the talc masses protruding from the surface. This talc forms crystalline masses similar to those formed by chlorite.

The section is an irregular mixture of pale yellowish serpentine and grayish-white talc with iron ore. The ore is principally associated with the talc, forming bands along the cleavage planes. The talc plates are partly isotropic and partly feebly polarizing, and are colorless or gray. The structure and relations of the serpentine and talc are such as to indicate that the serpentine has replaced the olivine, and the talc the pyroxene minerals.

Zöblitz, Saxony.

5001. A mixed reticulated greenish and brownish-red rock, containing roundish reddish-black to black spots.

Section: greenish- and brownish-red with grayish-black spots. The principal portion of the section is serpentine. This shows the reticulated structure in common and polarized light, frequently having between the colorless meshes greenish patches repre-

---

* All the High Bridge, New Jersey, serpentines were the gift of Mr. S. H. Dean.

senting the portions of the olivine last altered. In some portions the section is filled with reticulated veins of brown and cherry-red hematite. The dark spots are owing to portions being filled with innumerable granules of iron ore, arranged about some central lines, much like iron filings about the poles of a magnet. Talc fibres are common. Chrysotile veins cut the section in various directions.

From trail below Chip Flat, Sierra Co., Cal.

45 P. The specimens are green and more or less rubbed or "slickensided," as are the great majority of serpentine rocks. The only section is of a pale yellowish-green color traversed by black bands of iron ore. The serpentine shows a coarsely aggregate and fibrous polarization, and appears from its structure to replace, in part at least, olivine and enstatite. The ore crystals are octahedrons, some of which are translucent either as a whole or on the edges. The translucent portions are reddish-brown, and the opacity does not seem to depend upon the size, since some comparatively large crystals are translucent, while very minute ones are often opaque.

40 P. Similar to the preceding. This rock occurs apparently in two bands, enclosing slate, according to the collector, Professor W. H. Pettee.[*]

119 P. is of similar character. In the interior it is compact, massive, and dark, but on the exterior smoothed and coated with greenish and light greenish-yellow serpentine.

Depot Hill, near Camptonville, Sierra Co., California.

35 P. A compact greenish-gray rock with irregular bluish-black spots, and traversed by chrysotile veins.

Section: a compact grayish and greenish-yellow mass, composed principally of serpentine with iron ore, and dolomite. From the structure of the serpentine and the arrangement of the iron ore, it is probable that olivine and enstatite were former constituents of this rock, which was only found in a boulder.[†]

From a belt four hundred feet wide, between Whiskey Diggings and Hepsidam, Plumas Co., California.

89 P. A bluish-black and greenish mottled rock, showing a reticulated structure. It is traversed by yellowish-green serpentine veins.

Section: a gray groundmass spotted by magnetite and traversed by veins of magnetite and yellow serpentine. The groundmass has been so entirely changed to serpentine, showing the usual network structure, that none of the original silicates were observed. So far as can be judged from the structure, the rock originally contained olivine and enstatite, at least. Figure 5 of Plate VI. shows its present structure and the serpentine veins which traverse it.[‡]

Finland.

According to Lagorio, the Finland serpentine forms a fibrous mass of yellowish-gray to green color, showing the usual network (Maschenstructur). It contains no olivine grains, but some fissured ones of dolomite or calcite. The microscopic structure is very finely fibrous, and it forms masses in a limestone.[§]

[*] Aurif. Gravels, p. 434.   [†] Ibid., p. 429.   [‡] Ibid., p. 451.
[§] Micro. Analyse Ostbaltischer Gebirgsarten, 1876, p. 48.

Klopfberg, Austria.

This rock, according to Dr. F. Becke, is a light green to dark porous soft stone, bearing long, colorless tremolite crystals, chrome-bearing magnetic ore, and numerous soft silver-white talc scales. The rock is greatly altered, and in the section shows the usual network, arising from the alteration of olivine, which in the darker stone still exists in single grains, but in the light green specimens the olivine has disappeared, and grains of a rhombic carbonate appear in its place.*

Nezeros, Thessaly.

A dark, nearly black rock, rich in chromite, has been described by Dr. F. Becke as showing in the thin section the usual mesh structure formed by the serpentine and iron ores. It also contains a little colorless actinolite, possessing the prismatic cleavage of hornblende.†

Fatu Temanu, Timor.

A dark bluish-green rock with light green spots and magnetite grains. Microscopically this serpentine evidently was derived from olivine, and it shows a characteristic network especially marked through the arrangement of the ore particles which form the medial lines. Bordering them are light green bands enclosing the darker-colored interstitial portion. Much chrysotile occurs, and a whitish-green picrolite, forming in the section a finely fibrous cloudy mass.‡

Four miles from Westfield Centre, Westfield, Massachusetts.

1073. Section: greenish-yellow with grayish-white spots, and traversed by an irregular network formed from dust, grains, and crystals of black iron ore. The serpentine in polarized light shows aggregate and fibrous characters, while dolomite occurs sprinkled through much of the section's mass. The grayish spots seem to be formed of dolomite mixed with serpentine and talc.

The hand specimen is a dark grayish-black rock, with light greenish irregular patches of serpentine, talc, and dolomite. This structure is similar to that of the other specimens, **1074, 1075, 1076, 1077, 1078,** and **1079.** In the weathered surface forms the talc is better crystallized, showing its normal structure, while the dolomite is more abundant and better marked. In these specimens every gradation can be traced between the light-greenish serpentinous coloid-like masses to the well-differentiated aggregations of talc plates. These specimens show clearly the production of talc, dolomite, and serpentine from the metamorphosis of peridotites.

This rock (**1073**) weathers to a rough deep-pitted surface, colored grayish and coated with lichens. Here the difference is strongly marked between the internal molecular alterations and the superficial surface weathering.

I have been greatly indebted to the kindness of Mr. S. H. Dean, of High Bridge, N. J., for this and many others of the serpentines of Eastern North America described here.

1074. This section is similar to that of No. **1073.** The iron ore forms in places

---

* Min. Mitth., 1882 (2), iv. 341-343. † Min. Mitth., 1878 (1), i. 470-472.
‡ Wichmann, Jaarb. Mijnw. N. O. 1., 1882, pp. 214-216.

quite a rectangular grating, and much talc is present in curved and bent fibrous masses. The general structure of this section is shown in figure 2, Plate VII.

1081, also from Mr. S. H. Dean, was obtained by him from the bed of the Westfield River in Russell, Massachusetts. This is a leek-green serpentine, containing grains of chromite and closely resembling that from Chester and Texas, Pennsylvania. No section.

Lynnfield, Massachusetts.

1087. Section: pale yellowish-green, mottled with spots of clear grayish-white and with dust and grains of iron ore. In common light under the microscope, the greenish portion shows the dirty green spots commonly seen, formed from the alteration of the unfissured central portion of the olivine grains. In polarized light it shows the common reticulated meshwork of most alteration serpentine. The clear grayish-white portions are formed of interlacing and divergent fibres and plates, optically orthorhombic, and polarizing with clear, beautiful tints, varying from yellowish-white to yellow and red. The iron ore is crystalline granular, opaque, has but little lustre, and resembles chromite. The forms of the larger grains resemble those of picotite when only partially altered. The general structure is shown in Plate VI. figure 2.

The hand specimen is a dark grayish-green compact rock, mottled with black iron ore and talc scales. This specimen was kindly presented to the collection by Professor N. S. Shaler. Later the locality has been visited by Professor J. D. Whitney and myself, and other specimens answering in general characters to the above were obtained. While this serpentine is much jointed, no evidence of stratification was seen, and it was apparent that the approximately parallel jointing had been taken for stratification by previous observers. No contacts with the adjacent rock could be found. In a pit near the quarry the rock is a mottled dark grayish-black one, which in thin splinters is dark green.

A serpentine of much finer quality and of a dark green color, was found outcropping by the side of the road to the northwest. A dark green much broken and fissured serpentine outcrops opposite C. W. Horsey's blacksmith's shop, in Peabody, on the road near the line between that town and Lynnfield. While no definite field evidence regarding its origin could be obtained, the general appearance of the outcrops was that of an eruptive mass metamorphosed, nothing being observed that indicated either chemical or mechanical sedimentation.*

The Lynnfield serpentine shows when tested the presence of chromium, and the rock powder is magnetic.

From the road between La Vega and Jarabacoa, at the first crossing of the River Joa going from the former town, Province of La Vega, San Domingo.

141 G. This is a much altered foliated rock, composed essentially of light greenish-white and yellowish darker green serpentine. The foliated structure appears to be entirely due to the alteration and pressure to which the rock has been subjected. No section was made of this rock. Collected by W. M. Gabb.

* See also Crosby, Occas. Papers, Bost. Soc. Nat. Hist., 1880, iii. 115; Hitchcock, Final Report, Geol. Mass., 1841, p. 159.

Newport, Vermont.

95. This rock was collected by Mr. J. H. Huntington, near Mr. C. Gilpin's residence. It is a grayish-green rock having a greenish serpentine groundmass, holding grayish and brownish masses and crystals of a ferruginous carbonate, showing well-marked rhombohedral cleavage.

Section: a gray mass traversed and sprinkled with black iron ore. Composed of a coarsely fibrous serpentine, a dirty gray, feebly polarizing carbonate showing well-marked rhombohedral cleavage, and iron ore. The serpentine forms the principal portion of the section.

Celinac, Austria.

A light-green rock containing dark particles of amorphous silica. The section shows the usual network of serpentine with isotropic silica and picotite.*

Texas, Pennsylvania.

A clear leek-green serpentine, obtained from W. J. Knowlton, 169 Tremont Street, Boston, containing chromic iron in veins and crystals, or scattered granules.

Section: clear and grayish-white, with black spots of chromic iron. The clear portions show the fibrous polarization of serpentine, some of the fibres being distinctly optically orthorhombic in character. In the grayish portion lie plates and fibres of tremolite; while the chromite is opaque in transmitted light, except in the thinnest portions, which are translucent and reddish-brown. By reflected light the grains are dull, and without lustre. The larger grains are traversed by fissures filled with serpentine. A grain of pyrite was observed.

Chester, Pennsylvania.

1487. A clear leek-green compact rock containing grains of chromite. Weathers yellowish and greenish-gray. Section: clear grayish-white fibrous mass showing the usual aggregate fibrous polarization.

This and the preceding one show the extreme change in rocks to pure serpentine.

VARIETY.— **Porodite.**

Fatu Luka, Timor.

Large, rounded pieces of serpentine cemented by pale-whitish and finely spherulitic opal and a greenish paste. The serpentine is yellowish and grass-green, and shows the mesh structure. The history of these altered fragments is summed up by Wichmann as follows:— 1. The formation of the peridotite. 2. The formation of the serpentine, including the separation of the iron ore and the beginning of the *Maschenstructur*. 3. The decomposition of the iron ore and the formation of the yellow network. 4. The impregnation of the interstitial portion with the alteration-product,— chromite. 5. The alteration of the exterior into a finely fibrous compact gray substance.

The cement is mostly serpentine with a fine scaly material.†

---
* C. v. John. Jahr. Geol. Reichs., 1880, xxx. 449.   † Jaarb. Mijnw. N. O. I., 1882, pp. 216-222.

Strand, Timor.

Another porodite of similar character was described by Wichmann as a greatly decomposed fragmental rock, composed of rounded and angular fragments of dirty-brown and brownish-green serpentine, cemented by a sometimes lighter, sometimes darker, dirty-brown and greenish-brown mass. Microscopically this serpentine is similar to the preceding, but is more altered. The interior portion of some of the grains is filled with a dirty-brown hydrated oxide of iron.

Another porodite from *Fatu Luka, Timor*, was described by the same author as a dirty light-brown and brownish-green tufaceous rock with numerous serpentine and phæstine (enstatite) fragments. The rock effervesces feebly with acid. The serpentine shows under the microscope a network structure especially of the iron ore, while the interior grains are greenish. A somewhat altered bronzite containing ore grains occurs. The cement is of a brownish shade, homogeneous and isotropic.[*]

SECTION V. — *Peridotite.* — *Its Macroscopic Characters.*

THE meteoric forms show in general a fine, more or less granular groundmass of some shade of gray — varying from a light gray or grayish-white to a bluish or dark gray. Often they are porphyritic from enclosed chondri, pyrrhotite, and metallic iron. Again they are apt to show brownish-yellow spots of ferruginous staining, owing to the oxidation of the iron ores. The grayish color appears to be mainly due to the finely divided state of the component silicates, as well as to the natural color of the base and the enstatite. The olivine is in too minute grains to show its characteristic color, except in rare cases. The chondri frequently appear as gray, brown, bluish, and white grains in the groundmass, giving the appearance of a fragmental structure to the rock.

The completely or coarsely crystalline forms, like those from Estherville and Chassigny, present a gray to pale yellow crystalline mass closely resembling that of the least altered terrestrial peridotites if not identical with it.

The iron ores occur as irregular masses, sometimes of a semi-sponge-like structure, and in the form of metallic iron, pyrrhotite, chromite, and magnetite.

While the silicates are not usually sufficiently distinct to be determined macroscopically, yet they sometimes are, and olivine in such cases shows in pale green or yellowish grains, having a conchoidal fracture and the same general characters this mineral has when it is of terrestrial origin.

[*] Jaarb. Mijnw. N. O. I., 1882, pp. 216–222.

It has been above stated that the least altered of the terrestrial peridotites present an appearance and structure essentially similar to the meteorite of Chassigny and the portions of that from Estherville which are comparatively free from iron. They are of a grayish-green or green color, crystalline granular in structure, and usually contain more or less dark grains of picotite or some iron ore, disseminated throughout the mass. The first traces of change are in coloration, passing from a green to a yellowish-green, yellowish, and to a yellowish- or rusty-brown. The rocks are more or less vitreous or greasy in lustre. With increasing alteration, a reddish-brown to grayish-brown color predominates; and this finally passes into a dark greenish-black to black compact rock, somewhat resembling the basalts, but of a duller color, more resinous lustre, and more compact, as well as of a higher specific gravity and less hardness.

The crystalline granular groundmass of olivine or serpentine may or may not porphyritically enclose crystals and grains of enstatite, diallage, and augite. These minerals usually appear as greenish, grayish, or bronze-like crystals and grains scattered in the rock. They commonly weather to bronze-like, more or less cleavable and platy forms; and even on the fresh fracture of some specimens show in certain lights as an irregular network, brightly reflecting the light, and holding in its meshes the dark-greenish altered olivine.

The olivine groundmass when altered presents under the lens the appearance of yellowish or grayish granules cut and surrounded by a fine reticulated network of a darker material (serpentine); but when the change has progressed further, the groundmass becomes compact and apparently homogeneous.

As the more highly altered states are reached, the variations in the macroscopic appearance become exceedingly numerous; so much so, that only a few of them can be mentioned here. The color generally is some shade of green, varying from a dark green or greenish-black to a yellowish-green. Sometimes it is reddish (brownish- or cherry-red), owing to the state of its ferruginous contents. The pyroxene minerals, when occurring, vary in amount of alteration from the porphyritically sprinkled bronze- or copper-like crystals to silvery-white, and to grayish and greenish forms, which in turn pass into patches of serpentine of a deeper green color and more compact texture than the groundmass, but which finally become completely blended with, and entirely lost in, the serpentine groundmass. Oftentimes the pyroxene minerals are replaced by greenish to whitish talcose material and talc scales. In the process of alteration, segregations of serpentine, dolomite, magnetite, chromite, etc., occur, giving rise to veins of serpentine (chrysotile) and to veins and nodular masses of dolomite and iron ores lying in or traversing the serpentinous groundmass.

However dark the altered peridotites may be in color, the thin splinters, as a rule, are translucent and transmit a greenish or yellowish light. The more or less serpentinized peridotites are traversed by fissures, which are most abundant in those entirely changed to serpentine. The sides of these fissures usually are polished or coated with serpentine, talc, etc., forming "slickensides"; which, it is conceived, may have some connection with the chemical alteration of the rock itself.

Amongst the various forms produced by the extreme changes are a yellowish, more or less gummy-looking substance, and a grayish, yellowish, to chrome-green translucent serpentine. While these are oftentimes produced from the alteration of the rock *in situ*, they also appear to be formed by migrated serpentinous material, and in such cases to belong to the veinstones. These secondary massive products contain more or less iron ore in the form of chromite or magnetite. It is to these nearly pure serpentines, which result from the complete change or migration of the material, that the term *serpentine*, as it is used in works on mineralogy, properly applies. But from the general and microscopic characters of the material known as *serpentine* in lithology, it would appear that under that name is placed a mineral of variable composition, forming a series like feldspar or pyroxene, or else several distinct minerals are now so placed.

Further, in the process of alteration there often results a fissile or schistose structure, giving rise to a pseudo-lamination. In part this seems to be owing to the segregation of chrysotile, serpentine, iron ores, dolomite, etc., in approximately parallel lines; and in this case the fissility is often only apparent and not real. Sometimes the schistosity seems to be due to pressure during the time of alteration. Occasionally the rock has a brecciated or conglomerate structure, owing to the vein serpentine or dolomite surrounding less altered portions of the rock. With the formation of talc or actinolite in these altered peridotites, the transition to a true schist is evinced by various gradations, until a true talc schist or actinolite schist results. These schists are greenish in their normal condition, but often through decomposition of the iron, become stained and present a rusty brown and gray aspect closely simulating many mica schists.

Owing to the production of dolomite, there results, in part at least, ophicalcites and dolomitic limestones — the purity depending on the amount of alteration, and on the materials both carried into and removed from the rock during the process of alteration. These dolomitic limestones are usually gray, green, or yellow, but sometimes of quite a clear grayish-white color, and crystalline in structure. In the above, only a portion of the various forms produced in the process of alteration so common in peridotic rocks could be mentioned; but it is hoped that enough has been given to afford some idea of the general appearance of these rocks macroscopically.

Of necessity, from the mode of origin of the peridotites and their exposure to detrital agencies, various detrital or poroditic forms must result. Undoubtedly, when they are re-consolidated, it is exceedingly difficult to distinguish these true breccias, conglomerates, and sandstones from the pseudo-fragmental forms of similar structure that are produced in this rock species, as in every other, by the filling of fissures, or by the dissolving of portions of the rock and their replacement by other material, while interstitial portions of the rock remain *in situ*. The poroditic forms of the peridotites, so far as now known, are all of a serpentinous character, having been greatly altered; but it is suspected, and in many cases claimed, that other forms are of like detrital origin; however, conclusive proof of this is still wanting.

It is probable that part of our ophicalcites and brecciated serpentines are of a poroditic origin, while others appear to have been produced by changes in the massive rock *in situ;* that is, they do not properly belong to the fragmental rocks to which they are generally assigned. It is proposed here to distinguish these falsely appearing detrital forms by the terms pseudo-breccias, conglomerates, and sandstones; or, collectively, as pseudo-fragmental or detrital rocks; or, better still, by the introduction of the term *merotile* ($\mu\acute{\epsilon}\rho o\varsigma$, $\lambda\acute{\iota}\theta o\varsigma$), and its adjective form *merotitic*, for them, since they are composed of detached portions of the same rock.

SECTION VI. — *Peridotite.* — *Its Microscopic Characters.*

BEGINNING with the meteoric peridotites, the first variety is composed of rounded fissured olivine grains with brownish glass inclusions, brownish interstitial glass, and scattered crystals of chromite. In the next type enstatite enters as a constituent, and the chondritic structure appears. The groundmass is of a grayish color sprinkled with iron, pyrrhotite, and brownish ferruginous spots; and is composed of grains and crystals of olivine, enstatite, chromite, iron, and base, enclosing larger masses of these minerals and chondri. The base is fibrous-granular in structure, and varies from a light to a dark ash-gray, while it occurs with every gradation, from that not affecting polarized light to that in which the differentiation has been carried to such an extent that it shows a feeble coloration in this light, and at best is only a semi-base. The chondri are composed of olivine and base, enstatite and base, and enstatite, olivine, and base; all being more or less associated with iron ores, and generally passing gradually into the adjoining groundmass. The olivine chondri usually contain a darker base than the enstatite chondri, and are composed of grains and crystals of olivine cemented by the base, which in some cases produces forms somewhat resembling organized structures (Plate II. figure 4). The enstatite chondri show, like the olivine ones, a more or less spherical form. The enstatite chondri are usually composed of fan-like, eccentrically radiating ribs of enstatite cemented by the lighter gray fibrous base, and they sometimes simulate superficially certain organized structures (Plate II. figure 6; Plate III. figure 1). The olivine and enstatite chondri are composed of granules and crystals of enstatite and olivine cemented by the base (Plate II. figure 5).

The olivine of the meteorites is usually clear or pale greenish, although often stained by ferruginous material along its fissures. It is more or less fissured, contains inclusions of glass and iron ores, and generally is in rounded grains, and but rarely in well-defined crystals.

The enstatite is in grains and crystals, which are clear and transparent, but which sometimes display a faint green tinge, and contain glass inclusions. The mineral shows as a rule one longitudinal approximately parallel cleavage, with sometimes another — or a cross fracture — at right angles to the first cleavage (Plate III. figure 6). The iron is in irregular grains, having in the section in reflected light an appearance nearly like ground steel (Plate II. figures 4, 5, 6; Plate III. figure 3). Sometimes the iron is quite dark, and is united with pyrrhotite and possibly magnetite (Plate III. figures 2, 3, 4, 5, 6; Plate IV. figure 1). The pyrrhotite shows a dark bronze color and a rough granulated surface in reflected light, and frequently surrounds grains of metallic iron (Plate III. figure 3). The common ferruginous staining and the granular structure of the groundmass is shown to a greater or less extent in all the figures of meteoric peridotites given in the plates.

The chromite or picotite occurs in dark-brown to black, opaque to translucent grains and octahedrons.

An entirely crystalline form of saxonite occurs in the Manbhoom (India) meteorite, which Tschermak has described as composed of a greenish-yellow granular mixture, in which bronzite and olivine have a nearly equal color. Besides these, there are numerous grains of pyrrhotite and little grains of iron. In the thin section granular olivine is seen to be the principal constituent. This is traversed by fissures, and has few inclusions. Bronzite occurs in rounded or elongated grains, with a fibrous structure, and both it and the olivine have a pale-green color. Further, the rock contains colorless grains of plagioclase (?) and roundish opaque pyrrhotite and iron grains.*

The next variety is formed by the addition of diallage, but otherwise the structure remains the same. The diallage shows not only the common longitudinal cleavage, but it is also much cut by an irregular augitic cleavage, thus enabling its ready separation from enstatite in some cases. It otherwise is closely like the enstatite in its general characters and in its inclusions (Plate III. figures 5, 6).

Sometimes the lherzolite variety of the meteoric peridotites is found to be entirely crystalline, and in this case the chondri and base are wanting, and the rock is composed of a crystalline granular aggregate of olivine, enstatite, diallage, iron, pyrrhotite, and chromite. In this the olivine contains irregular masses and globules of iron; while the enstatite and diallage have the same inclusions, not only of iron, but also of olivine grains.

In the next type augite is added, but it makes no essential change in the general characters of the rock. In some of the peridotic meteorites, plagioclastic and possibly orthoclastic feldspar, peckhamite, schreibersite, graphite, etc., occur in subordinate quantities.

The microscopic study of meteorites is yet so incomplete that it is possible that other types and characters may be later added.

In two cases a fragmental or brecciated structure has been seen, giving us tufaceous meteorites, which, otherwise than this, show the common chondritic characters.

* Die mikros. Besch. meteoriten, 1883, i. 10; Sitz. Wien. Akad., 1883, lxxxviii. (1), 362, 363.

In the terrestrial peridotites we commence with *dunite* — a clear granular mass of fissured olivine grains, which are either colorless or slightly tinged yellow or green. Sprinkled through the olivine mass are dark to brownish, opaque to translucent, grains and crystals of chromite or picotite, and magnetite, as well as sometimes a few enstatite plates, either colorless or of a greenish tinge (Plate IV. figure 2).

In these a gradual change to serpentine begins by its production along the fissures of the olivine, forming a yellowish or greenish network, and this change goes on until the olivine is completely altered, and only the network structure remains (Plate IV. figures 3, 4; Plate V. figures 1, 2, 4; Plate VI. figure 2). Again the change extends so far that not even this trace of the original structure remains (Plate VI. figures 5, 6; Plate VII. figure 2). In the process of alteration to serpentine, that formed first along the fissures generally takes a different structure and color from that later produced by the alteration of the interior portion of the olivine grains — thus showing two, and sometimes three, stages in the progress of alteration. While the mode of alteration is thus conspicuous in the earlier stages, the final result is to produce a pure, clear, homogeneous serpentine, of a uniform yellowish or greenish tint, or even colorless; in which no trace remains of the original structure, to tell its derivation. The proof of these changes is found in following out the various gradations in the different peridotites, particularly in different portions of the same rock-mass.

By the gradual increase in the amount of enstatite present, we pass into the succeeding variety — *saxonite*, and this again, by the addition of diallage, gradually passes into the *lherzolite* variety, and this into the succeeding form (*buchnerite*) by the addition of augite. Again, we pass gradually to those forms in which the enstatite has disappeared, and only diallage (*eulysite*) or augite (*picrite*) remains with the olivine to form the rock. Every gradation exists between these forms, and they are closely allied in physical and chemical characters.

The enstatite appears as a clear, colorless mineral, or else as one slightly tinged with green. Sometimes it occupies a subordinate portion of the rock, then again it forms the chief part, holding the olivine inclosed in and subordinate to it. The enstatite is sometimes feebly pleochroic, and shows a well-marked longitudinal cleavage; the development of which, instead of forming a smooth fracture, usually occasions the tearing of a rough line, with stringy fibres extending from one side to the other. Besides the longitudinal cleavage, a cross fracture, at right angles to the principal cleavage, is often present.

The diallage possesses similar characters to the enstatite, and generally is undistinguishable from the latter except optically, but sometimes it shows two cleavages approaching those of augite, breaking the surface into rough, irregular rhombs, which serve to distinguish the diallage in question from enstatite. Again, diallage has not only its proper longitudinal cleavage, but also the well-marked cleavage of augite. This fact indicates that there is no real distinction between diallage and augite, but both form a continuous series.

The augite is pale-yellow or brown, shows its characteristic cleavage, and is sometimes feebly pleochroic. It occurs in grains and crystals, and sometimes encloses olivine grains.

Since the olivine, octahedral oxides, and their alteration-products in the varieties of peridotite are like those in the first-described variety, it remains simply to trace the alterations in these varieties as they are modified by the addition of other minerals than olivine. The pyroxene minerals, as a rule, are less liable to alteration than olivine, and are frequently determinable after the olivine has been entirely changed. This is indicated in Plate IV. figure 6, and in Plate VI. figures 3 and 4. The enstatite usually shows its alteration by the formation of a greenish product along its cleavage planes (Plate V. figure 3; Plate VII. figure 1). As the alteration progresses, the pyroxene minerals are transformed into a yellowish or grayish serpentinous mass, which may show aggregate polarization, or may retain that of the mineral from which it has been derived.

The various changes in the peridotites can perhaps be best followed from the plates. In Plate IV., figure 1 indicates a typical dunite composed of unchanged olivine grains, with only a cloudiness produced by the fissures by which the mass is traversed. Figure 3 shows another dunite containing brown picotites and exhibiting the formation of greenish and yellowish serpentine along the fissures of the olivine, with sometimes a complete serpentinization of the interstitial olivine grains. Figure 4 shows a saxonite in which the alteration to greenish serpentine has progressed so far as to leave only a subordinate portion of clear olivine grains untouched. Part of the enstatite has been changed to serpentine, while part is only partially altered, as shown in the upper left-hand portion of the figure.

In Plate V. figure 1, is shown the commencement of alteration in a lherzolite, in which the olivine and pyroxene minerals assume a gray tinge, and the whole mass is traversed by brown veins bearing iron dust along the medial line. Figure 2 shows further progress in the change; the brown veins increase in number and strength, and the ferruginous medial line becomes more strongly marked. Bordering these veins are bands of yellow serpentine, which in their turn are fringed on the inner side by orange, yellow, and brown serpentine, which again encloses grains of the still unaltered olivine. In figure 4 the change has progressed still further. The same brown veins with their ferruginous backbone are to be seen, but the yellow serpentine has engrossed the remainder, cutting out the orange-yellow serpentine and the still unchanged olivine grains seen in figure 2. Towards the base of figure 4 and on the right and left are to be seen the remains of two partly-altered grayish pyroxenes. Plate VI. figure 4 shows a still further change; in which the brown veins and the interstitial portions are only distinguished by slight shades of color. Inclosed in this is an enstatite, which retains its characteristic optical characters, but still it is altered and filled in by magnetite grains, which have separated out during the process of alteration. Figure 2 shows still farther change, in which the brown veins are only represented by their intermedial line of magnetite dust, which is bordered by a pale-yellowish or nearly colorless serpentine, holding interstitial rounded patches of serpentine, representing the last-altered olivine cores.

Plate V. figure 3 shows the mode of alteration in the enstatite, taken from the same section as figure 2. At the left and right of the upper portion of the figure are to be observed portions of the altered olivine mass as shown in figure 2, while a yellowish serpentine vein joins the two parts, and cuts the enstatite. Along the cleavage-planes of the enstatite the greenish and yellowish secondary product extends, while the intermediary portions are unchanged. Plate VII. figure 1 represents a still greater change in a crystal of enstatite from the same section. The colors are deeper, and fewer unchanged, intermediary portions exist, while the cross cleavage is well shown by the yellowish-green serpentine bands following its planes.

In Plate V. figure 5, we see the remains of serpentinized diallage crystals, showing optically the characters of serpentine surrounded by brown bands and all inclosed in pale-yellow and colorless serpentine. In figure 6 is shown another portion of the same section, in which the change has proceeded to a greater extent, leaving only the brown serpentinous masses to represent the altered minerals. Figure 1, Plate VI., shows a similar change. The figure at its base possesses a character similar to that of figure 4, but in the remaining portion is composed of clear, colorless serpentine, holding iron ores and yellowish serpentine pseudomorphs after olivine grains.

Figure 3 represents a serpentinized peridotite containing rejected iron ores and in the central portion the remains of enstatite crystals. In figure 5 we have an entire alteration of the rock to a light or colorless serpentine, filled with the precipitated iron ores, and traversed by yellow veins of serpentine. In figure 6 is to be seen a portion of the same section as that shown in figure 3. This is traversed by a yellowish, obliquely-banded, serpentine vein, while the adjacent bordering serpentine is filled with the ferruginous products rejected during the process of the formation of the serpentine vein. Plate VII. figure 2 shows a peridotite in which the change has gone so far that no trace remains of the original structure, while the precipitated ferruginous products largely assume the form of a rectangular grating in the yellow serpentine.

In figure 3 of the same plate, is shown an altered lherzolite in which enstatite forms the groundwork, inclosing the olivine. The enstatite shows the usual greenish alteration along the cleavage planes and throughout much of the interstitial portions. The olivine is chiefly distinguished by the rejection of large quantities of magnetite dust on the borders of the grains and their fissures. Sometimes the separation of the ferruginous material in this form has been carried so far as to render the olivine grains nearly or quite opaque. Figure 4 shows a further change in this lherzolite, in which the enstatite is partly replaced by greenish serpentinous material, and partly by dolomite and other secondary products. The olivine is altered and in part replaced by serpentine, magnetite, etc., although portions yet remain unchanged. Figure 5 indicates a still further alteration in this lherzolite, and one in which the enstatite and part of the olivine have been replaced by a groundmass of granular dolomite. The olivine grains now appear only in the greenish and brownish pseudomorphs after that mineral, inclosed in the dolomite groundmass. Figure 6 shows a yellowish secondary serpentine mass with inclosed colorless grains of unaltered olivine, and, so far as this portion of the section is concerned, is closely like that shown in Plate IV. figure 4, except in the former the serpentine is yellow, and in the latter it is green. But in addition, there occur in the serpentine, in the above-mentioned figure 6, gray and brownish particles and grains of secondary dolomite that evidently have replaced a portion of the groundmass, and in other parts of the section have produced an ophicalcite.

An interesting series of lherzolites is shown in the first five figures of Plate VIII. In figure 1 is represented a groundmass of enstatite enclosing fissured and unaltered olivine grains holding picotite. The pyroxene mineral is but slightly changed, showing this in one greenish band — extending a little distance from one of the upper olivines — also in the yellowish-brown tinge of the whole mass. We next pass into a form (fig. 2) in which the pyroxene minerals are more changed and of a deeper brownish color, while the boundaries between them and the olivine are less distinct. Again, the separation of the iron ore-dust along the fissures and borders of the olivines becomes strongly marked, and a series of black ore-bands extends across the lower portion of the section. In figure 3 the alteration is seen to be still greater, the color of the pyroxenes higher, and their cleavage planes nearly obliterated ; while in some cases a bluish border extends between them and the olivine grains. The olivines are much altered to a greenish serpentine, showing its network formation along the fissures, and with the iron ores holding in the interstices some still unaltered portions of olivine. However, in some of the grains the whole mass has been replaced by serpentine. Here, as elsewhere, it can be seen that while iron ores are the first products formed during the progress of the chemical changes which lead to the production of serpentine, these ores either disappear during the subsequent changes, or else are aggregated together in collections of greater or less size.

Figure 4 shows a still further progress in the alteration, the pyroxenes being greatly changed and in some parts replaced by a grayish mineral, as shown on the left of the centre. Only a very few portions of the olivine have escaped the general alteration to a yellowish serpentine, while the original fissures of the olivine are shown by the arrangement of the remnants of the ore bands. In figure 5 the alteration of the rock has progressed still further, the pyroxenes being entirely changed or nearly so ; and the olivine completely altered to a pale yellowish serpentine, in which only portions of the ore-bands are still visible.

This series of sections possesses an additional interest from its bearings on the *cozoön* question, for they were examined by Dr. Wm. B. Carpenter, in the presence of Mr. Alexander Agassiz and myself, regarding the occurrence of *cozoön* in them. They belong to the variety of peridotite commonly called schillerfels, and are usually looked upon as being of eruptive origin. It can be readily seen that the present writer regards the series as forming a progressive set of changes, coming down in regular order from the first to the fifth; but Dr. Carpenter took a different view. He found the remains of *eozoön* in every one, but the fossil was best preserved in the last section (fig. 5), and it was more and more illy defined in regular order, through metamorphic action, following the retrograde arrangement, going from figure 5 back to figure 1.

The same ground was also taken by Dr. Carpenter in reference to the sections shown in figures 5, 4, and 3, of Plate VII., although field evidence has shown this rock to be of eruptive origin.* *Eozoön* in various stages of preservation was found by him in other sections, even including some made from dolomitic veinstones. Sections of the felsite pebbles forming the Calumet and Hecla conglomerate, and other bands of conglomerate on Keweenaw Point, were shown Dr. Carpenter. The present writer in 1880 † called attention to the simulative appearance of organic structure assumed by their groundmass during the alteration of the rocks. On examining these sections, Dr. Carpenter thought that the rocks must be of organic origin, and these forms the remains of sponges and other protozoa. Now it is to be remembered that the original source of these pebbles has been found by Foster and Whitney, ‡ and later by Irving, § in eruptive felsites breaking through the copper-bearing rocks.

In the examinations made by Dr. Carpenter of the various sections laid before him, it was noticed that the more the rock was altered, or the nearer it approached a veinstone in character — or better, when it was a veinstone — the more perfect and the better preserved were the fossils.

Dr. Carpenter was frankly told the writer's views about the *eozoön*, the origin of the rocks in question so far as known, the supposed mode of production of these forms, and the object of their presentation to him; and he as frankly and unreservedly gave his opinions. Of course, since Dr. Carpenter's views have not been published over his own name, and were not the fruits of long-continued critical study on the specimens in question, they are not proper subjects for criticism — as his published views would be. The object for presenting them here, is simply to call attention to the fact

* *Ante*, pp. 136–139; also Bull. Mus. Comp. Zoöl., 1850, VII. 60–66.
† Bull. Mus. Comp. Zoöl., 1880, VII. 113–120.
‡ Geology of Lake Superior, Copper Lands, 1850, pp. 70, 71.
§ See. Ann. Rep. Director U. S. Geol. Survey, 1881, p. 33.

that zoölogists and palæontologists, however skilled they may be in the study of organized remains, tend to extend that kingdom in which they have most experience over every form of the mineral world simulating organic forms. So, too, it is not to be denied, on the other hand, that mineralogists and lithologists are likewise prone to unduly extend their kingdom. In all such cases of dispute, between the biologists on one hand and the petrographers on the other, every effort should be made to show that the conditions under which the rock containing the supposed organic remains was formed, were incompatible with one or the other view, instead of leaving the question to the weight of authority. For example, while the lithologist might insist for all time that these forms were produced by alteration, and that he could trace every step from the beginning to the end, the biologist might also insist that the forms were organic, and that he could trace every step from the most perfect form to those whose structure had been almost entirely obliterated by subsequent metamorphism. Both follow the same series, but each one traces it out in the reverse way from the other. Who shall decide between them? Plainly this can only be done satisfactorily by independent evidence which will disprove one side or the other. For example, the mode of occurrence of some of the rocks in which Dr. Carpenter found fossils, is that of eruptive bodies and veinstones; therefore, the proof of their origin decides the question, in these cases, adversely to the biologist.

The case of the *eozoön* affords another example of the successful application of the above method of determining the nature of a disputed form. It has been found by Professor Whitney and myself that limestone containing *eozoön*, acknowledged to be such by Carpenter, Dawson, and Hunt, cuts off dikes running through the country rock; thereby proving this eozoünal limestone to be a later deposit than the country rock, or a veinstone. This decides the case completely against the biologist, and removes from the decision every element of ambiguity or theoretical reasoning; since a veinstone formation of later date than the country rock is entirely incompatible with the growth of an organism such as the *eozoön* is claimed to be.*

In figure 6, Plate VIII., is shown one of the picrites in which the augite appears on the right hand of the section. This mineral exhibits in places, particularly at its base, a greenish alteration-product, and it incloses grains of olivine fissured and partly altered to serpentine. The remaining portion

* Bull. Mus. Comp. Zoöl., 1884, vii. 528-533.

of the section is composed of serpentine, olivine, biotite plates, iron ores, etc.

In the course of the conversion of peridotites into serpentine, it has been seen that the original characters of the rock were gradually obliterated, giving a texture to the serpentine that showed its mode of formation. But it was found that on further change, patches appeared which showed no trace of the mode of formation, and that these gradually occupied the entire rock-mass, yielding specimens whose microscopic characters gave no clue to their origin. In these extreme alterations a more or less schistose structure is often produced in the rock, and from this, the writer conceives, has arisen the view already referred to, that serpentine rocks are derived from schists as well as from massive rocks (*ante*, pp. 144–147). The absence of the reticulated or mesh structure in the serpentine, and the supposed want of chromite and picotite appear to be entirely due to the great alteration which produces a structure in the rock almost if not quite identical with that of serpentine veinstones. The only apparent difference between the mode of formation of these serpentines that are homogeneous and the serpentine veinstones, appears to be that in one the molecular or chemical changes have taken place in the body of the rock, while in the other a transference to a new locality has been superadded. There may be mentioned amongst the various products of alteration found in the peridotites — besides serpentine, dolomite, and iron ores — the following: actinolite, hornblende, smaragdite, quartz, zircon, spinel, garnet, feldspar, talc, chlorite, biotite, and various other micaceous minerals and carbonates.

For the special variations and further details, the reader is referred to the descriptions of the specimens from different localities. The points that seemed to the writer most important, in the case of nearly every peridotite or group of peridotites which has been microscopically studied, have been presented in the preceding pages. This was necessitated by the small number of Cordilleras peridotites at hand, and our still imperfect knowledge of the group, which seemed to demand somewhere a tolerably complete summary of the observed cases and their combination into a connected series.

SECTION VII. — *Chromite and Picotite.* — *Their Relations.*

AN interesting question is the relation of chromite to picotite. Professor H. Fischer described the former as opaque, yet sometimes magnetic from the contained magnetite;* but in a later paper he stated that chromite, in the finest dust and under a high power, was translucent and of a red-brown to red color.†

Dr. E. Dathe found that the chromite from Baltimore was, in thin splinters, translucent and of a brown color much like brown obsidian glass, and that this phenomenon could be observed with a low power. The same was also found by him to be true of the chromite from Waldheim.‡ From this, Dathe concluded that the ordinary microscopic distinction between picotite and chromite, based on the translucence of the one and the opaqueness of the other, was incorrect. M. J. Thoulet also found that the chromite from Röraas in Norway, and that from Negropont, were translucent, showing in transmitted light a color mixed with yellow and red. The grains were traversed by fissures which were impregnated with the surrounding rock material, — serpentine in the first case, calcite in the second. In reflected light the chromite shows a violet-rose color or a gray, and in the portions impregnated by magnetite the characteristic metallic-blue reflection of the latter mineral was observed.§

Although the translucency of chromite is considered by lithologists to have been first noticed by Fischer, it would appear to have been earlier remarked by C. H. Pfaff, who stated in 1825, in describing a compact mass of chromic iron from Massachusetts, that it was characterized by a thin violet rim on the plane of fracture.‖

In order to ascertain, so far as possible, the microscopic relations of picotite to chromite and the other iron ores, a number of sections have been re-examined with special reference to these points; and the powder of picotite and chromite from a number of different localities has also been microscopically studied.

* Kritische mikroskopisch-mineralogische Studien, 1869, pp. 5, 6, 20–22.
† Ibid. 1873, pp. 44, 77.
‡ Neues Jahr. Min., 1876, pp. 247–249.
§ Bull. Soc. Min. France, 1879, ii. 34–37.
‖ "Charakteristisch für dieses Chromeisen ist eine dünne violette Rinde auf den Ablösungsflächen. Die Masse war derb." Jour. Chemie Physik, 1825, xlv. 101–103.

The picotite from Viedessos is coffee-brown to yellowish-brown, translucent, and shows a smooth surface in reflected light. The chromite or picotite of St. Paul's Rocks is greenish-brown to brownish-yellow in color, translucent, and contains in association with it and in its interior, grains of pyrite and other iron ores of secondary origin. The chromite itself is here thought to also be an alteration-product.

The mineral in the Todtmoos peridotite shows in part a pale yellowish central portion surrounded and traversed by portions of a coffee-brown color which fade into a surrounding black opaque exterior. Number **142 G.**, from San Domingo, has its mineral in part colored deep coffee-brown, translucent, and traversed by dark opaque bands, part of which are magnetite. The mineral is in part entirely opaque. In numbers **3001** and **3002** from Colusa Co., California, the picotite or chromite is yellowish-brown in part, but most is opaque and gives a dull, grayish reflection. Some grains were found to be partly filled with pyrite, and some are traversed by black opaque bands along the fissures, while others again show a brownish surface in reflected light, traversed by bluish magnetite veins. One grain had a translucent centre, with a brown opaque border cut by magnetite veins.

The mineral in the Baste *schillerfels* is in part coffee-brown and in part opaque. The translucent grains contain opaque portions. In this, as in many of the others examined, the opacity appears to arise from, and to be proportionate to, the amount of alteration in the picotite or chromite.

In the Webster (N. C.) peridotite the smaller grains are coffee-brown and translucent, but the thicker interior portions are of a much darker color than the edges. The larger grains are coffee-brown and translucent on their edges, but opaque in the interior, and show a rough surface with a dull reflection. A few of the smaller grains have the same characters. The powder is coffee-brown and translucent on the thin edges. The mineral in the Andestad-See rock is of a coffee-brown color in the thinnest portions, and in minute grains, but the remaining portions are opaque, and give the usual dull reflection. Some of the grains are cut by fissures filled with serpentine. Part of the grains in the Tafjord rock are entirely translucent and have a yellowish-brown to a reddish-brown color; part are entirely opaque, and have a rough surface with a dull lustre; while part have the exteriors and some of the central portions translucent, and their remaining portions opaque. The Tron (Norway) rock has the centres of the grains translucent and of a deep reddish-brown color. The remaining portions are crystalline-granular, with a dull lustre. The Texas (Pa.) chromite in the sections is mainly opaque and traversed by fissures filled with serpentine. The surface of the chromite is rough, crystalline-granular, and the lustre dull; but in the thinnest portions the mineral is translucent and of a brown color. The powder in the thin portions is translucent and of a greenish and reddish-brown color. The color of the massive chromite is velvety black, and it has a resinous to vitreous lustre, like the chromite from North Carolina. The mineral in the serpentine from Windisch-Matrey (Tyrol) is mostly opaque and filled with magnetite, but a little of it was seen to be translucent and of a brownish color. The mineral in the Franklin (N. C.) peridotite is entirely opaque in the thin section, and its surface shows a dull lustre, is black, rough, and granulated; but its powder is translucent and of a deep yellowish-brown color on the thin edges.

The ores in the Herborn (Nassau) picrite are all opaque. Part have a bluish reflection, and part a dull one. The grains are in part mixed with pyrite. A brownish translucence seen at the borders of the ores in a few cases, is here considered to be owing to the coloration of the adjacent silicates by the iron oxides.

In the peridotites (mostly serpentines) from Gjørud and Christiania, Norway; Elba; Presque Isle and Ishpeming, Michigan; Westfield and Lynnfield, Massachusetts; High Bridge, New Jersey; Newport, Vermont; Deadwood, Hepsidam, Chip Flat, and Depot Hill, California; numbers **120 G.** and **252 G.**, San Domingo; and Tasmania, the ores seen are all opaque, while part are undoubtedly magnetite.

The general characters of the chromites or picotites and other iron ores in the peridotites of the "Assos Expedition" are as follows: **A. E. 324** has the centre of one grain of a yellowish-brown color with a velvety reflection. The border is granular, opaque, and traversed by fissures filled with serpentine. Some of the other grains are reddish-brown, and translucent in spots; the remaining portions of these grains, and the entire mass of the remaining grains are opaque.

A. E. 265 has its chromic ores in grains and octahedrons, which are translucent and of a deep brown color. They show a brilliant bluish lustre in reflected light.

A. E. 207 has part of its grains translucent on the thin edges, and of an orange-brown to a deep cherry-red color; while the remaining grains are opaque. Of part of the grains the reflection is dull; but of others, even of the translucent parts, it is bluish metallic; structure, granular.

Most of the isometric oxides in **A. E. 209** are opaque and in irregular granules and crystals. Some of the larger grains are traversed by an irregular network of crystalline grains, giving a bluish metallic reflection, and holding interstitial portions of a dull lustre. Part of these interior portions are opaque, and part are translucent and of a deep reddish-brown color.

In **A. E. 217, 473**, and **216** two different kinds of ore were observed. One is granular, opaque, and bluish-black in reflected light. The other is a dull, earthy-brown, amorphous mass in reflected light, but translucent and of a pale grayish-brown color by transmitted light. The two are frequently united in the same grain, and the first is here considered to be magnetite, while the second is a limonitic product of decomposition of iron ores.

A. E. 481 has its mineral in irregular opaque grains of a dull lustre, and traversed by cracks filled with serpentine.

A. E. 214, 270, 274, 482, 483, 483 (bis), 484, 485 have their ores all opaque and granular, giving a bluish reflection.

Through the kindness of Professors F. A. Genth and Edward S. Dana, a number of chromites were obtained for examination.

The following twenty-four were sent by Dr. Genth. All were found to be translucent, most showing this with a low power, but some required a high power. The color is a yellowish-brown in transmitted light, in the specimens from Westfield, Vermont; Chester, Massachusetts; Walter Green's mine, Delaware Co., Pennsylvania; Moro Phillip's mine in Marple Township, Delaware Co., Pennsylvania; Webster, Jackson Co., North Carolina; and Western North Carolina.*

The chromite from the Phillips mine, Nottingham, Chester Co., Pennsylvania, is of a yellowish-brown color tinged variously with green and reddish-brown. That from Media, Delaware Co., Pennsylvania, is in crystals, the powder of one of which is perfectly opaque, and that of another a deep yellowish-brown. In the following the color is a deep yellowish-brown and a reddish-brown: Davis Moore's mine, Middletown Township, Delaware Co., Pennsylvania; Wood's mine, Texas, Lancaster Co., Pennsylvania; the Red Pit, and Low's mine from same county; Soldier's Delight, Maryland; Culsagee,† Macon Co., North Carolina; Hampton's, Yancy Co., North Carolina;

* This last is from the specimen analyzed by Dr. Genth as being from Franklin, Macon Co., North Carolina, and containing 44.15 per cent. of chromic oxide. (See table of analyses.)

† There were two specimens from this locality, one in octahedral crystals, the other massive.

Troup Co., Georgia; Dudleyville, Alabama; California; near New Idria, Monterey Co., California; Ural Mountains; and Euboea, Greece. Another specimen from California had a yellowish and greenish-brown color, while one from Sweden, when very thin, was of a deep-brown coffee-color.

The seven following chromites were sent by Dr. Dana. Those from Lancaster Co., Pennsylvania; Cecil Co., Maryland; Franklin, North Carolina; and Bisersk, Ural Mountains, have a yellowish-brown color. Two specimens from Texas, Pennsylvania, require to be very thin to become translucent, and are of a yellowish-brown to reddish-brown color. One from Jamaica, West Indies, is greenish-yellow in its apparently freshest state, but in the partially changed condition it is reddish-brown.

A chromite obtained from Mr. Kerr, Commissioner from North Carolina at the New England Fair of 1883, in thin splinters is of a clear coffee-brown color with a greenish tinge. Its fracture is smooth, and presents a surface closely resembling a hardened black gum or pitch — for example, albertite — and has a lustre varying from resinous to vitreous. This was chipped from a large block sent to that exhibition. Most of the chromites examined have a pitchy or resinous look, with a velvet-black color closely resembling solid coal tar; but some are dull. While it may be said that in general more or less translucency exists in the powder of chromite, this apparently resides only in certain portions of the mineral, which is not translucent as a whole.

So far as the writer is aware, no tests have been made to compare the relative hardness of picotite and chromite, but the former has been assumed to have that of the normal spinel. In the same way the color of the streak of picotite does not appear to be known for itself; while that of chromite would seem to be due to its translucency.

In specific gravity the two minerals bear close relations. Chromite varies in its specific gravity as follows: 4.031, 4.0639, 4.11, 4.115, 4.1647, 4.319, 4.422, 4.439, 4.49, 4.50, 4.534, 4.56, 4.566, and 4.568; while the only determination of picotite found, places it at 4.08.

Both minerals have the same crystallographic form, the same color to their thin sections, and the same color and lustre in the massive state.

The term *coffee-brown* as used in this text and in the writings of others partakes of the same variability in shade that the infusion of coffee itself does, running from a yellowish or greenish-brown through a reddish-brown to a deep dirty- or muddy-brown. The depth of color, even in the same specimen, appears to be due in part to the thickness, and in part to alteration. For example, in some the yellowish-brown and reddish-brown shades are mingled in such a manner that it is evident that the latter shade is due to change in the state of the iron, and marks a stage in the progression towards opacity. In other cases the two tints are so related that the shade is seen to be due to the wedge-shaped form of the fragment examined.

The translucency is better observed in the powder than in the thin section, if the mineral tends to be at all opaque, since thinner edges are obtained by the process of fracture. The writer has found the quickest and simplest way to prepare the powder for microscopic examination, — to place a minute fragment, less than a pin's head in size, on a glass slide,* and then crush it on this slide under a clean knife-blade. The scattering of the powder can be prevented by placing a finger over the blade at the point under which the grain lies. In this way, by using a small blade, the finger projects over both sides and serves as a cushion to prevent the broken particles from flying off, gives a more uniform pressure, and saves the production of so much fine dust as to obscure our observations. Thus the powder can be directly examined on the slide on which it was crushed.

It does not appear practicable at the present time to enter upon any satisfactory discussion of the chemical relations existing between picotite and chromite; yet, as a contribution towards that desired end, a list of analyses of the two minerals has been arranged in order of the relative percentage of chromic oxide, and it will appear in the list of tables as Table I. One of the difficulties in the way of a satisfactory determination of the relations of chromite and picotite is the absence of analyses made from material carefully studied microscopically, as well as a like absence of analyses made from material of intermediate grades between the typical picotite and the typical chromite. For it will not escape the observer's attention that the analyses naturally group about these two poles, since typical specimens are selected for analysis. Another difficulty is the fact that only five analyses of picotite and one of chrompicotite are known, out of the one hundred and twenty analyses here collected. Hence it is that the series of analyses is far from being so continuous as it would probably be found to be if more attention had been paid to the question of the relations of these two minerals.

The percentage of chromic oxide begins as low as 4.74 per cent in one chromite, and in the picotites does not rise higher than 8 per cent, while the

* Any window-glass, if cut of proper size for the stage of the microscope, will do.

chromites next in order contain 9.80, 16.80, three between 17 and 18 per cent, then 21.16 and 31.20. The chrompicotite, however, contains 56.54 per cent of chromic oxide. The highest percentage is 77.00, in a doubtful analysis by C. H. Pfaff; while the next lower has 64.17 per cent.

The highest percentages of alumina in the chromites are 30.17, 27.83, and 24.71, but in general it diminishes in amount as the chromium increases. In picotite the alumina is high, being 50.34, 52.47, 53.93, 55.34, and 56.00 per cent, and in this occurs the only real chemical difference between picotite and chromite. In the chrompicotite the alumina is 12.13. The percentage of magnesia is about the same in both the chromites and picotites, and does not bear any observable proportion to any other element. The highest percentages are, in picotite 23.59, and in chromite 28.71 and 25.40.

The oxides of iron irregularly increase as the chromic oxide does, rising as high as 45.22, 48.46, and 62.02, while the lowest percentages are 2.30, 5.60, and 9.00; but picotite contains the following: 22.27, 21.42, 15.25, 24.60, and 24.90, and the chrompicotite 18.01. The silica and lime diminish irregularly as the chromic oxide increases. The highest percentages of silica are 26.01, 26.70, and 14.211; and of lime 24.36, 13.26, and 10.55.

The minor and rare elements are the oxides of nickel, manganese, and carbon.

The more general relations are perhaps best shown in the tables inserted here in the text.

TABLE I.

No. of Analyses.	23.						25.							27.					28.					17.			
Limits of Cr_2O_3 percentages.	4.74–39.12.						39.05–44.01.							45.00–52.12.					52.12–57.20.					55.00–77.00.			
Percentage limits of Elements.	None.	0–10.	10–20.	20–30.	30–40.	40–50.	50–60.	None.	0–10.	10–20.	20–30.	30–40.	40–50.	50–70.	None.	0–10.	10–20.	20–30.	30–40.	None.	0–10.	10–20.	20–30.	40–50.	None.	0–10.	10–20.	20–30.
MgO	1	4	14	4					4	5	14	2				3	11	11			3	12	13			4	10	3
Al_2O_3		5	7	5	1		5	1	3	10	9				1	15	3	8			22	6			1	6	6	
Fe_2O_3 & FeO		10	11	8	3					5	5	10	7		1		2	6	11	5	5		5	4	19	6		1	3	7	3
SiO_2	11	17	3	2				2	21	2						6	20	1			4	21	3			3	13		
CaO	12	8	2	1				17	8							24	3				24	5				14	3		

Table I. has placed in its upper line the number of analyses in each set; in the second line, the percentage limits of the chromic oxide in these analyses; while on the third line is placed the percentage limits of the magnesium, aluminum, ferric, ferrous, silicon, and calcium oxides. Below are given the number of analyses found in the above limits. Thus, for instance, in looking at the table it can be seen that in the first 23 analyses the limits of Cr_2O_3 are 4.74 and 38.12; while in these 23 analyses, there are to be found of analyses of MgO, one having no MgO; four having less than 10 per cent; fourteen carrying between 10 and 20 per cent; four carrying between 20 and 30 per cent; and none having any higher percentage. But in these same 23 analyses we see that there are five (picotites) which carry between 50 and 60 per cent of Al_2O_3.

TABLE II.

Percentage Limits.	None.	0–10.	10–20.	20–30.	30–40.	40–50.	50–60.	60–70.	70–80.	Not inclosed.
Cr_2O_3	...	7	4	1	16	36	43	12	1	...
Fe_2O_3	81	19	3	6	10	...	...	1	...	...
FeO	18	4	28	49	13	5	...	...	...	3
Al_2O_3	8	53	36	12	1	...	5	...	...	4
MgO	15	42	55	8	...	...	...	...	...	...
SiO_2	17	91	9	2	...	...	...	...	...	1
CaO	19	27	2	1	...	...	...	...	...	...

In Table II. there is given in the upper line the percentage limits for the different constituents, and below, the number of analyses whose constituents fall between those limits. Thus it will be seen that out of the 120 analyses, there are seven containing less than 10 per cent of Cr_2O_3, four between 10 and 20 per cent, etc.; while there are 81 analyses in which no Fe_2O_3 is reported and one which has between 60 and 70 per cent of it. From the above illustrations, the use of the tables will doubtless be readily understood.

In reply to a question of the present writer as to his views concerning the chemical relations of chromite and picotite, Dr. Genth states that, in common with many others, he thinks "that all the aluminates, ferrates, etc. of Mg, Zn, Mn, and Fe, which are isometric, are only varieties of the species $R\,R_2O_4$ — which so gradually change from one into the other, that it is often difficult to say where one begins and the other ends. Of typical forms we have only spinel ($Mg\,Al_2O_4$), magnetite ($Fe\,Fe_2O_4$), and magnoferrite ($Mg\,Fe_2O_4$). All the rest are mixtures. As for chromite, I have never seen a specimen which did not contain magnesia and alumina, although some of the analyses do not give any; but there are a great many poor analyses."

In the same manner, Rammelsberg classes together chromite and picotite, not even placing the latter under spinel.*

In the microscopic study of chromites and picotites we see a reason for the variability in their chemical analyses, and the nearly constant presence

* Handbuch der Mineralchemie, 1875, pp. 141–144.

of silica and other impurities. We further find various gradations in different specimens, and even partly in the same grain, between the yellowish- to reddish-brown mineral, and that which is opaque and crystalline-granular, with or without magnetite or some of the other iron ores, like limonite or hematite.

The above investigations apparently point to the following conclusions: —

That picotite in its freshest state is, in the thin sections, a yellowish- or greenish-brown, clear mineral which is subject to alterations, causing the color to deepen to a darker brown or muddy coffee-color, and even to a black and opaque mass. The changed forms vary from a dull, earthy mass to a crystalline-granular one which frequently contains more or less magnetite. Commonly, the more the rock is altered or changed to a serpentine, the less apt is one to find any of the translucent grains, and the greater is the amount of magnetite.

It is probable that picotite and chromite belong to the same mineral series, the term picotite being more commonly applied to the freshest states, and that of chromite to those forms more altered, and to the local aggregations arising from the migration of the chromic oxide during the alteration of the associated peridotic rock.

The results deduced from the microscopic study of minerals, lead to the conclusion that most of our mineral species are not definite compounds corresponding to a special chemical formula, but rather are varying and variable compounds. They are seen to contain inclusions of various kinds, and to exist in various stages of alteration and decomposition. This we see in the case of micaceous products which occur in certain greenish, fibrous, and scaly forms, produced from the alteration of various minerals. Now, while these forms are microscopically undistinguishable from one another in their earlier stages, they are seen to result in their further change, in the production of biotite, hornblende, chlorite, hydrous micas, etc. Now shall we give a distinct name to each of these variable and interminable micaceous forms, whenever from its analysis we can torture a chemical formula into being; or shall we recognize the variability, and use our mineral names simply as type-names about which the related products in their various stages are grouped? The latter is the method employed in this work. The variability of mineral species not only occurs in the micaceous minerals above mentioned, but it is seen in picotite and the ores of iron, the feldspars, serpentine, pyroxenes, amphiboles, and in almost every mineral or group of minerals that has been studied to a sufficient extent to afford us much information about its composition. Our minerals in Nature's laboratory appear to be produced and grow, to change and decay, to pass away and be succeeded by others, ever passing onward from the unstable towards the more stable; reaction after reaction, replacement after replacement, following one another according to the varying conditions, as they do in the chemist's laboratory. When we can learn the order of succession by alteration, and the various relations minerals thus hold to one another, we may hope for a natural system of mineralogy, which will display to us their origin and line of descent, with their relationships. In the establishment of such a system, the microscope and chemical reagents must go hand in hand, and the work is yet hardly begun.

An analysis of a chromite from Röraas, Norway, given in Table I., has had a strange history. It was attributed to Laugier by Rammelsberg in his Handwörterbuch des chemischen Theils der Mineralogie, 1841, pp. 163, 164, and in his Handbuch der Mineralchemie, 1860, pp. 171–174; and from these works of Rammelsberg it has been copied in the third, fourth, and fifth editions of Dana's System of Mineralogy, and elsewhere. The work from which the analysis is said to have been taken is the sixth volume of the Ann. Mus. d'Hist. Nat. It was proved by the present writer not to occur there, and after a long search, its history has been found to be as follows:—

The analysis was published in the Annales des Mines, 1829 (2), V. 316, as taken from the "An. du Bureau des mines de Suède, t. 9, 1825," but the name of the analyst was not given. Since the writer is unable to see, for the present at least, the Swedish journal referred to, the analysis has not been traced any further backwards. It was then copied by Beudant,* together with an analysis of Seybert, but in both cases without mention of the analyst or the source. Before this, however, it had been republished by Franz von Kobell,† without being attributed to any analyst, and without reference to the original source, but placed after a reference to an analysis by Laugier. This then evidently gave rise to Rammelsberg's mistake; while it also led Hausmann ‡ and Brooke-and-Miller § to attribute the analysis to Von Kobell himself, as they have done in their mineralogies. Thus this analysis

* Traité élémentaire de Minéralogie, 1832, ii. 667, 668.
† Charakteristik der Mineralien, 1831, ii. 255.
‡ Handbuch der Mineralogie, 1847, ii. 420.
§ An Elementary Introduction to Mineralogy, by the late William Phillips, 1852, p. 263.

has been credited over forty years to a chemist by whom it showed on its face it could not have been made, since Laugier was not in the habit of carrying his percentages into the decimals, at most, beyond one place.

This, and numerous other mistakes which have been found in the process of looking up the analyses for this work, are obviously due to the neglect of authors to verify the analyses which they take at second hand. The present writer has no doubt that he has contributed his quota of errors also, although he has endeavored to go to the fountain-head when possible; but with the accidents of twice copying and of passing the work through the press, the chance for errors to creep in are great; and they could only be entirely eliminated by again searching out the scattered literature, and comparing the originals with the tables in type — a labor which is impracticable at the present time.

SECTION VIII. — *Peridotite.* — *Its Chemical Characters.*

IN the appended table of chemical analyses (Table IV.), when the variety to which the meteorite belongs is known, the name of the variety is given, with an asterisk prefixed to indicate that it is a meteorite. When the variety is unknown, the simple designation, meteorite, is employed. The varieties of the terrestrial peridotites are given so far as possible; but when not known, the term used by the analyst to designate the rock is placed in the column of varieties.

The specific gravity of the unaltered peridotites is generally between 3.00 and 3.80, with the meteorites standing, as a whole, somewhat higher than the terrestrial forms, since they are less altered. As the alteration proceeds, the percentages in general fall, as was observed in the case of cumberlandite. Two of the carbonaceous meteorites fall very low on the scale, being 1.7025 and 1.94. These meteorites are thought to belong to this group in all respects except their carbonaceous matter, for sections of the Cold-Bokkeveld meteorite are seen as dense black masses, with brownish-gray spots of silicates and carbonaceous grains. The whole mass is very friable, and the silicates are in minute grains; but they appear to be chiefly, if not entirely, olivine and enstatite. The resemblance to a mass of mixed soot and olivine grains is striking — the latter being seen scattered here and there through the dark mass.

To return: the specific gravity of the altered forms, particularly of serpentine, lie almost entirely between 2.50 and 3.00. This decrease in specific gravity is generally accompanied with a diminution of the relative ferruginous contents, and an increase in that of the magnesia.

It was observed in the pallasites that only one contained over 30 per cent of silica, while it may be seen here that only three of the lherzolites fall below that percentage, and one of these is a carbonaceous meteorite which contains considerable organic matter and water. Another of these analyses is considered to be worthless. In the mention of the chemical analyses, reference, as a rule, is had to the first one when more than one is given for a single locality; for when several analyses are available, that one is placed first which is thought to be the more nearly correct, judging by the analyses and the analyst, when any especial difference exists. Of course, no such differences in composition occur in the same specimen, as some of the given analyses display, and many of these are poor and unreliable.

Only two of the analyses show for peridotite a higher percentage than 47 per cent — St. Paul's Rocks 47.15, and the Cabarras meteorite 56.168. This meteorite has in general been assigned to the basaltic division of the meteorites; but since, macroscopically, it has the characters of the peridotites, it has here been placed with them, in the belief that some error exists in the published analysis. It is to be hoped that a microscopic examination and further chemical analyses will be made of the Cabarras stone.

Only two meteoric and three terrestrial peridotites have a percentage of silica above 45, and below 47, per cent. One of the meteorites has two analyses in which the silica is respectively 46 and 48.25 per cent, made by Higgins in 1811. Had the second analysis been placed first, then the above statements would have varied accordingly.

From the above it can be seen that out of 193 different peridotites analyzed, all but 11 have their percentage of silica lying between 30 and 45, while the vast majority are included between 33 and 43 per cent. The meteorites preponderate in the lower percentages — the terrestrial rocks in the higher ones.

Except in the case of the picrites there cannot at present be said to be any gradation in the percentages of silica, according to the variety, from dunite up to picrite, although a tendency towards some arrangement has been observed. Of course, the more nearly the rock approaches to a purely olivine one or to a pure serpentine, the more nearly the percentage of silica will correspond to the typical analyses of those minerals.

The vast majority of analyses show a percentage of alumina less than 5, but the picrites tend to have more (mostly between 10 and 20), as also some of the others, thus approaching the basalts. The highest percentage is in the Muddor stone analyzed by Frank Crook — 26 per cent — a doubtful analysis.

The amount of iron in various states distinctly varies in the meteoric and terrestrial peridotites; so much so, that from the sum of the percentages the class can readily be inferred in most cases. In the meteorites the iron in every condition varies somewhere about the mean of 30 per cent — those forms having the lower percentages of silica, usually more than 30, and those having the higher percentages of silica, contain generally less than 30 per cent.

In the terrestrial peridotites the iron percentages are commonly below 10, and universally below 20 per cent. The more highly altered the rock, the less is the percentage of iron. This agrees with the microscopic observations, and shows that in the process of alteration much iron is removed and stored up elsewhere.

Lime is either absent in the peridotites, or less than 5 per cent in the vast majority. The cases in which higher percentages are found are apparently due to incorrect analyses, or, in the main, to the picrites and two serpentines which are associated with gabbro, and may possibly be altered forms of it — a conclusion to which their relatively high contents of alumina and lime point. The picrites show their near relation to the basalts in the same way. 19.50 per cent of lime (the highest) was found in the typical lherzolite from Viedessos, in an analysis published in 1813. It is thought that here the lime and magnesia were poorly separated, or else the peridotite has been in some way modified by the limestone through which it was erupted. No other peridotite contains over 13.61 per cent of lime.

The magnesia percentage is relatively high but variable, and it tends in the meteorites and picrites to lie below 30 per cent, and in the other peridotites to be above that. Of course, the nearer the rock comes to being a pure olivine one, or to be entirely altered to serpentine, the more nearly the percentages correspond to the typical ones for those minerals. Part of the variability in the percentage of magnesia is undoubtedly owing to poor analyses.

Chromium, nickel, and cobalt are quite commonly present, as are also phosphorus and sulphur in the meteoric forms. Sometimes copper and tin are found. The more highly altered the peridotites, the more apt is water to be present, and in the serpentine rocks it appears in general to vary from 8 to 16 per cent.

In general, the peridotites are relatively low in their percentages of silica, alumina, and lime; high in magnesia; and variable in iron and specific gravity; the unaltered forms being higher, in both cases, than the altered.

Section IX. — *Peridotite.* — *Its Origin.*

"Are the peridotites sedimentary or eruptive?" is an exceedingly important question, and one which, in the case of serpentine, has been frequently argued.

That the peridotites are sometimes eruptive, the cases cited by Bonney, Diller, and the present writer, for Cornwall, the Troad, and Lake Superior, are clear, explicit, and decisive — that they occur in dikes, in intrusive tongues, and in uplifting, altering, eruptive bosses, showing the same characters as do other eruptive rocks, especially those of a coarse-grained character like gabbro and granite. That the peridotites are in part eruptive we should, then, consider a settled fact; but another case still remains to be considered: the association of these rocks with schists.

Where schistose rocks are associated with the peridotites, especially the serpentine variety, their relations would appear to be accounted for in the following ways: —

1. They may occur as eruptive rocks which, with their associated country rocks, have later been altered, producing a general apparent blending of all into a single series; as it is well known has taken place with the older eruptive basaltic rocks — diorite, diabase, melaphyr — which has caused them also to be looked upon as interbedded sedimentary rocks, in common with their associated schists.

2. All may have come from the alteration of eruptive material, — the lenticular patches being the remnants of the altered rock. This would be in accordance with the well-known mode of alteration of olivine rocks, in which occur clear grains of unaltered olivine surrounded by the serpentine and other secondary minerals which often give to the rock a schistose character. We might as well claim that these clear olivine grains were produced by the metamorphosis of the serpentine and schistose material, when the reverse is known to be the case, as to claim that the patches of olivine rocks in schists

were produced by the metamorphosis of the schistose material, when the reverse is probably true.

3. All other eruptive rocks are subjected to denudation, and their débris piled up somewhere with other associated sedimentary beds; hence there is every reason to believe that we have detrital peridotitic rocks, the same as we have detrital basaltic ones.

All three of the preceding methods are probably correct for some cases, but which method is to be advocated in each case is to be determined by the study of the locality in question.

Although as yet it does not seem to be proved that peridotic volcanoes have existed, and peridotic ash may not have been formed, we should look for all the intermingling of the eruptive peridotic material with its own débris and with that of other rocks, the same as previously set forth in general terms for rocks of this origin (*ante*, pp. 22–24). We should then expect to find the peridotites occurring in dikes and eruptive masses, in altered schistose or foliated rocks, in detrital beds, and in every form and every association that it is possible for eruptive rocks and their débris to exist in. The study of these occurrences would, however, be expected to be just so much more obscure than is the study of the basaltic rocks, as the former are more basic and easily alterable than the latter.

That serpentines are produced from the alteration of peridotic rocks, is the testimony of all lithologists who have studied their structure with the microscope, and it is one of the most fixed facts in the science. That serpentines are not produced in other ways may perhaps be looked upon as an open question at the present time, although there would seem to be no proof of any other mode of origin. In the case of any mineral formed by secondary changes, more or less migration of the mineral material is apt to occur, and in this way the secondary serpentine is frequently found in veins, and in other localities outside of the rock from whose alteration it was produced.

That serpentines have come from chemical precipitates from ocean waters, is a view which certainly does not appear to have any proof in its behalf, and one which probably arose from the confounding of veinstone-serpentine or migrated serpentine material, with that produced by the alteration of peridotites *in situ*. The production of serpentine by the alteration of olivine and its removal and storage in fissures and adjacent rocks, brings in connection with the peridotites the difficult problems belonging both to eruptive rocks and veinstones; and the phenomena of both would appear to explain the mysteries hovering about the serpentine question.

The writer has been unable to find anything in the published reports of the Canada Geological Survey to substantiate the often repeated statement, that this survey had proved, prior to 1858, that the Canadian serpentines were in stratified sedimentary deposits. The geologists of that survey appear to have assumed, without proof, that the serpentines were so deposited, and worked out their geology on that supposition. Then, finally forgetting the basis on which the assumed stratification was placed, they afterwards declared that they had proved these rocks to be stratified; but the correctness of that statement is not here allowed. And in this connection it may be said that Dr. Hunt's "Geological History of the Serpentines" is looked upon here as having the same inaccuracies that all his other papers have been found to contain, when the present writer has had occasion to critically examine their contained statements, both of fact and opinion (*ante*, p. 38).*

The question now arises: Can serpentine result from the alteration of any rock except the peridotites? In the preceding pages it has been shown that olivine is the chief producer of serpentine, but that in olivine rocks enstatite and even diallage are changed to serpentine, although more slowly than the olivine. It has also been shown that in the cumberlandite more or less serpentine had been formed during the alteration of this olivine-magnetite rock. So, too, it is well known to lithologists that the olivine of the basaltic rocks is subject to alteration to serpentine, which, in the gabbros and other old basalts, produces a rock imperfectly serpentinous. It would seem, then, that any rock containing olivine or enstatite, may become more or less serpentinized, although it would appear that, outside of the peridotites proper, true serpentines that are not veinstones, rarely, if ever, occur.

The reader is further referred, for the literature and general discussions of the serpentine question by others, to Roth's "Ueber den Serpentin und die genetischen Beziehungen desselben," † Riess's "Ueber die Entstehung des Serpentins," ‡ and the lithological text-books of Rosenbusch and Zirkel.

The production of talcose rocks or talcose schists, as early advocated by Genth (*ante*, p. 119) appears to be one of the results of the alteration of

* See also "Azoic System," Bull. Mus. Comp. Zoöl., 1884, vii. No. 11; and Bonney, Geol. Mag., 1884 (3), i. 406–412.
† Abh. Berlin. Akad., 1869, ii. 329–361.
‡ Zeit. Gessam. Natur. Berlin, 1879 (3), iv. 1–18.

peridotites, especially those containing pyroxene minerals; but the present writer's studies would indicate to him that the most common source that yields by alteration our soapstone or steatite rocks, is to be sought in our gabbros and coarser crystalline diabases (diorites). The purer talcose rocks would appear to come from the former source (the peridotites), the more impure ones from the latter (the basalts).

From the evidence in the preceding pages, it is probable that some actinolitic and other schists result from the alteration of the peridotites, although in general the amphibole schists appear to belong to other groups.

The formation of impure dolomites from peridotites would seem to have been clearly shown in the preceding pages, but how far this will account for the common association of magnesian limestones with serpentine, is a problem for the future. One thing, however, appears clear, that such limestones are produced on a small scale, and sometimes on a more extended one in connection with the general alteration of peridotites into serpentine.

It is not the part or intention of the writer to explain the modes of change in these rocks. It is rather his part to give the facts observed, and for the mineral chemist to engage in the work of explanation, unless he can impeach the facts presented.

SECTION X. — *Peridotite.* — *Its Classification.*

As previously stated (*ante*, pp. 84, 85), all rocks of this class are here grouped under one species or type — *peridotite;* while for the modifications produced by the variation in mineral composition, varietal names are employed, in deference to the views of those who make species out of every mineral variation in rocks. Since, so far as practicable, these variety names are the same as the specific names of other lithologists, and have the same general limits, no difficulty will arise in their use, whether the person employing them looks upon each division as a specific or a varietal term.

In accordance with the methods of this work, *peridotite* is defined as including all meteoric and terrestrial rocks of every age, which are composed essentially of olivine, with or without pyroxene minerals, and iron ores including picotite.

It has not been customary to base any varietal distinction on the iron ores, or hardly to look upon them as essential, although they are universally present, or nearly so. The varietal distinctions (specific, of other lithologists) are founded on the pyroxene minerals and on the alteration-products. Thus *dunite* is the term given to the form of peridotite which is essentially composed of olivine; *saxonite* to that composed of olivine and enstatite; *lherzolite* to that composed of olivine, enstatite, and diallage; *buchnerite* to that composed of olivine, enstatite, and augite : *eulysite* to that composed of olivine and diallage; and *picrite* to that composed of olivine and augite.

Under these varieties are classed all the forms produced by alteration, so far as they may retain sufficient original characters for their identification; when they do not, then they are placed under a variety name belonging to the produced form. Thus, *serpentine* is given as the variety name for all the altered peridotites in which serpentine forms the essential constituent; *talc schist* to all in which talc holds a similar part; and in the same way any variety produced by alteration can be designated by its common name when its derivation is known.

It is, however, expected that future studies will lead to the discovery of every mineralogical combination that can be formed by the principal silicate constituents of peridotite. These combinations, so far as now known grade into one another, and it is to be expected that all other discovered ones will do the same. Hence, if the ordinary methods of nomenclature should be followed, the number of species or varieties of peridotite would be great and their separation difficult. However, the present writer, as he has previously stated, does not place any stress upon the subdivisions now made on a mineralogical basis in peridotite, but adopts them as a convenience only in the present state of lithological science; and they can readily be replaced by the general employment of the specific name — *peridotite*.

The *limburgite* of Rosenbusch has not been placed here with the peridotites, for its microscopic structure is like that of some of the porphyritic glassy basalts, and differs much from the peridotites. While its percentage of silica is like that of this species, its contents of alumina and lime ally it to a more acidic group; although it is not improbable that it belongs to the picrite variety. Except in its abundant olivine, limburgite microscopically closely approaches some of the andesites; but, taking its characters as a whole, the majority of them appear to be basaltic, and with that group it will here be classed until further evidence can be procured.

The fragmental states of the peridotites are indicated for the unaltered and altered forms by the respective varietal terms, *tufa* and *porodite*, or, if desirable, their adjective forms, *tufaceous* and *porodilic*.

Below is given a table showing the classification of all the rocks more basic than the basalts, so far as now known, but it admits of the ready addition of other varietal names, and even of specific ones, if future studies shall indicate such divisions. The three designated classes of varieties are of course not entirely distinct, since in alteration a mineralogical change enters, and that change or alteration is the basis of the two divisions of the fragmental forms, while these may partake of the mineral characters of the mineralogical varieties, and belong to them.

Table showing the Classification of the Rock Species preceding the Basalts.

Species.	Mineralogical varieties.	Alteration varieties.	Fragmental varieties.
Siderolite.	. . . . . .	. . . . . .	Porodite.
Pallasite.	Pallasite Cumberlandite.	Actinolite Schist.	
Peridotite.	Dunite. Saxonite. Lherzolite. Buchnerite. Eulysite. Picrite.	Serpentine. Talc Schist. Actinolite Schist.	Tufa. Porodite.

This seeming confusion or crossing of names is due to the present state of lithology, and the necessity of bringing the nomenclature into accordance with the general usage and prejudices of lithologists, since an abrupt departure from their nomenclature would only repel, and the inconsistencies can later be remedied by the dropping of all varietal names which the advance of the science shall render superfluous, as the writer now believes many of them to be. Thus, for instance, it is here considered that in peridotite, the terms *peridotite, serpentine,* and *talc* and *actinolite schist,* with the adjectives *tufaceous* and *porodilic,* will express every essential form of these rocks now known, and by their use alone a proper conception of their relations would be advanced.

CHAPTER IV.

THE BASALTS.

SECTION I. — *The Meteoric Basalts.*

VARIETY. — **Basalt.**

Stannern, Moravia.

TSCHERMAK has described the Stannern meteorite as a granular rock, showing an evident fragmental structure. According to him, it is not a homogeneous crystalline rock, but one composed of rock fragments of three different kinds: coarse-grained fragments, radiated finer-grained fragments, and compact fragments.

The coarser-grained fragments are chiefly composed of anorthite laminæ and augite columns united together. Some of the anorthite crystals show very fine twinning, but most have broad twin laminæ which are sometimes bent. Besides the colorless anorthite, and the brown to blackish augite, Tschermak observed a colorless isotropic mineral, which is probably the same as the mineral he had described as an isotropic labradorite (maskelynite) from the Shergotty meteorite. Minute grains of chromite, iron, and pyrrhotite occur inclosed between the other minerals; and black forms were seen in the augite.

The fragments, of an evidently radiated texture, are composed of anorthite laminæ interspersed with augite needles. Black grains occur in these fragments.

The compact fragments formed a gray mass, which in several points showed a radiated fibrous structure, and which contained the before-mentioned black grains.

The groundmass which unites these fragments is composed of anorthite and augite grains, and black particles.*

Tschermak later stated that this meteorite was closely like that from Juvenas, but finer-grained; but it did not contain either the unknown silicate or pyrrhotite found in that.†

The specimens of this rock in the Harvard College Mineral Cabinet, resemble in structure, on macroscopic examination, some diabases, but are of a much finer grain; the general crystalline arrangement is the same.

Constantinople, Turkey.

The Constantinople meteorite was found by Tschermak to be an ash-gray, nearly compact rock, composed of compact small fragments and fine radiating masses.

It was seen under the microscope to be composed of anorthite, pyroxene, pyrrhotite, and chromite. Its microscopic structure agrees with the Stannern meteorite, as also does its chemical composition.‡

* Min. Mitth., 1872, pp. 83–85.   † Die mikros. Besch. der Meteoriten, 1883, i. 7.
‡ Min. Mitth., 1872, pp. 85–87.

Jonzac, France.

The Jonzac meteorite is stated by Tschermak to have a fragmental structure, and under the microscope is seen to be composed of lamellæ of anorthite and columns of augite. The former has distinct bounding lines, while those of the augite are indistinct. Lying between these crystals are small grains of the same minerals, filling the interspaces. The anorthite is often cloudy from minute brown glass inclusions, and black grains arranged parallel to the length of the crystal. The augite when clear has a greenish-brown color, but it is often traversed by fissures, and rich in violet-blue, and brown, dust-like particles, — chromite and pyrrhotite, possibly. The meteorite further contains pyrrhotite, chromite, and iron.*

Petersburg, Lincoln Co., Tennessee.

The Petersburg meteorite is, according to Professor Shepard, of an "ash-gray color, with a slight intermixture of pearl-gray, for the basis of the stone." Porphyritically inclosed in this groundmass are crystals and grains, which, from Shepard's and Smith's descriptions, appear to be augite, plagioclase, and olivine. Some chromite and a garnet were reported.†

Tschermak states that it is composed of anorthite, augite, and a yellowish silicate like olivine.‡

The specimen in the Harvard College Cabinet macroscopically closely resembles the Staunern meteorite.

Frankfort, Franklin Co., Alabama.

The Frankfort meteoric stone, according to Professor Brush, presented a gray groundmass with a pseudo-porphyritic structure, having black, green, white, and dark-gray spots on it. Professor Brush determined the minerals as follows: the black one as chromite; the white as anorthite or chladnite (it is more probably feldspar than enstatite); the green and gray as olivine (probably some augite also); and, in addition, a little nickeliferous iron, and pyrrhotite (troilite). This rock seems to be a basalt, to which its chemical analysis refers it.§

VARIETY. — **Gabbro.**

Luotolaks, Finland, Russia.

The meteorite from Luotolaks was found by Professor F. J. Wiik to be composed of metallic iron; colorless anorthite; grayish-violet augite, inclosing long black microlites; and olivine, with little irregular cavities.∥ He refers this meteorite to the basic eruptives.

Tschermak describes it as a tufaceous mass, which, in an earthy, friable, gray groundmass, holds splinters and grains of greenish, whitish, and dark color, as well as basaltic (eucritic) fragments. He looks upon it as a volcanic ash. It contains, according to him, anorthite holding little rounded glass inclusions; augite in brownish grains, with black needle-formed inclusions; bronzite in very pale, greenish splinters, almost free from inclusions; olivine, chromite, pyrrhotite, and iron.¶

---

* Min. Mitth., 1874, pp. 168, 169.
† Am. Jour. Sci., 1857 (2), xxiv. 134–137; Safford's Geol. Reconn. of Tenn., 1856, pp. 125–127; Geol. of Tenn., 1869, pp. 520, 521.
‡ Min. Mitth., 1874, p. 170.   § Am. Jour. Sci., 1869 (2), xlviii. 240–244.
∥ Neues Jahr. Min., 1883, i. 384; Öfversigt Finska Vet. Soc. Forh., 1882, xxiv. 63, 64.
¶ Die mikros. Besch. der Meteoriten, 1883, i. 7, 8.

THE METEORIC BASALTS. — GABBRO. 197

Mässing, Bavaria.

The Mässing meteorite is said by Professor C. W. Gümbel to be of a grayish-white color in the interior, and to contain olivine in yellowish-green to clear-green, round, and irregular grains, which sometimes show parallel fissuring.

He refers to feldspar a white, glassy, transparent, or dusty, cloudy, strongly-fissured, rarely parallel-striped, evidently cleavable mineral. A wine-yellow to grayish-green, or pale, reddish-brown glassy mineral is regarded as belonging to the augite group. It is not dichroic, and is sometimes in long fibrous forms, and filled with numerous little bubbles. Besides these, chromite, pyrrhotite, and iron were found. All these are cemented by a fine, dust-like, granular, gray groundmass.*

Tschermak states that the Mässing meteorite is similar in character to that from Luotolaks, and contains anorthite, brownish, yellowish, and greenish-gray augite, bronzite, chromite, pyrrhotite, and greenish splinters of olivine.†

Juvenas, Ardèche, France.

According to Rammelsberg, this meteorite is composed of anorthite, augite, chromite, pyrrhotite, and possibly a little apatite, and titanite. It is similar to the Stannern form, but coarser.‡ Rose states that the nickeliferous iron is in a very minute quantity.§

The specimen in the Harvard College Cabinet looks macroscopically more like a gabbro than the Stannern form, and it has a coarser texture.

This meteorite is figured by Fouqué and Lévy, as being composed of anorthite, enstatite, augite, and magnetite,‖ and having a structure like some norites.

Tschermak states that it shows a crystalline to tufaceous structure under the microscope, and is evidently of a brecciated character.

The anorthite in it is well-crystallized, part being water-clear, and part cloudy and white, owing to rounded and fine needle-formed glass and other inclusions arranged parallel to the bounding planes. The crystals often show in polarized light a complicated twinning. Some of the inclusions hold bubbles and black grains. Rarely gas-pores were seen.

The augite is brownish-black, owing to numerous black, and rarely brown, needle-shaped and rounded inclusions. The brownish rounded inclusions are regarded as glass. Some irregular grains of a pale-brown color are referred to diallage. A pale-brownish silicate, sometimes having a fine lamellar structure was observed. Small amounts of pyrrhotite and nickeliferous iron were also found by Tschermak.¶

Shergotty, India.

A description of the microscopic characters of the Shergotty meteorite was given by Professor Tschermak in 1872. The stone is granular, with the grains nearly of the same size, and on the fractured surface it has a yellowish-gray color. In the thin section five different minerals were recognized: 1, a brownish cleavable mineral similar to augite; 2, a glass-clear isotropic mineral; 3, a yellowish, anisotropic mineral, very rare; 4, an opaque black mineral — magnetite; 5, an opaque metallic yellow mineral, extremely rare.

---

* Sitz. München Akad., 1878, viii. 32–40. † Die mikros. Besch. der Meteoriten, 1883, i. 8.
‡ Ann. Physik Chemie, 1848, lxxiii. 585–590; 1851, lxxxiii. 591–593.
§ Abh. Berlin. Akad. 1863, pp. 126–134. ‖ Min. Microg., 1879, plate LV. figure 1.
¶ Die mikros. Besch. der Meteoriten, 1883, i. 6, 7; Min. Mitth., 1874, pp. 169, 170.

Of these the first formed the principal portion of the stone. It is traversed by numberless fine fissures parallel to the cleavage. It is of a grayish-brown color, anisotropic, and shows only feeble pleochroism. In cleavage and optical characters it is similar to diopside. It is quite commonly twinned. While the mineral is regarded as augitic, Tschermak thinks, from its chemical composition, that it is different from any terrestrial compound.

The second mineral possesses conchoidal fracture, and is inclosed in and subordinate to the augitic mineral. Its form is that of a distorted cube. The hardness is a little less than that of orthoclase, while its chemical composition is similar to that of labradorite. Tschermak proposed for it the name *maskelynite*. The third mineral is intergrown with the first, is traversed by parallel fissures, and is orthorhombic in crystallization. It is referred to bronzite (enstatite).

The fourth mineral lies between the other minerals or is inclosed in the *maskelynite*. It is pitch-black, semi-metallic, with a conchoidal fracture, black streak, and is strongly magnetic. This mineral is regarded as magnetite. The fifth mineral is referred to pyrrhotite. The section as figured by Tschermak resembles some of the gabbros.*

Later, Tschermak speaks of the brownish mineral as augite, and of the maskelynite as a glassy state of plagioclase.†

Pawlowka, Saratow, Russia.

This meteorite has been described by Mr. Th. Tschernyschow, as composed of a brittle ash-gray groundmass, formed by a crystalline-granular mixture of feldspar, enstatite, and diallage, holding porphyritic grains of these minerals and olivine. The feldspar shows polysynthetic twinning, and is referred to anorthite. It is in irregular and ledge-formed masses. The diallage is either colorless or brownish-gray, with cleavage planes, and an absence of dichroism. The enstatite shows a fine parallel cleavage striation, and holds chromite (?) in black grains arranged parallel to the cleavage lines. Sometimes the feldspar predominates, and at others the pyroxenes; and of the latter, sometimes the enstatite and sometimes the diallage is most abundant.

The olivine occurs in clear-green grains. Besides the above minerals, there were seen also nickeliferous iron, pyrrhotite, and chromite, in grains and crystals. It also contains the cloudy-gray friction-product of Tschermak, but which the present writer regards as a base. ‡

This meteorite is placed, from the above description, with the basaltic meteorites, although the entire correctness of the microscopic diagnosis is perhaps questionable.

Le Teilleul, Manche, France.

This meteorite, according to Daubrée, is composed of plagioclase (anorthite), enstatite, diallage, olivine, iron, pyrrhotite, and chromite.

The feldspar is colorless, twinned, and presents similar inclusions to those found in the feldspar of gabbro. On chemical tests the feldspar is referred to anorthite. The enstatite shows two cleavages, is of a pale-greenish color, and contains opaque inclusions. The diallage is of a darker color than the enstatite, and contains inclusions of oxide of iron or troilite, as well as other forms similar to those common in diallage, and arranged parallel to one another. The olivine is colorless. §

---

* Sitz. Wien. Akad., 1872, lxv. (1), 122–135; Min. Mitth., 1872, pp. 87–95.
† Die mikros. Besch. der Meteoriten, 1883, i. 7.
‡ Zeit. Deut. geol. Gesells., 1883, xxxv. 190–192.
§ Comptes Rendus, 1879, lxxxviii. 544–547; Neues Jahr. Min., 1879, pp. 905, 906.

Bishopville, South Carolina.

The meteorite which fell at Bishopville, South Carolina, March, 1843, has been regarded as an interesting and peculiar one. Professor C. U. Shepard, in 1846,* described from it, under the name of *Chladnite*, a mineral which he regarded as a ter-silicate of magnesia, and as forming over two-thirds of the stone. The color is snow-white, rarely tinged with gray. Lustre pearly to vitreous, translucent, H. 6–6.5. Sp. Gr. 3.116. Fuses without difficulty before the blowpipe to a white enamel. He further describes as *apatoid*, small, yellow, semi-transparent grains having a hardness of 5.5, and very rare. A third mineral, which he names *iodolite*, is of a pale, smalt-blue color, vitreous lustre, and brittle. Hardness 5.5–6. Fuses easily with boiling into a blebby, colorless glass. The iodolite was found only in a small quantity.

Later, Shepard gave a fuller account of this stone, holding that it contained, chladnite 90 per cent, anorthite 6 per cent, nickeliferous iron 2 per cent, and 2 per cent of magnetic pyrites, schreibersite, sulphur, iodolite, and apatoid.†

The stone was next investigated by W. Sartorius von Waltershausen. He described the principal mass as a white siliceous mineral, forming a finely crystalline mass, with here and there little points showing metallic lustre, also grains of magnetite and brown oxide of iron. The hardness of the white mineral is given as 6, and the specific gravity as 3.039. His results indicated that the siliceous portion of the meteorite was composed of 95.011 per cent of chladnite, and 4.985 per cent of labradorite. The former he found to be monoclinic, and related to wollastonite in specific gravity, color, texture, hardness, and crystalline form.‡ Later, Professor J. Lawrence Smith stated that, from some of his investigations, "chladnite is likely to prove a pyroxene;" § and subsequently published a further discussion, in which he said of chladnite: "It is identical in composition with *Enstatite* of Kenngott."‖ Earlier than Smith's last paper, some investigations were made upon this meteorite by Professors Carl Rammelsberg and Gustav Rose. The former held that the yellowish-brown and bluish-gray particles (the apatoid and iodolite of Shepard) arose from the oxidation of the nickeliferous iron or the alteration of the pyrrhotite.

Rose's examination showed that the chladnite fused before the blowpipe only on the the edges to a white enamel.¶ Rammelsberg, in continuation of his work, further declared that no feldspar was to be found in the stone.** Through the courtesy of Mr. John Cummings and Professor A. Hyatt, the Curator of the Boston Society of Natural History, I have been permitted to make a microscopic examination of a small portion of this meteorite now deposited in the collection of that society.

The portion examined is a grayish-white mass, resembling, as Shepard remarked, a grayish-white granite (*albitic*), with brown and black spots.

Under the microscope it is seen to be composed of an entirely crystalline mass of enstatite, augite, feldspar, olivine, pyrrhotite, and iron.

The structure is essentially granitic, and it appears to belong to the gabbro (*norite*) variety of basalt.

The enstatite is clear and transparent. It shows a longitudinal cleavage parallel to the line of extinction, and in some specimens this is crossed by a cleavage at right angles. It

* Am. Jour. Sci., 1846 (2), ii. 380, 381.
‡ Ann. Chem. Pharm., 1851, lxxix. 369–374.
‖ Ibid. 1864, xxxviii. 225, 226.
** Ibid. 1870, pp. 121–123.

† Ibid. 1848 (2), vi. 411–414.
§ Am. Jour. Sci., 1855 (2), xix. 163.
¶ Abh. Berlin. Akad. 1863, pp. 117–122.

also has a cleavage which is often well marked, and divides the mineral into rhombic forms, with angles, as approximately determined by several measurements, of 73° and 107°. The principal cleavage is parallel to the longer diagonal of these rhombs. It is this rhombic cleavage, probably, which has led observers to believe that chladnite crystallized in the monoclinic and triclinic systems.

The enstatite is found to contain many glass inclusions with polyhedral outlines, the planes being presumably, as usual in such cases, the planes of the inclosing mineral. While many of these inclusions are arranged in the enstatite parallel to the cleavage planes, others are placed at every angle with those planes. The glass inclusions carry bubbles, microlites, and rounded lenticular forms. The latter are frequently at the end of the inclusion, and in some cases, show the cherry-brown color of some chromite. This material, besides forming inclusions in the glass, is in lenticular and irregular rounded grains in the enstatite itself. It sometimes extends in a series of grains across the entire enstatite mass, and at others is in isolated forms. These inclusions, microscopically, are seen to be composed of a centre of nickeliferous iron or pyrrhotite, surrounded by a band of dark material, — chromite or magnetite, possibly. These ferruginous materials are in many cases surrounded by a yellowish-brown staining of iron, which sometimes extends over considerable of the mass and along the fissures. Numerous vacuum or vapor cavities were observed, which were arranged in one plane of the enstatite. The inclusions are seen to be crossed and cut by the cleavage and fissure planes of the enstatite, showing that they were of prior origin to the fissures.

The feldspar stands next in abundance to the enstatite, and is in irregular masses held in its interspaces. It is water-clear, and almost invisible by common light. Much of it is seen to be plagioclastic, but the twinning bands are so exceedingly fine, and the polarization colors so bright, it does not, as a rule, show well this character, except with high powers, and when the mineral is near the point of extinction.

The feldspars contain numerous yellowish-brown, dark, and almost colorless inclusions, which are sometimes irregularly scattered, but more commonly are arranged in bands, similar to those of the fluid inclusions in quartz. These glass inclusions are of various dimensions, and many contain a small bubble. Some microlites were also seen.

In the feldspar at one end of a section, the eustatite was found in minute crystals extending outward from a centre, forming stellate or rosette-like forms. The structure is like that observed in terrestrial rocks, in minerals formed from alteration or solution. This apparently might have been produced in this case, either by the rapid crystallization of enstatite material in a liquid feldspathic mass, or by secondary alteration through water-action on the rock itself. The absence of any other signs of alteration, except of the ferruginous materials, seems to negative the latter supposition. The ferruginous alteration can probably be accounted for by the absorption of moisture by this friable fissured stone since it reached the earth.

The bands of inclusions were seen in several instances to extend from the feldspar through the enstatite, and in one case, to pass into another feldspar on the opposite side. This indicates that the cause of these inclusions was a general one for the rock-mass, and not limited to any one mineral. Eustatite was found in a few cases inclosed in the feldspar.

The monoclinic pyroxene or augite is less abundant, and its determination less sure than is the case with the enstatite and feldspar. It is crossed by fissures in a very irregular manner, but shows in some cases the approximately right-angled cleavage of augite. Its optical characters appear to be those of that mineral, but its polarization is more brilliant than terrestrial augite, and resembles olivine. All the transparent minerals of the section are clearer, and lighter-colored than their mundane representatives, and hence tend to show in polarized light clearer and more brilliant colors. The augite is not, however, quite so water-clear as the enstatite, but has a very faint tinge of yellowish-green. The ferruginous inclusions are the same in this as in the enstatite.

The determination of the olivine is more doubtful, since it is seen only in small irregular grains and masses, which hold the same relation to the other minerals that the olivine of terrestrial gabbros usually does to its associated minerals. From this, and the fact that it optically has the characters of olivine, it is here assigned to that species.

From the description of the mineral constituents of this meteorite, it would seem that, regarding the presence of the feldspar, Messrs. Shepard and Waltershausen were correct, while Rammelsberg was not. It shows the inability of the ablest mineralogical chemists to draw correct conclusions regarding the mineral constituents even of an unaltered rock. The trouble appears to reside in the instrument used — a defect in the method.

Chladnite ought no longer to be regarded as enstatite of the purest kind, as stated in most mineralogies, but rather as a mineral aggregate of which enstatite, feldspar, and augite are the principal constituents. While these observations gave an approximate solution of the Bishopville meteorite puzzle of twenty-seven years standing, it would be well if some one having larger amounts of this meteorite could make a chemical analysis of it as a whole, and also analyze the minerals by the modern microscopic, specific-gravity, chemical method.*

This stone, from the above observations, is, in its mineralogical composition, structure, bubble-bearing glass inclusions, and microlites, like a terrestrial eruptive rock, and it is presumable that it had a similar origin.

There are many who hold that the terrestrial eruptives are produced by the aqueo-igneous solution of chemical precipitates from the primeval ocean or thermal springs, or from sediments buried under the ruins of the earth's crust. Would it not, then, be in order for these scientists to explain the formation of this meteorite in the same way? Now if this body was thrown from the sun or a similar globe, by eruptive agencies, would it not then be proper for these writers to speculate how this sun commenced with a cold, inert surface, and a solid interior; and how, later, by its being blanketed by its own detritus, it had been raised to its present intensely heated condition? — a speculation which is in entire accord with methods formerly advocated by ardent Wernerians to account for the heated condition of the earth.

Since the publication of the preceding description of this meteorite, Tschermak has published independently another description. He recognized the presence of enstatite, plagioclase, and pyrrhotite.†

Manegaum, India.

The Manegaum meteorite was described by Maskelyne in 1863, as composed of a probable olivine and an opaque white or yellowish-white mineral. The latter occurs as a flocculent network, in round spherules, in fragments, and along the laminæ of the crystals of other minerals. Some pyrrhotite and chromite (?) were observed. ‡

In 1870, Maskelyne determined the supposed olivine to be enstatite, to which he

---

* Am. Jour. Sci., 1883 (3), xxvi. 32–36, 243.
† Die mikros. Besch. der Meteoriten, 1883, i. 9, 10; Sitz. Wien. Akad., 1883, lxxxviii. (1), 363–365.
‡ Phil. Mag., 1863 (4), xxvi. 135–139.

also referred the opaque flocculent white mineral. Minute amounts of iron were found. The analysis and composition as given are not satisfactory, and it is thought that a more extended microscopic examination would throw some light upon the subject. This, like the Shergotty meteorite, is probably closely like the gabbros in structure.*

Busti, India.

According to Tschermak, this is composed of crystals and fragments lying in a fine-grained, splintery groundmass, all composed of diopside, enstatite, plagioclase, nickel-iferous iron, oldhamite, and osbornite.

The diopside predominates, and has a gray to violet color, and contains rounded and needle-shaped crystals arranged parallel to the fibrous cleavage. These inclusions are the cause of the violet color.

The enstatite is in colorless splinters, and in gray cloudy forms replete with inclusions. These often show a polyhedral contour, and are filled with a pale-brownish glass, bearing bubbles. The plagioclase occurs only sparingly, and is colorless and nearly free from inclusions. The oldhamite only appears in a portion of the rock in rounded grains having a cubic cleavage; the osbornite in octahedrons in the nickel-iron, which occurs only sparingly.†

Shalka, India.

Tschermak describes this meteorite as composed of a clear-gray, somewhat friable mass, with inclusions of larger, greenish-gray, bronzite grains, and blackish chromites. Under the microscope the larger bronzites are seen to lie in a groundmass of bronzite fragments. This mineral often contains brown glass inclusions or opaque grains. The last are arranged in the fissures in the bronzite, and are referred to pyrrhotite. Some greenish-yellow grains, regarded by Rose as belonging to olivine, were placed by Tschermak under bronzite, on account of their cleavage and action in acid. ‡

Ibbenbühren, Westphalia.

The meteorite of Ibbenbühren consists of a grayish-white, granular mass, in which large and small grains of a light-yellowish-green mineral are unequally distributed. From the chemical analysis and physical character of this mineral, Von Rath referred it to bronzite, and to the same mineral he assigned the groundmass, regarding the entire meteorite as composed of bronzite (diallage). §

According to Tschermak,|| the bronzite forms the principal portion of the stone, and occurs in irregular grains of varying size. Some thin laminæ were referred to augite, and some little colorless grains filling the interspaces between the bronzite grains were looked upon as plagioclase, or possibly tridymite. The inclusions are in part reddish-brown glass, and in part opaque grains referred to chromite and iron.

Greenland.

On account of its interest in connection with the occurrence of metallic iron in basalts, a description of the iron-bearing basalt of Greenland is placed here in connection with these basaltic meteorites.

* Phil. Trans., 1870, pp. 211-213. † Die mikros. Besch. der Meteoriten, 1883, i. 9.
‡ Die mikros. Besch. der Meteoriten, 1883, i. 10. § Monats. Berlin. Akad., 1872, pp. 27-36.
|| Die mikros. Besch. der Meteoriten, 1883, i. 10.

The descriptions are in part taken from the writings of others, in part from sections belonging to the Whitney Lithological Collection, and in part from sections very kindly sent me by Professor J. Lawrence Smith on his own motion. These sections were the ones which had been used in the preparation of his "Mémoire sur le fer natif du Groenland, et sur la dolérite qui le renferme." *

One section, from Assuk, is composed of a gray groundmass, sprinkled with little rounded spots of a darker gray color, and porphyritically holding grains of feldspar, magnetite, and iron. The groundmass is composed of predominating minute augite crystals, in a matrix of clear glass, containing minute feldspars and elongated trichites, similar to those seen in quartz and iron ores. The structural appearance is that of a mass out of which the pyroxene material had mainly crystallized, leaving a colorless glass, which in part had yielded feldspar crystals before congelation. The feldspar crystals are, so far as observed, all plagioclase. A greenish secondary product not only occurs in association with the iron ores, but also in detached masses and bordering fissures. Its color varies from a bright grass-green to a dull dirty-green. Occasionally it is found to be isotropic, but oftener to exhibit aggregate polarization, and it may be classed under that convenient name for these variable secondary products — viridite. Little, rounded pale-pinkish isotropic grains occur. They are apparently foreign, and are considered to be garnet. A few large porphyritic crystals of feldspar were seen, which are filled in the interior portion with inclusions — microlites, magnetite, glass, etc.

The darker rounded masses observed in the section by the naked eye appear to be of the same composition as the rest of the section, but with smaller crystals on the whole, and with much finely-disseminated magnetite dust.

This rock has been described by Steenstrup † and Törnebohm, ‡ the former giving a plate. Törnebohm regards the augitic mineral as enstatite, stating that it is optically orthorhombic. In the section above described, the mineral is clearly monoclinic in its optical characters, although it is perfectly possible that a rhombic pyroxene exists in connection with the augite. The iron ores occur in small rounded and irregular grains, partly native iron, partly magnetite and pyrrhotite. Usually a border of magnetite surrounds the metallic iron.

The Ovifak basalt (dolerite) is described by Törnebohm as composed of plagioclase, augite, olivine, titaniferous iron, and a glassy interstitial material. The augite is in pale, clear-brown, almost colorless, irregular particles between the feldspars. Olivine is found sparingly in little grains, which as a rule are fresh and unchanged. Bubble-bearing glass inclusions occur in the augite, olivine, and feldspar. The titaniferous iron is in elongated staff-like masses. The interstitial glassy masses appear only sparingly in the angles, and as wedges between the above mentioned minerals. When fresh it is of a fawn color and usually filled with microlites or dark spheres. Besides these minerals there occur metallic iron, pyrrhotite, and a silicate rich in iron. This last varies from a green to a dark-brown color. The metallic iron appears, in part, in silver-white grains, often associated with magnetite, and sometimes with schreibersite. The pyrrhotite has in reflected light a yellowish-gray color, and is in larger and smaller grains associated with the other iron ores.

The silicate rich in iron falls into two divisions: one a beautiful grass-green color, isotropic, and allied to chlorophæite; the other a rusty-brown mass, sometimes isotropic, and sometimes anisotropic, and here referred to hisingerite. §

* Ann. Chimie Phys., 1879 (5), xvi. 452–505.   † Min. Mag., 1877, i, 143–148.
‡ Bihang Kongl. Svenska Vetens. Akad Handl., 1878, v., No. 10, pp. 18–21.   § Ibid. pp. 1–22.

Only a few additions will be made to Törnebohm's description from Dr. Smith's sections. The Ovifak sections have the usual structure of a diabase or dolerite; divergent crystals of plagioclase lying in and dissecting the irregular masses of pale brown augite, iron ores, olivine, etc., which form the interstitial material between the feldspars. The minerals are the same in general characters as those described by Törnebohm. In some cases the glass shows the globulitic structure common in basaltic glass.

This basalt is more or less altered in the different sections, presenting many of the characters of a diabase, and the green and brown silicates, replacing glass, olivine, iron, etc.

Much graphite occurs in scaly aggregations of a black color with a lustrous reflection in reflected light, and associated with a brown and violet-red mineral which has been referred by Törnebohm to spinel; but in the section examined by myself, part has been found not to be isotropic, and has been considered by Dr. Smith to be corundum (l. c. pp. 484–486).

The reader is further referred to the before-mentioned full and excellent description of Törnebohm for a more extended study of this basaltic rock; as well as to the writings of Tschermak.*

One section in the Lithological Collection shows a grayish-white groundmass filled by rounded grayish-black masses. These dark spots are seen under the microscope to be composed of plagioclastic feldspars, filled with an irregular network of granules and masses of magnetic and native iron, the whole closely resembling the structure of some portions of the Estherville meteorite (Plate III. fig. 6). The interstitial portions between the rounded feldspathic-iron masses are filled by the normal basalt, composed of ledge-formed plagioclase crystals, cutting a mass of yellowish-gray augite grains, violet-brown globulitic glass, magnetite, and the viriditic products.

In some parts of the section the large plagioclase crystals are free from the iron, and contain glass inclusions and minute pores. A little olivine, some large augites, and yellowish-brown bisingerite (?) was seen in this portion of the section which has a doleritic or diabasic structure, while other portions have that belonging distinctively to the fine-grained basalts.

Another section from the same hand-specimen shows in part of its mass the same basaltic structure as the preceding, of plagioclase, augite, magnetite, base, and secondary materials; but the remaining portion is a coarsely crystallized mass of olivine, plagioclase, augite, iron, and magnetite. The olivines are in irregularly rounded grains, traversed by fissures. They are sometimes clear, and at others stained yellowish, and are altered along the fissures to a yellowish and brownish serpentine. The augites are pale-yellowish, and with the olivines contain bubble-bearing glass inclusions, iron, magnetite, etc. The usual secondary products occur to some extent. Some of Professor Smith's sections have parts similar to these last two sections, except the coarsely crystalline olivine-bearing portion; but his are more altered, and contain a larger amount of secondary products.

Two of Dr. Smith's sections from Pfaff-Oberg are seen to be composed of lath-shaped, divergent plagioclase crystals, lying in a granular groundmass of augite, olivine, etc., with various secondary products. In one section is a large grain of iron, of an irregular cellular structure, and holding in its cells pyrrhotite, olivine, feldspar, etc.

The preceding descriptions show that the coarse and fine crystalline structure

* Min. Mitth., 1874, pp. 171–174.

is not dependent on age, or on any especial depth of the mass at the time of the crystallization; also that diabase, dolerite, and basalt are not distinct in age, but merely relative terms, indicating coarseness in crystalline texture and extent of alteration; for sections of these Greenland basalts could be pronounced, by taking certain portions of them, to be basalt, dolerite, diabase, and possibly gabbro.

Since this work is published in parts, it has seemed best to place in the first portion, so far as possible, all relating to meteorites, and to end the first part before taking up the terrestrial basalts.

Owing to the views of Professor Tschermak, that nearly all the meteorites are tufas, the preceding descriptions are affected by that view, since most of the microscopic study has been done by him. It appears to the writer that the basaltic meteorites display in general the structure of friable, rapidly crystallized basalts, apparently quickly cooled, and never bound together by the subsequent products of alteration; few if any of them being fragmental. From this point of view, their general structure in the basaltic variety would be described as divergent, lath-shaped plagioclase feldspars, lying in a groundmass of pyroxene (augite, diallage, and enstatite) grains, with some base, feldspar, and iron ores.

So far as the gabbro type of the meteorites is concerned, the description of the Bishopville form would serve as a general statement of their collective characters, varied by the predominance of any one of the mineral constituents. The Bishopville form is certainly not fragmental in structure, and it does not seem to the writer that the other meteoric gabbros are so; hence they may be defined as crystalline-granular masses of feldspar, pyroxene (augite, diallage, and enstatite), with various ores of iron, and with or without olivine. In these, however, certain of the constituents may predominate, to the partial or complete exclusion of others. This is no more than the observed variation occurring in different portions of the same terrestrial rock.

Although mineralogically the basaltic meteorites could be divided into many varieties, the same as the peridotites have been, it seems to the writer unnecessary. The terrestrial basalts were divided in the first place chiefly on structural characters and differences in external appearance, and the recently introduced terms, *norite*, *olivine-gabbro*, and *olivine-norite*, appear to be superfluous and unnecessary, although consistent with the common mineralogical nomenclature of rocks, since structurally all can readily be classed under the variety gabbro.

Many changes in the arrangement of the meteorites may hereafter be made by the writer, if ever opportunity should be afforded for an extended microscopic study of them. At present he has tried to arrange them as best he could with the means at his command.

Although all the chemical analyses found of the basaltic meteorites have been arranged in a table, they are too few and too imperfect for any satisfactory discussion.

SECTION II. — *The Pseudo-Meteorites.*

A NUMBER of supposed meteorites have been described, which so far as their general characters and chemical composition show, belong to the species trachyte and rhyolite. For these the meteoric origin has been denied in every case, and perhaps the Igast stone is the only one which has any claims to be considered even of doubtful meteoric origin.

Waterville, Maine.

This pseudo-meteorite has been studied by the present writer. It is in the form of a small triangular cinder-like mass, cellular, laminated, and on the fresh fracture, of an ash-gray color. The laminated appearance is produced by a series of flattened cells surrounded by a black vitreous mass.

The original surfaces are coated with a gray, red-brown, and bluish-black crust formed by fusion.

It was claimed that this stone was picked up shortly after falling, hence it became necessary to examine its characters to see how long it might have been exposed to atmospheric action. The portion of the fused crust which lay uppermost on the ground is seen under a lens to have been worn and polished the same as siliceous rocks are when long exposed to rain; while the remaining parts are found to be coated to some extent by earthy material, the same as rocks are when lying in a dry, sandy soil. Its cavities contain in places a fine, brown, matted mass, formed by the fibres of growing plants, and under the microscope their vegetable character can readily be distinguished.

The specimen, then, when picked up by Captain Crosby, could not have been a newly detached mass, but had been for a long while partially buried in the soil, and of course could not have been a portion of the meteor seen shortly before the specimen was found. It remains, then, to consider the very improbable supposition — is it a fragment of a meteorite which fell at some former period? Microscopically it is seen to be a cellular, glassy mass, which has begun to devitrify, and presents the appearance of a slag-like body which has been long exposed to the action of atmospheric agencies. The sections were cut across the lamination, and showed a fluidal structure parallel to it. A few quartz grains which were cracked and fissured were seen. Near the fissures numerous ferruginous globulites had been developed, and the quartz showed evident signs of having been exposed to strong heat.

Adjacent to the flattened, as well as some other cells, is a black and brown ferruginous material.

The sections show not the slightest characters belonging to any meteorite that has yet been examined microscopically, either by myself or by others, so far as can be ascertained by their published descriptions. It is apparently a slag.*

Richland, South Carolina.

This so-called meteoric stone is reported to have fallen in 1846. This when cut was, according to Professor C. U. Shepard, of a "uniform yellowish-white color, much resembling that of common fire-brick. A few minute grains of transparent quartz are visible throughout its substance, which is otherwise perfectly homogeneous. It is close-grained and rather firm in texture." This description, and the chemical analysis given by Shepard, coupled with one by Rammelsberg denotes a structure similar to that of the rhyolites, for such a description could be given of many of them.†

Rammelsberg regards the Richland stone as a clay, or possibly a fragment of a brick. A microscopic examination by a competent lithologist ought to readily determine the character and origin of this stone.

Igast, Livonia, Russia.

This stone is looked upon by Professors Grewingk and Schmidt as an authentic meteorite, and they made a chemical analysis of it, showing that it contained a little over eighty per cent of silica.‡

Professor F. J. Wiik also accepts it as a meteorite, and states that in the thin sections it shows a fine-granular, dark-colored groundmass, the dark color owing to little magnetite, porphyritically inclosing larger crystals of quartz, orthoclase, and oligoclase. The quartz contains fluid cavities with movable bubbles, and the plagioclase shows fine parallel cleavage lines as well as the usual twinning. By a high magnifying power is shown in the groundmass little colorless elongated crystals, and minute crystalline grains.

Professor E. Cohen regards it as a doubtful meteorite. §

Lasaulx describes this as a stone rich in a basaltic glass base, in which lie inclosed numerous grains of plagioclase, microcline, and quartz. The groundmass is composed largely of a brown glass, rich in magnetite grains, some showing quadratic sections, and others a dendritic structure. The groundmass further contains numerous little spear- or ledge-shaped plagioclase crystals, and yellowish-green irregular grains of augite — all showing fluidal structure. The entire groundmass appears as the product of the fusion of quartz and feldspar, the rudiments of which are now inclosed, with the later crystallization of plagioclase and augite out of the molten magma.

Many of the crystals show distinct rounding through the fusion of their edges. The larger plagioclase fragments are mostly ragged, slashed, and irregular, while the minute quartz grains are commonly perfect, and smoothly rounded. The plagioclase crystals are generally clear and free from inclusions; only an external rim of disjointed glass inclusions lies about them. The brown glass penetrates into the fissure in the

---

* Am. Jour. Sci., 1883 (3), xxvi. 36–38. † Proc. Am. Assoc. Adv. Sci., 1850, iii. 147, 148.
‡ Archiv Nat. Liv-, Ehst-, Kurlands, 1864, iii. 421–554.
§ Neues Jahr. Min., 1883, i. 384; Finska Vet. Soc. Forh., 1882, xxiv. 63. Archiv Nat. Liv-, Ehst-, Kurlands, 1882, ix. 158.

crystals, and in general the rock appears similar in character to one produced by the partial fusion of an inclosure of sandstone, granite, or some other rock, in basalt.

After further description, Lasaulx decides against its meteoric character, and apparently justly.[*]

Waterloo, Seneca Co., New York.

The so-called meteorite of Waterloo, described by Shepard,[†] is considered by Rammelsberg to be a clay.[‡]

Concord, New Hampshire.

The meteoric stone of Concord, described by Professor B. Silliman, Jr., [§] is now preserved in the collection at Yale College.

A macroscopic examination by the writer convinces him that it is a portion of the consolidated scum or froth of some slag, and this opinion seems to be held by others. [||]

It would be a matter of the greatest interest to prove the fall of meteorites more acidic than the basaltic variety, and it is not impossible that further microscopic studies will reveal that some already known are of the andesitic type.

[*] Sitz. nieder. Gesell., Bonn, 1882, xxxix. 108–110.
[‡] Jour. Prakt. Chemie, 1862, lxxxv. 87, 88.
[||] G. W. Hawes, Geol. of N. H., part iv., p. 24.
[†] Am. Jour. Sci., 1851 (2), xi. 39, 40.
[§] Am. Jour. Sci., 1847 (2), iv. 353–356.

EXPLANATION OF THE TABLES.

TABLE I. — Chromite and Picotite. pp. ii–v.

THIS table contains one hundred and twenty analyses of chromite and picotite, arranged in the ascending order of the percentage of chromic oxide. Since the object of the table is to show the mutual relations of the two minerals, and their variations, many of the analyses given of chromite are of the more impure forms, — commercial ores (!).

TABLE II. — Siderolite. pp. vi–xv.

This table contains one hundred and ninety-three analyses of meteoric and terrestrial irons, arranged in the descending order of their percentage of iron. The irons which are supposed to be meteorites, but which have not been known to fall, have been marked by an interrogation point placed after the term Meteorite. No variety names proper occur in this species; but for convenience the meteoric irons known to have fallen, the supposed meteoric irons, and the terrestrial irons, are distinguished from one another by terms placed in the "Variety" column.

When several analyses are given for the same locality, no attempt is made to arrange them beyond this: the analysis first found in the search for the analyses is placed first, and the others follow in the order in which they were seen; except in cases in which the analyses *strikingly differed* in value, owing either to internal evidence or to the reputation for accuracy of the analyst; then the best is placed first, but the order of the others still remains in the order in which they were found.

TABLE III. — Pallasite. pp. xvi, xvii.

This table contains twenty-four analyses of meteoric and terrestrial pallasites. The doubtful meteorites are designated as in the preceding table, while the terrestrial forms are given their proper variety name, — Cumberlandite. But few of these analyses are accurate exponents of the constitution of the rock mass, the majority being rough approximations only. The analyses are arranged in ascending order of the percentages of silica.

TABLE IV. — Peridotite. pp. xviii–xxxi.

This table contains two hundred and forty-four analyses of terrestrial and meteoric peridotites. In the "Variety" column is given the name of the variety so far as known, and when the specimen is a meteorite it has been designated by an asterisk prefixed to the variety name. The meteorites whose variety is not known are designated by the term Meteorite, and the terrestrial peridotites, whose variety is also unknown, are given the names which the analysts have applied to them.

The analyses have been arranged in the order of the percentages of silica; but when more than one exists for the same locality, they have been arranged as stated for Table II.

The specific gravities in this and the other tables have been taken from any available source, when the analyst has given none; but it has been found impracticable to designate the source from which they were obtained, although many are from C. Rumler's determinations, which with analyses are to be found in the works and tables of Partsch, Buchner, Rammelsberg, and Roth, to which I am deeply indebted.

Many analyses of meteoric forms have been made in such a manner that no determination of the complete chemical constitution is possible, owing to the omission of necessary data for recalculation, and all such have been omitted. Many others have been recalculated with more or less approximation to correctness, varying according to the data; matters in which the numerous analyses of Dr. J. Lawrence Smith have been particularly unfortunate. The recalculations have mostly been made by the aid of a four-place table of logarithms, and therefore partake of its imperfections.

TABLE V. — Part I. The Meteoric Basalts. pp. xxxii, xxxiii.

This part contains thirty-one analyses, arranged in order of their percentages of silica.

TABLES.

TABLE I. — Analyses of

Name.	Locality.	Analyst.	Publication.
Chromite.	Kynouria, Greece.	A. Christomanos.	Berichte Chem. Gesell. Berlin, 1877, i. 343–350.
Picotite.	Kosakover, Bohemia.	F. Farsky.	Verh. Geol. Reichs., 1876, pp. 207, 208.
Picotite.	Kosakover, Bohemia.	" "	" " " " " "
Picotite.	Hofheim, Bavaria.	Hilger.	Neues Jahr. Min., 1866, p. 399.
Picotite.	L. Lherz, France.	F. Sandberger.	Neues Jahr. Min., 1866, p. 388.
Picotite.	L. Lherz, France.	A. Damour.	Bull. Soc. Géol. France, 1862 (2), xix, 414.
Chromite.	Near Athens, Greece.	A. Christomanos.	Berichte Chem. Gesell. Berlin, 1877, i. 343–350.
Chromite.	Piræus, Greece.	" "	" " " " " "
Chromite.	Alt-Orsowa, Hungary.	Alfr. Hofmann.	Neues Jahr. Min., 1873, p. 873.
Chromite.	Delos, Grecian Archipelago.	A. Christomanos.	Berichte Chem. Gesell. Berlin, 1877, i. 343–350.
Chromite.	Seres, Macedonia.	" "	" " " " " "
Chromite.	Gythion, Greece.	" "	" " " " " "
Chromite.	Cerigo, Ionian Isles.	" "	" " " " " "
Chromite.	Hungary.	J. Clouet.*	Ann. Chimie Phys., 1869 (4), xvi. 90–100.
Chromite.	Mt. Hymettus, Greece.	A. Christomanos.	Berichte Chem. Gesell. Berlin, 1877, i. 343–350.
Chromite.	Australia.	J. Clouet.	Ann. Chimie Phys., 1869 (4), xvi. 90–100.
Chromite.	Salamis, Greece.	A. Christomanos.	Berichte Chem. Gesell. Berlin, 1877, i. 343–350.
Chromite.	Corinth, Greece.	" "	" " " " " "
Chromite.	Vrysi, Greece.	" "	" " " " " "
Chromite.	Vache Island, W. Indies.	P. Berthier.	Ann. Chimie Phys., 1821, xvii. 55–64.
Chromite.	Var, France.	J. Clouet.	Ann. Chimie Phys., 1869 (4), xvi. 90–100.
Chromite.	Loukissia, opp. Chalcis, Greece.	A. Christomanos.	Berichte Chem. Gesell. Berlin, 1877, i. 343–350.
Chromite.	Loutraki, Greece.	" "	" " " " " "
Chromite.	Locris, Greece.	" "	" " " " " "
Chromite.	Pernehora, Greece.	" "	" " " " " "
Chromite.	Peky, Greece.	" "	" " " " " "
Chromite.	Bare Hills, Baltimore, Md.	Henry Seybert.	Am. Jour. Sci., 1822 (1), iv. 321–323.
Chromite.	Alt-Orsowa, Hungary.	Alfr. Hofmann.	Neues Jahr. Min., 1873, p. 873.
Chromite.	Christiania, Norway.	J. Clouet.	Ann. Chimie Phys., 1869 (4), xvi. 90–100.
Chromite.	Shetland Isles.	"	" " " " " "
Chromite (Magnetic Chrome Sand).	Chester, Penn.	T. H. Garrett.	Am. Jour. Sci., 1852 (2), xiv. 47.
Chromite.	Drontheim, Norway.	J. Clouet.	Ann. Chimie Phys., 1869 (4), xvi. 90–100.
Chromite.	Volterra, Tuscany.	C. Bechi.	Am. Jour. Sci., 1852 (2), xiv. 62.
Chromite.	California.	J. Clouet.	Ann. Chimie Phys., 1869 (4), xvi. 90–100.
Chromite.	Cerasia, Eubœa.	A. Christomanos.	Berichte Chem. Gesell. Berlin, 1877, i. 343–350.
Chromite.	Haziskos, Greece.	" "	" " " " " "
Chromite.	Var, France.	L. N. Vauquelin.	Jour. Mines, 1801, x. 521–524.
Chromite.	Volo, Thessaly.	A. Christomanos.	Berichte Chem. Gesell. Berlin, 1877, i. 343–350.
Chromite.	Troezene, Greece.	" "	" " " " " "
Chromite.	Epidaurus, Greece.	" "	" " " " " "
Chromite.	Nauplia, Greece.	" "	" " " " " "
Chromite.	Dryope, Greece.	" "	" " " " " "
Chromite.	Olympus, Thessaly.	" "	" " " " " "
Chromite.	Franklin, Macon Co., N. C.	F. A. Genth.	Geol. of North Carolina, 1881, ii. 81.
Chromite.	Shetland Isles.	J. Clouet.	Ann. Chimie Phys., 1869 (4), xvi. 90–100.
Chromite.	Volo, Thessaly.	A. Christomanos.	Berichte Chem. Gesell. Berlin, 1877, i. 343–350.
Chromite.	Poros, Greece.	" "	" " " " " "
Chromite.	Baltimore, Maryland.	Hermann Abich.	Ann. Physik Chemie, 1831, xxiii. 335–342.
Chromite.	Baltimore, Maryland.	J. Clouet.	Ann. Chimie Phys., 1869 (4), xvi. 90–100.
Chromite.	Haziskos, Greece.	A. Christomanos.	Berichte Chem. Gesell. Berlin, 1877, i. 343–350.
Chromite.	Tinos, Grecian Archipelago.	" "	" " " " " "
Chromite.	Ural.	....	Kokscharow's Material Min. Russ., 1866, v. 163.
Chromite.	Australia.	Schultz.	Rammelsberg's Handbuch der Mineralchemie, 2d ed., 1875, p. 142.
Chromite.	Wilmington, Delaware.	J. Clouet.	Ann. Chimie Phys., 1869 (4), xvi. 90–100.
Chromite.	Bolton, Canada.	T. Sterry Hunt.	Report Prog. Geol. Canada, 1847–48, p. 164.
Chromite.	Lützelberg, Kaiserstuhl, Bavaria.	A. Knop.	Neues Jahr. Min., 1877, pp. 697–699.
Chromite.	Limne, Eubœa.	A. Christomanos.	Berichte Chem. Gesell. Berlin, 1877, i. 343–350.
Chromite.	Andros, Grecian Archipelago.	" "	" " " " " "
Chromite.	India.	J. Clouet.	Ann. Chimie Phys., 1869 (4), xvi. 90–100.
Chromite.	Mourtin, Eubœa.	A. Christomanos.	Berichte Chem. Gesell. Berlin, 1877, i. 343–350.
Chromite.	Alt-Orsowa, Hungary.	J. Clouet.	Ann. Chimie Phys., 1869 (4), xvi. 90–100.
Chromite.	Ural.	....	Kokscharow's Material Min. Russ., 1866, v. 163.
Chromite.	Ekaterinburg, Russia.	J. Clouet.	Ann. Chimie Phys., 1869 (4), xvi. 90–100.
Chromite.	Lake Memphramagog.	T. Sterry Hunt.	Report Prog. Geol. Canada, 1847–48, p. 164.
Chromite.	Haziskos, Greece.	A. Christomanos.	Berichte Chem. Gesell. Berlin, 1877, i. 343–350.
Chromite.	Sagmata, Greece.	" "	" " " " " "
Chromite.	Ural.	....	Kokscharow's Material Min. Russ., 1866, v. 163.
Chromite.	Salonica, Turkey.	A. Christomanos.	Berichte Chem. Gesell. Berlin, 1877, i. 343–350.
Chromite.	Samos, Grecian Archipelago.	" "	" " " " " "

* This and all others of Clouet's analyses are stated to be the mean of a number of analyses.

Chromite and Picotite.

Sp. Gr.	Al$_2$O$_3$.	MgO.	Cr$_2$O$_3$.	Fe$_2$O$_3$.	FeO.	SiO$_2$.	CaO.	Miscellaneous.	Total.
....	30.17	17.27	4.74	....	2.30	26.01	13.26	CO$_2$+H$_2$O = 4.45.	98.20
....	50.51	17.87	5.75	....	22.27	3.77	....	....	100.00
....	52.47	18.23	7.01	....	21.42	1.25	....	....	100.38
....	53.93	23.69	7.23	11.40	3.85	....	....	....	100.00
....	55.31	10.18	7.90	....	24.90	1.98	....	....	100.00
4.08	56.00	10.30	6.00	....	24.90	2.00	....	....	101.20
....	20.80	11.78	9.80	2.72	7.00	4.85	5.50	FeCO$_3$ = 37.75.	100.20
....	14.73	6.12	10.80	29.06	12.05	6.17	10.55	CO$_2$ = 2.27, H$_2$O = 1.90.	90.05
....	16.110	21.101	17 096	22.409	....	14.211	8.300	....	99.317
....	3.85	25.40	17.73	....	16 81	26.70	7.20	CO$_2$ = 2.80.	100.49
....	1.12	28.71	17.88	....	5.60	9.82	....	CO$_2$ = 35.05.	100.28
....	trace.	10.60	21.16	trace.	11.10	12.04	24.36	CO$_2$ = 18.14.	100.46
....	0.48	10.92	31.20	27.72	14.79	11.20	....	Mn$_3$O$_2$ = 4.18.	100.50
....	16.77	14.85	31.48	....	20.00	7.30	....	....	100.00
....	20.50	12.08	32.75	....	23.84	7.67	2.01	CO$_2$ = 1.03.	98.88
....	18.00	17.40	33.20	....	23.40	8.00	....	....	100.00
....	19.81	9.18	33 60	trace.	24.71	4.63	8.80	CO$_2$ = trace.	100.63
....	22.70	13.65	34.75	0.90	10.81	9.43	2.02	....	100.35
....	24.71	7.81	35.60	....	25.02	3.56	1.55	CO$_2$ = 0.02.	99.47
....	21.80	....	36.00	37.20	....	5.00	....	....	100.00
....	13 15	12.53	37 00	....	34.79	2.53	....	....	100.00
....	17.00	3.08	37.31	3.80	35.12	2.82	trace.	Mn$_3$O$_4$ = 1.12.	100 25
....	7.70	16.22	38.12	1.06	27.40	8.53	....	....	98.73
....	27.83	10.47	39.05	0.85	18.05	2.10	....	Mn$_3$O$_4$ = 1.45.	99.80
....	5 02	14.07	39.53	0.75	27.70	11.64	....	....	99.42
....	20.14	10.00	39.60	....	28.20	1.91	....	....	100.35
4.0630	13.002	....	39.514	36.004	....	10 596	....	....	99.116
....	20.026	17.065	39.574	10.558	....	4.19	....	....	98 023
....	4.80	13.23	40.00	....	37.77	4.20	....	....	100.00
....	10.15	16.86	41.00	....	23.14	8.85	....	....	100.00
....	....	....	41.55	62.02	....	1.25	....	....	104.82
....	12.00	21.28	42.00	....	10.72	5.00	....	....	100.00
....	19.84	....	42.13	....	33.93	4.75	....	....	100.65
....	13.60	14.88	42.20	....	28.84	1.48	....	....	100.00
....	10.07	15.27	42.60	trace.	19.02	9.31	2.20	....	99.07
....	22.64	12.72	42.80	....	19.38	2.02	1.13	....	100.64
....	20.30	....	43.00	34.70	....	2.00	....	....	100.00
....	21.12	3.18	43.20	....	30.02	2 31	trace.	....	100.33
....	0.60	12.85	43.23	....	29.90	6.95	4.70	CO$_2$ = 0.88.	99.03
....	11.53	21.00	43.40	trace.	20.56	4.87	....	....	101.42
....	20.15	7.77	43.50	....	20.92	6.92	trace.	....	99.26
....	10.23	15.25	43.70	....	21.27	5.42	trace.	Mn$_2$O$_3$ = 1.95.	100.32
....	23 81	0.77	43.80	....	31.55	....	trace.	....	99.96
4.313	22.41	15.67	44.15	5.78	11.76	....	....	....	99.77
....	7.47	17.30	44.20	....	24.93	6.10	....	....	100.00
....	19.14	3.00	44.79	....	31.85	2 00	....	10	100.84
....	9.09	11.89	44.81	....	21.41	5.50	5.74	CO$_2$ = 1 25.	100.29
....	17.85	9.96	44.91	....	18.97	0.83	....	....	98.25
....	5.40	4.09	45.00	....	42.31	3.20	....	....	100.00
....	22.22	11.64	45.10	....	14.50	0.40	....	....	99.95
....	10 72	6 28	45.32	....	23.97	12.42	trace.	....	98.71
....	3.00	23.77	45.40	....	21.88	5.26	....	....	99.91
4.534	7.29	6.28	45.46	....	43.30	....	....	....	102.42
....	6.00	2.06	45.50	....	42.78	3.00	....	....	100.00
....	3.20	15.03	45 00	....	35.68	....	....	....	99.81
....	20.00	20.55	46.87	....	12.98	....	....	....	100.26
....	8.71	14.28	47.30	....	23.17	6.20	....	....	99.70
....	3.33	4 27	47.60	....	45.22	....	....	....	100.32
....	0.30	6.00	47.50	....	35.70	1.50	....	....	100.00
....	8 03	2.88	47.66	trace.	34.87	5.53	....	....	98.71
....	•12.00	15.09	48.72	....	18.33	5.26	....	....	100.00
....	10.20	4.08	49.00	....	29.90	7 00	....	....	100.08
....	6.77	13.40	49.40	....	23.27	7.07	....	....	100.00
....	11.30	18.18	49.75	....	21.28	....	....	....	100.46
....	21.57	8 00	50.04	....	15.70	3.12	....	....	98.44
....	14 25	1.80	50.60	0.97	23.96	2.75	4.80	CO$_2$ = 0.75.	90.78
....	5.00	11.53	50.80	....	27.00	4.00	....	....	99.23
....	11.87	15.72	50.80	....	15.92	4.90	....	....	99.21
....	6.14	17.05	51.60	....	22.75	3.50	....	....	100.00

ANALYSES OF CHROMITE AND PICOTITE.

TABLE I.

Name.	Locality.	Analyst.	Publication.
Chromite.	Vache Island, W. Indies.	J. Clouet.	Ann. Chimie Phys., 1860 (4), xvi. 90–100.
Chromite.	Chester Co., Penn.	Henry Seybert.	Am. Jour. Sci., 1822 (1), iv. 321–323.
Chromite.	Ural.	....	Kokscharow's Material Min. Russ., 1866, v. 163.
Chromite.	Philadelphia, Penn.	P. Berthier.	Ann. Chimie Phys., 1821, xvii. 55–64.
Chromite.	Tanagra, Greece.	A. Christomanos.	Berichte Chem. Gesell. Berlin, 1877, i. 343–350.
Chromite.	Polyhieron, Macedonia.	" "	" " " " "
Chromite.	Monterey Co., Cal.	E. Goldsmith.	Proc. Phila. Acad. Nat. Sci., 1873, p. 365.
Chromite.	Papades, Eubœa.	A. Christomanos.	Berichte Chem. Gesell. Berlin, 1877, i. 343–350.
Chromite.	Jannina, Epirus.	" "	" " " " "
Chromite.	Styria.	J. Clouet.	Ann. Chimie Phys., 1869 (4), xvi. 90–100.
Chromite.	Karahissar, Asia Minor.	" "	" " " " "
Chromite.	Orenbourg, Russia.	"	" " " " "
Chromite.	Winaga, Ural.	A. Laugier.	Ann. Mus. Hist. Nat., 1815, vi. 325–331.
Chromite.	Ural.	....	Kokscharow's Material Min. Russ., 1866, v. 163.
Chromite.	Hibbard's, near Media, Delaware Co., Penn.	F. A. Genth.	Sec. Geol. Survey Penn., B, 1874, p. 48.
Chromite.	Ural.	....	Kokscharow's Material Min. Russ., 1866, v. 163.
Chromite.	Albania.	A. Christomanos.	Berichte Chem. Gesell. Berlin, 1877, i. 343–350.
Chromite.	Tinos, Grecian Archipelago.	" "	"
Chromite.	Röraas, Norway.	....	Ann. Mines, 1829 (2), v. 316 (ante, p. 185).
Chromite.	Vatondos, Eubœa.	A. Christomanos.	Berichte Chem. Gesell. Berlin, 1877, i. 343–350.
Chromite.	Broussa, Asia Minor.	" "	" " " " "
Chromite.	Plattsburg, N. Y.	P. Collier.	Am. Jour. Sci., 1881 (3), xxi. 123.
Chromite.	Texas, Lancaster Co., Penn.	Franke.	Rammelsberg's Handbuch der Mineralchemie, 2d ed., 1875, p. 142.
Chromite.	Smyrna, Asia Minor.	A. Christomanos.	Berichte Chem. Gesell. Berlin, 1877, i. 343–350.
Chromite.	Krieglach, Steiermark.	M. H. Klaproth.	Mineral Korper, 1807, iv. 132–136.
Chromite.	Pyli, Eubœa.	A. Christomanos.	Berichte Chem. Gesell. Berlin, 1877, i. 348–350.
Chromite.	Shetland Islands.	T. Thomson.	Ann. Mines, 1827 (2), i. 280.
Picotite (Chrompicotite).	Dun Mountain, New Zealand.	Theodor Petersen.	Jour. Prakt. Chemie, 1869, cxv. 137–140.
Chromite.	Texas, Lancaster Co., Penn.	C. F. Rammelsberg.	Handbuch der Mineralchemie, 2d ed., 1875, p. 142.
Chromite.	Broussa, Asia Minor.	A. Christomanos.	Berichte Chem. Gesell. Berlin, 1877, i. 343–350.
Chromite.	Tarasska, Ural.	....	Kokscharow's Material Min. Russ., 1866, v. 163.
Chromite.	Mt. Rossipnain, Ural.	....	" " " " "
Chromite.	Viatka, Russia.	J. Clouet.	Ann. Chimie Phys., 1869 (4), xvi. 90–100.
Chromite.	Alt-Orsowa, Hungary.	Alfr. Hofmann.	Neues Jahr. Min., 1873, p. 873.
Chromite.	Oita, Japan.	T. Haga.	Jahresb. Chemie, 1881, p. 1302.
Chromite.	Ural.	....	Kokscharow's Material Min. Russ., 1866, v. 163.
Chromite.	Asia.	Alfr. Hofmann.	Neues Jahr. Min., 1873, p. 873.
Chromite (Crystallized).	Baltimore, Maryland.	Hermann Abich.	Ann. Physik Chemie, 1831, xxiii. 835–342.
Chromite.	Haziskos, Greece.	A. Christomanos.	Berichte Chem. Gesell. Berlin, 1877, i. 343–350.
Chromite (Chrome Sand).	Chester, Penn.	Isaac Starr.	Am. Jour. Sci., 1852 (2), xiv. 47.
Chromite.	Mourtia, Eubœa.	A. Christomanos.	Berichte Chem. Gesell. Berlin, 1877, i. 343–350.
Chromite.	Baltimore, Maryland.	L. E. Rivot.	Ann. Chimie Phys., 1850 (3), xxx. 200–203.
Chromite.	Texas, Chester Co., Penn.	T. H. Garrett.	Am. Jour. Sci., 1852 (2), xiv. 46.
Chromite.	Ural.	....	Kokscharow's Material Min. Russ., 1866, v. 163.
Chromite.	Ural.	....	Kokscharow's Material Min. Russ., 1866, v. 162.
Chromite.	Berezof, Siberia.	A. Moberg.	Jour. Prakt. Chemie, 1848, xliii. 114–128.
Chromite.	Massachusetts.	C. H. Pfaff.	Jour. Chemie Physik, 1825, xlv. 101, 102.

ANALYSES OF CHROMITE AND PICOTITE.

Continued.

Sp. Gr.	Al_2O_3	MgO.	Cr_2O_3	Fe_2O_3	FeO.	SiO_2	CaO.	Miscellaneous.	Total.
....	....	....	51.53	....	48.40	....	....	....	100.00
....	0.723	....	51.562	35.14	....	2.001	....	MnO = trace.	99.326
....	0.20	12.12	51.60	....	24.06	6.35	....	....	100.33
....	9.70	....	51.60	37.20	....	2.90	....	....	99.00
....	13.90	7.81	51.90	....	24.72	2.05	0.41	....	100.69
....	11.01	17.45	52.12	....	16.76	2.60	....	....	99.94
4.1647	2.18	12.29	52.12	15.24	....	12.12	....	....	99.00
....	5.88	12.62	52.50	trace.	24.72	3.90	trace.	....	99.71
....	3.02	6.72	52.88	1.22	24.27	12.95	trace.	....	100.00
....	8.00	11.58	53.00	....	24.02	2.50	....	....	100.00
....	7.62	12.81	53.00	....	24.92	2.15	....	....	100.00
....	8.05	10.98	53.00	....	24.92	3.05	....	....	100.00
....	11.00	....	53.00	....	34.00	1.00	....	MnO = trace, Loss = 1.00.	100.00
....	0.90	14.86	53.16	....	21.06	10.10	....	....	100.08
4.78	5.98	6.53	53.36	7.41	26.04	....	....	NiO_2 = 0.14, CoO_2 = trace, MnO = 0.39.	100.45
....	1.30	15.26	53.00	....	19.88	11.35	....	....	101.84
....	17.75	2.03	53.90	....	25.60	0.86	....	....	100.14
....	11.14	7.01	54.00	....	18.08	7.30	....	$CaCO_3$ = 2.44.	100.00
....	9.02	5.357	54.08	25.661	....	4.833	....	....	98.951
....	7.85	9.92	54.42	....	24.88	4.41	....	....	101.48
....	11.82	6.04	54.53	trace.	25.75	1.95	....	....	10 12
....	5.60	0.941	54.044	....	31.567	3.731	3.405	....	100.278
....	5.75	9.39	55.14	....	28.88	....	....	....	99.16
....	4.82	10.58	55.50	trace.	26.25	2.62	0.60	....	100.37
4.60	6.00	....	55.50	38.00	....	2.00	....	Ignition = 2.00.	98.50
....	2.06	7.21	55.84	....	24.80	0.52	....	....	96.43
....	13.00	....	56.00	31 00	....	trace.	....	....	100.00
4.115	12.13	14.08	56.54	....	18.01	....	....	MnO = 0.46, CoO+NiO = trace.	101.22
....	0.86	9.89	56.55	....	30.23	....	....	....	97.53
....	2.53	12 37	56.70	....	26.00	2.04	....	....	100.54
....	5.80	12.38	56.80	....	20.16	4.20	....	....	99.34
....	4.80	12.75	57.20	....	20.06	5.80	....	....	100.61
....	{ 4.60	0.33	56.92	....	27.00	5.20	....	....	100.05
....	{ 6.20	12.38	56.60	....	20.07	5.00	....	....	100.25
....	10.00	11.62	58.00	....	18.18	2.20	....	....	100.00
....	14.406	2.018	58.096	21.337	....	3.030	....	MnO = 0.002.	99.586
4.50	0.80	0.17	59.86	....	28.27	1.58	....	....	90.12
....	0.90	10.20	59.60	....	22.41	6.80	....	....	100.06
....	10.001	3.130	60.022	20.192	....	....	0.026	MnO = 5.20.	99.171
....	11.85	7.45	60.04	....	20.13	....	....	....	99.45
....	8.40	2.19	60.50	....	28.75	0.45	trace.	....	100.29
....	0.928	....	60.836	38.052	....	0.610	....	NiO = 0.10.	100.425
....	13.45	5.31(?)	61.50	....	18.95	0.775	....	....	99.985
....	1.06	....	62 37	30.04	....	2.21	2.02	....	99.60
4.608	....	....	63.89	38.66	....	....	....	NiO = 2.28.	104.33
....	0.50	12.12	63.80	....	20.34	3.00	....	....	99.76
....	....	{ 5.04	64.00	....	....	1.03	....	Al_2O_3+FeO 29.33	99.40
....	....	{ 6.15	62.25	....	....	0.05	....	30.05	99.40
....	....	6.28	63.40	....	....	2.60	....	28.00	100.88
....	10.83	6.08	64.17	....	18.42	0.91	....	....	101.01
....	....	....	77.00	0.00	....	....	....	Al_2O_3+SiO_2 = 15.00.	101 00

A CLASSIFIED LIST OF COMPLETE (BAUSCH)

TABLE II.

Variety.	Locality.	Analyst.	Publication.	Sp. Gr.	Fe.	Ni.	Co.	P.	S.	P,Fe,Ni.
Meteorite ?	Walker Co., Ala.	C. U. Shepard.	Am. Jour. Sci., 1847 (2), iv. 74, 75.	7.265	99.89					
Meteorite ?	Scriba, N. Y.	C. U. Shepard.	Am. Jour. Sci., 1841 (1), xi. 306-360.	7.50	99.08					
Meteorite ?	Bonanza, Coahuila, Mexico.	C. U. Shepard.	Am. Jour. Sci., 1867 (2), xliii. 384, 885.	7.825	97.90					
Meteorite ?	Campbell Co., Tenn.	J. L. Smith.	Am. Jour. Sci., 1855 (2), xix. 153.	7.05	97.54	0.25	0.60	0.12		
Meteorite ?	Bedford Co., Pa.	C. U. Shepard.	Am. Jour. Sci., 1828 (1), xiv. 183-186.	7.337	97.44					
Meteorite ?	Petropawlowsk, Siberia.	{ Sokolowskij. { Iwanow.	Archiv. Kunde Russland, 1841, i. 317. Ibid., 1841, i. 723-725.	7.76	97.29 { 98.09 { 94.12	2.07 7.00 6.06				
Meteorite ?	Durango, Mex.	{ M. H. Klaproth. { J. F. John.	Beiträge, 1807, iv. 101, 102. Jour. Chemie Physik, 1821, xxxii. 203, 264.	7.885	96.75 91.50	3.25 0.50	2.00			
Meteorite ?	Prambanan, Java.	{ M. van der Boon Mesch. { E. H. von Baumhauer.	Archives Néerl., 1866, i. 468. Ibid., pp. 465-468.	7.4816 7.861	96.71 { 93.77 { 94.95	2.86 5.91 4.83				
Meteorite ?	Yanhuitlan, Oaxaca, Mexico.	L. R. de la Loza.	Proc. Phila. Acad. Nat. Sci., 1876, p. 120.	7.824	96.5818 2	1.852				
Meteorite ?	Ashville, Buncombe Co., N.C.	C. U. Shepard.	Am. Jour. Sci., 1839 (1), xxxvi. 81-84.	6.50-7.50, 8.00	96.50	2.60	trace.		trace.	
Meteorite ?	Mexico.	F. A. Genth.	Am. Jour. Sci., 1851 (2), xviii. 239, 240.	8 31	96.17 95.92	3.07 3.57	0.42			
Meteorite ?	Hacienda St. Rosa, Mexico.	H. Wichelhaus.	Ann. Physik Chemie, 1863, cxviii. 631-634.		96.072	3.263	0.55	1.040		
Meteorite ?	Black Mt., Buncombe Co., N.C.	C. U. Shepard.	Am. Jour. Sci., 1847 (2), iv. 82, 83.	7.261	96.04	2.52	trace.			
"	Ruff's Mt., Newberry, S. C.	C. U. Shepard.	Proc. Am. Assoc. Adv. Sci., 1850, iii. 152-154.	7.01-7.10	96.00	3.121	trace.		trace.	
"	Murfreesborough, Rutherford Co., Tenn.	G. Troost.	Am. Jour. Sci., 1848 (2), v. 351, 352.		96.00	2.40				
"	Sarepta, Saratow, Russia.	J. Auerbach.	Sitz. Wien. Akad., 1864, xlix. (2), 497.		95.937	2.057				1.315
Meteorite ?	Coahuila, Mex.	J. L. Smith.	Am. Jour. Sci., 1855 (2), xix. 160, 161.	7.81	95.82	3.18	0.35	0.24		
"	Losttown, Cherokee Co., Ga.	C. U. Shepard.	Am. Jour. Sci., 1869 (2), xlvii. 234.		95.759	3.66	trace.			
"	Heidelberg, Baden, Ger.	R. Wawmkiewicz.	Ann. Chemie Pharm., 1862, cxxiii.252-255.		95.472	0.10		1.250	0.24	
"	San Gregorio, Mexico.	J. L. Smith.	Am. Jour. Sci., 1871 (3), ii. 335-338.	7.84	95.01	4.22	0.51	0.08		
"	Chesterville, Chester Co., S.C.	C. U. Shepard.	Am. Jour. Sci., 1849 (2), vii. 449.	7.818	95.00	5.00	trace.			
"	Ivanpah, Cal.	C. U. Shepard.	Am. Jour. Sci., 1880 (3), xix. 381, 382.	7.65	94.98	4.52		0.07		
"	Auburn, Macon Co., Ga.	C. U. Shepard.	Am. Jour. Sci., 1869 (2), xlvii. 230-233.	7.0-7.17	94.58	8.015		0.120		
Meteorite ?	Duel Hill, Madison Co., N. C.	B. S. Burton.	Am. Jour. Sci., 1877 (3), xii. 439.	7.46	94.24	5.17	0.37	0.14		
"	Denton Co., Tex.	{ W. P. Riddell. { A. Madelung.	Trans. St. Louis Acad., 1860, i. 623. Buchner, Meteoriten, 1863, p. 193.	7.6698 7.42	94.0246 6 92.099	5.42982 7.50	trace. trace.	0.001		
Meteorite ?	Cachiuyal, Atacama, Chili.	J. Domeyko.	Comptes Rendus, 1876, lxxxi. 507.		93.92	4.93	0.89	0.085		
"	Wayne Co., Ohio.	J. L. Smith.	Am. Jour. Sci., 1864 (2), xxxviii. 385, 386.	7.901	93.01	6.01	0.73	0.13		
"	San Francisco del Mezquital, Durango, Mexico.	A. A. Damour.	Comptes Rendus, 1868, lxvi. 573, 574.	7.855	93.39	5.80	0.30	0.23		

Siderolite.

C.	Cu.	Sn.	Cr.	Si.	Al.	Ca.	Mg.	Mn.	Cl.	As	Insol.	Loss.	Undet.	Miscellaneous.	Total.
....	....	....	....	....	trace.	trace.	trace.	....	....	....	....	....	....	....	99.89
....	....	....	....	0.20	trace.	0.09	....	....	....	....	....	....	....	According to Heddle it contains nickel, potassium, and traces of sodium, silicon, sulphur, carbon, phosphorus? and tin? Phil. Mag., 1862(4), xxiv. 541.	99.97
....	....	....	....	....	....	....	....	....	....	....	....	....	....	Ni, Cr_2O_3, Co, Mg, and P=210.	100.00
1.50	trace.	....	....	1.05	....	....	....	....	....	....	....	....	....	....	100.52
....	....	....	....	....	....	....	....	....	1.56	....	....	....	Graphite	....	99.00
....	....	....	....	....	....	....	....	....	....	....	....	....	....	....	99.36
....	....	....	....	....	....	....	....	....	....	....	....	....	....	....	100.08
....	....	....	....	....	....	....	....	....	....	....	....	....	....	....	101.08
....	....	....	Cr_2O_3 trace.	....	....	....	....	....	....	....	....	....	....	....	100.00
....	....	....	....	....	....	....	....	....	....	....	....	....	....	....	100.00
....	....	....	....	....	....	....	....	....	....	....	....	....	....	Co, Si, and loss = 0.43.	100.00
....	....	....	....	....	....	....	....	....	....	....	....	....	....	Co and Si = {0.32, 0.22}	100.00 / 100.00
0.00018	....	....	....	SiO_2 0.0058	Al_2O_3 0.61015	CaO 0.80815	....	....	....	....	....	....	....	....	100.00
....	....	....	Cr_2O_3 trace.	0.50	....	....	....	....	0.20	trace?	....	....	....	....	99.80
....	....	....	....	....	....	....	....	....	....	....	....	....	....	....	99.86
....	....	....	....	....	....	....	....	....	....	0.57	....	....	....	....	100.00
....	....	....	....	....	....	....	....	....	....	....	....	....	....	....	100.981
....	....	....	....	....	....	....	....	....	1.44	....	....	....	....	....	100.00
....	....	....	trace.	....	....	....	trace.	....	....	....	....	....	....	....	99.121
....	....	....	....	....	....	....	....	....	....	1.80	....	....	....	....	100.00
....	....	0.017	....	0.02	....	....	....	....	....	....	....	....	....	....	99.946
....	trace.	....	....	....	....	....	....	....	....	....	....	....	....	....	99.69
....	....	trace?	trace.	....	....	....	trace.	....	....	0.58	....	....	....	....	99.990
....	0.287	....	....	....	....	....	....	....	....	0.735	....	....	....	....	98.10
....	trace.	....	....	....	....	....	....	....	....	....	....	....	....	....	99.82
....	....	....	trace.	....	....	....	....	....	....	....	....	....	....	....	100.00
0.10	....	....	....	....	....	....	....	....	....	....	....	....	....	The carbon occurs as graphite.	99.67
....	....	....	....	....	....	....	....	....	....	....	....	....	....	....	100.00
....	....	....	....	....	....	....	....	....	2.276 0.15	....	....	....	....	....	100.07
....	trace.	....	....	....	....	....	....	....	....	....	....	....	....	....	99.78262
....	....	....	....	....	....	....	....	....	0.22814	....	....	....	....	....	99.68
....	....	....	....	SiO_2 0.20	CaO	MgO	....	....	....	....	....	....	....	....	99.82
....	....	....	....		0.30		....	....	....	....	....	....	....		
....	trace.	....	....	....	....	....	trace.	....	....	....	....	....	....	....	100.48
....	....	....	....	....	....	....	....	....	....	....	....	....	....	....	99.89

viii A CLASSIFIED LIST OF COMPLETE (BAUSCH)

TABLE II.

Variety.	Locality.	Analyst.	Publication.	Sp. Gr.	Fe.	Ni.	Co.	P.	S.	P,Fe,Ni.
Meteorite?	Lion River, Great Namaqualand, South Africa.	C. U. Shepard.	Am. Jour. Sci., 1863 (2), xv. 1–4.	7.45	93.30	6.70	....	trace.	trace.	....
"	Schwetz, Weichsel River, Prussia.	C. Rammelsberg.	Ann. Physik Chemie, 1851, lxxxiv. 153,154.	7.77	93.18	5.77	1.05	....	....	....
"	Nelson Co., Kentucky.	J. L. Smith.	Am. Jour. Sci., 1800 (2), xxx. 240.	....	93.10	6.11	0.41	0.05	....	....
"	Nenntmannsdorf, Saxony.	F. E. Geinitz.	Neues Jahr. Min., 1876, pp. 608–612.	6.21	93.04	6.16	....	0.22	....	....
		G. E. Lichtenberger.	Sitz.Isis, Dresden, 1873, p. 4.	....	94.50	5.31	....	....	....	....
"	Lick Creek, Davidson Co., N.C.	J. L. Smith and J. B. Mackintosh.	Am. Jour. Sci., 1880 (3), xx. 324–326.	....	93.00	5.74	0.52	0.36	trace.	....
"	Coahuila, Mexico.	J. L. Smith.	Am. Jour. Sci., 1860 (2), xlvii. 383–385.	7.092	92.95	6.02	0.48	0.02	....	....
"	Not known.	C. U. Shepard, Jr.	Am. Jour. Sci., 1881 (3), xxii. 119.	7.589	92.028	6.071	0.539	....	....	0.562
"	Pittsburg, Penn.	F. A. Genth.	Am. Jour. Sci., 1876 (3), xii. 72, 73.	7.741	92.809	4.065	0.395	0.251	0.037	....
"	Tabarz, Thuringia, Germany.	W. Eberhard.	Ann. Chem. Pharm., 1855, xcvi. 286–289.	7.737	92.757	5.803	0.791	0.862	....	0.277
"	Guilford Co.,N.C.	C. U. Shepard.	Am. Jour. Sci., 1841 (1), xl. 369, 370.	7.67	92.75	3.145	trace.	....	....	....
"	Angara, Jeniseisk, Siberia.	M. A. Göbel.	Bull. Acad. St. Peters., 1874, xix. 544–554.	....	92.6346	7.1088	trace.	0.103	....	....
*	Caille, Var, France.	L. E. Rivot.	Ann. Mines, 1854 (5), vi. 554, 555.	7.428	92.30 92.70	6.20 5.00	trace. trace.	....	....	....
		J. Boussingault.	Comptes Rendus, 1872, lxxiv. 1287–1289.	7.64	80.53 80.73	9.76 9.00	....	....	....	....
		V. de Luynes.	Ann. Mines, 1844 (4), v. 161–164.	....	87 63	7.37	....	....	....	....
"	Southeastern Missouri.	C. U. Shepard.	Am. Jour. Sci., 1869 (2), xlvii. 233, 234.	7.015–7.112	92.090	2.004	trace.	trace.	....	5.00
"	Rio Juncal, Atacama, Chili.	A. A. Damour.	Comptes Rendus, 1868, lxvi. 569–571.	7.097	92.03	7.00	0.02	0.21	....	....
		Fickentscher.	Buchner, Meteoriten, 1863, p. 144.	7.731	91.90	5.71	....	....	....	....
"	Bemdego Creek, Bahia, Brazil.	W. H. Wollaston.	Phil. Trans., 1810, pp. 270–285.	7.73	95.10	3.00	....	....	....	....
		Wohler & Martius.	Phipson, Meteorites, 1867, p. 94.	7.408	88.46	8.59	....	....	....	0.37
"	Sizipilec, Mexico.	C. H. L. v. Babo.	Buchner, Meteoriten, 1863, p. 141.	....	91.89	6.32	1.58	....	....	....
Meteorite.	Braunau, Bohemia.	Duflos & Fischer.	Ann. Physik Chemie, 1847, lxxii. 475–480.	7.7142	91.882	5.517	0.529	....	....	....
Meteorite?	Dakota.	C. T. Jackson.	Am. Jour. Sci., 1863 (2), xxxvi. 259–261.	7.952	91.735 91.735	6.592 7.08	trace. trace.	0.01 0.01	....	....
"	Cosby Creek, Cocke Co., Tennessee.	C. A. Joy.	Ann. Chem. Pharm., 1853, lxxxvi. 39–43.	....	91.635	5.846	0.809	0.105	....	....
		C. Bergmann.	Ann. Physik Chemie, 1857, c. 254, 255.	7.257	91.698	6.704	0.392	0.089	....	....
		C. U. Shepard.	Am. Jour. Sci., 1842 (1), xliii. 354–363.	0.222	93 80 94.083	4.66 4.444	....	....	....	....
"	Chulafennee, Cleburne Co., Ala.	J. B. Mackintosh.	Am. Jour. Sci., 1880 (3), xx. 74.	....	91.608	7.368	0.50	0.17	....	....
"	Atacama, Chili.	E. Ludwig.	Denks. Wien. Akad., 1872, xxxi. 187–195.	7.7586	91.53	7.14	0.41	0.45	....	....
		J. Boussingault.	Comptes Rendus, 1872, lxxiv. 1288, 1299.	7.73	91.50	8.58	....	....	....	....
"	Lenarto, Hungary.	A. Wherle.	Rammelsberg, Handwörterbuch, 1841, p. 423.	7.79	90.00	8.50	0.065	....	....	....
		P. A. v. Bolger.	Zeit. Phys. Math., 1830, vii. 120.	....	85.04	8.12	3.59	....	....	....
Meteorite.	Rowton, Shropshire, Eng.	W. Flight.	Phil. Trans., 1882, pp. 891–896.	....	91.25 91.016	8.582 0.077	0.371	....	....	....
Meteorite?	Santa Rosa, New Granada.	Rivero and Boussingault.	Ann. Chemie Phys., 1824, xxv. 438–443.	7 60 7.30	91.23 91.76 91.41	8.21 6.36 8.59	....	....	....	....

ANALYSES OF METEORIC AND TERRESTRIAL ROCKS.

Continued.

C.	Cu.	Sn.	Cr.	Si.	Al.	Ca.	Mg.	Mn.	Cl.	As.	Insol.	Loss.	Undet.	Miscellaneous.	Total.
....	....	trace.	....	....	....	....	....	....	....	....	....	....	....	K_2O = trace.	100.00
....	....	....	....	....	....	....	....	....	....	....	0.008	....	....	....	100.008
....	trace.	....	....	....	....	....	....	....	....	....	....	....	....	....	99.67
....	....	....	....	....	....	....	....	....	....	....	....	....	....	....	99.42
....	....	....	....	....	....	....	....	....	....	....	....	....	....	....	99.90
....	trace.	....	....	....	....	....	....	trace.	....	....	....	....	....	Mean of closely agreeing analyses.	99.02
....	trace.	....	....	....	....	....	....	....	....	....	....	....	....	....	99.07
....	....	....	....	....	....	....	....	....	....	....	....	....	....	....	100.095
....	0.034	....	....	....	....	....	0.141	....	....	....	....	....	....	....	98.332
....	....	....	....	....	....	....	....	....	....	....	....	....	....	....	100.38
....	....	....	....	....	....	....	....	....	....	....	....	....	....	Fe_2O_3+FeO = 0.75. Analysis imperfect.	96.645
trace.	....	....	....	0.0421	....	trace.	0.0565	....	....	....	trace.	....	....	....	100.00
....	....	....	trace.	0.90	....	....	....	....	....	....	....	....	....	....	99.40
....	....	....	trace.	0.90	....	....	....	....	....	....	....	....	....	....	99.20
0.12	....	....	....	....	....	....	....	....	....	0.50	....	....	....	....	100.00
0.12	....	....	....	....	....	....	....	....	....	0.25	....	....	....	....	100.00
....	....	trace.	....	....	....	....	....	trace.	....	....	....	....	....	....	100.00
trace.	....	....	trace.	SiO_2 trace.	....	....	trace.	....	....	....	....	....	....	Trace of Fe_2O_3.	99.70
....	....	....	....	....	....	....	....	....	....	....	....	....	....	....	99.86
....	....	....	....	....	....	....	....	....	....	....	0.46	1.93	....	....	100.00
....	....	....	....	....	....	....	....	....	....	....	....	....	....	....	100.00
0.07	....	....	....	....	....	....	....	....	....	....	....	1.96	....	....	100.00
....	....	....	....	....	....	....	....	trace.	....	....	....	....	....	....	99.70
....	....	....	Cr_2O_3	....	....	....	....	....	....	....	....	....	....	Cu+Mn+As+Ca+Mg +Si+C+Cl+S=2.072	100.00
....	....	0.003	trace.	....	....	....	....	....	....	....	....	....	....	....	98.34
....	....	0.003	trace.	SiO_2 0.070	....	....	....	....	....	....	....	....	....	....	98.888
....	0.219	....	....	0.070	....	....	....	0.002	....	....	....	....	....	Graphite = 0.798.	99.673
0.175	....	....	....	....	....	....	....	....	....	....	....	....	....	....	99.198
....	....	....	....	....	....	....	....	....	....	....	0.10 0.10	....	....	....	98.56 / 98.577
....	....	....	....	....	....	....	....	....	....	....	....	....	....	....	99.646
....	trace.	....	....	....	....	....	....	....	....	....	....	....	....	....	99.53
....	trace.	....	....	....	....	....	....	....	....	....	0.30	....	....	....	100.38
....	0.002	....	....	....	....	....	....	....	....	....	....	....	....	....	100.10
....	....	....	....	0.01	0.77	1.63	0.23	0.01	....	....	....	....	....	....	100.00
....	trace.	....	....	....	....	....	....	....	....	....	....	....	....	Analysis incomplete.	100.208
....	trace.	....	....	....	....	....	....	....	....	....	....	....	....	" "	100.123
....	....	....	....	....	....	....	....	....	....	....	0.28	....	....	....	99.72 / 98.12 / 100.00

A CLASSIFIED LIST OF COMPLETE (BAUSCH)

TABLE II.

Variety.	Locality.	Analyst.	Publication.	Sp. Gr.	Fe.	Ni.	Co.	P.	S.	P,Fe,Ni.
Meteorite ?	Lagrange, Oldham Co., Ky.	J. L. Smith.	Am. Jour. Sci., 1861 (2), xxxi. 265, 266.	7.80	91.21	7.81	0.25	0.05	....	....
Meteorite.	Charlotte, Dickson Co., Tenn.	J. L. Smith.	Am. Jour. Sci., 1875 (3), x. 349–352.	7.717	91.15	8.01	0.72	....	....	....
Meteorite ?	Jewell Hill, Madison Co., N. C.	J. L. Smith.	Am. Jour. Sci., 1860 (2), xxx. 240.	....	91.12	7.82	0.43	0.08	....	....
"	Mexico.	J. L. Smith.	Am. Jour. Sci., 1808 (2), xlv. 77.	7.72	91.103	7.557	0.763	0.02	trace.	....
"	Red River, Texas.	B. Silliman, Jr., and T. S. Hunt.	Am. Jour. Sci., 1846 (2), ii. 372–374.	7.40 7.82	90.911	8.402	....	....	....	....
		C. U. Shepard.	Am. Jour. Sci., 1829 (1), xvi. 217–219.	7.543	90.02	9.674	....	....	....	....
"	Obernkirchen, Germany.	F. Wöhler.	Göttingen, Nachrichten, 1863, pp. 364–367.	7.12	90.95	8.01	0.04	....	....	....
"	Smith's Mt.,Rockingham Co.,N.C.	J. L. Smith.	Am. Jour. Sci., 1877 (3), xiii 213, 214.	7.78	90.88	8.02	0.50	0.03	....	....
		F. A. Genth.	Am. Jour. Sci., 1877 (3), xiii. 214.	....	90.08	9.07	....	0.14	....	....
"	20 miles from Fort Pierre,Nebraska.	A. Madelung.	Buchner, Meteoriten, 1863, p. 107.	7.741	90.704	7.607	0.889	trace.	....	....
		H. A. Prout.	Trans. St. Louis Acad., 1860, i. 711, 712.	7.735	94.288	7.185	....	....	trace.	....
"	Rasgata,New Granada.	Rivero and Boussingault.	Ann. Chimie Physique, 1824, xxv. 442, 443.	7.60	90.76	7.87	....	....	....	....
		F. Wöhler.	Ann. Chem. Pharm., 1852, lxxxii. 243–248.	7.88–7.77	92.85	6.71	0.25	0.35	trace.	0.37
"	Colorado.	C. T. Jackson.	Am. Jour. Sci., 1867 (2), xliii. 280, 281.	7.092	90.05	7.867	0.01	....	....	....
"	Russell Gulch,Gilpin Co., Col.	J. L. Smith.	Am. Jour. Sci., 1806 (2), xlii. 218, 219.	7.72	90.61	7.84	0.78	0.02	....	....
"	Franklin Co.,Kentucky.	J. L. Smith.	Am. Jour. Sci., 1870 (2), xlix. 331–335.	7.002	90.58	8.53	0.36	0.05	....	....
		A. Löwe.	Neues Jahr. Min., 1840, p. 199.	....	90.471 91.001	7.321 7.323	....	....	trace. trace.	....
"	Szlanicza, near Arva, Magura Mts., Hungary.	C. Bergmann.	Ann. Physik Chemie, 1857, c. 256–290.	....	77.182	4.730	....	0.434	15.350	....
		A. Patera.	Neues Jahr. Min., 1849, p. 109.	7.814	89.42 83.15 94.12	8 61 5.94 5.43	....	....	....	....
"	Xiquipilco, Mex.	Evan Pugh.	Ann. Chem. Pharm., 1856, xcviii. 383–386.	....	90.43 87.89	7.62 9.06	0.72 1.07	0.15 0.62	0.03	0.56 0.34
		W. J. Taylor.	Am. Jour. Sci., 1856 (2), xxxii. 374–376.	....	90.72	8.49	0.44	0.18	FeS.	....
		H. B. Nason.	Jour. Prakt. Chemie, 1857, lxxi. 123.	....	90.133	7.241			0.370	trace.
"	Toluca, Mexico.	E. Uricoeches.	Jour. Prakt. Chemie, 1854, lxiii. 317, 318.	....	90.40	5.02	0.04	0.16	....	2.00
		F. Wöhler.	Ann. Chem. Pharm., 1857, lxxxii. 243–247.	....	86.073	0.016	0.700	....	....	1.000
"	Salt River, Kentucky.	W. H. Brewer.	Proc. Am. Assoc. Adv. Sci., 1851, iv. 36–38.	....	90.23 90.51 91.07 91.14	0.08 0.05 0.08 0.05	....	....	....	....
"	Lenarto, Hungary.	W. S. Clark.	Clark, Metallic Meteorites, 1852, p. 40.	7.73	90.153	6.553	0.502	....	0.482	....
		A. Wehrle.	Clark, Metallic Meteorites, 1852, p. 40.	7.98	90.883	8.45	0.665	....	....	....
		P. A. v. Holger.	Buchner, Meteoriten, 1863, p. 153.	7.72–7.80	85.04	8.12	3.59	....	....	....
"	Marshall Co.,Kentucky.	J. L. Smith.	Am. Jour. Sci., 1860, xxx. 240.	....	90.12	8.72	0.32	0.10	....	....
"	Seeläsgen, Austria.	A. Duflos.	Ann. Physik Chemie, 1848, lxxiv. 61–65.	7.63–7.71	90.00 Fe+Mn	5.308	0.434	....	....	....
		C. Rammelsberg.	Ann. Physik Chemie, 1848, lxxiv. 443–448.	7.7345	92.327	6.228	0.667	....	....	....
"	Brazos River,Tex.	W. P. Riddell.	Trans. St. Louis Acad., 1860, i. 623.	....	80.003	10.007	trace.	....	....	....
Meteorite.	Hraschina, near Agram, Croatia.	A. Wehrle.	Clark, Metallic Meteorites, 1852, pp. 42–44.	7.785	89.784	8.880	0.067	....	....	....

ANALYSES OF METEORIC AND TERRESTRIAL ROCKS.

Continued.

C.	Cu.	Sn.	Cr.	Si.	Al.	Ca.	Mg.	Mn.	Cl.	As.	Insol.	Loss.	Undet.	Miscellaneous.	Total.
....	trace.	....	....	....	....	....	....	....	....	....	....	....	....		99.82
....	0.06	....	....	....	....	....	....	....	....	....	....	....	....		99.94
....	trace.	....	....	....	....	....	....	....	....	....	....	....	....		99.45
trace.	....	....	....	....	....	....	....	....	....	....	....	....	....		99.443
....	....	....	....	....	....	....	....	....	....	....	0.50	....	....		99.878
....	....	....	....	....	....	....	....	....	....	....	....	0.306	....		100.00
....	....	....	....	....	....	....	....	....	....	....	....	....	....		99.00
....	0.03	....	....	....	....	....	....	....	....	....	....	....	....		99.46
....	0.11	....	....	....	....	....	....	....	....	....	....	....	....		100.00
....	trace.	....	....	....	....	....	....	....	....	....	0.053	....	....		99.313
....	....	....	....	....	0.35	0.05	....	....	....	....	....	....	....		102.473
....	....	....	....	....	....	....	....	....	....	....	....	....	....		98.63
....	trace.	trace.	....	....	....	....	....	....	....	....	....	....	....	Silicates = 0.08.	100.11
....	....	0.02	....	....	....	....	....	0.95	....	....	....	....	....		99.497
....	trace.	....	....	....	....	....	....	....	....	....	....	....	....		99.26
....	trace.	....	....	....	....	....	....	....	....	....	....	....	....	Co, C, Si, etc. 1.404	99.52 / 99.196
....	....	....	....	....	....	....	....	....	....	....	....	....	....	0.938	99.622
0.00	....	....	trace.	....	....	....	....	....	....	....	....	....	....	Graphite = 1.17.	99.997
....	....	....	....	....	....	....	....	....	....	....	....	....	....	Co, C, Si, etc. = 1.41.	99.41 / 99.07 / 99.55
....	0.03	....	....	....	....	....	....	....	....	....	....	....	....	Graphite, etc. 0.34	99.88
....	trace.	....	....	....	....	....	....	0.20	....	....	....	....	....	0.22	99.41
....	....	....	....	0.25	....	....	....	....	....	....	....	....	....	Schreibersite, graphite, etc. 0.88	100.46
....	....	....	....	....	....	....	....	....	....	....	0.216	2.034	....		100.00
....	trace.	....	....	....	....	....	trace.	....	....	....	....	....	....	1.11	99.72
....	trace.	....	Cr₂O₃ trace.	....	....	....	trace.	....	....	....	....	....	....	0.973	98.234
....	....	....	....	....	....	MgO	....	....	....	....	0.20	....	....		100.17
....	....	....	....	....	....	trace.	....	....	....	....	0.26	....	....	Na₂O	99.82
....	....	....	....	....	....	trace.	....	....	....	....	0.20	....	....	trace.	101.01
....	....	....	....	....	....	....	....	....	....	....	0.26	....	....	trace.	100.45
....	0.08	0.082	....	....	....	....	0.145	....	....	....	1.226	....	....		99.228
....	....	....	....	....	....	....	....	....	....	....	....	....	....		99.998
....	....	....	....	0.01	0.77	0.68	0.23	0.61	....	....	....	....	....		99.00
....	trace.	....	....	....	....	....	....	....	....	....	....	....	....		99.26
....	0.104	....	....	1.157	....	....	0.912	....	....	....	0.834	....	....		98.749
0.52	0.049	....	....	0.026	....	....	....	....	....	....	0.188	....	....		100.00
....	....	....	....	....	....	....	....	....	....	....	....	....	....		100.00
....	....	....	....	....	....	....	....	....	....	....	....	....	....		.99.887

xii   A CLASSIFIED LIST OF COMPLETE (BAUSCH)

TABLE II.

Variety.	Locality.	Analyst.	Publication.	Sp. Gr.	Fe.	Ni.	Co.	P.	S.	P,Fe,Ni.
Meteorite.	Hraschina, near Agram, Croatia.	M. H. Klaproth.	Beiträge Mineralkorper, 1807, iv. 99–101.	7.75–7.80	96.50	3.50	....	....	....	....
		P. A. v. Holger.	Rammelsberg, Handworterbuch, 1841, 422.	7.824	83.20	11.84	1.26	....	....	....
		W. S. Clark.	Metallic Meteorites, 1852, pp. 61, 62.	7.728	80.762	8.807	0.025	....	....	....
Meteorite?	Burlington, Otsego Co., N. Y.	C. H. Rockwell.	Am. Jour. Sci., 1844 (1), xlvi. 401–403.	....	92.201	8.140	....	....	....	....
		C. U. Shepard.	Am. Jour. Sci., 1847 (2), iv. 77, 78.	....	95.20	2.125	....	....	....	....
"	Ocatitlan, Oaxaca, Mexico.	C. Bergmann.	Jour. Prakt. Chemie, 1857, lxxi. 57, 58.	7+	89.71	8.53	0.56	0.17	....	....
"	Cooperstown, Robertson Co., Tennessee.	J. L. Smith.	Am. Jour. Sci., 1861 (2), xxxi. 260.	7.85	89.50	9.12	0.35	0.04	....	....
"	Putnam Co., Ga.	C. U. Shepard.	Am. Jour. Sci., 1854 (2), xvii. 331, 332.	7.60	80.52	8.82	trace.	....	....	....
"	San Luis Potosi, Mexico.	P. Murphy.	Proc. Phil. Acad. Sci., 1876, pp. 123, 124.	7.38	89.51	8.05	1.94	....	0.45	....
"	Carthage, Tenn.	E. Boricky.	Neues Jahr. Min., 1866, pp. 808–810.	7.478–7.50	89.465	7.721	0.245	0.003	0.401	....
"	Washington Co., Wisconsin.	G. Bode.	Ann. Rep. Smith. Inst., 1860, pp. 417–419.	7.3272	89.22	10.70	trace.	0.60	....	....
		J. L. Smith.	Am. Jour. Sci., 1869 (2), xlvii. 271, 272.	7.82	91.03	7.20	0.53	0.14	....	....
"	Butler, Bates Co., Missouri.	J. L. Smith.	Am. Jour. Sci., 1877 (3), xiii. 213.	7.72	89.12	10.02	0.26	0.12	....	....
"	Istlahuaca, Mex.	M. Böcking.	Neues Jahr., Min., 1856, p. 304.	7.982	89.073	7.20	0.978	....	0.855	0.072
		C. Rammelsberg.	Mon.Berlin.Akad.,1870, p. 444.	....	89.06	10.65	0.08	....	0.17	....
"	Cambria, Niagara Co., New York.	B. Silliman, Jr., and T. S. Hunt.	Am. Jour. Sci., 1846 (2), ii. 374–376.	....	92.583	5.708	....	....	....	....
		D. Olmsted, Jr.	Am. Jour. Sci., 1845 (1), xlviii. 388–392.	7.5267	95.54 / 94.224	5.037 / 6.353	....	....	....	....
"	Rokitan, Bohemia.	J. Stolba.	Sitz.Wien. Akad., 1864, xlix. (2), 480–485	6.005	89.00	8.84	....	....	1.03	....
		K. R. v. Hauer.	Sitz.Wien. Akad., 1864, xlix. (2), 480–485.	6.394	90.00	....	....	....	....	....
"	Victoria West, Cape Colony, South Africa.	J. L. Smith.	Am. Jour. Sci., 1873 (3), v. 107–110.	7.602	88.83	10.14	0.53	0.26	....	....
		J. W. Mallet.	Am. Jour. Sci., 1871 (3), ii. 10–15.	7.853 / 7.855 / 7.839	88.706 / 88.365 / 89.007	10.163 / 10.242 / 9.964	0.396 / 0.426 / 0.387	0.341 / 0.362 / 0.375	0.019 / 0.008 / 0.026	....
"	Staunton, Augusta Co., Virginia.	J. R. Santos.	Am. Jour. Sci., 1878 (3), xv. 337, 338.	7.686	91.439	7.559	0.508	0.008	0.018	....
		J. J. Berzelius.	Ann. Physik Chemie, 1834, xxxiii. 135–137.	7.74–7.87	88.231	8.517	0.762	....	trace.	2.211
		M. H. Klaproth.	Beiträge Mineralkorper, 1815, vi. 306–308.	7.80–7.83	97.50	2.50	....	....	....	....
"	Elbogen, Bohemia.	J. F. John.	Jour. Chemie Physik, 1821, xxxii. 253–261.	7.76	87.50	8.75	1.85	....	....	....
		A. Wehle.	Buchner, Meteoriten, 1863, pp. 151, 152.	7.78	89.90	8.435	0.609	....	....	....
		P. A. v. Holger.	Buchner, Meteoriten, 1863, pp. 151, 152.	....	94.69	2.47	1.59	....	....	....
"	Nöbdenitz, Altenburg, Germany.	H. B. Geinitz.	Neues Jahr. Min., 1868, pp. 459–463.	7.06	88.125	1.34	trace.	....	....	....
		G. Troost.	Am. Jour. Sci., 1845 (1), xlix. 342–344.	....	87.58	12.42	....	....	....	....
"	Babb's Mill,Green Co., Tenn.	C. U. Shepard.	Am. Jour. Sci., 1847 (2), iv. 76, 77.	7.548	85.30	14.70	....	....	....	....
		W. S. Clark.	Metallic Meteorites, 1852, pp. 65, 66.	7.839	80.594	17.10	2.037	....	....	....
"	Tejupilco, Mex.	M. Böcking.	Neues Jahr. Min., 1856, p. 304.	7.326	87.002	0.801	0.766	....	0.79	0.73
"	Howard Co., Ind.	J. L. Smith.	Am. Jour. Sci., 1874 (3), vii. 391–395.	7.821	87.02	12.20	0.65	0.20	....	....
"	Misteca, Oaxaca, Mexico.	C. Bergmann.	Jour. Prakt. Chemie, 1857, lxxi. 57.	7.20, 7.58, 7.62	87.122	10.049	0.745	1.23	0.553	....

ANALYSES OF METEORIC AND TERRESTRIAL ROCKS.

Continued.

C.	Cu.	Sn.	Cr.	Si.	Al.	Ca.	Mg.	Mn.	Cl.	As.	Insol.	Loss.	Undet.	Miscellaneous.	Total.
....	....	....	....	....	....	....	....	....	....	....	....	....	....		100.00
....	....	....	....	0.08	1.38	....	0.48	0.64	....	....	....	....	....	K = 0.43.	100.00
....	trace.	....	....	....	....	....	....	trace.	....	....	0.703	....	....		99.977
....	....	....	....	....	....	....	....	....	....	....	....	....	....		100.487
....	....	....	....	....	....	....	MgO	....	....	....	0.50	....	....	Loss+S = 2.175.	100.00
0.07	trace.	....	....	....	....	....	trace.	....	....	....	....	....	....		99.12
....	trace.	....	....	....	....	....	....	....	....	....	....	....	....		99.10
....	....	....	Cr₂O₃ trace.	....	....	....	....	....	....	....	....	....	....	Sn + P + S + Mg + Ca = 1.66.	100.00
....	....	....	....	....	....	....	....	....	....	....	....	0.05	....		100.00
....	....	....	....	0.002	....	....	....	....	trace.	....	....	....	....	1.102	99.719
....	....	....	....	....	....	....	....	....	....	....	....	....	....		100.70
....	trace.	....	....	....	....	....	....	....	....	....	0.45	....	....		99.35
....	0.01	....	....	....	....	....	....	....	....	....	....	....	....		99.43
....	trace.	....	....	....	....	....	....	trace.	....	....	0.039	....	....		99.207
....	0.01	....	....	....	....	....	....	....	....	....	....	....	....		100.00
....	trace.	....	....	....	....	....	....	....	....	trace.	1.40	....	....		99.991
....	....	....	....	....	....	....	....	....	....	....	....	....	....		100.577
....	....	....	....	....	....	....	....	....	....	....	....	....	....		100.577
....	....	....	....	SiO₂ 1.10	....	CaO trace.	....	....	....	....	....	....	....	Graphite = 0.87.	99.74
2.40	....	....	....	....	....	....	....	....	....	....	....	....	....		99.50
....	trace.	....	....	....	....	....	....	....	....	....	....	....	....		99.78
0.172	0.003	0.002	....	SiO₂ 0.007	....	....	....	trace.	0.003	....	....	....	....		99.872
0.185	0.004	0.002	....	0.011	....	....	....	....	0.002	....	....	....	....		99.650
0.122	0.003	0.003	....	0.050	....	....	....	trace.	0.004	....	....	....	....		99.947
0.142	0.021	trace.	....	0.108	....	....	....	....	trace.	....	....	....	....		99.063
....	....	....	....	....	....	....	0.270	trace.	....	....	....	....	....		100.00
....	....	....	....	....	....	....	....	....	....	....	....	....	....		100.00
....	....	....	trace.	....	....	....	....	trace.	....	....	....	....	....		98.10
....	....	....	....	....	....	....	....	....	....	....	....	0.050	....		100.00
....	....	....	0.12	....	0.19	....	....	0.88	....	....	....	....	....		99.04
....	9.013	1.321	trace.	SiO₂ trace.	....	....	....	....	....	....	trace.	....	....		99.709
....	....	....	....	....	....	....	....	....	....	....	....	....	....		100.00
....	....	....	....	....	trace.	trace.	trace.	....	....	....	....	....	....		100.00
....	....	....	....	trace.	....	....	....	trace.	....	....	0.124	....	....		99.850
....	0.009	....	....	....	....	....	....	....	....	....	....	0.022	....		99.204
....	trace	....	....	....	....	....	....	....	....	....	....	....	....		99.08
....	....	....	....	....	....	....	....	....	....	....	....	....	....	C+Fe = 0.524.	99.117

xiv   A CLASSIFIED LIST OF COMPLETE (BAUSCH)

TABLE II.

Variety.	Locality.	Analyst.	Publication.	Sp. Gr.	Fe.	Ni.	Co.	P.	S.	P,Fe,Ni.
Meteorite?	Bohumilitz, Bohemia.	P. A. v. Holger.	Zeit. Physik Math.,1831, ix. 323–328.	7.61–7.71	80.07 83.67	8.12 7.88	0.50 0.60	....	....	....
		J. J. Berzelius.	Ann. Physik Chemie, 1833, xxvii. 118–132.	....	92.473 93.775	5.667 5.812	0.235 0.213	....	....	....
		J. Steinman.	Am. Jour. Sci., 1831 (1), xix. 384–386.	7.146	04.00	4.01	....	....	0.81	....
"	Zacatecas, Mexico.	C. Bergmann.	Neues Jahr. Min., 1850, p. 297.	7.48	85.09	9.80	0.78	....	0.84	1.65
		S. N. Manross.	Ann. Chemie Pharm., 1852, lxxxi. 252–255.	7.55	92.83	7.38	....	....	....	0.42
		H. Müller.	Quart. Jour.Chem. Soc., 1859 (1), xi. 236–240.	7.20 7.50 7.625	89.84 91.30 90.01	5.90 5.82 5.06	0.02 0.41 0.42	.... 0.25 0.23	0.13 .... 0.07	....
		A. E. Nordenskiöld.	Geol. Mag., 1872 (1), ix. 518.	6.36, 6.80	84.40	2.48	0.07	0.20	1.52	....
		T. Nordström.	Geol. Mag., 1872 (1), ix. 518.	7.05, 7.08	86.34	1.64	0.35	0.07	0.22	....
		G. Lindström.	Geol. Mag. 1872 (1), ix. 518.	0.24	93.24	1.24	0.56	0.03	1.21	....
		F. Wöhler.	Neues Jahr. Min., 1879, p. 843.	5.62	80.64	1.19	0.47	0.15	2.82	....
		R. Nauckhoff.	Min. Mitth., 1874, p. 125.	....	58.25	2.10	0.80	....	0.16	....
				6.87	91.71	1.74	0.53	....	0.10	....
				....	91.17	1.82	0.51	....	0.78	....
				....	52.02	1.39	0.76	....	0.08	....
				....	50.77	1.60	0.39	....	?	....
Terrestrial Iron.	Southern Greenland.			7.02	96.89	2.55	0.54	....	0.20	....
		J. Lorenzen.	Zeit. Deut. Geol. Gesell., 1883, xxxv. 695–703.	7.57	92.41	0.45	0.18	....	trace.	....
				7.26	95.15	0.34	0.06	....	....	....
				....	95.67	....	trace.	....	0.00	....
				7.02, 7.29	92.46	0.92	1.93	0.07	0.59	....
				....	92.68	2.54	0.58	....	0.01	....
				7.06	92.23	2.73	0.84	....	....	....
				....	94.11	2.85	1.07	....	....	....
		G. Forchhammer.	Ann. Physik Chemie, 1854, xciii. 155–159.	7.073	93.80	1.56	0.25	0.18	0.67	....
		J. L. Smith.	Ann. Chimie Phys.,1879 (5), xvi. 432–505.	0.42 7.46 6.80 7.00	93.16 90.17 88.13 92.45	2.01 6.50 2.13 2.88	0.80 0.79 1.07 0.43	0.32 .... 0.26 0.24	0.41 .... 0.36 1.25	....
Meteorite?	Claiborne, Clarke Co., Alabama.	A. A. Hayes.	Am. Jour. Sci., 1845 (1), xlviii. 145–156.	6.82	83.572	12.005	....	....	....	....
		C. T. Jackson.	Am. Jour. Sci., 1838 (1), xxiv. 332–337.	5.75, 6.40, 6.50	60.56	24.708	....	....	2.00	....
		E. Uricoechea.	Ann. Chem. Pharm., 1854, xv. 232.	6.035–7.944	81.20	15.00	2.50	0.00	trace.	....
"	Cape of Good Hope.	Baumhauer and Seelheim. A. Wehrle.	Archives Néerland., 1867, ii. 376–384. Zeit. Physik Math., 1835 (2), iii. 222–220.	7.708 7.605	82.77 85.808	14.32 12.275	2.52 0.887	0.26	....	....
		M. Böcking.	Ann. Chemie Pharm., 1855, xcvi. 248–240.	7.004	81.90	15.23	2.01	0.08	trace.	0.88
		P. A. v. Holger.	Zeit.Physik Math.,1830, viii. 288.	7.318	78.00	15.28	1.00	....	....	....
"	Los Angeles, Cal.	C. T. Jackson.	Am. Jour. Sci., 1872 (3), iv. 495, 496.	7.0053	80.74	15.73	....	....	....	....
"	Santa Catharina, Brazil.	Guignet and Almeida.	Comptes Rendus, 1876, lxxxiii. 917–919.	7.75	64.00	30.00	....	....	....	....
"	Oktibbeha Co., Mississippi.	W. J. Taylor.	Am. Jour. Sci., 1857 (2), xxiv. 293–295.	0.854	37.09	59.09	0.40	0.10	....	....

ANALYSES OF METEORIC AND TERRESTRIAL ROCKS.

Continued.

C.	Cu.	Sn.	Cr.	Si.	Al.	Ca.	Mg.	Mn.	Cl.	As.	Insol.	Loss.	Undet.	Miscellaneous.	Total.
....	....	....	....	....	0.32	0.41	0.13	0.46	....	....	1.34	....	....	Be = 0.10.	98.16
....	....	....	....	....	0.42	1.08	0.10	0.58	....	....	4.78	....	....	Be = 0.12.	99.16
....	....	....	....	....	....	....	....	....	....	....	1.625	....	....	....	100.00
....	....	....	....	....	....	....	....	....	....	....	2.20	....	....	....	100.00
....	....	....	....	....	....	....	....	....	....	....	....	....	....	Graphite, etc. = 1.12.	100.00
0.16	0.03	....	....	....	....	....	0.19	trace.	....	....	....	....	....	C + Fe = 0.33. Chromite = 148.	100.62
....	....	0.03	....	....	....	....	....	....	....	....	....	....	....	....	100.16
....	....	....	....	....	....	....	....	....	....	....	3.08	....	....	....	99.63
....	trace.	....	....	SiO_2	....	....	trace.	....	....	....	2.19	....	....	....	99.97
....	....	....	....	0.50	....	....	....	....	....	....	2.17	....	....	....	100.50
10.16	0.27	....	....	....	trace.	trace.	0.04	....	0.72	....	0.05	....	....	K_2O = trace. Na_2O = trace. SiO_2 = trace.	100.00
8.71	0.19	....	....	SiO_2 0.96	0.24	0.48	0.20	....	1.16	....	4.37	....	....	K_2O = 0.07. Na_2O = 0.14.	100.00
2.30	0.10	....	....	....	....	....	trace.	....	0.10	....	....	....	....	K_2O=0.08, Na_2O=0.12, Insol.+SiO_2=0.50,Li=0.07.	99.70
3.69	....	....	....	SiO_2	Al_2O_3	CaO	MgO	....	....	....	....	....	....	Silicates + Cr + Cu=0.08, O = 11.19.	100.13
1.64	0.13	....	....	0.26	1.45	0.50	0.33	....	0.16	....	6.07	....	Li = 0.28	FeO+Fe_2O_3=30.43, Na_2O=0.09, NiO+CoO=0.41.	102.04
1.57	0.16	....	....	SiO_2 0.31	Al_2O_3 1.21	....	....	....	....	....	2.89	....	....	....	99.52
1.70	0.10	....	....	SiO_2 0.46	Al_2O_3 2.12	....	....	....	....	....	0.77	....	....	....	99.43
1.27	0.19	....	....	SiO_2 0.50	Al_2O_3 1.08	....	....	....	....	....	8.03	....	....	....	95.41
1.20	0.23	....	....	SiO_2 0.30	8.79	....	....	....	....	....	22.23	....	....	....	89.60
0.28	0.33	....	....	SiO_2 0.46	....	....	....	....	....	....	1.48	....	....	....	99.73
0.87	0.48	....	....	SiO_2 0.90	Al_2O_3 0.00	....	....	....	....	....	4.57	....	....	....	100.46
0.95	0.14	....	....	SiO_2 0.08	Al_2O_3 0.01	....	-	....	....	....	1.00	....	....	....	99.74
1.94	0.06	....	....	SiO_2 1.40	....	....	....	....	....	....	1.00	....	....	....	100.25
3.11	0.10	....	....	SiO_2 0.24	....	....	....	....	....	....	1.00	....	....	....	100.57
2.40	0.20	....	....	SiO_2 0.31	....	....	....	....	....	....	0.08	....	....	....	98.80
0.29	0.36	....	....	SiO_2 0.64	Al_2O_3 0.61	....	....	....	....	....	1.09	....	....	....	99.63
....	0.23	....	....	....	....	....	....	....	....	....	0.61	....	....	....	98.87
1.60	0.45	....	....	SiO_2 0.38	....	....	....	....	....	....	....	....	....	....	98.57
2.34	0.12	....	....	SiO_2 1.54	....	....	....	....	0.02	....	....	....	....	....	99.18
....	0.13	....	....	....	....	....	....	....	....	....	....	....	....	....	99.13
2.33	0.48	....	....	SiO_2	....	....	trace.	....	0.08	....	....	....	....	Silicates = 4.30.	99.03
1.74	0.18	....	....	1.31	....	trace.	trace.	....	....	....	....	....	....	....	100.48
....	....	....	....	....	....	....	....	....	0.907	....	....	....	0.401	FeS_2 = 2.305.	100.00
....	....	....	....	....	....	....	....	....	1.48	....	....	....	....	Cr_2O_3+Mn = 3.24.	99.988
....	trace.	trace.	....	....	....	....	....	....	....	....	0.95	....	....	....	99.80
....	trace.	....	....	....	....	....	....	....	....	....	....	....	....	....	99.87
....	....	-	....	....	....	....	....	....	....	....	....	....	....	....	98.77
....	trace.	trace.	....	....	....	....	....	....	....	....	....	....	....	....	99.50
....	....	....	....	....	....	1.41	0.15	....	1.76	....	1.84	....	....	....	100.00
....	....	0.01	....	....	....	....	....	....	....	....	....	....	....	P, etc. = 3.52.	100.00
....	....	....	....	....	....	....	....	....	....	....	....	....	....	....	100.00
....	0.90	....	....	0.12	0.20	0.09	....	....	....	....	....	....	....	....	99.19

A CLASSIFIED LIST OF COMPLETE (BAUSCH)

TABLE III.

Variety.	Locality.	Analyst.	Publication.	Sp. Gr.	SiO_2.	Fe.	Fe_2O_3.	FeO.	TiO_2.	Al_2O_3.
Meteorite?	Tucson, Arizona.	J. L. Smith.	Am. Jour. Sci., 1855 (2), xix. 101, 102.	6.52,6.91, 7.13		3.02	85.54			trace.
"	Tucson, Arizona.	G. J. Brush.	Proc. Cal. Acad. Sci., 1863, iii. 30–35.	7.20		3.63	81.56		0.12	trace.
"	Bitburg, Eifel, Prussia.	J. F. John.	Jour. Chemie Physik, 1826, xlvi. 386.	6.52		5.50	78.82			
		F. Stromeyer.	Jour. Chemie Physik, 1826, xlvi. 386.	6.14			81.60			
"	Brahin, Minsk, Russia.	A. Laugier.	Buchner, Meteoriten, 1863, p. 120.	6.20		{ 6.30 { 3.00	87.35 91.50			
"	Atacama, Chili.	Von Kobell and Rivero.	Korrespondenz-Blatt Vereines Regensberg, 1851, v. 112.	6.16		13.00	60.27		4.00	0.01
			Clark, Metallic Meteorites, 1852, pp. 17–19.	5.46		20.39	45.20		6.05	0.01
Cumberlandite.	Långhult, Sweden.	B. Fernqvist.	Åkerman's Iron Man., Sweden, 1876, p. xxxii.			14.95		52.85	8.50	8.95
Meteorite?	Singhur, Deccan, India.	H. Giraud.	Edin. Phil. Jour., 1849, xlvii. 56, 57.	4.72–4.90	Silicates 19.50	60.16				
"	Anderson, Hamilton Co., Ohio.	L. P. Kinnicutt.	Ann. Rep. Peabody Mus. Arch., 1884, iii. 381–384.	4.72		20.01	44.50		7.03	
		J. J. Berzelius.	Ann. Physik Chemie, 1834, xxxiii. 123–135.	5.44		20.43	44.021		6.86	
"	Krasnojarsk, Siberia.	M. H. Klaproth.	Dict. d'Hist. Nat., 1818, xxvi. 250.			20.50	58.50			
		A. Laugier.	Mém. Mus. Hist. Nat., 1817, iii. 341–352.			16.00		68.20		
		E. Howard.	Dict. d'Hist. Nat., 1818, xxvi. 250.			27.00	52.50			
"	Atacama, Chili.	C. A. Joy.	Am.Jour.Sci.,1864(2),xxxvii. 243–248.	4.35		20.660	48.208		10.417	3.872
Cumberlandite.	Iron Mine Hill, Cumberland, R. I.	T. Drown.	Communicated by M. Standish, Esq., 128 Broadway, New York City.	3.56–4.05		20.85		45.62	9.93	5.55
		R. H. Thurston.	Bull. Mus. Comp. Zoöl., 1881, vii. 185.			22.87		44.88	0.90	10.64
		C. T. Jackson.	Geol. Survey R. I., 1880, pp. 52–54.	3.62–3.88		23.00		27.60 12.40	15.30	13.10
Cumberlandite.	Taberg, Sweden.	B. Fernqvist.	Åkerman's Iron Man., Sweden, 1876, p. xxxii.			21.25		43.45	6.00	5.55
Meteorite?	Sierra de Chaco, Atacama, Chili.	I. Domeyko.	Ann. Mines, 1864 (6), v. 431–451.	5.64		23.34	Fe+Ni 39.00	FeS 14.10	14.32	4.10
"	Rittersgrün, Saxony.	C. Winkler.	Nova Acta Leop. Acad., Halle, 1878, xl. 335–282.	4.29		26.787	Fe+Ni 50.406	FeS 7.226	3.53	0.70
"	Lodran, India.	G. Tschermak.	Sitz. Wien. Akad., 1870, lxi. (2), 465–475.			29.41	Fe+Ni 32.50	FeS 7.40	7.417	0.168
"	Hainholz, Prussia.	C. Rammelsberg.	Mon. Berlin. Akad., 1870, pp. 322–325.	4.61		33.24	4.12	22.20	3.51	0.72

Pallasite.

CaO.	MgO.	MnO.	P_2O_5.	S.	Cr_2O_3.	Ni.	Co.	Cu.	Sn.	H_2O.	Loss.	Miscellaneous.	Total.
......	2.04	......	P. 0.12	......	0.21	8.55	0.61	0.03	......	......	......	Analysis of a portion freest from silicates.	100.12
Ca. 1.16	2.43	......	P. 0.49	trace.	Cr. trace.	0.17	0.44	0.08	......	......	......	Cl = trace.	99.08
......	......	Mn. 0.20	......	4.50	......	8.10	3.00	......	......	......	......	Si = 0.08.	100.00
......	......	......	......	5.10	......	11.90	1.00	......	......	......	......	......	100.00
......	2.10	......	......	1.85	Cr. 0.50	2.50	......	......	......	......	......	......	100.50
......	2.00	......	......	1.50	trace.	1.50	......	......	......	......	......	......	90.00
......	15.68	......	......	......	......	5.73	......	......	......	......	Insol. 0.20	Recalculated on the supposition that the silicates compose one third of the mass as they appear to do in the specimen seen by the present writer.	98.68
......	23.53	......	......	......	......	4.30	......	......	......	......	Insol. 0.15	Recalculated on Clark's supposition that the silicates compose one half of the mass.	99.63
1.50	10.25	0.30	0.118	0.019	......	......	......	......	......	1.40	......	......	99.187
......	......	......	......	......	......	4.24	......	......	......	......	......	Analysis very imperfect.	92.05
......	22.80	0.06	P. trace.	......	......	5.33	0.22	trace.	......	......	......	Recalculated on the supposition that the silicates compose one half of the mass.	90.94
......	25.67	0.22	......	......	......	5.366	0.228	0.033	......	......	Insol. 0.24	Mg = 0.025, Mn = 0.060, C = 0.021, SnO = 0.00. Recalculated on the supposition that the silicates comprise one half of the mass.	101.27
......	19.25	......	......	......	......	0.75	1.00	......	......	......	......	......	100.00
......	15.00	......	......	5.20	0.50	5.20	......	......	......	......	3.00	......	118.10
......	13.50	......	......	......	......	0.75	......	......	......	......	0.50	......	90.25
1.518	4.278	0.970	P. 0.115	2.003	0.477	5.298	0.838	0.04	SnO_2 0.189	......	......	Mn = 3.75, NiO+CoO = 0.07.	100.076
0.73	16.45	......	trace.	trace.	......	......	......	......	......	......	......	......	90.09
0.65	5.67	......	......	......	......	......	......	......	......	3.05	......	Zn = 20. Mean of several analyses.	100.00
......	4.00	......	......	......	......	......	......	......	......	2.00	......	......	100.00
1.65	18.30	0.40	0.127	0.013	......	......	......	CuO 0.02	......	2.60	......	......	99.60
2.51	3.56	Na_2O 0.22	......	......	......	......	......	......	......	......	......	Recalculated, but, owing to some doubts regarding the original, the recalculation is probably faulty.	100.95
0.60	6.31	Na_2O 0.48	......	......	......	......	......	0.018	......	......	......	Fe_4Ni_4P P_2P Fe_2Si Cr_2O_3+FeO 0.149, 0.274, 0.160, 0.323. Recalculated.	97.032
0.181	22.28	......	......	......	0.174	......	......	......	......	......	......	Recalculated.	90.402
......	30.52	......	......	......	......	1.05	......	......	......	2.86	......	Cr_2O_3+FeO = 0.50.	98.72

A CLASSIFIED LIST OF COMPLETE (BAUSCH)

TABLE IV.

Variety.	Locality.	Analyst.	Publication.	Sp. Gr.	SiO_2.	Al_2O_3.	Fe.	Fe_2O_3.	FeO.	CaO.
Meteorite.	Orgueil, France.	F. Pisani.	Comptes Rendus, 1864, lix. 132–135.	....	26.08	0.90	....	8.30	21.60	1.85
		S. Cloez.	Comptes Rendus, 1864, lix. 37–40.	2.50	26.081	1.2496	....	14.230	19.003	2.322
Meteorite.	Murcia, Spain.	S. Meunier.	Comptes Rendus, 1868, lxvi. 639–642.	3.546	29.224	0.51	13.03	....	5.228	0.09
Meteorite.	Noblcborough, Maine.	J. W. Webster.	Boston Jour. Phil., 1824, i. 386–389.	2.05 † } 3.092 }	20.50	4.70	14.00	....	....	trace.
Meteorite.	Cold Bokkeveld, South Africa.	E. P. Harris.	Sitz. Wien. Akad., 1850, xxxv. 5–12.	2.69	30.80	2.05	2.50	....	20.94	1.70
		M. Faraday.	Phil. Trans., 1839, pp. 83–87.	2.94	28.90	5.22	....	....	33.22	1.04
		J. J. Berzelius.	Ann. Physik Chemie, 1834, xxxiii. 113–123.	1.94	31.22	2.30	....	....	29.03	0.32
Meteorite.	Alais, Gard, France.	Commission French Academy.	Ann. Physik, 1806, xxiv. 195–208.	1.7025	30.00	....	....	....	38.00	....
		L. J. Thenard.	Buchner, Meteoriten, 1863, p. 20.	....	21.00	....	....	....	40.00	....
Meteorite.	Ornans, France.	F. Pisani.	Comptes Rendus, 1868, lxvii. 063–065.	3.509	31.23	4.32	4.12	....	24.71	2.27
Meteorite.	Little Piney, Missouri.	C. U. Shepard.	Am. Jour. Sci., 1840 (1), xxxix. 254, 255.	3.50	31.57	0.49	16.00	....	17.25	....
Meteorite.	Dacca, India.	T. Hein.	Sitz. Wien. Akad., 1866, liv. (2), 558–561.	3.55	32.05	2.54	10.38	....	28.83	1.12
*Saxonite.	Gnadenfrei, Silesia.	Galle and Lasaulx.	Mon. Berlin. Akad., 1879, pp. 756–771.	3.644 } 3.712 } 3.785 }	32.11	1.60	25.16	....	14.88	2.01
Meteorite.	Kernove, Morbihan, France.	F. Pisani.	Comptes Rendus, 1869, lxviii. 1489–1491.	3.747	32.95	3.10	22.25	....	11.70	1.80
Picrite.	Bystryc, Teschen.	J. Pösch.	Sitz. Wien. Akad., 1866, liii. (1), 272.	....	83.01	15.83	....	2.75	7.62	13.61
Meteorite.	Klein-Wenden, Germany.	C. Rammelsberg.	Ann. Physik Chemie, 1844, lxii. 449–464.	3.7006	33.08	3.75	23.90	....	6.00	2.83
Meteorite.	Heredia, Costa Rica.	I. Domeyko.	Anales de la Universidad de Chile, 1850, xvi. 325–330.	....	83.10	1.25	24.50	....	16.97	1.19
Meteorite.	Petrowsk, Stawropol, Russia.	H. Abich.	Bull. Acad. St. Petersbourg, 1860, ii. 403–422, 433–430.	3.48 } 3.71 }	33.16	4.22	4.32	....	18.59	1.20
Meteorite.	Eichstädt, Bavaria.	A. Schwager.	Sitz. München Akad., 1878, viii. 25–32.	3.70	33.31	2.31	....	....	....	0.74
		M. H. Klaproth.	Mem. Acad. Berlin, 1803, pp. 42–45.	3.599	37.00	....	19.00	16.50	....	....
*Buchnerite.	Grosnaja, Terek, Caucasus.	Plohn.	Min. Mitth., 1878, pp. 153–164.	3.45–3.55 }	33.78	3.44	....	....	28.66	3.22
					34.02	3.46	....	4.78	20.07	3.24
Serpentine.	Calagrande, Tuscany.	A. Cossa.	Ric. Chim. Roc. Italia, 1881, p. 132.	2.902–3.025	33.863	7.502	....	12.073	15.345	4.514
Meteorite.	Saurette, Vaucluse, France.	A. Laugier.	Ann. Mus. Hist. Nat. 1842, iv. 249–257.	3.4852	34.00	....	38.03	....	....	....
Meteorite.	Kaba, Hungary.	F. Wöhler.	Sitz. Wien. Akad., 1858, xxxiii. 205–209.	....	34.24	5.38	2.88	....	26.20 Al_2O_3+FeO	0.66
Meteorite.	Menz, Alt-Strelitz, Mecklenburg.	J. L. Smith.	Am. Jour. Sci., 1876 (3), xii. 207–209.	3.65	34.75	....	16.54	17.34	....	1.44
*Lherzolite.	Zsadány, Banat.	W. Pillitz.	Zeit. Analyt. Chemie, 1879, xviii. 58–68.	....	34.88	2.23	18 23	....	11.09	3.45
Serpentine.	Chester, Mass.	E. Hitchcock.	Geol. Mass., 1841, p. 160.	....	34.91	....	....	10.27	....	....
Meteorite.	Epinal, Vosges, France.	L. N. Vauquelin.	Ann. Chimie Phys., 1822, xxi. 324–328.	3.660	35.00	....	22.00	31.37	....	....
Meteorite.	Khettree, Rajputana, India.	D. Waldie.	Jour. Asiat. Soc. Bengal, 1860, xxxviii. (2), pp. 252–258.	3.743 } 3.612 }	35.17	1.77	18.70	....	11.16	2.37
Meteorite.	Vernon Co., Wisconsin.	J. L. Smith.	Am. Jour. Sci., 1876 (3), xii. 207–209.	3.66	35.24	1.07	15.72	....	15.54	1.41
Meteorite.	Borkut, Hungary.	J. Nuricsány.	Sitz. Wien. Akad., 1856, xx. 398–406.	5.242	35.28	2.74	27.03	....	4.71	1.05
*Dunite.	Chassigny, Haute Marne, France.	A. A. Damour.	Comptes Rendus, 1862, lv. 591.	3.57	35.30	....	....	....	26.70	....

* The prefixed asterisk indicates that the specimen is a meteorite.

Peridotite.

MgO.	MnO.	Na₂O.	K₂O.	Cr₂O₃.	Ni.	Co.	Cu.	Sn.	P.	S.	H₂O.	Miscellaneous.	Total.
17.00	0.36	2.26	0.19	Cr₂O₃+FeO 0.49	NiO+CoO 2.26	....	....	....	....	5.75	....	H₂SO₄ = 1.64, H₂SO₃ = 0.58, Cl = 0.08, H₂O + organic matter = 10.81.	100.00
8.6711	1.9302	1.323	0.3265	Cr₂O₃ 0.2392	NiO 2.6057	CoO 0.0904	....	....	....	4.6466	7.812	H₂SO₄ = 2.3345, Cl = 0.0776. Organic matter = 6.41. Ammonia = 0.1642. H₂O = 7.812.	99.472
27.926	....	0.35	trace.	Cr₂O₃+FeO 0.02	1.36	....	....	....	trace.	....	....	FeS = 20.52.	99.758
24.80	....	....	....	4.00	2.30	....	....	....	....	18.30	....		98.50
22.20	0.97	1.23		0.76	NiO 1.30	trace.	0.03	....	trace.	3.38	....	C = 1.67. Bituminous matter = 0.25.	98.70
19.20	....	trace.	....	0.70	0.82	trace.	....	....	....	4.24	6.50		100.44
22.21	0 26 Mn.	....	....	C₂O₃+FeO 0.63	NiO 1.38	....	....	0.80	....	....	....	Insol. = 8.69.	......
11.00	2.00	....	....	Cr₂O₃ 2.00	Ni 2.00	....	....	....	....	....	....	C = 2.50. H₂O + loss = 9.50.	100.00
9.00	2.00	....	....	1.00	NiO 2.50	....	....	....	....	3.50	....	C = 2.50. H₂O + loss = 18.50.	100.00
24.40	trace.	0.55		FeO+Cr₂O₃ 0.40	NiO 2.88	....	trace.	....	trace.	2.09	....	Fe, Ni = 1.85.	99.42
25.88	....	trace.	....		Ni, Cr, Co 4 28	....	....	....	....	....	....	S+Pt+loss = 4.73.	100.00
22.90	....	1.50	0.07		1.03	....	0.11	....	0.05	0.78	....	NiO = 0.80.	98.47
17.08	trace.	0.70	....	0.57	3.02	trace.	....	....	P₂O₅ trace.	1.87	....		99.85
23.68	....	1.41		Cr₂O₃+FeO trace.	1.55	....	trace.	....	....	2.15	....		100.77
7.28	....	0.59	1.81		....	....	....	....	....	....	4.23	CO₂ = 11.97, Li₂O = trace. Rock altered.	98.70
23.64	0.07	0.26	0.38	0.62	2.87	....	0.05	0.08	0.02	2.00	....		100.01
20.30	....	0.68	0.04		1.51	....	....	....	....	....	....	Recalculated.	99.87
29.24	....	1.40	0.60		NiO 3.81	....	....	SnO₂ 1.10	....	1.00	....	C = trace.	99.24
18.86	....	1.04	0.40	0.15	0.04	....	....	....	....	1.42	....	Fe+P = 24.64.	99.15
21.50	....	....	....		1.50	....	....	....	....	....	....	Loss, etc. = 4.50.	100 00
23.55	....	0.63	0.30	....	....	....	....	....	....	....	0.17	FeS = 5.37, CO₂ = 0.08. Fresh portion.	100 00
23.72	....	0.63	0.30	....	....	....	....	....	....	....	0.17	CO₂ = 0.68. Exterior portion.	100.07
18.092	trace. Mn.	....	....	....	....	....	....	....	P₂O₅ 1.31	....	....	TiO₂ = 0.686. Ignition = 5.868.	99.013
14.50	0.53	....	....		0.33	....	....	....	....	9.00	....	H₂O+loss = 3.31.	100.00
22.39	0.05	....	0.30	Cr₂O₃+FeO 0.89	1.87	trace.	0.01	....	trace.	....	....	FeS = 3.55, C = 0.58.	98.50
22 33	....	0.04	....	....	1.36	....	0.02	trace.	....	trace.	....	FeS = 4 24. Recalculated.	98.00
10.46	trace.	0.31	4.31	0.94	2.77	trace.	0.08	....	0.45	2.64	....	C = 0.21, Mn = 1.04, Cr₂O₃+FeO = 0.56.	102.70
44.91	....	....	....	....	....	....	....	....	....	....	9.45	Loss = 0.40.	100.00
4.25	....	....	....		NiO 0.50	....	....	....	....	2.25	....	CaO+K₂O = 1.25.	96.87
26.80	....	0.87	trace.	0.40	1.26	0.21	....	....	0.12	1.76	....	Cr = 0.10. Loss = 2.00.	101.31
22.05	....	1.01	....	....	1 28	....	0.07	trace.	....	trace.	....	FeS = 4.00. Recalculated.	100.51
19.92	....	1.91	0.66	Cr₂O₃+FeO 0.64	1.84	....	0.08	....	0.08	0.80	....	Ni+Mn = 0.78. Recalculated.	98.46
31.70	0.45	....	0.66	0.75	....	....	....	....	....	....	....	Chromite+Pyroxene = 3.77.	99.39

1 Probably a misprint for 3.05. Buchner, Meteoriten, 1863, p. 46.

A CLASSIFIED LIST OF COMPLETE (BAUSCH)

TABLE IV.

Variety.	Locality.	Analyst.	Publication.	Sp. Gr.	SiO$_2$.	Al$_2$O$_3$.	Fe.	Fe$_2$O$_3$.	FeO.	CaO.
*Dunite.	Chassigny, Haute Marne, France.	L. N. Vauquelin.	Ann.Chimie Phys.,1816, i. 45-54.	....	33.90	....	....	....	31.00	....
Meteorite.	Warrenton, Missouri.	J. L. Smith.	Am. Jour. Sci., 1877 (3), xiv. 222-224.	3.47	35.63	0.13	1.78	....	30.44	1.41
		F. Crook.	Chem. Const. Met. Stones. pp. 21-26.	3.50	35.647	2.607	8.00	....	34.193	1.770
Meteorite.	Ensisheim,Elsass, Germany.	C. Barthold.	Jour. Physique, 1800, i. 169-170.	3.233	42 00	17.00	20.00	....	....	2.00
		Foucroy and Vauquelin.	Ann. Mus. Hist. Nat., 1804, iii. 108-112.	3.4884	56.00	....	....	....	30.00	1.40
Serpentine.	Radauberg, Harz.	A. Streng.	Neues Jahr. Min., 1862, pp. 541, 542.	2.71	35.67	2 98	....	0.04	4.95	0.18
Meteorite.	Ställdale,Dalecarlia, Sweden.	G. Lindström.	Öfversigt Kongl. Veten. Forhan., 1877, p. 35.	3.733-3.745	35.71	2.11	21.10	....	10.20	1.61
Meteorite.	Albarello, Modena.	P. Maissen.	Gazzetta Chemica,1880, x. 20.	....	35.013	4.479	4.332	....	24.313	2.073
Meteorite.	Buschof,Kurland, Russia.	Grewingk and Schmidt.	Archiv Nat. Liv-, Ehst-, Kurlands, 1864, iii. 421-554.	3 527 / 3.511	36.011	2.484	7.918	....	20.978	0.709
Serpentine.	Proctorsville,Vermont.	A. A. Hayes.	Proc. Bost. Soc. Nat. Hist., 1856, v. 340.	....	36.10	1.18	....	....	....	....
		G. Werther.	Schriften Königsberg Gesell.,1866,ix.35-40.	3.719	36.26	1.22	31.07	....	....	2.61
*Lherzolite.	Pultusk, Poland.	C. Rammelsberg.	Mon.Berlin.Akad.,1870, pp. 448-462.	....	35.85	1.96	15.55	3.85	12.12	1.56
		G. vom Rath.	Neues Jahr. Min., 1869, pp. 80-82.	3.537-3.782	41.54	1.17	11.57	....	14.04	0.28
Meteorite.	Muddoor, India.	F. Crook.	Chem. Const. Met. Stones, pp 35-36.	....	30.256	26.28	10.601	....	17.97	0.81
		F. Stromeyer.	Ann. Physik, 1812, xlii. 105-110.	3.61	36.32	1.604	24.415	....	5 574	1.522
Meteorite.	Erxleben,Prussia.	C. F. Bucholz.	Jour. Chemie Physik, 1813, vii. 143-174.	3.5004	36.625	2 25	13.75	....	....	0.75
		M. H. Klaproth.	Beiträge Mineralkorper, 1810, vi. 303-306.	3 60 / 3.64	35.50	1.25	31.00	....	....	0.50
		A. Kuhlberg.	Archiv Nat. Liv-, Ehst-, Kurlands, 1867 (1), iv. 1-32.	3.793 / 3.721	36 324 / 36.582	2.650 / 2.385	16.324 / 17.572	....	13.929 / 12.385	trace. / trace.
Meteorite.	Lixna, Russia.	T. von Grotthus.	Ann. Physik Chemie, 1852, lxxxv. 577.	3.756	33.20	1.30	20.00	....	22.00	0.50
		A. Laugier.	Ann.Chimie Phys.,1824, xxv. 210-221.	3.6608	34.00	1.00	....	....	40.00	0.50
		J. L. Smith.	Am. Jour. Sci., 1875 (3), x. 302, 303.	3.57	36.34	0.63	11.16	....	22.28	....
*Saxonite.	Iowa Co., Iowa.	Gümbel and Schwager.	Sitz. München Akad., 1875, v. 313-380.	3.75	36.98	1.18	10.27	....	22.30	1.80
Meteorite.	Nulles, Tarragona, Spain.	L. de la Escosura.	Phil. Mag., 1862 (4), xxiv. 536-538.	3.818	36.43	0.84	22.50	13.55	....	....
Meteorite.	Ohaba, Transylvania.	F. Bukeisen.	Sitz. Wien. Akad.,1858, xxxi. 70-84.	3.11	36.60	0.28	21.40	....	1.75	trace.
Meteorite(?)	Mainz, Hesse.	F. Seelheim.	Jahrb. Vereins Natur. Nassau, 1857, xii. 465-410.	3.26	36.70	13.49	....	....	31.89	trace.
Meteorite.	Nanjemoy, Maryland.	G. Chilton.	Am.Jour.Sci., 1825 (1), x. 131-135.	3.06	36.72	0.10	....	....	60.30	0 90
Meteorite.	Hizen, Japan.	T. Shimidzn.	Trans. Asiat.Soc.Japan, 1882, x. 190-203.	3.02	36.75	1.89	15.35	....	8.84	1.94
		G. Lindström.	Ann. Physik Chemie, 1870, cxli. 205-224.	3.097	36.83	2.38	20.08	....	10.85	2.38
Meteorite.	Hessle, Sweden.	A. E. Nordenskjöld.	Ann. Physik Chemie, 1870, cxli. 205-224.	3 071 / 4 004 / 4.048	36.75 / 37.08	2.00 / 1.11	16 42 / 16.29	....	13.86 / 13.40	1 50 / 2.66
*Tufa.	Chantonnay, Vendée. France.	C. Rammelsberg.	Zeit. Deut. geol. Gesell., 1870, xxii. 889-892.	3.44-3.49	36.80	2.47	0.77	....	15.90	1.38
Meteorite.	Blansko,Moravia.	J. J. Berzelius.	Ann. Physik Chemie, 1834, xxxiii. 8-25 / 1865, cxxiv. 213-234.	8.40	37.077	2.386	16.089	....	14.045	1.248
Serpentine.	Duporth, Cornwall, England.	J. H. Collins.	Min. Mag., 1877, i. 224.	2.64	37.09	19.90	....	15.54	2.02	trace.
		J. A. Phillips.	Min. Mag., 1877, i. 224.	2 86	35.74	12.23	....	4.08	13.84	trace.

* The prefixed asterisk indicates that the specimen is a meteorite.

ANALYSES OF METEORIC AND TERRESTRIAL ROCKS.

Continued.

MgO.	MnO.	Na₂O.	K₂O.	Cr₂O₃.	Ni.	Co.	Cu.	Sn.	P.	S.	H₂O.	Miscellaneous.	Total.
32.00	....	....	....	2.00	....	....	....	....	....	....	....	....	98.00
26.74	....	0.24	....	0.06	0.21	0.01	....	....	....	....	....	NiO = 1.17, CoO = 0.24, FeS = 3.47. Recalculated.	100.53
13.13	0.210	0.376	0.223	0.400	1.26	....	....	....	1.013	2.05	....	....	99.564
14.00	....	....	....	....	....	....	....	....	....	....	2.00	....	97.00
12.00	....	....	....	....	2.40	....	....	....	....	....	3.50	....	105.50
35.03	0.11	0.77		0.87	....	....	CuO trace.	....	....	0.03	trace.	12.04 Cr₂O₃+FeO = 1.37.	100.04
23.16	0.25	0.02	0.15	0.40	1.61	0.17	....	....	....	0.01	2.27	Cl = 0.04, NiO = 0.20, P₂O₅ = 0.30.	100.00
22.773	trace.	1.037	0.44	trace.	0.73	0.105	....	....	....	....	2.364	Loss = 0.84.	99.909
27.174	0.062	0.26	0.325	0.225	1.513	trace.	....	....	....	0.011	2.184	Graphite+SnO₂+loss = 0.146	100.00
34.00	....	....	....	Cr₂O₃+FeO 0.92	....	....	....	....	....	....	0.51	CO₂ = 17.05, FeO+Mn+etc. = 3.40.	90.91
23.47	....	0.60	....	1.30	1.69	....	....	....	....	....	1.77	....	99.97
24.95	....	0.95	0.39	2.21	....	....	....	....	....	....	....	Recalculated.	99.39
26.73	0.49	1.34	....	Cr₂O₃+FeO 0.29	0.65	....	....	....	trace.	0.87	....	Insol. = 0.04. Recalculated.	99.01
27.483	....	0.33	0.285	0.158	1.162	....	....	....	....	1.543	....	....	99.318
23.584	0.705	0.741	....	0.246	1.579	....	....	....	....	2.952	....	....	99.642
23.0875	0.8125	....	....	....	0.50	....	....	....	....	....	....	FeS = 21.625.	100.00
26.50	0.25	....	....	1.00	0.25	....	....	....	....	....	....	S+loss = 3.75.	100.00
24.540	0.025	0.680	trace.	Cr₂O₃+FeO 0.759	1.725	....	....	....	0.120	2.204	....	Mn = 0.647.	99.827
25.006	0.034	0.760	trace.	0.682	1.090	....	....	....	0.163	2.052	....	Mn = 0.302.	107.974
10.80	....	....	....	0.90 Cr₂O₃	2.00	....	....	....	....	....	3.50	Mn = trace.	100.20
17.00	....	....	....	1.00	1.50	....	trace.	....	....	....	0.80	Mn = trace.	101.80
19.70	....	1.40	trace.	....	1.30	0.08	....	....	....	....	....	Li₂O = trace, FeS = 5.82. Recalculated.	98.71
18.21	0.25	0.82	0.57	0.49	2.05	....	....	....	....	....	....	FeS = 5.25. Recalculated.	99.85
19.47	0.30	....	....	Cr₂O₃+FeO 0.50	1.43	....	....	....	....	....	....	FeS = 2.34, Insol. = 0.79.	98.20
23.45	0.15 Mn.	0.98		Cr₂O₃+FeO 0.56	1.80 NiO	....	....	trace.	P₂O₅	....	....	FeS = 18.14.	100.11
16.12	trace.	....	1.21	0.46	2.08	....	trace.	trace.	0.00	....	1.51	Fe, Ni = 2.13, FeS = 3.80.	100.05
5.20	....	....	....	....	NiO 4.10	....	....	....	....	....	2.54	Recalculated.	109.66
23.80	0.51	0.97	0.16	Cr₂O₃+FeO 0.51	1.75			0.15 CuO+SnO	P₂O₅ 0.84	....	....	NiO = 0.30, FeS = 5.91, Mn = 0.18.	99.01
23.21	0.42	0.94	....	0.07	2.15	0.02	0.02	....	0.15	1.88	....	C = trace, Cl = 0.04.	100.84
20.06	....	1.03	....	....	1.98	trace.	0.01	....	trace.	0.37	....	C = 0.52.	100.00
21.06	....	2.11	....	....	2.33	trace.	0.02	....	trace.	trace.	....	C = 0.85.	100.00
25.15	0.27	1.11		0.66	1.16	....	....	....	....	2.24	....	....	97.00
23.898	0.489	0.740	0.187	Cr₂O₃+FeO 0.616	0.866	0.06	0.079	....	....	0.056	....	NiO = 0.207. Analysis recalculated by Von Reichenbach.	99.243
15.00	trace.	trace.	trace.	....	....	....	....	....	P₂O₅ 0.21	....	8.65	TiO₂ = trace.	99.31
22.13	0.98	0.25	trace.	....	....	....	....	....	....	0.18	10.01	....	100.04

TABLE IV.

Variety.	Locality.	Analyst.	Publication.	Sp. Gr.	SiO₂.	Al₂O₃.	Fe.	Fe₂O₃.	FeO.	CaO.
Picrite (Palæopicrite).	Fichtelgebirge, Bavaria.	H. Loretz.	Gumbel's Die paläozoischen Eruptivgesteine des Fichtelgebirges, 1874, p 40.	....	37.12	4.00	....	8.92	7.02	0.14
Serpentine.	Reichenstein, Silesia.	G. L. Ulex.	Zeit. Deut. geol. Gesell., 1867, xix. 243.	....	37.16	1.43	....	10.06		....
Lherzolite.	Presque Isle, Michigan.	J. D. Whitney.	Am. Jour. Sci., 1859 (2), xxviii. 18.	....	37.25	....	....	6.75	14.14	....
Meteorite.	Adare, Limerick Co., Ireland.	R. Apjohn.	Jour. Chem. Soc., 1874 (2), xii. 104–106.	3.021–4.23	37.26	2.03	16.24	....	8.95	8.61
Meteorite.	Alessandria, Piedmont.	G. Missaghi.	Ann. Physik Chemie, 1863, cxviii. 361–363.	3.815	37.403	8.65	19.37	....	12.851	3.144
Olivinfels.	Kalobelmen, Norway.	Hauan.	Verh. Geol. Reich., 1807, pp. 71, 72.	....	37.42	0.10	....	....	8.88	....
*Saxonite.	Gopalpur, India.	A. Exner.	Min. Mitth., 1872, pp. 41–43.	....	37.44	2.52	20.96	....	11.94	1.00
*Saxonite.	Tourinnes-la-Grosse, Louvain, Belgium.	F. Pisani.	Comptes Rendus, 1864, lviii. 169–171.	3.525	37.47	3.05	11.05	....	13.89	2.61
Serpentine.	Lynnfield, Massachusetts.	C. T. Jackson.	Proc. Bost. Soc. Nat. Hist., 1850, v. 318.	....	37.50	....	....	....	2.50	....
Meteorite.	Kakova, Hungary.	E. P. Harris.	Chem. Const. Meteorites, 1859, pp. 22–34.	3.384	37.02	2.25	7.11	....	22.47	0.60
Meteorite.	Bandong, Java.	C. L. Vlaanderen.	Comptes Rendus, 1872, lxxv. 1676–1678.	3.519	37.05	3.06	4.95	4.30	10.87	1.06
Meteorite.	Dundrum, Tipperary Co., Ireland.	S. Haughton.	Proc. Roy. Soc., 1866, xv. 214–217.	3.066–3.57	37.80	0.85	19.57	....	7.92	1.82
Meteorite.	Smolensk, Russia.	M. H. Klaproth.	Ann. Physik, 1809, xxxiii. 210, 211.	3.70	38.00	1.00	17.00	25.00	....	0.75
		J. Scherer.	Ann. Physik, 1808, xxix. 214.	3.0046	39.00	....	17.75	17.50	....	....
*Tufa.	Orvinio, Italy.	L. Sipöcz.	Sitz. Wien. Akad., 1875, lxx. (1), 464.	{ 3.075 { 3.600	38.01 36.82	2.22 2.31	22.34 22.11	....	6.55 0.41	2.33 2.31
Meteorite.	Pohlitz, Reuss, Germany.	F. Stromeyer.	Jour. Chemie Physik, 1819, xxvi. 251, 252.	3.4038	38.0574	3.4688	17.4890	....	4.8959	....
Meteorite.	Castalia, Nash Co., North Carolina.	J. L. Smith.	Am. Jour. Sci., 1875 (3), x. 147, 148.	2.001†	38.06	2.12	14.02	....	13.10	....
Serpentine.	Blanford, Mass.	E. Hitchcock.	Geol. Mass., 1841, p. 160.	....	38.00	....	....	....	6.75	....
Meteorite.	Saint Mesmin, Aube, France.	F. Pisani.	Comptes Rendus, 1866, lxii. 1326.	....	38.10	3.00	4.94	....	17.21	1.00
Meteorite.	Château-Renard, France.	A. Dufrénoy.	Comptes Rendus, 1841, xiii. 47–53.	3.50	38.13	3.82	7.70	....	20.44	0.14
		A. Schwager.	Sitz. München Akad., 1878, viii. 16–24.	3.4506	38.14	2.51	....	....	25.70	2.27
Meteorite.	Mauerkirchen, Bavaria.	F. Crook.	Chem. Const. Meteoric Stones, pp. 26–30.	....	41.532	1.705	....	....	23.32	2.115
		Imhof.	Sitz. München Akad., 1878, viii. 17.	3.452	25.40	....	2.33	40.24	....	....
Serpentine.	Varzi, Italy.	A. Cossa.	Ric. Chim. Roc. Italia, 1881, pp. 102–164.	....	38.22	trace.	....	....	14.05	trace.
Serpentine.	Kynance Cove, Cornwall, Eng.	S. Haughton.	Phil. Mag., 1855 (4), x. 254.	....	38.29	....	....	....	13.50	....
Meteorite.	Charsonville, Loiret, France.	L. N. Vauquelin.	Ann. Mus. Hist. Nat., 1811, xvii. 1–15.	3.712 3.57–3.65	38.40	3.00	25.80	....	....	4.20
Meteorite.	Drake's Creek, Summer Co., Tennessee.	E. H. Baumhauer.	Ann. Physik. Chemie, 1845, lxvi. 468–503.	3.469	38.503	4.807	12.810	....	10.029	0.70
		H. Seybert.	Am. Jour. Sci., 1830 (1), xvii. 326–328.	3.484-8.487	40.00	2.466	12.00	....	12.20	....
Meteorite.	Aukoma (Pillistfer), Livland, Russia.	Grewingk and Schmidt.	Archiv Nat. Liv-, Ehst-, Kurlands, 1864, iii. 421–554.	3.047	38.503	2.491	25.007	....	2.519	0.48
*Saxonite.	Waconda, Kansas.	J. L. Smith.	Am. Jour. Sci., 1877 (3), xiii. 211–213.	3.40–3.60	38.61	1.00	4.00	....	22.61	trace.
Serpentine.	Monteferrato, Italy.	A. Cossa.	Ric. Chim. Roc. Italia, 1881, pp. 148, 149.	2.55	38.70	0.58	....	3.19	7.26	trace.
Meteorite.	Richmond, Virginia.	C. Rammelsberg.	Mon. Berlin. Akad., 1870, pp. 453–457.	3.3713	38.71	2.17	0.45	....	16.17	2.53
Meteorite.	Ausson, Haute Garonne, France.	A. A. Damour.	Comptes Rendus, 1859, xlix. 31–36.	3.51–3.57	38.72	1.85	8.63	....	16.93	0.80
		E. P. Harris.	Chem. Const. Meteorites, 1859, pp. 44–61.	3.50	58.40	2.25	7.13	....	18.00	trace.

* The prefixed asterisk indicates that the specimen is a meteorite.

ANALYSES OF METEORIC AND TERRESTRIAL ROCKS.

Continued.

MgO.	MnO.	Na₂O.	K₂O.	Cr₂O₃.	Ni.	Co.	Cu.	Sn.	P.	S.	H₂O.	Miscellaneous.	Total.
25.92	0.40	0.40	0.49	....	....	....	....	....	P₂O₅ 0.10	....	5.04	TiO₂ = 0.40, CO₂ = 0.00.	98.60
36.24	....	....	....	....	....	....	....	....	....	....	12.15	FeAs = 2.70.	100.34
28.07	....	1.10	....	....	....	....	....	....	....	....	10.80	Analysis of soluble portion only.	98.86
13.50	5.50	0.70	0.12	Cr₂O₄+FeO 1.75	2.73	0.10	....	....	....	....	....	FeS = 0.54, V = trace. Recalculated.	99.12
11.176	Mn trace.	....	....	....	0.845	1.077 NiO	trace.	....	....	3.831	....	....	98.327
48.22	0.17	....	....	....	....	0.23	....	....	....	....	....	Ignition = 4.71.	99.75
10.72	0.20	0.02	0.21	trace.	1.80	0.10	....	....	....	1.74	....	....	98.00
24.40	trace.	2.26		Cr₂O₄+FeO 0.71	1.30	....	....	0.17	....	2.21	....	....	99.72
41.00	....	....	....	Cr₂O₄+FeO	....	....	....	....	....	....	15.00	CaCO₃ = 4.00.	100.00
24.74	0.42	1.76	0.51	0.07	1.24	0.10	trace.	....	0.01	trace.	....	Graphite = 0.14. Recalculated.	101.13
13.24	....	2.11	1.07	Cr₂O₃+FeO 4.41	1.03	0.14	....	....	....	2.18	....	....	98.33
23.53	0.10	0.96	0.50	Cr₂O₄+FeO 1.50	1.03	....	....	....	....	....	....	FeS = 4.05. Recalculated.	98.99
14.25	....	....	....	....	0.40	....	....	....	....	....	....	Loss, etc. = 5.00.	100.00
20.00	....	....	....	....	1.25	....	....	....	....	....	....	Loss, etc. = 4.50.	100.00
24.11	....	1.40	0.31	....	2.15	....	....	....	....	1.04	....	....	101.42
21.60	....	0.96	0.26	....	3.04	....	....	....	....	2.04	....	....	100.95
20.9300	1.1467	....	....	0.1298	1.9057	....	....	....	....	2.6957	....	....	99.1602
29.43	....	0.55	trace.	....	1.12	0.06	trace.	....	trace.	0.46	....	Li₂O = trace.	98.02
40.19	....	....	....	....	....	....	....	....	....	....	14.77	Loss = 0.20.	100.00
25.64	....	3.13		Cr₂O₄+FeO 2.18	....	....	....	....	....	....	....	FeS = 2.99.	99.00
17.07	....	0.80	0.27	....	1.55	....	....	....	....	0.39	....	....	99.97
21.73	....	1.00	0.48	0.30	....	....	....	....	0.14	2.09	....	Fe+Ni = 0.36.	100.75
24.202	....	0.242	0.145	Cr₂O₄+FeO 0.725	....	....	....	....	....	0.705	....	Fe+Ni = 3.745.	98.430
28.75	....	....	....	....	1.20	....	....	....	....	....	....	S+loss = 2.08.	100.00
32.83	....	....	....	trace.	....	....	....	....	....	....	14.05	....	99.75
34.24	....	....	....	....	....	....	....	....	....	....	12.00	....	98.12
13.00	Mn 0.00	....	....	Cr 1.50	6.00	....	....	....	....	5.00	....	....	98.70
22.789	2.31	0.504	0.025	1.374	1.495 NiO	0.162	0.005	....	....	1.804	....	CuO+SnO₂+NiO = 2.528.	100.00
23.830	....	....	....	....	0.833	2.100	....	....	....	....	2.433	....	95.031
23.066	0.018	0.341	0.24	0.487	1.878	trace.	....	....	0.013	3.492	....	Graphite+TiO₂+loss = 0.115.	100.00
25.15	Mn 0.46	1.07	trace.	....	0.64 NiO	0.10	trace.	....	trace.	....	....	Li₂O = trace, FeS = 3.85. Recalculated.	98.38
36.44	....	....	....	0.30	trace.	....	....	....	....	....	....	Ignition = 13.23.	99.70
27.30	....	....	....	....	1.18	....	....	....	....	....	....	....	98.15
22.56	trace.	0.57	0.11	Cr₂O₄+FeO 1.83	0.06	....	....	....	....	....	....	P+Fe+Ni, etc. = 2.00, FeS = 3.74. Recalculated.	99.05
25.08	0.24	0.10	0.18	Cr₂O₃ 0.78	1.02	0.00	....	....	....	trace.	2.10	FeS = 2.51. Recalculated.	98.01

† Probably a misprint for 8.001.

TABLE IV.

Variety.	Locality.	Analyst.	Publication.	Sp. Gr.	SiO$_2$.	Al$_2$O$_3$.	Fe.	Fe$_2$O$_3$.	FeO.	CaO.
Meteorite.	Ausson, Haute Garonne, France.	Filhol and Leymerie.	Comptes Rendus, 1859, xlviii. 193–198.	3.30	50.28	1.82	8.30	2.32	15.38	0.55
Picrite.	Schönau, Neutitschein, Moravia.	F. E. Szameit.	Sitz. Wien. Acad., 1860, liii. (1), 200.	3.020	38.72	10.10	....	6.30	0.14	10.37
Serpentine.	Neurode, Silesia.	G. vom Rath.	Ann. Physik Chemie, 1855, cxv. 553.	2.012	38.78	3.06	....	14.19	....	4.51
Serpentine.	River Oisain, Tirol.	Pufahl.	Samml. Geol. Mus. Leiden, 1884, ii. 100.	....	38.81	1.14	....	5.80	2.10	0.32
Serpentine.	Lizard, Cornwall, England.	J. A. Phillips.	Phil. Mag., 1871 (4), xii. 101.	2.59	38.80 / 38.58	2.95 / 3.06	....	1.86 / 1.95	5.04 / 5.10	trace. / trace.
Meteorite.	Rakowska, Tula, Russia.	P. Grigoriew.	Zeit. Deut. geol. Gesell., 1880, xxxii. 417–420.	3.582	38.87	2.60	5.67	....	13.44	2.36
Dunite.	Söndmore, Norway.	W. C. Brögger.	Neues Jahr. Min., 1880, ii. 187–192.	3.32	38.87	....	....	....	8.45	0.09
Picrite.	Söhle, Neutitschein, Moravia.	G. Tschermak.	Sitz. Wien. Akad., 1866, liii. (1), 203; 1867, lvi. 274, 275.	2.961	38.00	10.80	....	4.90	7.00	6.00
Serpentine.	Prato, Italy.	A. Cossa.	Ric. Chim. Roc. Italia, 1881, pp. 151, 152.	2.57–2.50	38.04	....	....	1.18	8.25	trace.
Meteorite.	Linn Co., Iowa.	C. Rammelsberg.	Mün. Berlin. Akad., 1870, pp. 457–450.	....	38.00	2.00	13.51	....	14.52	1.18
		C. U. Shepard.	Am. Jour. Sci., 1848 (2), vi. 403–405.	....	52.34	....	8.98	....	20.42	....
Meteorite.	Cynthiana, Kentucky.	J. L. Smith.	Am. Jour. Sci., 1877 (3), xiv. 224–227.	3.41	38.00	0.22	5.36	....	19.73	2.20
*Buchnerite.	Alfianello, Brescia, Italy.	H. von Foullon.	Sitz. Wien. Akad., 1883, lxxxviii. (1), 433.	....	39.14	0.93	11.31	....	17.42	1.00
Meteorite.	Sétif, Algeria.	S. Meunier.	Comptes Rendus, 1868, lxvi. 513–519.	3.595	39.20	1.04	....	....	14.18	2.66
Serpentine.	Rio Marina, Elba.	A. Cossa.	Ric. Chim. Roc. Italia, 1881, pp. 134, 155.	2.50	39.21	trace.	....	7.87	2.63	trace.
Meteorite.	Utrecht, Holland.	E. H. Baumhauer.	Ann. Physik Chemie, 1845, lxvi. 465–408.	3.57–3.05	39.301	2.252	11.008	....	15.290	1.48
Serpentine.	Longone, Elba.	A. Cossa.	Ric. Chim. Roc. Italia, 1881, pp. 130, 137.	2.61	39.38	trace.	....	8.26	3.67	trace.
Meteorite.	Parnallee, India.	E. Pfeiffer.	Sitz. Wien. Akad., 1863, xlvii. (2), 460–463.	3.115	39.408	2.573	9.83	....	15.288	0.56
Serpentine.	Rio Alto, Elba.	A. Cossa.	Ric. Chim. Roc. Italia, 1881, pp. 135, 136.	2.61	39.58	....	....	7.65	4.13	trace.
Dunite.	Karlstätten, Austria.	Kouya.	Sitz. Wien. Akad., 1867, lvi. 277.	3.011	39.61	1.08	....	....	8.42	trace.
Meteorite.	Honolulu, Hawaii, Sandwich Isls.	A. Kuhlberg.	Archiv Nat. Liv., Ehst-, Kurlands, 1867 (1), iv. 1–32.	3.5900 / 3.3964	39.65	1.03	6.45	....	19.15	....
Meteorite.	Villeneuve, Alexandria, Italy.	Bertolio.	Comptes Rendus, 1868, lxvii. 322–320.	3.29	39.661	0.415	20.70	....	12.234	0.678
Meteorite.	Girgenti, Sicily.	G. vom Rath.	Ann. Physik Chemie, 1869, cxxxviii. 541–545.	3.594	39.72	1.44	10.40	....	16.47	1.70
Serpentine.	Valle Tournanche, Piedmont.	A. Cossa.	Ric. Chim. Roc. Italia, 1881, p. 120.	2.80	39.76	....	....	5.11	6.37	....
Serpentine.	Montemezzano, Italy.	A. Cossa.	Ric. Chim. Roc. Italia, 1881, p. 150.	2.56	39.77	trace.	....	1.76	8.46	trace.
Olivinfels.	Kraubat, Steiermark.	H. Wieser.	Min. Mitth., 1872, p. 79.	2.889	39.87	0.80	....	9.76	0.64	0.44
Serpentine.	Portoferraio, Elba.	A. Cossa.	Ric. Chim. Roc. Italia, 1881, pp. 137, 138.	2.53	39.932	trace.	....	6.809	3.75	....
Meteorite.	Swajahn, Kurland, Russia.	A. Kuhlberg.	Archiv Nat. Liv., Ehst-, Kurlands, 1867 (1), iv. 1–32.	3.4341	39.97 / 40.414	3.06 / 3.798	6.15 / 8.322	....	19.45 / 15.424	....
Meteorite.	Nerft, Russia.	A. Kuhlberg.	Ann. Physik Chemie, 1866, cxxxvi. 448,449.	....	40.00	3.52	8.36	....	15.98	0.05
Meteorite.	Pohgel, Kurland, Russia.	A. Kuhlberg.	Archiv Nat. Liv., Ehst-, Kurlands, 1867 (1), iv. 1–32.	3.555	40.05 / 30.556	3.94 / 3.299	10.15 / 8.835	....	14.11 / 14.002	trace. / 0.185
Serpentine	Ballinahinch Quarry, Connemara, Ireland.	J. A. Galbraith.	Jour. Geol. Soc. Dublin, 1852, v. 138.	....	40.12	trace.	....	....	3.47	trace.
Meteorite.	Schönenberg, Bavaria.	C. W. Gümbel.	Sitz. München Akad., 1878, viii. 40–46.	....	40.13	5.57	13.77	....	17.12	2.31
Meteorite.	Sokol Banja, Servia.	S. M. Losanitch.	Berichte Chem. Gesell. Berlin, 1878, xi.96–98.	3.502	40.14	....	5.82	....	25.54	....

* The prefixed asterisk indicates that the specimen is a meteorite.

ANALYSES OF METEORIC AND TERRESTRIAL ROCKS.

Continued.

MgO.	MnO.	Na₂O.	K₂O.	Cr₂O₄.	Ni.	Co.	Cu.	Sn.	P.	S.	H₂O.	Miscellaneous.	Total.
10.74	....	2.10	....	....	0.72	....	....	....	....	1.82	....	Recalculated.	99.73
18.59	....	1.50	1.57	....	....	....	....	....	....	....	3.96	TiO₂ = trace, CO₂ = 2.93, Organic material = trace.	100.27
20.96	0.90	0.11	0.29	....	....	....	....	....	....	....	....	Ignition = 7.74.	99.55
35.91	trace.	0.12	trace.	0.62	....	CuO 0.04	....	P₂O₅ 0.03	....	....	14 87	TiO₂ = 0.16.	99.92
34.61	trace.	0.77	0.83	0.08	NiO 0.28	....	....	....	....	....	15.52	....	100.80
84.32	trace.	0.76	0.30	0.08	0.30	....	....	....	....	....	15.52	....	99.97
24.00	0.24	2.04	0.37	Cr₂O₄+FeO 0.81	1.43	0.32	....	....	0.12	....	....	Mn = trace, C = 0.13, FeS = 0.10.	....
51.86	0.12	....	....	....	....	....	....	....	....	....	....	....	100.29
23.60	....	1.30	0.80	....	....	....	....	....	....	....	4.50	CO₂ = 1.80.	99.10
37.28	....	....	....	0.29	NiO trace.	•	....	....	....	....	....	Ignition = 13.00.	99.84
26.05	....	0.38	trace.	....	1.08	....	....	....	....	2.32	....	Recalculated.	100.00
9.75	....	0.26		....	1.46	....	....	....	....	....	....	FeS = 5.00. Recalculated.	98.21
26.56	....	0.40	....	0.15	0.50	0.07	....	....	....	....	....	FeS = 5.50. Recalculated.	101.77
25.01	....	0.75	0.10	....	1.09	....	....	....	....	2.71	....	....	100.42
25.03	....	....	....	0.12	....	....	....	....	....	....	....	Fe+Ni = 8.32, FeS = 8.04.	99.84
36.92	trace.	....	....	0.27	....	....	....	....	....	....	....	Ignition = 12.54.	99.44
21.366	....	1.395	0.152	0.050	1.242	....	0.025	....	0.005	1.807	....	MnO + NiO = 0.009, CuO + SnO₂ = 0.256.	100.00
85.02	trace.	....	....	trace. Cr₂O₄+FeO	....	....	....	....	....	....	....	TiO₂ = trace, Ignition = 12.85.	99.78
22.819	0.54	1.907	0.547	trace.	0.904	0.06	trace.	trace.	0.10	2.712	0.684	CoO₂ = 0.00, Zn = trace, NiO = 0.724.	100.00
36.37	trace.	....	....	trace.	....	....	....	....	....	....	....	Ignition = 12.72.	100.45
42.29	....	0.01	0.02	....	....	....	....	....	....	....	5.80	....	97.92
24.51	Mn. 0.21	0.88	trace.	Cr₂O₄+FeO 1.35	1.63	....	....	....	0.04	2.20	....	....	98.00
14.770	....	4.151	....	0.036 Cr₂O₄+FeO	NiO 5.371	....	trace.	....	P₂O₅ 0.607	0.503	....	Cl = 0.105, Loss = 0.587.	100.00
24.61	trace.	....	....	1.00	1.05 NiO	....	....	....	....	2.06	....	Recalculated.	98.45
38.16	....	....	....	trace.	trace.	....	....	....	....	....	9.96	....	99.72
37.33	....	....	....	0.27	....	....	....	....	....	....	....	Ignition = 12.10.	99.71
40.99	trace.	1.28	....	....	NiO 0.66	....	....	....	....	....	6.48	....	100.11
36.824	trace.	....	....	0.183 Cr₂O₄+FeO	....	....	....	....	....	....	....	TiO₂ = trace, Ignition=13.047.	100.635
24.91	trace.	0.64	0.09	0.04	1.45	....	....	....	0.01	1.88	....	Mn = 0.05.	98.80
26.489	0.045	0.508	0.038	0.478 Cr₂O₄+FeO	1.255	....	....	....	0.006	1.293	....	Mn = 0.08.	98.269
25.50	0.03	1.65	0.08	0.55 Cr₂O₄+FeO	1.82	trace.	....	....	0.05	2.02	....	Mn = 0.10.	99.40
24 35	0.04	0.765	0.123	0.05	1.58	....	....	....	0.06	2.35	....	Mn = 0.09.	98.238
26 0.51	0.021	0.630	0.072	0.848	0.981	....	....	....	0.050	2.505	....	Mn = 0.107.	98.811
40.04	....	....	....	....	....	....	....	....	....	....	13.36	CO₂ = 2.00.	98.99
13.81	....	2.20	0.73	0.60	1.47	....	....	....	0.30	1.98	....	....	100.00
25 78	0.12	0.26	0.06	0.04	0.02	0.07	....	....	trace.	1.40	....	Recalculated.	100.21

TABLE IV.

Variety.	Locality.	Analyst.	Publication.	Sp. Gr.	SiO$_2$.	Al$_2$O$_3$.	Fe.	Fe$_2$O$_3$.	FeO.	CaO.
Meteorite.	Bachmut, Jekatherinoslaw, Russia.	A. Kuhlberg.	Archiv Nat. Liv-, Ehst-, Kurlands, 1867 (1), iv, 1–32.	3.566	40.209 / 38.971	2.884 / 2.554	8.105 / 8.028	....	22.374 / 15.256	0.069 / trace.
		F. v. Giese.	Ann. Physik, 1815, l. 117, 118.	3.4235	44.00	3.00	21.00	....	....	....
		F. Wöhler.	Sitz. Wien. Akad., 1862, xlvi. (2), 302-306.	....	33.71	2.78	12.00	....	14.17	1.24
*Buchnerite.	Tieschitz, Moravia.	J. Habermann.	Denks. Wien. Akad., 1879, xxxix. 187-201.	3.50	40.23	1.93	10.26	....	19.48	1.54
Serpentine.	Föhrenbühl, Bavaria.	G. Schulze.	Zeit. Deut. geol. Gesell., 1883, xxxv. 451.	....	40.30	1.30	....	1.35	8.50	trace.
Serpentine.	Orford, Canada.	T. S. Hunt.	Am. Jour. Sci., 1858, xxv. 219.	2.597	40.30	....	....	....	7.02	....
*Saxonite.	Goalpara, India.	N. Teclu.	Sitz. Wien. Akad., 1870, lxii. (2), 852-864.	3.444	40.36	....	8.49	....	13.82	0.60
Picrite.	Dillenburg, Nassau.	G. Angelbis.	Inaug. Dissert., Bonn, 1877, p. 9.	3.108	40.37	9.86	....	4.70	8.34	4.74
Serpentine.	Heiligenblut, Carinthia.	R. v. Drasche.	Min. Mitth., 1871, p. 8.	2.79	40.39	1.68	....	0.98	3.32	4.78
Serpentine.	Lizard Point, Cornwall.	T. S. Hunt.	Am. Jour. Sci., 1858, xxvi. 236.	....	40.40	0.05	....	....	....	....
Serpentine.	Favaro, Piedmont.	A. Cossa.	Ric. Chim. Roc. Italia, 1881, pp. 125-127.	2.66	40.43	trace.	....	9.55	4.23	3.51
Serpentine.	Levanto, Italy.	C. T. Heycock.	Geol. Mag., 1879 (2), vi. 367.	2.705	40.47	4.35	....	7.01	....	0.84
Meteorite.	Doroninsk, Siberia.	J. Scheerer.	Mém. Acad. St. Pétersbourg, 1813-14, vi., Hist., p. 46.	3.6154	40.50	3.26	....	18.50	....	6.25
Serpentine.	Fahlun, Sweden.	R. F. Marchand.	Neues Jahr. Min., 1845, p. 831.	2.58	40.52	0.21	...;	....	3.01	....
		J. L. Jordan.	Neues Jahr. Min., 1845, p. 831.	....	40.32	....	....	....	3.33	....
Serpentine.	Sprechenstein, Tyrol.	E. Hussak.	Min. Mitth., 1882 (2), v. 67.	....	40.55	2.70	....	10.40	....	4.40
Meteorite.	Rochester, Indiana.	J. L. Smith.	Am. Jour. Sci., 1877 (3), xiv. 219-222.	3.55	40.61	0.10	9.45	....	16.56	2.41
Meteorite.	Dhurmsalla, India.	S. Haughton.	Proc. Roy. Soc., 1866, xv. 214-217.	3.309	40.69	0.50	6.88	....	11.20	....
Picrite.	Freiberg, Neutitschein, Moravia.	P. Juhasz.	Sitz. Wien. Akad., 1870, liii. (1), 265.	2.96	40.70	10.41	....	3.52	6.39	8.48
Serpentine.	Talof Copper Mine, Ural.	Ivanoff.	Neues Jahr. Min., 1847, p. 207.	2.65	40.80	3.02	....	....	2.20	0.42
Serpentine.	Ober-Steiermark, Austria.	H. Hofer.	Jahrb. Geol. Reichs., 1866, xvi. 443-446.	....	40.81	1.00	....	1.98	5.02	1.32
Serpentine.	Col de Pertuis, Vosges, France.	A. Delesse.	Ann. Mines, 1850 (4), xviii. 341.	2.749	40.88	0.92	....	....	7.30	1.50
Serpentine.	Corio, Piedmont.	A. Cossa.	Ric. Chim. Roc. Italia, 1881, pp. 123, 124.	2.64	40.88	trace.	....	2.05	10.21	trace.
Serpentine.	Verrayes, Piedmont.	A. Cossa.	Ric. Chim. Roc. Italia, 1881, pp. 115-118.	{ 2.587 / 2.600 / 2.516 }	40.90 / 40.86	....	....	....	4.70 / 4.50	0.02 / 0.03
Serpentine.	Sprechenstein, Tyrol.	E. Hussak.	Min. Mitth., 1882 (2), v. 70.	....	40.90	2.08	....	7.08	....	0.30
Meteorite.	Zaborzyca, Volhynia, Russia.	A. Laugier.	Ann. Chimie Phys., 1824, xxv. 210-221.	....	41.00	0.75	....	45.00	....	2.00
Meteorite.	Searsmont, Maine.	J. L. Smith.	Am. Jour. Sci., 1871 (3), ii. 200, 201.	3.701	41.04	0.86	13.16	....	13.84	....
Serpentine.	Heiligenblut, Carinthia.	R. von Drasche.	Min. Mitth., 1871, p. 9.	2.91	41.05	1.67	....	8.82	3.15	3.76
Meteorite.	Krahenberg, Bavaria.	Keller.	Sitz. München Akad., 1878, viii. 47-58.	....	41.12	3.22	10 37	....	17.42	2.06
		A. Schwager.	Sitz. München Akad., 1878, viii. 47-58.	....	30.08	2.08	1.43	....	28.53	13.35
Dunite.	Bonhomme, Vosges, France.	B. Weigand.	Min. Mitth., 1875, p. 187.	....	41.13	0.84	....	3.86	2.77	trace.
Serpentine.	Neurode, Silesia.	Fickler.	Sitz. Wien. Akad., 1867, lvi. 274, 275.	2.88	41.13	13.56	....	....	6.19	6.72
Meteorite.	Stewart Co., Georgia.	J. L. Smith.	Am. Jour. Sci., 1870 (2), l. 330-341.	3.65	41.15	2.17	6.09	....	14.85	0.04
Serpentine.	Syria.	S. Haughton.	Phil. Mag., 1855 (4), x. 254.	....	41.24	....	....	....	7.41	....
Serpentine.	Villa Rota, Italy.	A. Delesse.	Ann. Mines, 1848 (4), xiv. 79.	2.644	41.34	3.22	....	....	5.54	....

* The prefixed asterisk indicates that the specimen is a meteorite.

ANALYSES OF METEORIC AND TERRESTRIAL ROCKS.

Continued.

MgO.	MnO.	Na₂O.	K₂O.	Cr₂O₃.	Ni.	Co.	Cu.	Sn.	P.	S.	H₂O.	Miscellaneous.	Total.
20.115	0.036	0.612	trace	Cr₂O₃+FeO 0.044	1.195	....	....	....	0.042	2.516	....	Mn = 0.228.	98.936
26.025	0.045	0.734	trace	0.039	1.208	....	....	....	0.051	2.221	....	Mn = 0.185.	97.782
18.00	....	....	....	....	2.50	....	....	....	....	....	....	S+Cr₂O₃ = 1.00, Mn = 1.00.	99.50
27.33	1.00	0.45	0.13	2.00	1.09	....	....	....	0.02 P₂O₅	1.81	....	Mn = 1.00. Recalculated by A. Kuhlberg.	98.76
20.55	....	1.52	....	....	1.31	....	....	....	0.22	1.05	....	....	99.02
34.21	....	....	....	0.90	....	....	....	....	....	....	18.00	....	99.56
30.07	....	....	....	trace.	NiO trace.	....	....	....	....	....	13.35	....	100.00
37.45	....	....	....	....	....	....	....	....	....	....	....	C = 0.72, H = 0.13. Recalculated by Tschermak.	101.08
21.03	....	3.61	0.82	....	....	....	....	....	....	....	5.04	....	99.77
30.12	....	....	....	....	....	....	....	....	....	....	9.86	....	100.13
37.43	....	....	....	Cr₂O₃+FeO 7.47	NiO 0.15	....	....	....	....	....	....	Ignition = 13.00.	100.00
31.82	....	....	....	trace.	NiO 0.06	....	....	....	....	....	10.05	....	100.25
34.59	0.15	....	....	....	NiO 0.49	....	....	....	....	....	....	H₂O+FeS = 11.61.	100.11
9.00	1.25	....	....	2.00	10.00	....	....	....	....	....	8.12	Loss = 1.13.	100.00
42.05	....	....	....	....	....	....	....	....	....	....	13.85	C = 0.80.	99.04
41.70	....	....	....	....	....	....	....	....	....	....	13.54	....	98.95
33.50	....	....	....	....	....	....	....	....	....	....	9.32	....	100.00
28.73	....	0.57	....	0.05	0.42	0.05	....	....	....	....	....	FeS = 3.00. Recalculated.	101.85
26.50	1.26	0.39	0.21	Cr₂O₃+FeO 4.16	1.54	....	....	....	....	....	....	FeS = 5.61. Recalculated.	99.14
23.34	....	1.71	0.71	....	....	....	....	....	....	....	4.04	CO₂ = trace.	99.30
40.50	0.20	....	....	....	....	....	....	....	....	....	12.02	....	99.24
37.09	0.64	....	....	0.32	....	....	....	....	....	....	10.20	....	98.53
37.08	trace.	....	....	0.08	....	....	....	....	....	....	....	Ignition = 10.70.	100.00
34.54	....	....	....	trace.	NiO 0.51	....	....	....	....	....	11.74	....	98.02
41.51	trace.	....	....	0.02	NiO 0.08	....	....	....	P₂O₅ trace.	....	13.40	....	100.43
41.37	trace.	....	....	0.03	0.00	....	....	....	trace.	....	13.08	....	100.05
37.45	Mn	....	....	....	....	....	....	....	....	....	12.15	....	100.56
14.90	trace.	....	....	0.75	1.00	....	....	....	....	....	4.00	....	109.40
20.10	....	0.86		Undt.	1.52	0.06	Undt.	....	Undt.	....	....	Li₂O = trace. Recalculated.	98.01
33.70	....	....	....	....	....	....	....	....	....	....	....	Ignition = 8.45.	100.60
16.02	0.78	0.17	1.22	0.99	1.30	....	SnO₂ 0.18	0.46	2.35	....	....	....	100.82
5.07	0.82	1.81	1.48	0.89	....	....	....	....	1.81	....	....	....	99.25
41.88	trace.	trace.	trace.	trace.	NiO trace.	....	....	....	....	....	....	....	100.50
22.52	....	0.96	0.83	Cr₂O₃+FeO 2.19	....	....	....	....	....	....	8.30	....	102.40
28.13	....	1.00	trace.	....	0.85	0.05	....	....	....	....	....	FeS = 6.10, Li₂O = trace. Recalculated.	100.59
36.29	....	....	....	....	....	....	....	....	....	....	14.16	....	99.09
37.61	trace.	....	....	trace.	....	....	....	....	....	....	12.06	....	99.57

xxviii   A CLASSIFIED LIST OF COMPLETE (BAUSCH)

TABLE IV.

Variety.	Locality.	Analyst.	Publication.	Sp. Gr.	SiO$_2$.	Al$_2$O$_3$.	Fe.	Fe$_2$O$_3$.	FeO.	CaO.
Picrite.	Schriesheim, Baden.	C. W. C. Fuchs.	Neues Jahr. Min., 1864, pp. 326–332.	2.82	41.44	0.03	....	13.87	6.20	7.20
Serpentine.	Hillswick Ness, Scotland.	M. F. Heddle.	Min. Mag., 1890, iii. 21.	2.522	41.46	0.01	....	2.422	1.163	trace.
Serpentine.	Windisch-Matrey, Tyrol.	R. v. Drasche.	Min. Mitth., 1871, p. 4.	2.09	41.57	0.67	....	2.63	5.31	1.22
Dunite.	Franklin, Macon Co., N. C.	T. M. Chatard.	Geol. North Carolina, 1881, p. 42.	....	41.58	0.14	....	....	7.40	0.11
Meteorite.	Mezö-Madaras, Transylvania.	{ Wöhler and Atkinson. C. Rammelsberg.	Phil. Mag., 1856 (4), xi. 141–143. Zeit. Deut. geol. Gesell., 1871, xxiii. 734–737.	3.50	41.02 37.64	3.15 3.41	18.10 12.12	....	4.01 15.44	1.80 1.68
Serpentine.	Kühstein, Bavaria.	G. Schulze.	Zeit. Deut. geol. Gesell., 1883, xxxv. 447.	....	41.63	1.40	....	3.85	4.07	3.57
Lherzolite.	Germagnano, Piedmont.	A. Cossa.	Ric. Chim. Roc. Italia, 1881, pp. 112, 113.	3.116	41.66	4.25	....	2.95	10.38	1.76
Serpentine.	Dillenburg, Prussia.	C. Schnabel.	Rammelsberg, Handwörterbuch, 4, Supp., 1847, p. 200.	....	41.70	7.04	....	....	26.95	3.34
Serpentine.	Malenker Thal, Granbünden.	L. R. v. Fellenberg.	Neues Jahr. Min., 1867, p. 197.	2.09	41.72	3.19	....	....	7.06	....
Meteorite.	Renazzo, Ferrara, Italy.	A. Laugier.	Ann. Chimie Phys., 1827, xxxiv. 139–142.	3.2442	41.75	....	....	43.00	....	....
Meteorite.	Krähenberg, Bavaria.	G. vom Rath.	Ann. Physik Chemie, 1860, cxxxvii. 328–336.	3.4975	41.78	0.06	6.31	....	19.53	1.04
Dunite.	Webster, Jackson Co., N. C.	F. A. Genth.	Am. Jour. Sci., 1862 (2), xxxiii. 199–203.	{ 3.28 3.252	41.80 40.74	trace. trace.	....	....	7.39 7.26	0.06 0.02
Lherzolite.	Muhsdorf, Saxony.	Leuckart.	Neues Jahr. Min., 1876, pp. 232, 233.	....	41.99	0.734	....	9.143	1.650	1.841
Serpentine.	Raduu, Harz.	A. Streng.	Neues Jahr. Min., 1862, p. 540.	2.88	42.02	13.89	....	....	3.10	8.01
Meteorite.	Guernsey Co., Ohio.	J. L. Smith.	Am. Jour. Sci., 1861 (2), xxxi. 87–98.	3.55	42.24	0.28	9.31	....	25.03	0.02
*Lherzolite.	New Concord, Ohio.	J. L. Smith. D. M. Johnson. A. Madelung.	Am. Jour. Sci., 1861 (2), xxxi. 87–98. Am. Jour. Sci., 1860 (2), xxx. 109–111. Buchner, Meteoriten, 1863, p. 105.	3.55 3.5417	42.25 51.25 40.391	0.28 5.325 2 30	9.309 8.803 5.778	.... 5.819	25.03 25.204 18.133	0.018 0.785 2.523
Serpentine.	Goujot, Vosges, France.	A. Delesse.	Ann. Mines, 1850 (4), xviii. 342.	....	42.26	1.51	....	....	7.11	0.80
Serpentine.	Polinewaja, Russia.	A. A. Lösch.	Zeit. Kryst., 1881, v. 591.	....	42.34	1.68	....	0.20	1.98	....
Lherzolite.	Harz, Germany.	F. Köhler.	Neues Jahr. Min., 1862, p. 541.	2.008	42.36	2.18	....	....	....	0.03
Meteorite.	Middlesborough, Yorkshire, Eng.	W. Flight.	Phil. Trans., 1882, pp. 896–900.	....	42.39	1.73	7.80	....	23.76	....
Serpentine.	Findel Glacier, Zermatt, Switzerland.	V. Merz.	Vierteljahr. Nat. Gesell. Zurich, 1861, vi. 300–372.	....	42.53 42.27 42.44 42.45 42.13	....	....	....	2.22 1.88 1.80 2.12 2.23	....
Lherzolite.	Germagnano, Piedmont.	A. Cossa.	Ric. Chim. Roc. Italia, 1881, p. 111.	3.20	42.70	2.84	....	1.03	7.44	8.18
*Lherzolite.	Mocs, Transylvania.	F. Koch.	Min. Mitth., 1883 (2), v. 245.	{ 3.000 3.077	42.74	trace.	7.93	....	20.86	2.78
Schillerfels.	Altihal, Transylvania.	J. Barber.	Sitz. Wien. Akad., 1867, lvi. 266–275.	2 028	42.77	7.48	....	3.34	4.79	6.50
Dunite.	Dun Mt., near Nelson, New Zealand.	A. Schrötter. A. Madelung.	Zeit. Deut. geol. Gesell., 1864, xvi. 341–344. Zeit. Deut. geol. Gesell., 1864, xvi. 341–344.	3.296 3.296	42.80 42.09	....	....	....	9.40 10.09	....
Picrite.	Söhle, Neutitschein, Moravia.	V. Šlechta.	Sitz. Wien. Akad., 1866, liii. (1), 270.	....	42.85	10.42	....	0.27	6.86	11.84
Serpentine.	Zermatt Thal, Switzerland.	S. Haughton.	Phil. Mag., 1855 (4), x. 254.	....	42.88	....	....	....	3.80	....
Serpentine.	Aberdeen, Scotland.	J. D. Hannay.	Min. Mag., 1879, ii. 194.	....	42.91	0.05	....	0.77	2.90	0.02
Picrite.	Ty Croes, Anglesey.	J. A. Phillips.	Quart. Jour. Geol. Soc., 1883, xxxix. 356.	2 88 {	42.94 42.70	10.87 10.98	....	3.47 3.40	10.14 10.13	9.07 9.15

* The prefixed asterisk indicates that the specimen is a meteorite.

ANALYSES OF METEORIC AND TERRESTRIAL ROCKS.

Continued.

MgO	MnO	Na$_2$O	K$_2$O	Cr$_2$O$_3$	Ni	Co	Cu	Sn	P	S	H$_2$O	Miscellaneous	Total
18.42	....	0.24	0.93	....	....	....	....	....	....	....	5.60	....	100.03
41.763	0.23	....	....	....	....	....	....	....	....	....	12.43	....	99.478
36.60	....	....	....	....	NiO trace.	....	....	....	....	....	....	CO$_2$ = 0.51, Ignition = 11.88.	100.45
49.28	....	....	....	....	NiO 0.34	....	....	....	....	....	....	Ignition = 1.72.	100.00
23.83	0.28	2.34	0.50	....	1.45	0.05	....	....	....	....	....	Graphite = 0.26, S+P+Cr$_2$O$_3$ = 2.02.	100.00
24.11	0.18	1.76	trace.	0.64	1.04	....	....	....	....	2.27	....	NiO = 0.06. Recalculated.	100.85
33.97	trace.	....	....	1.20	....	....	....	....	....	....	9.02	CO$_2$ = 0.80.	100.23
31.82	....	....	....	0.22	....	....	....	....	....	....	4.95	....	101.00
10.20	....	....	....	....	....	....	....	....	....	....	11.58	....	100.87
42.15	....	....	....	0.18	NiO 0.25	....	....	....	....	....	5.55	....	101.55
16.00	....	....	....	1.50	NiO 1.25	....	....	....	....	1.00	....	....	104.50
24.44	trace.	1.00	....	Cr$_2$O$_3$+FeO 0.01	0.54	....	....	....	....	2.17	....	Recalculated.	98.08
40.13	....	....	....	....	NiO 0.35	....	....	....	....	....	....	Cr$_2$O$_3$+FeO+SiO$_4$ = 0.58, Ignition = 0.82.	100.21
49.18	....	....	....	....	0.30	....	....	....	....	....	....	Cr$_2$O$_3$+FeO+SiO$_2$ = 1.83, Ignition = 0.70.	100.18
31.40	trace.	....	....	....	....	....	....	....	....	....	7.004	....	99.951
20.07	....	0.35	0.44	Cr$_2$O$_4$+FeO 4.68	....	....	....	....	....	....	6.04	....	100.20
21.81	Mn trace.	0.93		....	1.32	0.01	trace.	....	trace.	0.06	....	Recalculated.	101.01
21.01	Mn trace.	0.986		....	1.322	0.045	trace.	....	0.001	0.113	....	Recalculated.	101.264
8.873	....			trace.	2.30	....	....	....	trace.	1.184	0.035	....	103.819
23.51	Mn trace.	....	....	....	0.235	....	....	....	....	....	....	NiO = 0.812.	99.601
38.00	trace.	....	....	trace.	....	....	....	....	....	....	....	Ignition = 9.42.	100.00
40.83	....	....	....	trace.	....	....	....	....	....	....	....	....	100.13
28.00	0.85	....	....	Cr$_2$O$_3$+FeO 13.27	....	....	....	....	....	....	12.07	....	100.26
20.82	....	Undt.	Undt.	....	2.00	0.08	....	....	....	....	....	Recalculated.	98.08
42.29	....	....	....	....	....	....	....	....	....	....	13.04	....	100.78
43.10	....	....	....	....	....	....	....	....	....	....	13.50	....	100.84
42.07	....	....	....	....	....	....	....	....	....	....	13.48	....	100.00
42.50	....	....	....	....	....	....	....	....	....	....	13.70	....	100.83
42.00	....	....	....	....	....	....	....	....	....	....	13.60	....	100.80
37.56	....	....	....	0.25	....	....	....	....	....	....	3.54	....	98.54
15.95	1.12	1.20	0.21	Cr$_2$O$_3$+FeO 1.56	1.38	trace.	....	....	0.41	2.01	....	Mn = 0.57, Li$_2$O = trace, Cl = 0.10.	99.51
30.11	....	0.50	0.10	trace.	....	....	....	....	....	....	3.28	....	98.87
47.58	....	trace.	....	....	NiO trace. Ni trace.	....	....	....	....	....	0.57	CoO = trace.	100.15
46.00	....	....	....	....	....	....	....	....	....	....	0.49	....	100.17
9.01	....	1.65	1.01	....	....	....	....	P$_2$O$_5$ trace.	....	....	2.70	Cl = trace, CO$_2$ = 5.88. Rock altered.	99.00
40.62	....	....	....	....	....	....	....	....	....	....	12.64	....	99.84
40.01	0.18	....	....	....	....	....	....	....	....	....	11.89	....	99.96
16.32	trace.	0.00	0.15	....	....	....	....	P$_2$O$_5$ trace.	....	....	3.44	TiO$_2$ = trace, CO$_2$ = 2.65.	99.95
16.22	trace.	0.93	0.10	....	....	....	....	trace.	....	....	3.43	TiO$_2$ = trace, CO$_2$ = 2.65.	99.89

TABLE IV.

Variety.	Locality.	Analyst.	Publication.	Sp. Gr.	SiO_2.	Al_2O_3.	Fe.	Fe_2O_3.	FeO.	CaO.
Lherzolite.	Dreiser Weiher, Eifel.	C. Rammelsberg.	Ann. Physik Chemie, 1870, cxli. 512–519.	....	42.06	1.74	....	....	8.50	2.20
Meteorite.	Lissa, Bohemia.	M. H. Klaproth.	Beiträge Mineralkorper, 1810, v. 246–253.	3.66	43.00	1.25	29.00	....	....	0.50
Serpentine.	Westfield, Mass.	E. Hitchcock.	Geol. Mass., 1841, p. 160.	....	43.08	....	....	8.08	....	....
Serpentine.	Germagnano, Piedmont.	A. Cossa.	Ric. Chim. Roc. Italia, 1881, pp. 121, 122.	2.615	43.44	0.42	....	0.91	2.84	....
Serpentine.	Gornoschit, Russia.	F. v. Schaffgotsch.	Rose, Reise nach dem Ural, 1857, i. 245.	....	43.734	0.813	....	....	6.111	....
Serpentine.	East Goshen, Chester Co., Penn.	S. P. Sharples.	Am. Jour. Sci., 1866 (2), xlii. 272.	....	43.80	....	....	....	1.38	....
Meteorite.	Sienna, Italy.	M. H. Klaproth.	Mém. Acad. Berlin, 1803, pp. 38–42.	3.34–3.40	44.00	....	2.25	....	25.00	....
Serpentine.	Haaf-Grunay Island, Scotland.	M. F. Heddle.	Min. Mag., 1879, ii. 106.	....	44.008	....	....	0.108	0.286	....
*Lherzolite.	Knyahinya, Hungary.	E. H. von Baumhauer.	Archives Néerland., 1872, vii. 146–153.	3.515	44.30	3.067	....	....	16.379	2.727
Meteorite.	Danville, Alabama.	J. L. Smith.	Am. Jour. Sci., 1870 (2), xlix. 90–93.	3.308	44.47	1.68	2.58	....	23.44	0.22
Meteorite.	Uden, North Brabant.	Baumhauer and Seelheim.	Ann. Physik Chemie, 1862, cxvi. 184–188.	3.4025	44.579	4.10	....	....	22.400	2.276
Serpentine.	Saxony.	A. Vogel.	Gelehrte Anzeig. München, 1844, xix. 115, 116.	.... {	41.70 43.10	1.24 1.94	....	....	13.20 15.60	....
Meteorite.	Harrison Co., Indiana.	J. L. Smith.	Am. Jour. Sci., 1859 (2), xxviii. 409–411.	3.465	44.80	2.23	4.26	....	24.80	0.77
Meteorite.	L' Aigle, Orne, France.	E. H. von Baumhauer.	Archives Néerland., 1872, vii. 154–160.	3.607	44.81	2.34	....	....	16.34	4.08
		Foucroy and Vauquelin.	Ann. Mus. Hist. Nat., 1804, iii. 101–108.	3.40–3.626	53.00	....	....	36.00	....	1.00
Meteorite.	Sauguis-Saint-Etienne, Mauléon, France.	S. Meunier.	Comptes Rendus, 1868, lxvii. 873–877.	3.360	44.870	....	....	....	4.022	0.50
Lherzolite.	Vicdessos, France.	H. A. v. Vogel.	Jour. Mines, 1813, xxxiv. 71–74.	3.25–3.333	45.00	1.00	....	12.00	....	19.50
Meteorite.	Forsyth, Georgia.	C. U. Shepard.	Am. Jour. Sci., 1848 (2), vi. 406, 407.	....	45.00	1.02	8.00	....	29.90	4.77
Meteorite.	Bremervörde, Hannover.	F. Wöhler.	Ann. Chemie Pharm., 1856, xcix. 244–248.	3.54	45.40	2.34	21.61	....	4.36	Undt.
Lherzolite.	Baldissero, Piedmont.	A. Cossa.	Ric. Chim. Roc. Italia, 1881, p. 105.	2.260	45.08	6.28	....	....	9.12	2.15
Picrite (Pi-kropicrite).	Ottenschlag, Austria.	A. Gamroth.	Min. Mitth., 1877, p. 278.	....	45.03	15.00	....	1.87	11.45	8.92
Meteorite.	Moresfort, Tipperary Co., Ireland.	W. Higgins.	Phil. Mag., 1811, xxxviii. 262–268.	{ 3.07 3.6478	46.00 48.25	....	42.00 30.00	....	....	....
Lherzolite.	Corio, Piedmont.	A. Cossa.	Ric. Chim. Roc. Italia, 1881, pp. 109, 110.	3.225	46.46	2.85	....	....	15.22	3.25
		J. S. Brazier.	Neues Jahr. Min., 1879, pp. 390–394.	....	47.15	0.90	....	3.40	0.56	1.51
Peridotite.	St. Paul's Rocks, Atlantic Ocean.	L. Sipöcz.	Rep. Challenger Exp., Narrative, 1882, ii., App. B.	3.287	43.84	1.14	....	....	8.76	1.71
		J. S. Brazier.	Rep. Challenger Exp., Narrative, 1882, ii., App. B.	....	43.50	0.88	....	....	1.92	8.01
Meteorite.	Cabarras Co., North Carolina.	C. U. Shepard.	Proc. Am. Assoc. Adv. Sci., 1850, iii. 140–152.	3.00–3.60	56.108	1.707	....	....	18.108	trace.

* The prefixed asterisk indicates that the specimen is a meteorite.

ANALYSES OF METEORIC AND TERRESTRIAL ROCKS.

Continued.

MgO.	MnO.	Na$_2$O.	K$_2$O.	Cr$_2$O$_3$.	Ni.	Co.	Cu.	Sn.	P.	S.	H$_2$O.	Miscellaneous.	Total.
42.59	....	....	....	Cr$_2$O$_3$+FeO 1.00	....	....	....	....	....	....	....	....	99.19
22.00	Mn 0.25	....	....	....	0.50	....	....	....	....	....	....	S+loss = 3.50.	100.00
33.74	....	....	....	....	....	....	....	....	....	....	13.93	Loss = 0.42.	100.00
41.15	....	....	....	....	....	....	....	....	....	....	12.06	....	100.82
37.716	....	....	....	....	....	....	....	....	....	....	11.620	....	100.00
40.48	....	....	....	....	....	....	....	....	....	....	13.45	....	99.20
22.50	0.25	....	....	....	0.00	....	....	....	....	....	....	Loss = 5.40.	100.00
36.711	....	trace.	....	trace.	....	....	....	....	....	....	13.20	....	100.511
22.16	....	1.00	0.658	Cr$_2$O$_3$+FeO 0.80	....	....	....	....	....	....	....	FeS = 2.22, Fe+Ni = 5.00. Recalculated.	98.282
25.69	trace.	0.49	0.03	trace.	0.28	0.01	trace.	....	trace.	0.98	....	Li$_2$O = trace. Recalculated.	00.84
20.667	0.43	0.94	0.49	Cr$_2$O$_3$+FeO 0.76	NiO 0.29	....	....	....	....	....	....	Ni+Fe+S=1.707, FeS=0.718.	99.424
23.50	....	....	....	....	0.145	....	....	....	....	....	11.20	C = 0.192.	99.277
29.20	....	....	....	....	0.17	....	....	....	....	....	12.40	C = 0.20.	99.01
26.28	trace.	0.40	0.05	....	0.05	0.02	trace.	....	trace.	trace.	....	Recalculated.	104.80
19.93	....	1.23	0.85	Cr$_2$O$_3$+FeO 0.00	....	....	....	....	....	....	....	Fe+Ni = 8.00, FeS = 1.80. Recalculated.	101.93
9.00	....	....	....	....	3.00	....	....	....	....	2.00	....	....	104.00
39.400	....	trace.	0.454	0.012	....	....	....	....	....	....	....	Al$_2$O$_3$+Fe$_2$O$_3$ = 0.604, Fe+Ni = 8.05, FeS = 3.044.	100.574
10.00	trace.	....	....	0.50	....	....	....	....	....	....	....	Loss = 6.00.	100.00
8.37	....	....	....	....	0.96	....	....	....	....	....	....	Cr$_2$O$_3$+loss = 0.14. Recalculated.	99.06
22.40	Undt.	1.18	0.37	Cr$_2$O$_3$+FeO 0.31	1.89	Undt.	....	....	Undt.	Undt.	....	Graphite = 0.14.	100.00
34.70	....	....	....	0.26	....	....	....	....	....	1.21	....	....	99.46
14.82	....	1.93	0.22	....	....	....	....	....	....	....	0.58	....	106.81
12.25	....	....	....	....	1.50	....	....	....	....	4.00	....	....	105.75
9.00	....	....	....	....	1.75	....	....	....	....	4.00	....	....	102.00
30.08	....	....	....	trace.	....	....	....	....	....	....	0.72	....	99.28
36.69	....	....	....	....	....	....	....	....	....	....	....	Loss = 0.50, CaS = 0.20.	100.00
44.33	0.12	....	....	0.42	NiO 1.06	....	....	....	....	....	1.06	....	101.89
38.48	....	....	....	....	....	....	....	....	....	....	....	CaSO$_4$ = 0.06, Ca$_3$P$_2$O$_8$ = 0.28, CaCO$_3$ = 0.47, Ignition = 4.20.	100.00
10.400	....	trace.	trace.	....	....	....	....	....	....	....	....	Fe+Ni = 6.32, FeS = 3.807, Loss = 3.394.	100.00

A CLASSIFIED LIST OF COMPLETE (BAUSCH)

TABLE V. — Basalt.

Variety.	Locality.	Analyst.	Publication.	Sp. Gr.	SiO_2.	Al_2O_3.	Fe.	Fe_2O_3.
Basalt.	Jonzac, France.	A. Laugier.	Mém. Mus. Hist. Nat., 1820, vi. 233–240.	3.12, 3.0773, 3.0607	40.00	6.00		36.00
		C. Rammelsberg.	Ann. Physik Chemie, 1851, lxxxiii. 591–593.	2.90–3.20	48.50	12.65		
Basalt.	Stannern, Iglau, Moravia.	M. H. Klaproth.	Beiträge Mineralkorper, 1810, v. 257–263.	2.95–3.16	48.25	14.50	23.00	
		J. Moser.	Ann. Physik, 1808, xxix. 309–327.	3.077–3.1520	40.25	7.02		27.00
		L. N. Vauquelin.	Ann. Chimie, 1809, lxx. 321–330.	3.10	50.00	9.00		29.00
Basalt.	Constantinople, Turkey.	E. Ludwig.	Min. Mitth., 1872, pp. 85–87.	3.17	48.50	12.63		
Basalt.	Petersburg, Lincoln Co., Tenn.	J. L. Smith.	Am. Jour. Sci., 1861(2), xxxi. 264–266.	3.20	49.21	11.05	0.50	
		C. Rammelsberg.	Ann. Physik Chemie, 1848, lxxvii. 585–590.		40.23	12.55	0.16	1.21
Gabbro.	Juvenas, Ardèche, France.	A. Laugier.	Ann. Chimie Phys., 1821, xix. 264–273.	3.000–3.148	40.00	10.40		23.50
		L. N. Vauquelin.	Ann. Chimie Phys., 1821, xviii. 421–423.		40.00	13.40		
Gabbro.	Shergotty, India.	E. Lumpe.	Min. Mitth., 1871, pp. 55, 56.		50.21	5.90		
		F. Crook.	Chem. Const. Met. Stones, pp. 30–33.		36.211	1.871	8.143	
	Charkow, Russia.	J. Scheerer.	Mém. Acad. St. Pétersbourg, 1813–14, vi. Hist., p. 47.	3.00	51.00		19.80	
		Schnaubert and Giese.	Ann. Physik, 1809, xxxi. 316–322.	3.4902	48.00		21.78	
Basalt.	Frankfort, Franklin Co., Alabama.	G. J. Brush.	Am. Jour. Sci., 1869 (2), xlviii. 240–244.	3.31	51.03	8.05	trace.	
	Kuleschowka, Poltawa, Russia.	J. Scheerer.	Mém. Acad. St. Pétersbourg, 1812, v., Hist., pp. 22, 23.	3.530	52.00	1.60	10.00	18.40
		C. Rammelsberg.	Mon. Berlin. Akad., 1870, pp. 316–322.	3.412	52.04			
Gabbro.	Shalka, India.	N. S. Maskelyne.	Phil. Trans., 1871, clxi. 366, 367.		45.37			
		H. Piddington.	Jour. Asiat. Soc. Bengal, 1851, xx. 299–314.	3.00	68.00	0.50		26.80
Gabbro.	Busti, India.	N. S. Maskelyne.	Phil. Trans., 1870, cxl. 193–211.		52.871			
		W. Dancer.	Phil. Trans., 1870, cxl. 193–211.		52.73			
Gabbro.	Massing, Bavaria.	A. Schwager.	Sitz. München Akad., 1878, viii. 32–40.	3.3036	53.115	8.204	0.523	
		Imhof.	Sitz. München Akad., 1878, viii. 84.	3.305	31.00		1.80	32.54
Gabbro.	Manegamm, Khandeish, India.	N. S. Maskelyne.	Phil. Trans, 1870, clx. 211–213.	3.198	53.629			
	Vavilovka, Kherson, Russia.	R. Prendel.	Mém. Sci. Nat. Cherbourg, 1877–78, xxi. 203–207.		53.81	8.75		0.41
Gabbro.	Ibbenbüren, Westphalia.	G. vom Rath.	Sitz. nieder. Gesell. Bonn, 1871, xxviii. 142–145.	3.40–3.43	54.40	1.06		
		C. Rammelsberg.	Mon. Berlin. Akad., 1861, pp. 895–900.		57.52	2.72		
Gabbro.	Bishopville, South Carolina.	J. L. Smith.	Am. Jour. Sci., 1864 (2), xxxviii. 225, 226.		60.12 / 59.83			0.30 / 0.50
		W. S. v. Waltershausen.	Ann. Chemie Pharm., 1851, lxxix. 369–374.	3.090	67.140	1.478		1.706
		C. U. Shepard.	Am. Jour. Sci., 1846 (2), ii. 380, 381.	3.116	70.41			

Part I. The Meteoric Basalts.

FeO.	CaO.	MgO.	MnO.	Na$_2$O.	K$_2$O.	Cr$_2$O$_3$.	Ni.	P$_2$O$_5$.	S.	H$_2$O.	Miscellaneous.	Total.
......	7.50	1.60	2.60	......	......	1.00 Cr$_2$O$_3$+FeO	......	......	1.50	......	....	102.40
19.82	11.27	6.87	0.81	0.62	0.23	0.54	......	......	......	......	FeS = trace....................	100.61
......	9.50	2.00	......	......	......	......	......	......	......	......	Loss = 2.75..................	100.00
......	12.12	2.50	0.75	......	......	Cr$_2$O$_3$ trace.	......	......	......	......	Loss = 3.70.................	100.00
......	12.00	......	1.00	......	......	......	......	......	......	......	....	101.00
20.90	10.30	6.16	trace.	0.46	0.16	Cr$_2$O$_3$+FeO 0.44	......	......	......	......	FeS = trace..................	99.82
20.41	9.01	8.13	......	0.82	......	......	trace.	P trace.	0.06	......	....	99.23
20.38	10.23	6.44	......	0.63	0.12	0.24	......	0.28	0.00	......	TiO$_2$ = 0.10...............	101.61
......	0.20	0.80	6.50	......	0.20	1.00	......	......	......	0.50	Cu = 0.10....................	92.20
......	8.00	......	......	......	......	......	......	......	......	......	Na$_2$O+K$_2$O+Cu+Cr$_2$O$_3$+S = 11.00, Fe+Mn = 27.00.	100.00
21.85	10.41	10.00	......	1.28	0.57	......	......	......	......	......	....	100.22
27.125	0.435	24.114	......	0.223	0.109	0.237	1.30	P trace.	trace.	......	Co = trace....................	99.778
......	......	20.50	......	......	......	......	1.50	......	......	......	Mn$_2$O$_3$ = 4.20, Loss = 3.00.	100.00
......	......	22.05	......	......	......	......	1.00	......	......	......	Mn$_2$O$_3$ = 6.00..............	99.43
13.70	7.03	17.59	......	0.46	0.22	0.42	trace.	......	0.23	......	....	90.02
......	......	9.00	......	......	......	......	1.20	......	4.25	......	CaO+MnO+loss = 2.95.......	100.00
10.78	0.55	20.38	......	0.40	......	0 26	......	......	......	......	Mean analysis of the crust and interior.	99.08
10.06	2.214	15.636	......	......	......	......	......	......	......	......	Cr$_2$O$_3$+FeO = 17.717.......	99.097
......	......	......	......	......	......	2.00	......	......	0.10	0.12	As = trace. Analysis of the crust.	98.12
0.194	12.397	28.321	......	0.573	0.239	......	......	......	......	......	Li$_2$O = 0.019, CaS = 4.133, CaSO$_4$ = 0.442.	100.18
4.28	1.18	37.22	0.01	......	trace.	......	NiO 0.78	......	0.02	......	CaCl = 0.01, Na$_2$S = 0.76, Li$_2$O = trace, Ca$_3$PO$_8$ = trace, CaSO$_4$ = 1.58.	99.47
19.138	5.786	8.485	......	1.928	1.188	0.979	trace.	......	0.374	......	....	99.72
......	......	23.25	......	......	......	......	1.36	......	......	......	Loss, etc. = 10.06............	100.00
20.476	1.495	23.32	......	......	......	Cr$_2$O$_3$+FeO 1.029	......	......	......	......	....	99.940
......	2.07	18.54	trace.	1.14	......	trace.	0.70	......	......	......	FeS = 5.26...................	99.68
17.31	1.22	26.12	0.28	......	......	......	......	......	......	......	....	100.77
1.25	0.66	34.80	0.20	1.14	0.70	......	......	......	......	......	Ignition = 0 80...............	99.70
......	......	39.45	......	0.74	trace.	......	......	......	......	......	Li$_2$O = trace...............	100.61
......	......	39 22	......	0 74	trace.	......	......	......	......	......	Li$_2$O = trace...............	100.23
......	1.818	27.115	trace.	......	......	......	......	......	0.671	......	....	99.928
......	......	28.25	......	1.30	......	......	......	......	......	......	....	100.06

PLATE I.

Fig. 1. **Pallasite.** ATACAMA, BOLIVIA.

PAGES

A tracing made from the polished surface of a specimen. The coloring is conventional in this and in the next three figures. The yellow portions are the olivine grains, while the gray reticulated portion indicates the metallic iron and pyrrhotite, — since no distinction of the different constituents was possible in a tracing except to divide them into silicates and metallic portions. 70

Fig. 2. **Pallasite.** KRASNOJARSK, SIBERIA.

Tracing, as in Fig. 1. . . . . 71, 72

Figs. 3, 4. **Pallasite.** RITTERSGRÜN, SAXONY.

Tracings of two opposite sides of the same polished slab. All these tracings are of natural size and form, so far as it was possible to make them. 72, 73

Fig. 5. **Pallasite, — Cumberlandite.** IRON MINE HILL, CUMBERLAND, RHODE ISLAND.

A slightly magnified portion of a section. The dark portions represent magnetite, and the light parts the olivine with a minute portion of feldspar. While in the four preceding figures the sponge-like structure of the metallic parts with the enclosed silicates could alone be shown, in this and in the following figures the minerals are in general differentiated, and the fidelity of the lithographer's work, in representing the form, structure, fissuring, coloring, etc. of the natural section, will be appreciated by all familiar with such rocks. This figure shows the same sponge-like structure as the preceding figures, but with the metallic iron replaced by its oxidized form. 75, 76

Fig. 6. **Pallasite, — Cumberlandite.** IRON MINE HILL, CUMBERLAND, RHODE ISLAND.

This figure is from a section of the same rock-mass as the preceding, and shows the same general structure; but the olivine of Fig. 5 is here replaced by serpentine, which retains the outlines of the former, and marks its fissures by secondary magnetite grains. 78, 79

PLATE I

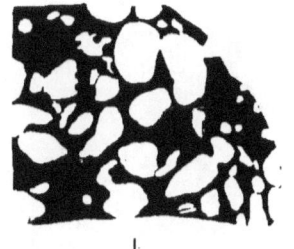

1.

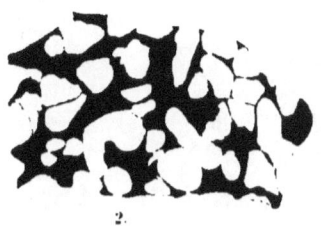

2.

3.

4.

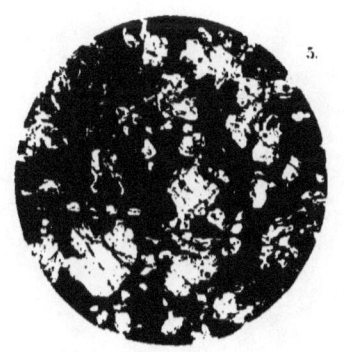

5.

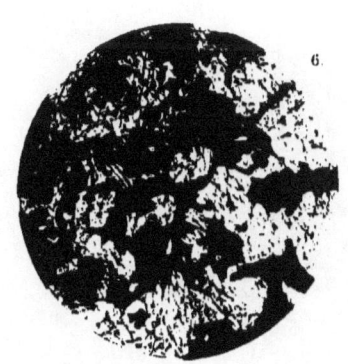

6.

PLATE II.

FIG. 1. Pallasite, — Cumberlandite. IRON MINE HILL, CUMBERLAND, RHODE ISLAND.

PAGES

This figure illustrates a more highly magnified intermediate stage in the same rock-mass, lying between that presented in Figs. 5 and 6 of Plate I. The dark portion represents the magnetite sponge which holds the lighter silicates. The brownish portion represents the smoky, fissured, somewhat altered olivine, which is surrounded by a grayish and white actinolite, produced by the alteration of the olivine on its borders. The ragged character of the magnetite borders, as shown in the figure, also indicates that it is associated in the change, or affected by the alteration. 77, 78

FIG. 2. Pallasite, — Cumberlandite. TABERG, SWEDEN.

This shows the same general structure of magnetite enclosing silicates, principally olivine, as the three preceding figures. The reddish-brown spots at the bottom of the figure represent a secondary mica (biotite) produced in connection with the magnetite. 81

FIG. 3. Pallasite, — Cumberlandite. TABERG, SWEDEN.

This figure represents a more highly altered portion of the same section as that shown in Fig. 3. The magnetite is less in amount, having been partially removed, and the reddish-brown biotite more abundant, while the silicate portions are more altered. 81

FIG. 4. Peridotite, — Saxonite. IOWA COUNTY, IOWA.

The grayish and brownish parts represent the granular groundmass of olivine and enstatite sprinkled with ferruginous particles and enclosing the steel-gray masses of metallic iron. The orange-brown represents the ferruginous staining. A little to the right of the centre of the figure is represented an olivine chondrus composed of the colorless olivine grains held in a grayish base. 86–88

FIG. 5. Peridotite, — Saxonite. IOWA COUNTY, IOWA.

This represents one of the larger chondri, composed of olivine and enstatite, which blends at the lower portion of the figure with the general groundmass. The enstatite and olivine grains are held in a gray base, which is here given too dark a shade. The metallic iron and the ferruginous staining are represented by the steel-gray and orange-brown colors. 86–68

FIG. 6. Peridotite, — Saxonite. KNYAHINYA, HUNGARY.

This shows a granular groundmass of chondri and olivine and enstatite grains, partially stained by ferruginous material to an orange- and yellowish-brown. One chondrus is shown extending from the centre towards the right of the figure, which consists of a fan-shaped mass of grayish fibrous base, held in and cut by enstatite bars. At the base is shown a portion of another chondrus composed of radiating bands of enstatite and base. Towards the bottom of the figure, and at the left of the centre, is shown an elongated fissured enstatite crystal. The metallic iron grains are indicated as before. 88–91

MEM MUSEUM COMP ZOOL. VOL. XI.   PLATE

PLATE III.

Fig. 1. **Peridotite,—Lherzolite.** Pultusk, Poland.

PAGES

This shows a portion of a section with two chondri at the base of the figure, while the remaining upper portion is made up of an aggregate of chondri, olivine, enstatite, diallage, pyrrhotite, and iron grains. The larger and darker chondrus is composed of aggregately polarizing fibrous enstatitic material. This chondrus shows rounded indentations, and on its left is another form, composed of alternating colorless enstatite ribs and bands of gray base with minute iron granules. The dark portions of the figure represent the iron and pyrrhotite, and the yellowish-brown the ferruginous staining. 94, 95

Fig. 2. **Peridotite,—Lherzolite.** Pultusk, Poland.

This displays the structure of a chondrus composed of olivine, enstatite, iron, etc., cemented by a gray base. This chondrus occupies the chief portion of the figure, but towards the bottom its gradual passage into the groundmass is shown. The ferruginous materials are colored as in Fig. 1. . . . . 94, 95

Fig. 3. **Peridotite,—Lherzolite.** Pultusk, Poland.

The brownish-black central portion is pyrrhotite surrounding a steel-gray pear-shaped mass of metallic iron. Surrounding the pyrrhotite is the chondritic groundmass of the meteorite, partially stained yellowish-brown. 94, 95

Fig. 4. **Peridotite,—Saxonite.** Waconda, Kansas.

This shows a mixed granular groundmass of olivine, enstatite, iron, and pyrrhotite, which is more or less stained a yellowish- and reddish-brown from the oxidation of the iron. 93, 94

Fig. 5. **Peridotite,—Lherzolite.** Estherville, Emmet Co., Iowa.

This shows a grayish and a greenish-yellow groundmass of olivine, enstatite, and diallage, with dark-colored iron and pyrrhotite, surrounding a larger crystal of diallage. 97–101

Fig. 6. **Peridotite,—Lherzolite.** Estherville, Emmet Co., Iowa.

This represents a semi-sponge-like mass of iron and pyrrhotite with enclosed grains of olivine, diallage, and enstatite. On the left is figured a crystal of enstatite with its inclusions and characteristic cleavage; while on the right is a crystal of diallage showing its cleavages. The yellowish-brown ferruginous staining is to be seen in some portions of the figure. . . . 97–101

PLATE III

MEM MUSEUM COMP ZOOL VOL.XI.

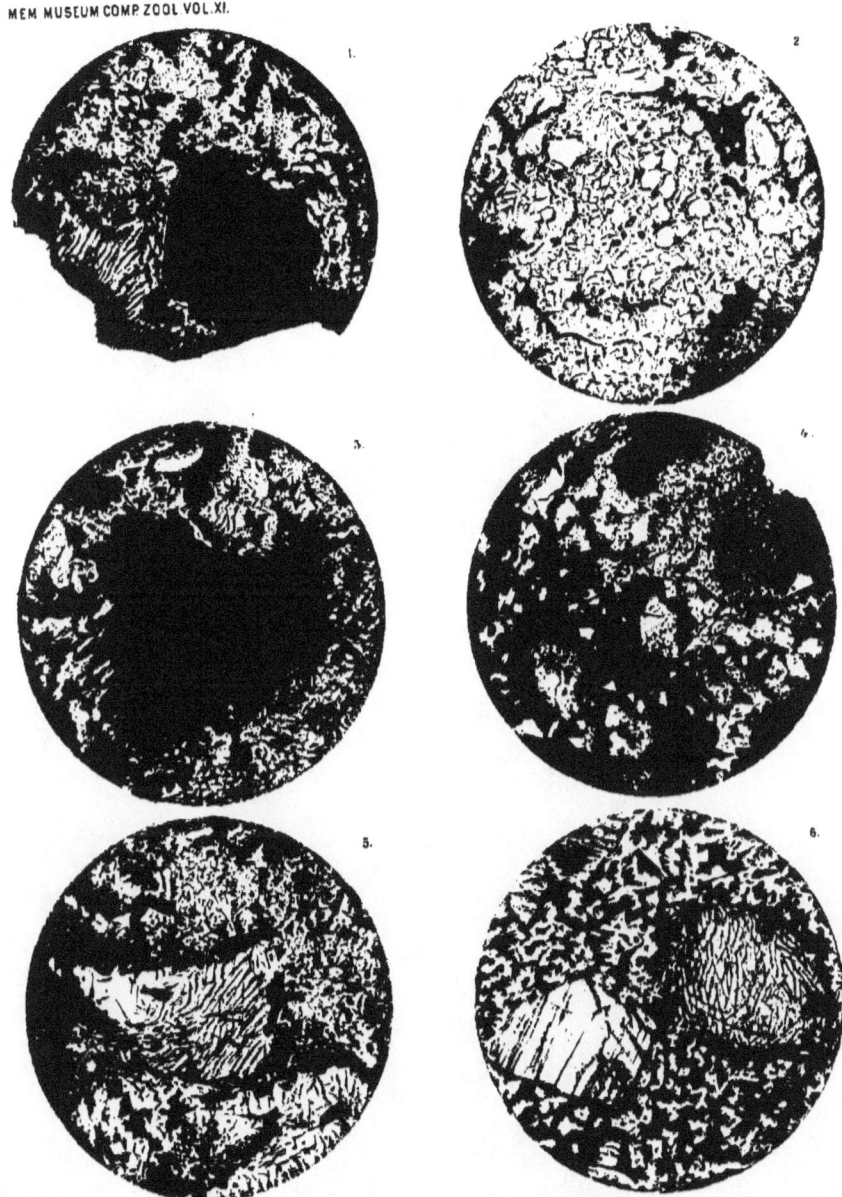

PLATE IV.

FIG. 1. Peridotite,—Lherzolite. NEW CONCORD, GUERNSEY CO., OHIO.

PAGES

This shows a grayish, crystalline, granular mass of olivine, enstatite, and diallage, containing dark grains of iron and pyrrhotite. The groundmass is stained by the oxidation of the iron to a reddish- and yellowish-brown. 95, 96

FIG. 2. Peridotite,—Dunite. FRANKLIN, NORTH CAROLINA.

This figure represents a granular mass of olivine traversed by fissures, giving it a grayish appearance. A little below the centre, and also on the left of the figure, are two dark chromite grains. This, with the ten preceding figures, presents the structure of the unaltered peridotites.   118

FIG. 3. Peridotite,—Dunite. WEBSTER, NORTH CAROLINA.

This represents an early stage in the alteration of the peridotites, in which a greenish and yellowish fibrous serpentine has been formed along the fissures of the olivine, leaving colorless grains in the interstices of the serpentine network. A further stage in the alteration is the change of some of the interstitial grains to a pale yellow serpentine. The reddish-brown grains sprinkled with black granules show the picotite, while the minute black grains in and about the serpentine indicate the magnetite produced during the process of the conversion of the olivine into serpentine. 119, 120

FIG. 4. Peridotite,—Saxonite. ANDESTAD SEE, AURE, NORWAY.

This figures a further change in a peridotite, in which the chief portion is altered to a greenish serpentine containing clear grains of unaltered olivine. In the upper portion of the figure is a partially altered enstatite traversed by fissures and containing much secondary magnetite dust. This enstatite is also partially altered to serpentine. Dark magnetite dust is shown in connection with the olivine grains, while dark grains of chromite are figured in the serpentine. 126, 127

FIG. 5. Peridotite,—Serpentine. HIGH BRIDGE, NEW JERSEY.

This represents an extreme stage in the process of the alteration of a peridotite, in which is shown a yellowish and grayish serpentine mass blotched with aggregations of dark iron-ore grains. Extending across the figure is an irregular pronged grayish band, formed by serpentinized olivine traversed by numerous fissures filled with dust-like granules of iron ore. Enclosed in this gray band are greenish spots of partially altered olivine grains. 157

FIG. 6. Peridotite,—Lherzolite. JAINA RIVER, SAN DOMINGO.

This shows a grayish-white serpentine mass holding dark patches of iron ore. The yellowish-brown mass to the right of the centre is a diallage crystal altered to serpentine, the four white spots indicating the unchanged portions. The other yellowish-brown and greenish spots are serpentinized pyroxenes and olivines, while the gray irregular band on the left is a partially altered mass of diallage and feldspar. 140

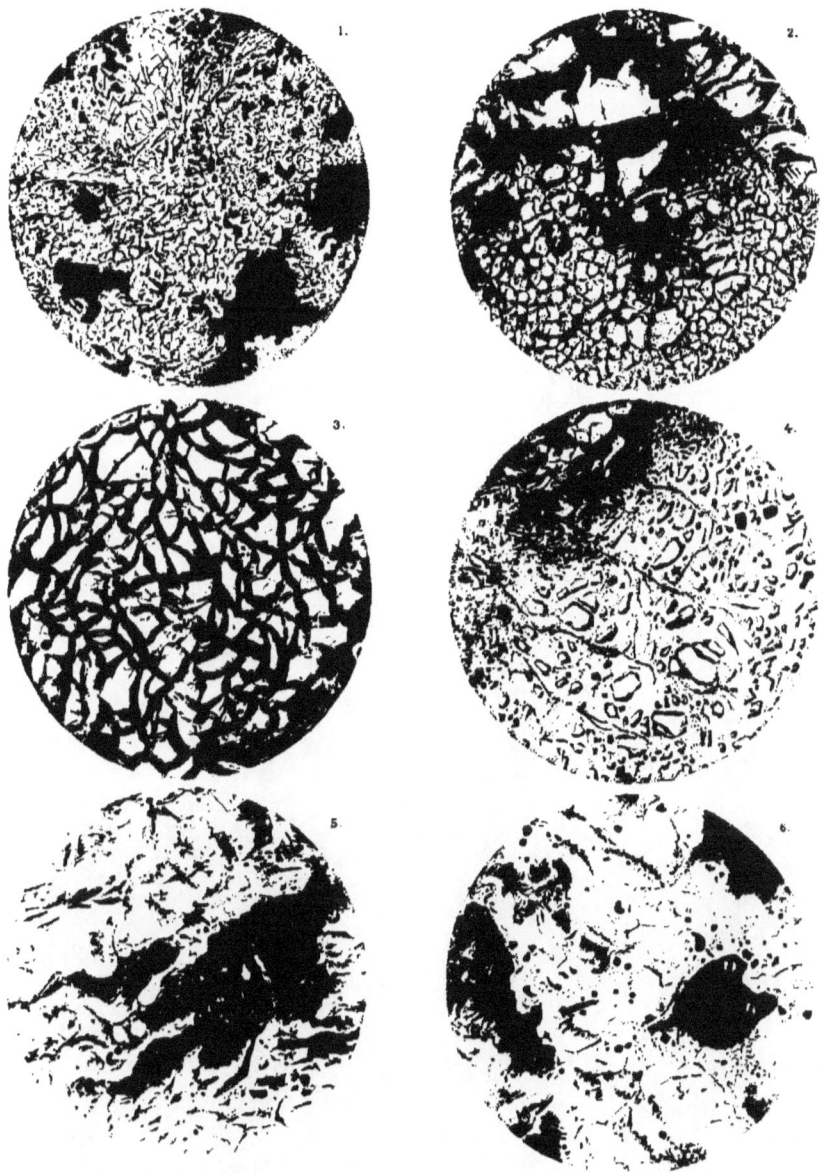

PLATE V.

FIG. 1. Peridotite, — Lherzolite. COLUSA CO., CALIFORNIA.

PAGES

This represents one of the earlier stages in the alteration of a peridotite, showing a fissured granular mass of olivine, enstatite, and diallage traversed by a network of pale grayish serpentine, which borders the fissures. The mass is traversed by brown bands of serpentine, containing iron-ore dust along the medial lines. Dark grains of picotite or chromite lie in the upper part of the figure. 129–131

FIG. 2. Peridotite, — Lherzolite. COLUSA CO., CALIFORNIA.

This shows a further alteration in the same type of rock as Fig. 1. In this the outline of the olivine can be distinguished by the yellow serpentine bands, while a later formation of serpentine shows in the orange-brown interior portions which retain in part grains of colorless unaltered olivine. The brown serpentine bands with their medial line of iron-ore dust are more abundant and better marked than in Fig. 1 ; while much of this secondary black dust is disseminated through the section. 131, 132

FIG. 3. Peridotite, — Lherzolite. COLUSA CO., CALIFORNIA.

The principal portion of the figure represents a crystal of enstatite from the same section as that given in Fig. 2. The cleavage lines with their bordering gray and brown alteration products run, more or less vertically, — the latter containing considerable fine black ore-dust. On the right and left of the upper portion of the figure are shown portions of serpentinized olivine, like that given in Fig. 2. The two portions are connected by a yellowish branching vein of serpentine. The dark brown and black grains are picotite or iron ores. 131, 132

FIG. 4. Peridotite, — Serpentine. LA VEGA, SAN DOMINGO.

This indicates a further stage of alteration than that shown in Fig. 2. The brown bands with their medial ore-dust remain, and are connected by finer brown bands marking the fissures in the original olivine ; while the interstitial olivine has been replaced by yellow serpentine. Towards the bottom of the figure, on the right and left, are represented two grayish-white altered enstatites. The series is continued in Figs. 2, 4, and 5 of Plate VI., and in Fig. 2 of Plate VII. 154

FIG. 5. Peridotite, — Serpentine. HIGH BRIDGE, NEW JERSEY.

A grayish-white mass of serpentine containing disseminated dark iron-ore grains and dust ; and traversed by a band of serpentinized enstatite or diallage crystals, which are surrounded and cut by a brown serpentine holding black ore-dust 156, 157

FIG. 6. Peridotite, — Serpentine. HIGH BRIDGE, NEW JERSEY.

This is from the same section as Fig. 6, and contains the same serpentine groundmass which, in places, is stained yellow. Scattered through the groundmass are iron ores and brown serpentine pseudomorphs after olivine containing ore-dust, and showing part of the original olivine fissures by the traversing bands of grayish-white serpentine 156, 157

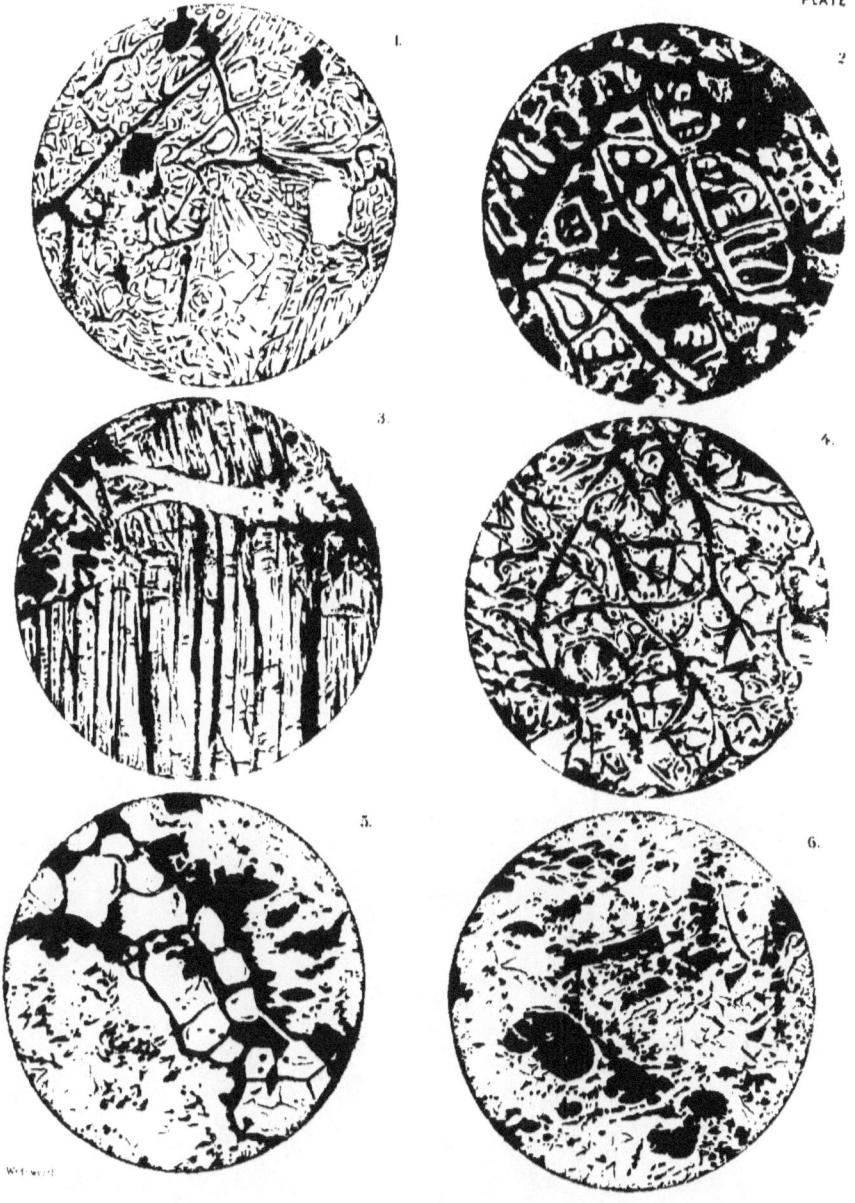

PLATE VI.

Fig. 1. Peridotite, — Serpentine. SANTIAGO, SAN DOMINGO.

                                                                                         PAGES

This shows at the base a brownish and yellowish reticulated serpentine mass, while above lie yellowish and brown pseudomorphs of serpentine after olivine grains which are surrounded and cut by colorless serpentine. In all the serpentine masses, particularly the upper portion, are disseminated black grains and dust of iron ore. 153, 154

Fig. 2. Peridotite, — Serpentine. LYNNFIELD, MASSACHUSETTS.

This forms one of a series with Figs. 1, 2, and 4 of Plate V. In this the brown serpentine bands no longer appear, but their former position is marked by the lines of black iron ore. The pale flesh-tint indicates serpentine which encloses the yellowish central rounded spots of serpentine which has replaced the last altered olivine grains. At the top and bottom of the figure are to be seen patches of pale serpentine in which the alteration has been carried so far that the yellowish portions have disappeared and the color been rendered uniform, — the constant tendency in the serpentinization of peridotites. The black grains are the iron ores. . .   160

Fig. 3. Peridotite, — Lherzolite, — Serpentine. PLUMAS CO., CALIFORNIA.

This shows a yellowish and grayish serpentine in which are lying black iron ore and the fibrous remains of eustatite crystals, which are best seen in the centre of the figure.[1]   142

Fig. 4. Peridotite, — Lherzolite, — Serpentine. INYO CO., CALIFORNIA.

This exhibits a brownish reticulated serpentine, holding in its interstices serpentine of a lighter color. This belongs to the same series as Fig. 2. In the serpentine lies a large fibrous crystal of altered enstatite, filled with black granules of iron ore precipitated during the process of alteration. The same ore is also to be seen in the serpentine.   132

Fig. 5. Peridotite, — Serpentine. PLUMAS CO., CALIFORNIA.

This shows a grayish-white reticulated mass of serpentine containing disseminated black iron-ore dust of a secondary nature ; also some larger black primary grains of iron ore. The upper half of the figure is traversed by veins of yellow serpentine, one of which cuts an iron-ore grain.   158

Fig. 6. Peridotite, — Lherzolite, — Serpentine. PLUMAS CO., CALIFORNIA.

This figure is from the same section as Fig. 3, and illustrates the formation of a serpentine vein. This, in the form of a brownish-yellow obliquely banded serpentine, crosses the central portion of the figure, while heaped up on both sides are to be seen the aggregations of expelled iron ores mixed with yellow and colorless serpentine.[1]   142

[1] Whitney's Auriferous Gravels, 1880, p. 459.

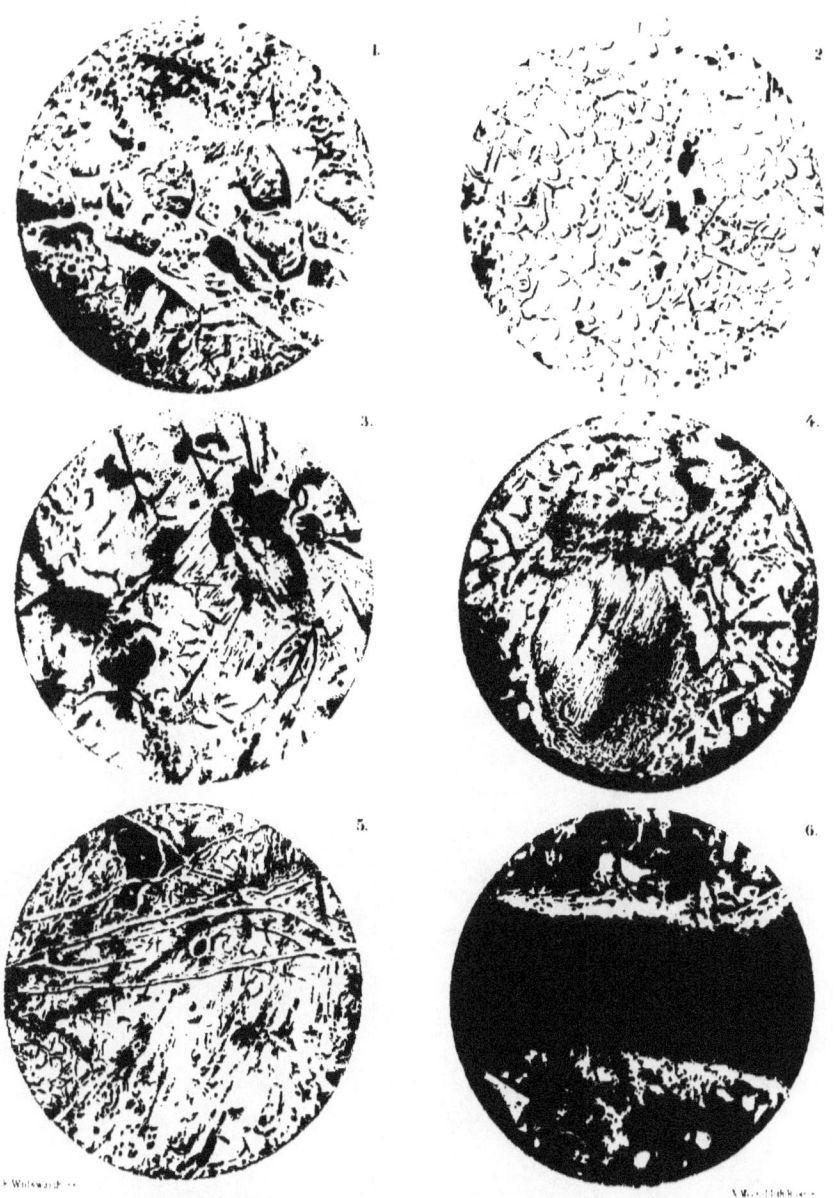

PLATE VII.

Fig. 1. Enstatite. Colusa Co., California.

PAGES

This is figured from the same rock as Figs. 2 and 3, Plate V. It indicates the manner in which enstatite is altered to serpentine. The longitudinal cleavage runs from side to side, and is crossed by the vertical fractures. The unchanged enstatite is colorless, but upon the borders of the cleavage planes and cross fractures the mineral has been altered to a greenish and yellowish serpentine. A yellowish serpentine vein runs from the upper left-hand portion of the figure to the centre of the base. 131, 132

Fig. 2. Peridotite, — Serpentine. Westfield, Massachusetts.

This continues the series formed by Figs. 1, 2, and 4 of Plate V., and Figs 2, 4, and 5 of Plate VI. Here the serpentine is of a pale yellow without trace of the usual network, and much of the black iron ore has been arranged in the form of a rectangular grating. 159, 160

Fig. 3. Peridotite, — Lherzolite. Presque Isle, Michigan.

This shows a grayish and greenish partially serpentinized enstatite containing black iron ore and holding rounded olivines. These are fissured and rendered opaque in portions owing to the precipitations of magnetite dust along the borders of the fissures. Greenish and yellowish serpentine is also to be observed in connection with both the enstatite and olivine.   136

Fig. 4. Peridotite, — Lherzolite, — Serpentine. Presque Isle, Michigan.

This is drawn from a portion of the same continuous rock-mass as Fig. 3, and represents a more highly altered state of the rock. The enstatite and diallage are largely replaced by greenish serpentine, bluish-green and yellowish biotite (?), gray dolomite, and black iron ores. The olivines are in part still more opaque from the rejected iron ore, and they have so far been changed to serpentine that comparatively few clear, unaltered, interstitial fragments remain. The structure is confused, and the distinctness of the minerals confused by the alteration. . 136, 137

Fig. 5. Peridotite, — Lherzolite, — Dolomite. Presque Isle, Michigan.

This is from the same continuous mass of rock as Figs. 3 and 4, and displays a further stage in the alteration. The groundmass is formed by a grayish mass of secondary granular dolomite, which holds yellowish, bluish-green, and brown psendomorphs of serpentine and ferruginous material after olivine. 137

Fig. 6. Peridotite, — Serpentine. Fitztown, Berks Co., Pennsylvania.

This shows a yellow serpentine mass containing grayish and colorless grains of olivine. The brown masses represent secondary dolomite grains formed in the serpentine, but the lithographer has given them much too dark a color, since the grains figured are of a cloudy-gray to brownish-gray color. 152

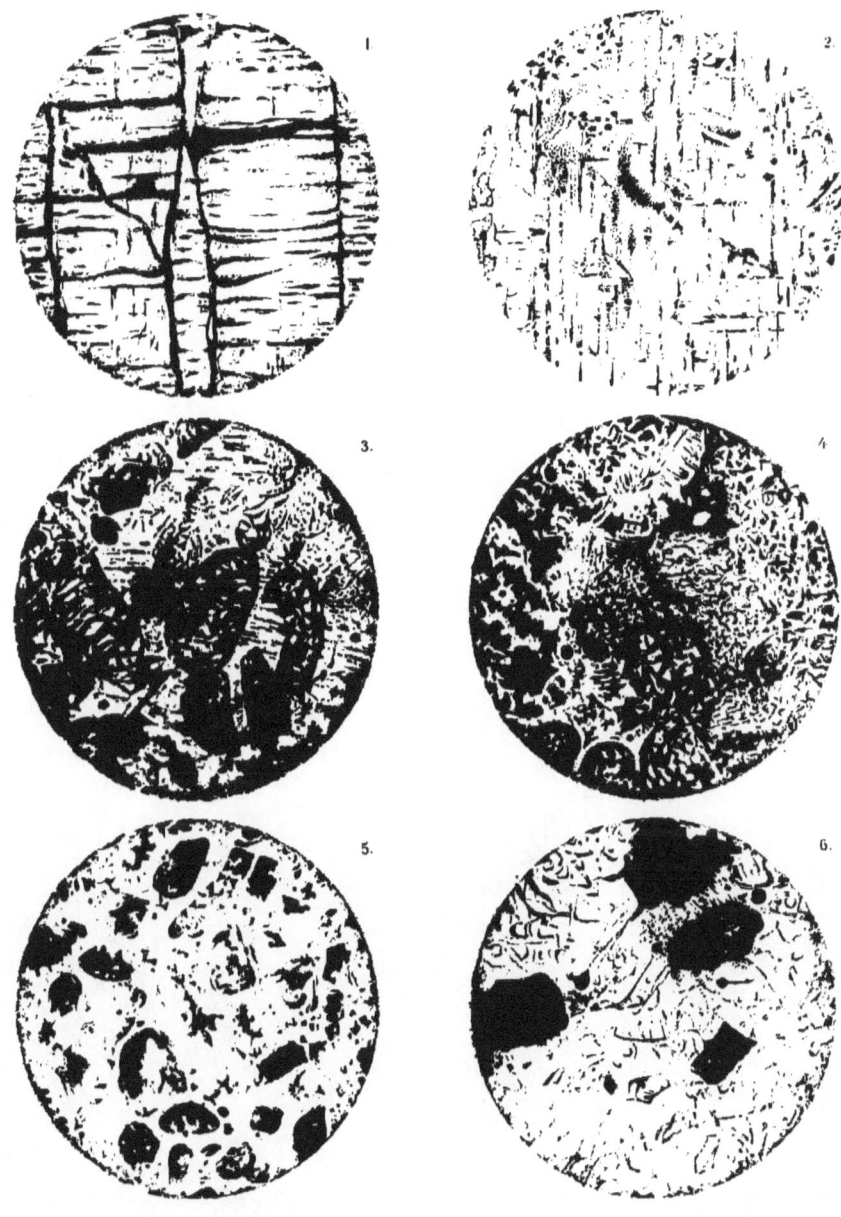

PLATE VIII.

Fig. 1. Peridotite, — Lherzolite. Baste, Harz.

The first five figures of this plate form a series in the order of their numbers, showing progressive alteration in the same type of rock. Fig. 1 shows a yellowish enstatite mass holding colorless fissured grains of olivine, some of which contain brown picotite grains. The olivine cracks sometimes extend into the adjacent enstatite, and even across this into the contiguous olivine. The greenish color of the enstatite near the upper right-hand olivine grain marks an alteration state. The color of the enstatite probably marks the beginning of a change. 133, 134

Fig. 2. Peridotite, — Lherzolite. Baste, Harz.

This shows a further change in the same rock as Fig. 1. The color of the pyroxene minerals is deeper and much iron-ore dust has appeared, as one of the first products of alteration, along the fissures of the olivine. Bands of black ore-dust and yellowish serpentine cross the lower portion of the figure. Yellowish and greenish serpentine replaces portions of the silicates. . 133, 134

Fig. 3. Peridotite, — Lherzolite. Christiania, Norway.

A brownish altered enstatite and diallage mass, holding greenish serpentine pseudomorphs after olivine. The structure produced by the formation of the serpentine along the olivine fissures is distinctly shown, while colorless interstitial fragments of olivine remain in portions of the pseudomorphs. The bluish band on the right of the figure marks a border of alteration between the original olivine and enstatite. Much black iron-ore dust is to be seen, particularly in the altered olivine, but it is not so abundant as it is in Fig. 2. . . . . 134, 135

Fig. 4. Peridotite, — Lherzolite, — Serpentine. Gjørud, Norway.

The pyroxene minerals are changed, having a brownish color, while in part they are replaced by a grayish-white to colorless magnesium-carbonate, as shown on the left of the figure. The olivine is altered more than it was in the preceding figure, only a very few granules remaining unchanged in the yellow serpentine. The iron-ore dust has diminished in amount, but sufficient remains to mark the original fissures in the olivine. The lithographer in his endeavor to be exact, has reproduced on the left and towards the bottom of the figure three bubbles which were in the balsam, but which, it is needless to say, were not in the original drawing. 135

Fig. 5. Peridotite, — Lherzolite, — Serpentine. Baste, Harz.

This shows a brownish altered pyroxene mass containing yellow serpentine pseudomorphs after olivine. The change has progressed further here than in the preceding. The serpentine has a more uniform and paler color, the iron ore diminishes in amount, and the olivine is entirely changed. 133, 134

Fig. 6. Peridotite, — Picrite. Herborn, Nassau.

On the right of the figure is a brownish augite crystal containing olivine grains, some of which is altered to greenish, bluish, and brownish serpentine and biotite. Part of the olivines show the commencement of alteration only by the production of iron-ore dust and colorless serpentine along the fissures. At the base of the augite is shown a greenish alteration product, while a large olivine is attached to the upper portion. The groundmass is a yellowish, grayish, bluish, and greenish serpentine, holding partially altered olivines, brown biotite scales, and black iron ores. 150

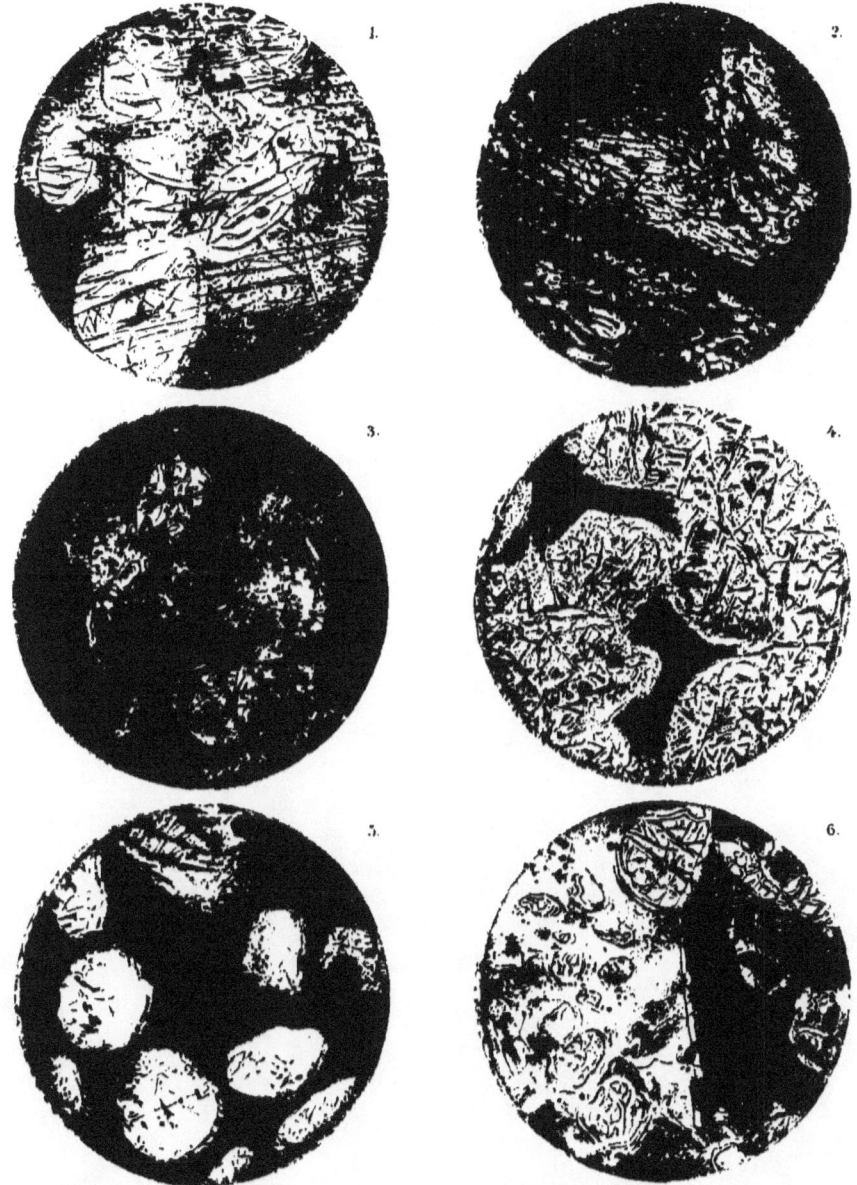